FLOYD DELL

FLOYD DELL

The Life and Times
of an American Rebel

DOUGLAS CLAYTON

I V A N   R .   D E E

Chicago   1 9 9 4

FLOYD DELL. Copyright © 1994 by Douglas Clayton. All rights
reserved, including the right to reproduce this book or portions
thereof in any form. For information, address: Ivan R. Dee, Inc.,
1332 North Halsted Street, Chicago 60622.
Manufactured in the United States of America and printed
on acid-free paper.

Library of Congress Cataloging-in-Publication Data:
Clayton, Douglas, 1956–
Floyd Dell : the life and times of an American rebel /
Douglas Clayton.
p. cm.
Includes bibliographical references and index.
ISBN 1-56663-059-2 (alk. paper)
1. Dell, Floyd, 1887–1969—Biography.   2. Politics and
literature—United States—History—20th century.   3. Authors,
American—20th century—Biography.   4. Journalists—United
States—Biography. 5. Radicals—United States—Biography.
I. Title.
PS3507.E49Z62   1994
818'.5209—dc20

[B]   94-18653

To Christine

CONTENTS

Acknowledgments ix
Preface xi
ONE: Midwest Boyhood 3
TWO: Tri-City Rebel 19
THREE: Literary Journalist 43
FOUR: "A New Era" 65
FIVE: South Side Bohemian 80
SIX: "Revolutionaries Without a Revolution" 102
SEVEN: Love in Greenwich Village 131
EIGHT: Wartime 155
NINE: Postwar Novelist 176
TEN: "Literature and the Machine Age" 195
ELEVEN: Under Fire 214
TWELVE: Radical Renegade 233
THIRTEEN: Great Depression 255
FOURTEEN: New Deal 273
FIFTEEN: Man of Letters 288
SIXTEEN: True Riches 307
Notes 314
Index 327

ACKNOWLEDGMENTS

I OWE THANKS to many people. William Graham read an early draft of this book; Michael Keller read a much later draft. Both these friends offered indispensable guidance and encouragement as I embarked on later revisions. Among those who talked or wrote to me about Dell are William L. O'Neill, Daniel Aaron, Paul Whyte Ferris, Charles Yarnoff, Steven Watson, and Mark Krupnick. Gerald Graff led me to work on Dell in the first place; he read portions of the manuscript and helped me refine my ideas on Dell's career and his critical writings. Christopher Dell spoke to me on numerous occasions about his father's life and granted me access to private papers by and about his father. For two splendid days in August 1992 Christopher and his wife Kate entertained me in their home in Winchester, New Hampshire, regaling me with stories about Floyd Dell's life. And I thank Christopher's daughter, Jerri Dell, who also shared with me her extensive knowledge and fond memories of Floyd Dell.

I am grateful to Saundra Taylor, Curator of Manuscripts at the Lilly Library, Indiana University, for permission to quote from the Upton Sinclair and Max Eastman collections; to Patricia Willis, Curator of Manuscripts, Yale Collection of American Literature at the Beinecke Rare Book and Manuscript Library, Yale University, for permission to quote from the Arthur Davison Ficke and William Lyon Phelps collections; to Nancy M. Shawcross, Curator of Manuscripts, Special Collections, Van Pelt Library, University of Pennsylvania, for permission to quote from the Theodore Dreiser papers; and to Diana Haskell, Lloyd Lewis Curator of Midwest Manuscripts, Rare Book Room, Newberry Library, for permission to quote from the Sherwood Anderson and Floyd Dell papers. I am also grateful to the staffs at the Davenport Public Library, the Pike County Historical Society, the Chicago Public Library, Northwestern University Library, and the Museum of the City of New York for their assistance. Most of all, I wish to thank Diana Haskell, Robert Karrow, Margaret Kulis, and the staff at the Newberry Library for the countless ways, large and small, in which they have assisted my work with the Floyd Dell papers.

I am deeply indebted to Ivan Dee for his years of counsel, patient reading of two drafts of the book, and careful editing of the final manuscript. My greatest debt is to Christine Clayton, who read every draft of the manuscript and offered me, as always, invaluable support and advice. To her goes gratitude and love.

D. C.

Lincoln, Nebraska
May 1994

PREFACE

ON A BRILLIANT spring morning in April 1918, Floyd Dell and four other writers and editors from the radical magazine the *Masses* walked into a federal courtroom in New York City to stand trial under the Espionage Act. The act had been passed a year earlier to stifle dissent against America's entrance into World War I. All five of the *Masses* defendants—Dell, editor Max Eastman, cartoonist Art Young, business manager Merrill Rogers, and the poet Josephine Bell—were charged with "conspiring to cause mutiny and refusal of duty in the military and naval forces, and to obstruct recruiting and enlistment to the injury of the service." The *Masses* trial became one of the most celebrated prosecutions of radical dissenters in a year when war hysteria and general intolerance of antiwar sentiments reached all-time highs. The maximum sentence under the Espionage Act was twenty years in prison. Dissidents in other trials had been sentenced to stiff fines and jail sentences. Dell and his fellow defendants had good reason to believe that they too were headed for long prison terms.

Yet for all its gravity, the *Masses* trial had an absurd, illusory air. It was, according to Dell, like "a scene from 'Alice in Wonderland' rewritten by Dostoievsky." After all, these were writers and editors who were on trial, not hard-core labor organizers or violent revolutionaries. Dell walked the halls between sessions with his lover, the poet Edna St. Vincent Millay, listening to her recite her latest poems. One day the two arrived late at court, having stayed too long in bed; Dell stepped with embarrassment to his seat beside the other defendants. When it was his time to testify he did so with unmistakable self-assurance, stating his initial view of the war as a contest between corrupt capitalist powers and asserting the rights of conscientious objectors. But afterward he admitted that the whole episode, including his own performance, had seemed phantasmic, even grotesque. A few months later he wrote, "I sometimes wondered then, in the midst of some legal argument, suddenly: What am I doing here? Why was I not at home writing a story? The scene became, in such moments, utterly unreal. The fact was that I was an artist—not a politician. How in the world did I come to be mixed up in this political *cause célèbre?*"

Dell might just as well have asked how he had come to adopt the dual identity of a literary artist and political radical. In the decades before the *Masses* trial, he had been one of the most ambitious and influential intellectuals of the sort that his friend Randolph Bourne called "literary radicals." He was to remain a prominent literary radical for more than a decade afterward. To adapt a well-worn phrase from Lionel Trilling, Dell went often to the crossroads where literature and politics meet.

Yet literary radicalism was a continuing puzzle for Floyd Dell, a source of productivity and insight but also of worry and confusion, throughout his entire career. He could imagine no intellectual persona that was not made up of both literary and political passions. And yet part of him always remained skeptical about this joint endeavor. He was radical enough to arrive at center stage in a trial of antiwar dissidents; but he was sufficiently detached to see the whole thing as a piece of absurd—bizarre, ghastly, gripping, comic— theater.

When the *Masses* defendants were set free several weeks later as a result of a hung jury, Dell returned impatiently to his dual life as writer and radical. In this and many other regards, the trial proved emblematic of Dell's career. As at the trial, he managed for many years the oddly paired roles of radical and skeptic, insider and outsider, enthusiast and questioner. And as with the trial's conclusion, he always emerged from the periodic crises of his literary leftism with both his idealism and irony intact. The passion and skepticism he brought to the cause of left-wing culture and the avant-garde guaranteed that his journey through American literary culture would be provocative and productive. They also made Dell peculiarly well qualified to tell his rebellious generation's story.

*   *   *

FLOYD DELL'S key role in the insurgent culture of the early century is beyond dispute. When cultural rebellion ignited in America—in Chicago between 1909 and 1913, and in New York between 1913 and the early 1920s—he was at its center. Writers and artists within that chaotic, immensely productive vanguard mixed cultural and social rebellion in an effort to overturn the conventions and injustices they felt governed American life. Dell—novelist, critic, editor, poet, playwright, bohemian, socialist, critic of patriarchal institutions, proponent of free love, and champion of feminism, progressive education, and Freudianism—was an indispensable figure in that rebellion.

The sheer range of Dell's writings and activities attests to his talents and ambitions. His books include eleven novels and several collections of stories, poems, essays, and plays. His first novel, *Moon-Calf* (1920), was often compared with Sinclair Lewis's *Main Street* and F. Scott Fitzgerald's *This Side of Paradise* for its focus on an alienated, disoriented youth. It was a best-seller that established Dell as one of the first important postwar novelists. He also wrote a biography of Upton Sinclair and books on feminist leaders, educational reform, the politics of the avant-garde, and the revolutionary changes taking place in modern marriages and families.

Dell worked at some of the most influential literary and political journals in Chicago and New York during the 1910s and 1920s. He edited the *Masses* with Max Eastman and John Reed, promoted writers from Charlotte Perkins Gilman to Ezra Pound, and had a lifelong affair with democratic socialism. He was a central figure in the Chicago Literary Renaissance and a notorious Greenwich Village bohemian during the Village's heyday in the 1910s. His private life attracted nearly as much attention in the Village as his literary and political writings. Dorothy Day, who knew Dell when he lived in Greenwich Village, remarked that his "love encounters should really take place on the stage of the Hippodrome before a packed house."

In 1917 and 1918 he was a playwright, director, and actor with the ground-breaking Provincetown Players. Later he co-authored a successful Broadway play that was eventually turned into two Hollywood movies. He was friends with Theodore Dreiser, Sherwood Anderson, and Upton Sinclair, editing various of their novels and tirelessly publicizing their works. At the time he was tried in 1918 under the Espionage Act, he epitomized the radical intellectual at

odds with the political status quo. Two decades later he was sufficiently reconciled to the United States government to work as a
writer and editor in the Works Progress Administration.

This partial account of Dell's writings and activities makes plain
why his prominent place in radical American culture of the early
century has never been in doubt. His exact contribution to it has
been more difficult to describe. Literary and social historians have
portrayed him as an archetypal radical of the age—"a textbook case,"
as the author of one anecdotal history of American bohemia phrased
it. Certainly the temptation to see Dell as a versatile representative of
the era's eclectic radicalism—with its heady mix of politics and
culture, socialism and bohemianism, art and journalism, public and
private revolt—is very great.

Yet Dell bore a complex, often strained relation to many of the
political and cultural causes championed by his contemporaries. His
views were often ambivalent, satiric, ironic—though fond and affectionate. From first to last he aimed to develop a radical point of view
that would avoid the rigid doctrine, impenetrable theory, mandarin
self-importance, and appalling humorlessness that has so often
marked left-wing intellectuals. He always sought to redefine cultural
radicalism and modern literature in ways that would eliminate the
contradictions, absurdities, and hypocrisies buried beneath avant-
garde platforms. Without doubt Dell's work as a novelist and critic
reflected the extraordinarily diverse radical culture of his times. But
it was also marked by an incisive quarrel with that culture.

The conflict can be seen at every stage of his career. As a central
figure in bohemian enclaves in Chicago and New York, Dell
regularly pointed out the hidden conformism (and conservatism)
coursing through these ostensibly uninhibited communities. Although he was closely identified for decades with the avant-garde, he
frequently attacked the disdainful elitism and carefully cultivated
incoherence of much modern art; both, he argued, revealed the
self-serving, retrograde politics of many avant-gardists. The author of
pioneering critical works on the close relation between culture and
politics, Dell resisted what he called Marxism's "Grand Economic
Explanation of Everything, which is rigor mortis to the mind." In
the 1930s, when many of his friends and former colleagues were
embracing Marx and the Soviet Union, Dell renounced both. In the
1940s and 1950s he kept his distance from all the reigning movements (left-wing and otherwise) in American literary culture: the

remaining Stalinists, the handful of Trotskyites, the converts to McCarthyism and other reactionary causes, the swelling ranks of apolitical professors.

This pattern of commitment and independence, of cooperation and dissent within the left-wing cultural community was central to Floyd Dell's life as a public intellectual. He knew himself to be a radical of a recognizably American sort: charged with good faith and optimism, but independent, skeptical, quarrelsome, and allergic to dogmas, schools, and systems. Often he found inspiration in leftist institutions and communities. But he guarded his independence, his suspicion of every shiny new orthodoxy, radical or otherwise, that rolled off the assembly line. His unwillingness to submit to radical systems and doctrines alienated him from his more dogmatic contemporaries, just as it has made him (and others of his generation) seem "lyrical" and "innocent" to more recent generations of academic critics and radicals. Today, in light of the moral and political collapse of Soviet communism and widespread concerns about the routinization (and professionalization) of the academic left, Dell's independence and skepticism seem more formidable than ever before.

Yet Dell never let that skepticism drown the optimism that was also essential to his life and writings. He once famously remarked that the *Masses* "stood for fun, truth, beauty, realism, freedom, peace, feminism, revolution." Add to that impressive list a few more items—literature, politics, irony, laughter, hope—and one begins to get a sense of the myriad elements that contributed to Floyd Dell himself. He exemplified what Irving Howe once called the characteristic sentiment of his age—"its characteristic lilt and bravado"— even as he stood apart from his contemporaries, chronicling their achievements and foibles. Remarkably, he managed to serve his generation as a leader, its ablest chronicler, and its finest satirist. That unlikely trio of callings makes Dell a figure who deserves our attention today. That—and the fact that he lived a fascinating, eventful life.

FLOYD DELL

ONE

Midwest Boyhood

FLOYD DELL spent several boyhood years in Quincy, Illinois, a small industrial city perched atop steep bluffs along the Mississippi River. Summer evenings found him alone on a bluff above the river, eyes trained on the western bank, the sun setting in brilliant colors farther westward. A few blocks behind him was his family's home: half of a small house in a run-down neighborhood, propped beside an unsightly gully. Dell lived there with his two elderly parents—his father often out of work, his mother holding desperately to an illusion of the family's respectability—and his three grown-up siblings. At the foot of the bluff, cramped in beside the river, were factories and railroad tracks. Dell's father worked off and on in several of these factories, as did his older brothers and sister. In 1900, when he was thirteen, Dell insisted that he too take his place in the family's struggle for economic survival and join the ranks of industrial laborers.

During solitary evenings on the bluff, however, Dell kept his back to the family's run-down home and stared resolutely beyond the industrial scene below. It was not that he could forget his family's poverty and desperation. For years he had struggled between resignation and indignation as he faced that poverty. By age fifteen he had pored through the writings of radicals from Karl Marx to Illinois's notorious freethinker Robert Ingersoll in an effort to discover reasons for despising the society in which his family had failed. At sixteen he joined the Socialist party, a decision that confirmed his emerging image of himself as a member of the working class, a youth irrevocably opposed to the capitalist economic order and middle-class respectability.

Still, real hatred for the turn-of-the-century Midwest eluded Floyd Dell. If there was much in that world that angered and humiliated the boy, there was also much he loved. In the landscape and the people he discovered a scene that was, as he wrote many years later, both "grim and generous." Sprawled atop the Quincy bluffs, the boy was enchanted by the loveliness of the river and anxious about the industrial scene below. And while a steady diet of romantic verse had fed his feelings of alienation from Midwestern life, Dell was never oblivious to the impressive number of adults—librarians, teachers, local radicals, intellectuals—who befriended him and encouraged his awakening talents.

Twenty years later, in October 1920, Dell published *Moon-Calf*, his first novel and a largely autobiographical account of his early years in the Midwest. Published two days after Sinclair Lewis's *Main Street*, Dell's novel was frequently likened to Lewis's work: both portrayed young idealists at odds with their Midwestern environments. Dell was delighted by *Moon-Calf*'s nationwide success. But he objected to the argument, made in many reviews, that his book, like Lewis's, was essentially sympathetic to its idealistic protagonist and hostile to Midwestern society. In a number of public statements he insisted upon his sympathy for the Midwestern scene and his corresponding impatience with "young idealism." At other times he seemed to realize that in writing the book he had indulged a tangled mix of emotions about both the Midwestern towns and the awkward hero of *Moon-Calf*. He sensed that the book's merit was bound up in his ability, at long last, to capture that delicate balance of alienation and affection that had always characterized his feelings for the Midwest.

A month after *Moon-Calf* appeared, Dell received a letter from his friend of many years, Theodore Dreiser, who recognized the blend of realism and affection that Dell had woven into his novel. "I have just finished *Moon-Calf*," Dreiser began, "and it impresses me as not only an intimate & faithful picture of middle west American life—catholic & generous to a degree—but as a delightful piece of writing as well." Much in contrast to his own harrowing books, Dreiser detected the fond flavor of Dell's Midwestern novel. "There is about it really that high poetry & mood which we ask of life and find, if at all, in our own response." He called the book "a fine armful of cut flowers out of our great valley."

What Dreiser and other readers recognized in *Moon-Calf* was that

Dell had found a fruitful literary subject in the Midwest, particularly in his own awkward, uncertain boyhood there. Dell was thirty-three years old when *Moon-Calf* appeared, and he had spent the preceding decade battling in the service of almost every conceivable faction of the party of progress and the future. Socialism, literary innovation, feminism, bohemianism, progressive education—these and other causes had counted Dell among their most fervent partisans. But in *Moon-Calf* he turned away from the future and discovered in his inchoate boyhood matter fit for a novelist. Like Sherwood Anderson—whom Dell befriended in Chicago in 1913, and whose own first book, *Windy McPherson's Son*, found a publisher due to Dell's tireless efforts—Floyd Dell was to return often in his writings to his Midwestern origins. For all his passion for the future, it was his bewildering past in towns and cities along the Mississippi River that first sparked Dell's imagination.

FLOYD JAMES DELL was born June 28, 1887, in Barry, Illinois, a small town a dozen miles inland from the Mississippi, across the river from Mark Twain's hometown of Hannibal, Missouri. In 1887 Barry was beginning to show signs of the strain of wild economic swings and a precipitous rush to urbanization that characterized late-nineteenth-century America. The depression of 1873 had undermined the confident growth that Barry experienced briefly in the years after the Civil War. Businesses were ruined, families slipped into poverty, people left town for jobs in cities elsewhere along the Mississippi or beyond.

These were decades when the United States was transforming itself from a decentralized, rural continent into an urban, industrialized, insistently modern nation. Most Americans continued to live in small towns during these decades, but they were also dimly aware that small, independent communities were becoming more and more irrelevant in a country of massive industries and transcontinental business and transportation networks. Farmers and farm workers were leaving the country in search of factory jobs in fast-growing cities. Independent businessmen, mainstays of social order and respectability in small-town communities, seemed doomed in an economy increasingly dominated by corporations and investment banks. "In a manner that eludes precise explanation," the historian Robert Wiebe writes, "countless citizens in towns and cities across the land sensed that something fundamental was happening to their lives, something they had not willed and did not want." This transformation, only vaguely perceptible to residents of out-of-the-way towns like Barry, doomed these same towns to decades of attrition and shrinking expectations.

Dell's parents, Kate and Anthony Dell, were unwitting participants in this metamorphosis. For Floyd, their youngest child, the family's indigence inspired a lifelong effort to understand the larger conditions that shape a family's tiny destiny. Though he had little sympathy for systematic master plans, Dell was aware, from youth on, that family narratives are connected in hard-to-define but important ways with vast social developments. His family's poverty became a constant reminder of how individual lives are buffeted by shadowy circumstance.

THE HIGHLIGHT OF Anthony Dell's life arrived early, when he was a Union Army soldier in the Civil War. He enlisted with Company K, Second Illinois Cavalry, not long after the war began, and fought in several battles. The last of these was in Texas, where he was wounded, left for dead by his own retreating comrades, and taken prisoner by the Confederate army, to be released only at the end of the war. When he arrived in Barry after his release, he was welcomed by the townspeople as a military hero—a reputation he continued to cherish throughout the following decades.

Anthony Dell had been born on a farm in Madison County, Illinois, nearly as far downriver as St. Louis, in 1839. His parents were of Pennsylvania Dutch origins, with likely a touch of Irish blood in the family as well. He was short, compactly built, good-natured, but feisty and ungovernable. Fittingly, he was nicknamed "Banty" when he was young, for he reminded everyone of a quarrelsome bantam. From his father he had received his radical Republican politics, particularly his loathing for slavery. Abolitionist sympathies were unpopular in southern Illinois in the years before the outbreak of the Civil War, but public disapproval only encouraged Anthony Dell's combative will. He railed regularly against the Democratic party's tolerance of Southern slavery, which he regarded as an unpardonable affront to American political ideals. He went to war in 1861 convinced that the cause was just—not to mention a splendid opportunity for manly adventure.

In the years after 1865 Anthony remained in many regards "a military man," creating an identity for himself that centered on his experiences as a soldier. In *Moon-Calf* and *Homecoming*, the autobiography he wrote in the early 1930s, Floyd Dell fondly portrayed his father's nostalgia for his army days. What Dell also captured in these books, however, was the way this nostalgia opened a rift between Anthony Dell and his wife, and how it subtly unsuited him for civilian life generally. Dell clearly patterned the character Adam Fay in *Moon-Calf* after his own father:

> Adam was only one of many young "veterans" who had begun to find the feminine society of their wives a little tame. There was a flavour of old-time adventure in their own companionship, spiced as it was with selected reminiscence. They looked back to those old times as the best part of their lives; and they felt in each other's society a free and easy sympathy and understanding that they missed at home.

Throughout Dell's boyhood, his father was often to be found sitting at the kitchen table or in the living room, strangely detached from the family's domestic life, reading Ulysses S. Grant's memoirs or expatiating on his own military exploits.

This came much later, though, after several national depressions and much professional disappointment. In the years just after the Civil War, Anthony Dell had good reasons for feeling confident about the future. Soon after his return to Barry he met and married Kate Crone, a slender, quiet woman of Irish descent, whose family had been farmers for generations in the countryside outside of Barry. She was twenty-four years old when she married Anthony in 1870, and had already worked for several years as a schoolteacher in town. Unlike her blustery husband, she was dreamy and circumspect, a lover of books, art, and poetry.

For a brief span of years, Anthony and Kate Dell rose easily in Barry society. Anthony's business flourished for a half-decade. He assumed the dress and demeanor of rising respectability: he added a few comfortable pounds, he dressed well, he became much impressed with his own dignity. Soon the Dells had a son, Charles, born in 1872. Kate had hired help to keep up with the house and child-raising. Barry was a promising town with a small group of independent businessmen, among whom Anthony was prominent.

The Panic of 1873, though, rattled Barry and signaled trouble for the Dells. Anthony held on to his butcher shop for a couple of years after the depression set in, but the business was never the same again. Two more children were born: Harry in 1874, then Cora a few years later. The family clung to its view of itself as resiliently independent and middle class. But within a few years Anthony had lost his business and accepted a wage earner's position in another man's butcher shop.

In the midst of this family trauma Floyd was born in 1887. By then his mother and father were in their forties. Financial difficulties, together with Anthony and Kate's vastly different temperaments, had long since come to define the tenor of their marriage and home. Dell's father was still able to find fairly regular employment, but he had already become a man baffled by financial difficulties. Kate Dell continued to indulge her interests in literature and the arts, but these were no longer the gracious adornments of a respectable middle-class home. Rather, Kate turned to literature as a refuge from the frustrations and uncertainties of her daily life. The gap between the parents did not bode well for their youngest son, who came to identify his mother and father with conflicting sides of his own temperament. For years he was to have difficulty sorting out the contradictory feelings he had for both of his willful, unhappy parents.

DELL PASSED HIS first six years oblivious to his parents' mounting misfortunes. In part this was an inevitable blindness to social distinction shared by all children. But there were other reasons as well: his parents' desperate pride; their refusal to countenance any suggestion that their straitened circumstances might prove permanent; the solicitous desire to shield their little boy from premature knowledge of poverty and shame.

All the while the family's situation was becoming more precarious. Not long after Floyd's birth, his father lost his job at the butcher shop where he worked. He managed, a short while later, to get a job at the Barry Woolen Mills. The transition was unnerving to Anthony Dell. Although he was soon made a foreman at the mill, his position there meant the loss of his professional status as a butcher. Money in the Dell household was scarcer than ever. Floyd's two older brothers were only teenagers when they were forced to leave school and go to work to help support the family.

Soon his sister Cora was also out of school, adding her wages to the family resources. Years later Dell described this surrender to the job market, imposed on his three older siblings by brutal necessity: "The first jobs from which they were not fired, furnished them their trades for the rest of their lives. That was the method of vocational choice by which one of my big brothers, a sensitive artist, with a love of drawing, became a harnessmaker; and the other, who was good at figures, a sash-and-door factory employee, running a saw which presently took off a thumb."

Both Anthony and Kate Dell tried to forget their worries through absorption in their youngest son. Anthony marched with his young son through the house and around the yard, training the boy in the manual of arms. The lad was enthralled by his father's political passions: his obstreperous support for the Republican party and hatred of the Democrats. Anthony enjoyed taking his son to political meetings on the Barry town square, where Floyd was mesmerized by the political speeches. At annual Decoration Day celebrations, when his father and other veterans were honored by the town, Floyd was flush with pride.

It was to his mother, though, that Floyd formed his strongest attachment. She read stories and poems to him constantly and awakened him to a childish appreciation of natural and artistic beauty. Later in life Dell was to identify his early passion for literature almost exclusively with his mother. He also credited her with the emergence of his social conscience. She was, he later remembered, "the Lawgiver. I learned from her the sense of *ought*. If I followed obscure unruly impulses, if I were selfish, greedy, lazy, quarrelsome, afraid, unwilling, then I was afflicted with her sorrowful eyes, not to be endured. My shame was a worse punishment than any outward one that could be inflicted. I *had* to be all that she expected me to be."

Questions about the boy's upbringing aggravated differences between his parents. Dell's father deplored the mother's power over the child. Her emphasis on art, beauty, and rigid moral standards, the long blond curls that she insisted on maintaining until the lad was five years old—these matters Anthony Dell regarded as unwholesome influences for a young boy. The older children led lives largely independent of the parents, working full-time jobs and seeking entertainment outside the house. Perhaps for this reason Kate Dell attached herself with special energy to her youngest child, whose quick intelligence seemed perfectly suited to her own bookish and artistic interests.

In the fall of 1892 Floyd entered school, where, after initial difficulties in adjusting to classroom discipline and decorum, he flourished in his studies. He was small and frail but pugnacious like his father. Amidst children from all sectors of Barry society, he remained blithely unaware that he and his family were sinking into unmistakable poverty. The family's condition worsened in the summer of 1893 when economic depression gripped the entire United States. In Barry, one of its severest effects was the closing of the woolen mills where Anthony Dell had worked for several years. Bereft of job and prospects, Anthony remained at home now, devoting his time to endless rereadings of Grant's memoirs. One by one the older sons and Cora moved to Quincy, an industrial town upriver, where they were able to find work in factories. Kate Dell fed those who remained behind potato soup every night. The soles of Floyd's shoes wore through; his father resoled them with scraps of cardboard.

By the fall of 1893, what was left of the family had retreated into its home, rarely venturing out or making contact with the outside world. When school started, Floyd was sick, and his mother kept him home for the first week. Then she decided, likely out of shame, to keep him out of school for the remainder of the fall. Floyd spent the days contentedly at home, reading and playing with his parents, unaware of why he was not allowed to go back to school. As Christmas approached and his parents failed to mention the holiday at all, he became more baffled. Without friends or contacts with the outside world, the six-year-old boy was not even sure if Christmas *was* coming, or whether he should be surprised by his parents' silence. As he was heading off for bed on the evening of December 24, he meekly inquired if it was not in fact Christmas Eve. His parents were thrown into paroxysms of embarrassment. Kate Dell stiffly ignored his questions; Anthony joked lamely that yes, it might in fact be Christmas Eve, but he'd forgotten it altogether. Floyd went to his bedroom alone, shocked to discover what he had long failed to notice: his family was desperately poor, and his parents were overwhelmingly ashamed.

In the next five years the Dells moved often within Barry, each time to narrower quarters in increasingly run-down houses. Anthony Dell worked odd jobs, hauling dirt and picking apples in local orchards. After Christmas 1893 Floyd stayed at home, confined to his bed with a mysterious stomach ailment for the remainder of the school year. Separated from schoolmates, he began to tumble into a world of books, illness, and solitary fantasy. Once he returned to school in the fall of 1894, he discovered a new refuge in the Barry Public Library. There he began reading everything that came to hand, from children's books to the novels of Daniel Defoe and Victor Hugo. He disliked Dickens and Thackeray, whose novels he found "clever but unreal." But he developed a bottomless appetite for what he called "true romantic literature"—*The Arabian Nights* and the visionary scientific and social novels of Jules Verne and H. G. Wells. Mark Twain's books were early favorites, especially *A Connecticut Yankee in King Arthur's Court* and *Innocents Abroad*, novels that satirized the social hierarchies and injustices of medieval and modern Europe. "I spent all the time I could at the public library," Dell later wrote, "preferring its peace rather than the environment of a home where there was always some painful reminder of our poverty."

By the time he was eight or nine he was beginning to rebel against his mother's suffocating love and equally stifling ethical standards. Floyd was even more torn by contradictory feelings for his father. Part of him adored Anthony, who remained a blustery presence in the household. But he also felt "cruelly disillusioned" in a father who had failed so manifestly in his responsibilities to his family. He later described his father as "no model, no hero, no masculine influence in his son's boyhood, no guide along the pathway of life, no evoker of ambition." As an adult, Dell suspected that his own inconsistent career in love and work had had its roots in his ambivalent feelings about his father. "For such a boy," he wrote, "one would be inclined to predict trouble."

His one defense against utter disappointment was an obstinate unwillingness to cultivate any ambition for worldly happiness. The discovery of his family's poverty gave rise to an odd resolution for a young boy: he would wish for nothing—not a piece of candy to be bought in a store, nor any distinction or prestige to be attained in later life. Stoic resolve was mixed with a desire, fueled by his voracious reading habits, to retreat into a private world of the imagination. As he headed toward adolescence, this inward, constricted nature of Dell's life was aggravated by confusions about sex. A shy, bookish boy, Floyd had declined invitations from other poor children to venture into the woods for forbidden sexual play. When he discovered that some of the well-to-do boys and girls at the Barry Public School—children whose wealth and refinement had led him to idealized images of their behavior—also took part in such games, he was shocked. Stubbornly he retreated into vague, childish fantasies of innocent companionship between himself and girls—fantasies that crowded out any hint of sexual desire or initiative.

The Spanish-American War, which flared up in 1898, briefly distracted Dell from his stoic resolutions, particularly when his eldest brother, Charles, shipped out for training camp in Florida. In his imagination Floyd followed Charles to Florida and beyond, picturing himself as a heroic journalist, dodging bullets in the midst of battle. The war, as Dell later remembered, "created in the public mind the romantic figure of the war-correspondent. It romanticized the Reporter." This glamorous figure, blended with fantasies about Charles's experiences, temporarily intoxicated Floyd. Still, he never allowed himself to entertain these dreams wholeheartedly. "If it had not been too daring a thought, I should have then formed the ambition of sometime becoming a Newspaper Man." But it was altogether too daring a thought. How could a poor boy in Barry entertain hopes of pursuing the sole career "in which a fellow could actually make a living and have a good time"?

The war over, Charles returned to Barry, never having left Florida for combat duty, and having there contracted a bad case of rheumatism. When he returned to his parents' house to convalesce, Charles passed the time reading cheap novels about Diamond Dick and Nick Carter—books that his eleven-year-old brother already found puerile. By the spring of 1899 Charles had recovered sufficiently to return to his job in Quincy, joining Harry and Cora there. Later that summer, despairing of any possibility for steady employment and renewed respectability in Barry, Dell's parents decided to follow their three elder children to Quincy. There, at least, was the promise of better-paying jobs for Anthony.

QUINCY, ILLINOIS, thirty or so miles upriver, was a vastly different place from Barry when the Dell family arrived there in late summer 1899 with their meager belongings and threadbare dreams. In every regard larger and more energetic than Barry, with more than thirty thousand inhabitants, Quincy represented a modest first step for Dell toward the protean American urban scene of the next century.

The city had been founded in 1825—a full decade before the incorporation of Chicago, three hundred miles northeast—with the intention of establishing a trade center on the Mississippi River. Built largely on bluffs that protected much of the town from flood waters, and located beside a small baylike area ideally suited for the creation of a commercial harbor, Quincy had developed by 1870 into a diverse, bustling town. In the years just after the Civil War it was Illinois's second largest city, a place, like Chicago, that seemed destined to grow with the Midwest itself. But by the 1880s and 1890s the city's growth was beginning to slow due to the decline of river trade and the corresponding rise of the railroads, none of which ran main lines through Quincy. Nevertheless, when the Dells moved there Quincy was still an energetic place, much like the "brisk, handsome, well-ordered city" Mark Twain had described in 1883 in *Life on the Mississippi*. Factories and businesses had begun to replace river trade as the main sources of economic growth in the city. In 1899 Quincy still exuded a healthy sense of its own importance, dotted with expansive public parks and filled with large, gracious homes and imposing public buildings.

Quincy was also home to cultural institutions and events that distinguished it from Barry. Twain had written that the city was uncommonly "interested in art, letters, and other high things." Such cultural achievements were partly due to the city's original Yankee settlers but also to the German and Irish immigrants that flooded into Quincy after 1850. The Germans played an especially important role in Quincy during these years, when more than ten thousand German immigrants arrived in the city, at one time constituting 40 percent of its population. Besides their contributions to the city's industries and businesses, they added much to Quincy's diverse cultural and intellectual life. By the 1880s German immigrants to Quincy had established ten parochial schools and two colleges, a modern hospital, musical and literary organizations, and three newspapers. Institutions like these created a lively intellectual setting unlike any Dell had encountered.

To note these admirable features of Quincy at the turn of the century is by no means to suggest that the town was uniformly prosperous and harmonious. The Dells, like other working people who looked for jobs in Quincy's shops and factories, continued to know poverty after they arrived in town. An industrial city, Quincy experienced the growing sense of class conflict that characterized

American urban life at the turn of the century. In a charged and self-conscious political setting of this sort, Dell began to find ways to put his own frustrations and his beleaguered family's plight into some sort of perspective.

The Dell family was reassembled, after a fashion, when all six family members moved into five dingy rooms in half of a house in a poor district on the south edge of town. The place was soon crammed with all the worn-out belongings that Anthony and Kate Dell had collected in thirty years of marriage: "old wooden bedsteads, moth-eaten couches, battered bureaus, rickety chairs with cane seats repaired with heavy twine, ancient stoves, an extension table with many 'leaves,' the family portraits 'enlarged' in crayon, a trunkful of books, including the Family Dispensary and all the school books ever used by the children, and a vast quantity of rags, which my mother intended to make into a carpet." There was also an odd keepsake that the family called the "whatnot," a contraption that Dell later described as "a series of little triangular shelves tied together with string and made to hang in a corner of the parlor." Weighed down with photos, inexpensive china, bottles, glassware, bills, letters, newspapers, and fliers, the "whatnot" was for Dell the finest symbol of his family's precarious pretensions to genteel respectability.

Liberated from Barry, Dell began to find breathing room for his buried ambitions. He made his way to Quincy's new library, located just off the town square. Here he was taken under the wing of a solicitous librarian who granted him the rare privilege to roam at will through the stacks, where he discovered armloads of unexpected books. He also began to flourish at the Franklin School, the large brick junior high school that he attended from 1899 until 1901. He was dazzled by the Elizabethan and romantic poetry he studied in class. In the spring of 1901, when he was in eighth grade, he organized the Franklin School Literary and Athletic Society, to which he was elected president. The society, comprised entirely of boys Dell's age, devoted itself not at all to athletic activities but rather to discussing books, holding debates, publishing a newspaper, and creating a school library. When he was graduated from Franklin School in June 1901, his prestige there had risen sufficiently for him to speak at the graduation ceremonies: an address on "The Influence of Oratory upon History," parts of which were later printed, with his picture, in a Quincy newspaper.

The speech contained hints of rebellious political sympathies. In 1900 Dell had read through a socialist newspaper that his brother Charles brought home from work. It turned out to be the Socialist party's official organ, *The Appeal to Reason*. Floyd found it outrageously unpatriotic and jeered that the paper ought to be called "The Appeal to Treason." Later that summer, though, while on a trip back to Barry, Floyd was introduced to a socialist farmer who convinced him that "Socialism was not a matter of economics only, but of a different kind of life, based upon service for the common good and not on money. 'It is the kind of world a poet would want to live in,' he said, looking at me. 'Or a hero.'"

This romantic view of socialism was fortified by a pamphlet Dell discovered while working in a harness factory soon afterward. The little book avoided all mention of economic issues. "It told about Greek ideals of beauty in art and life," Dell recalled, and it emphasized "the gloriously alive and happy nature of Greek manhood and womanhood." All this it subsumed under the heading "Socialism." This was a type of socialism—heavy on aesthetic beauty and light on the mundane details of economic renovation—that appealed to a boy who was "less a rebel than a Utopian."

Slowly, Dell began to warm to the socialist messages he encountered in the countryside and in Quincy—both romantic and more bluntly economic sorts. The Midwestern socialist and populist movements of the late nineteenth century, emerging out of a growing resentment against centralized Eastern capital and the spread of poverty in Midwestern cities and throughout the countryside, provided a backdrop of rebellion that began to work upon Dell's imagination in lasting ways. Once over his initial shock at socialism's subversive reputation, Floyd began to discover in it ideas that would help him account for his family's unhappy decline. Socialism offered reasons for his family's failure to succeed—reasons that placed blame on economic conditions and injustice, not on the family's lack of discipline and resolve. Through socialism Floyd found a key to understanding what had previously prompted only bewilderment, shame, and inarticulate rage.

As an adult Dell recalled his early encounter with socialism as it affected his troubled feelings toward Anthony Dell: "I was engaged at this time in a desperate search for grounds of emotional reconciliation with my father." Romantic socialism furthered that reconciliation: it both identified impersonal economic causes for his father's plight and cast an unflattering light on the middle-class cult of respectability that had always provided the standards against which Anthony Dell appeared a failure. The socialism Dell was discovering enabled him to acknowledge forms of heroism—for instance, the way Anthony Dell stood up to managers at the factories where he sometimes worked—other than the conventional "heroism" of economic success and community status. "What if my father had not supported his family in respectable style?" Dell remembered asking himself at the time. "I could be proud of him! That, certainly, was how I suddenly felt. American respectability had taken my father away from me. Socialism was giving me a chance to get him back."

Socialism also helped him shed the emotional and ethical constraints that bound him so tightly to his mother. Floyd had felt a peculiar responsibility to his mother—a feeling mixed with tenderness and pity—as she suffered for the family's lack of social respectability. Floyd had actually been driven to work by the desire to provide Kate Dell with the money needed for the household and, to whatever extent possible, for a life of some graciousness. The aspersions that socialism seemed to cast on respectability now helped lighten the crushing responsibility Floyd felt toward his mother. It lifted from him "the obligation of doing or being something by which she should be enabled to sit on a cushion in the parlor."

At the menial jobs he took each summer in factories, department stores, and newspapers, Dell came across still more information about socialism. Finally, in 1903, he overheard a socialist streetsweeper giving a speech in a park, and the man's fervor prompted Dell to join the Socialist party local. "That was a glorious evening," he recalled, "in which I heard from the lips of the street-sweeper, in broken English, that my dreams and I were part of a living movement that was preparing to take the world into its hands to shape anew." Together with another sixteen-year-old rebel, a middle-class youth named Harry, Dell made his way to the local's headquarters where he discovered a tiny group of believers that allowed the two boys to join the Socialist party, even though the rules stated that one had to be eighteen to qualify for membership. It was a dull group, but it offered Dell the chance to anchor himself in a political organization that might give his life direction.

His readings extended beyond socialist rags like *The Appeal to Reason* to vaguely socialist, utopian novels like Edward Bellamy's *Looking Backward* and William Morris's *News from Nowhere*. He also was reading poetry and every book he could find on archaeology and anthropology—books which gave off an aroma of exotic places. He bought his first volumes: Emerson's *Essays*, Carlyle's *Past and Present*, and Ik Marvel's *Reveries of a Bachelor*, a book of cynical observations on love. From Marvel he discovered that "love exists for its own sake. . . . Love does not have to be eternal; it does not have to lead to marriage; it is beautiful all the same—and the more girls one can remember, the more beautiful it is." Soon he was reading other kinds of scandalous books. Frank Norris's novel *The Octopus* appeared in 1901, and Dell seems to have read it at once. He was also reading books on atheism, which seemed to Floyd the only sensible response to the superstitions of religion.

Dell was also plowing through writings by the Russian anarchist Peter Kropotkin. His youthful, incongruous views of anarchism reveal more about Dell's state of mind at the time than they do about the contents of any of the books he was reading. Russian anarchism he imagined as "a kind of Slavic Forest of Arden, or Sherwood Forest, where Robin Hood and Maid Marian robbed and killed the rich and helped the poor." Anarchism seemed to him to promise a delightful "combination of student life and military life; the goal of effort was freedom—freedom from superstition, from hypocrisy and from tyranny; students and soldiers, they studied, conspired, taught, killed, and endured their punishment, not as individuals but as comrades in a cause greater than themselves." Men and women would live together in a joyous fashion without a sexual component. "Here was an atmosphere of happy comradeship between girls and men, such as did not exist for me in any American reality I had ever known. . . . In this Nihilist realm, [men and women] studied, worked and fought side by side."

Dell realized years later that his enthusiasm for anarchism, together with that for socialism and atheism, was fueled by an underlying desire to rebel against middle-class America: a class to which his parents had always desperately aspired. His induction into the Socialist party in the summer of 1903 seemed to sum up his rejection of the world he had been raised to respect but which had remained inaccessible to him.

> My life seemed now to have some meaning, to be a whole. . . . I was an enemy of the established order, Church and State both, out to destroy it. I was one of the working-class. I need not

pretend to belong to the respectable world, nor try to struggle for a place in it. I could accept my destiny as a workingman with a good grace, for it was by my class that this whole sham civilization would be destroyed, and a new one erected all over the world.

Rebellion and alienation seemed to penetrate all his life. Wiry and high-strung, Dell was the very image of an estranged youth. Together with the stories he had begun to write, patterned on those of Edgar Allan Poe, he wrote several plays (one on Benedict Arnold, another on the abolitionist John Brown) that revealed his sympathy for rebels or outcasts. Even his awkward infatuation in the summer of 1903 with a girl named Margaret was spurred on by his discovery that she and her parents were socialists and admirers of Robert Ingersoll. Working side by side in a hot, noisy candy factory, Floyd and Margaret had shy feelings for each other that were inseparable from the radical politics they shared. Dell championed the working class even as he trembled at the touch of her slender bare arms. This combination of physical attraction and political sympathy delighted Dell. But he was helpless before his own lack of initiative—he could not even bring himself to kiss Margaret. "I enjoyed each moment of her presence," Dell remembered years later, "but was incapable of making any claim upon more of it than came to me without any effort." Then, late that same summer, his parents decided again to move the family, this time to Davenport, Iowa, in search, as always, of better jobs. Economic hardship had come between the two young people—that was something they, as fervent socialists, were fully prepared to understand. But Floyd never said goodbye to Margaret, and he left town with the unnerving feeling that he had failed the girl and himself.

TWO

Tri-City Rebel

Politics and literature emerged as twin elements in Dell's identity during his five years in Davenport. Harry Hansen, a journalist who knew Dell in Davenport (and later in Chicago and New York), realized that some unstable mix of the two typified Dell in these years: "Floyd Dell was in high school when I first heard of him; the story was that the high school had a freak poet, who actually sold verses to 'McClure's' but who was eternally damned because he was a Socialist."

Dell's contradictions were fueled by Davenport, which was home to an impressive number of radicals, intellectuals, and literary people in 1903. Like Quincy, most of Davenport was located on hilly land overlooking the Mississippi; it too was covered with parks and impressive buildings. But Davenport was bigger than Quincy, and in 1903 it was still growing rapidly, its population doubling from thirty to sixty thousand in the first decades of the new century. Across the river were two industrial cities comparable in size: Rock Island, which Dell found "commonplace and uninteresting," and Moline, which he described as "a nightmare—the inconceivably hideous product of unrestricted commercial enterprise; its center was occupied by the vast, bare, smoke-begrimed structures of the greatest plow-factory on earth." Davenport appeared older and more settled than its two Illinois counterparts, lovelier and more gracious, with a livelier intellectual scene.

Important in this regard was the city's large population of central European immigrants, many of whom had arrived in Davenport in the years after the failed revolutions of 1848. Of these the greatest number were German. Many were Jewish. They had brought with them progressive political traditions and a serious devotion to European culture. In *Moon-Calf* Dell has Rabbi Nathan (based on one of his Davenport mentors, Rabbi William Fineshriber) rhapsodize about Port Royal, the town that stands, transparently, for Davenport: "Port Royal has a quality of its own. I suppose this is partly due to the pioneers from New England, who brought with them ideals and a respect for learning; but it is more due, I think, to the Germans, who left home because they loved liberty, and brought with them a taste for music, discussion and good beer." According to Rabbi Nathan, the Germans lent Port Royal "a general readiness to believe that ideas are matters of real importance. The effect of all this has been to give Port Royal a somewhat European air."

There was more to Davenport as well. German newspapers, businesses, and cultural institutions flourished alongside sizable Swedish, Irish, and Hungarian populations and a small black community that had been founded by freed slaves searching for a relatively tolerant place to live after the Civil War. There was also what Dell called "some native American mysticism in the picture, a mysticism of the sort which blossomed in the '30s and '40s, a curious religious expression of romantic libertarian ideas." Nor was the city without industrial blight and poverty: much of its river shore was occupied by an ugly factory district. Although "Davenport was a city with some handsome tree-lined residential streets," Dell wrote in the 1950s, "the part of town where I lived was not a place of handsome residences."

It was a potent blend of influences for an impressionable young man. His family's persistent poverty assured Dell's continued interest in socialism while the city's robust intellectual scene inspired him to pursue his rising literary ambitions. Gradually he began to imagine a flamboyant identity for himself, one made up equally of radical politics and vanguard literary tastes. It was an intoxicating combination, one that promised to liberate him altogether from the respectable world that had crushed and humiliated his parents. And yet it also made Dell anxious. Did it not reflect irreconcilable contradictions in his own temperament? Even when he was eighteen he realized that it might in the end "prove a troublesome combination to compose into an everyday working personality."

*   *   *

UPON ARRIVAL IN Davenport the Dells settled in their usual haphazard fashion in half of still another run-down house. Despite the timid hopes that had accompanied them on their trip up the river from Quincy, they found little respite from economic worries in Davenport. Anthony worked fitfully in factories and at odd jobs. Floyd was enrolled in the public high school. Both parents believed he was destined for the academic success and social respectability that had eluded everyone else in the family. In fact he was a successful student, completing his junior year in stellar fashion. But he was becoming indifferent to school learning. His fellow students regarded him as an odd bird, learned and aloof. Harry Hansen, several years older than Dell and already working on a Davenport newspaper, met him at this time:

> Floyd Dell was a lean lad with a bit of fuzz on his cheeks; rather negligent of his clothes and somewhat diffident in his manner; unobtrusive in a group, with a sort of smile that might be half interest, half disdain. And yet he was the best and most fluent talker of all if you hit his subject—though his subjects were hardly those that the average adolescent cares or knows anything about. Strange comment on philosophy; quotations from poets with unfamiliar names; stories from books with unconventional foreign titles.

Dell told Hansen about James Huneker, the fin-de-siècle aesthete-critic who championed literary and intellectual rebels from continental Europe. He also introduced Hansen to the writings of A. E. Housman, whose collection of lyrics, *A Shropshire Lad*, was Dell's favorite. The poems were otherwise unknown in Davenport at the time. Dell discovered "some expression of the confused passions of my own heart" in Housman's wistful, elegiac verse—something more suited to his own emotional state than the "godlike eloquence" of poets like Browning or Shelley. "Housman understood the troubled mind of youth," he felt. "In this book the torment, the pride, the folly, the despair, the beautiful agony of youth, lived again."

Independent of his studies at school, Dell was swallowing poets whole, reading and memorizing great chunks of poetry, discovering a poet or so each week. Within a year of his family's arrival in Davenport, he had "read and knew vastly by heart Wordsworth, Shelley, Walt Whitman, Kipling, Wilde, the Rossettis, Tennyson,

Wilfred Scawen Blunt, Herrick, Milton, Heine, Swinburne, John Donne, Marvell, Drayton, Shakespeare's Sonnets; some Persian and Chinese poetry of which I made my own rhymed versions; among living Americans I was enthusiastic about Bliss Carmen and William Vaughn Moody." He was reading nonpoets as well—"Darwin, Emerson, [the German biologist and philosopher Ernst Heinrich] Haeckel, Marx (or Engels), H. G. Wells, Bernard Shaw, Kropotkin, Max Stirner."

And Dell was producing verse as romantic in temper as that of any of his idols. Some of it was notably accomplished for so young a poet. Most of the poems he wrote in traditional verse forms—a preference he was to retain all his life. The poetry expressed above all else his feelings of alienation from society; often there were romantic premonitions of his own superiority to that society. He was still determined to find points of contact with the world through socialist theory and action. Yet he was also overcome with the impression of his own disconnection from the everyday world. The two developments occurred at once—and not without his awareness of the problem. In his personal copy of Emerson's essays, Dell underlined Emerson's famous remark that "a foolish consistency is the hobgoblin of little minds"; he was equally fond of Whitman's declaration from *Song of Myself*: "Do I contradict myself? Very well then, I contradict myself." Nevertheless, he was uncomfortable with this clash between the politics that placed him in the world and the poetry that removed him from it. He hoped at times to resolve the contradiction by writing "Socialist poetry." But the poems he wrote almost always expressed feelings of alienation from the everyday world.

Before long he met a sponsor for his poetry: Marilla Freeman, librarian at the new Davenport library. An ambitious woman who overawed Dell at first with her beauty and energy, she had noticed Floyd as he wandered about the stacks, resurrecting his old library-haunting habits in a new town and building. Marilla was a charismatic promoter of books and ideas, a woman devoted to expanding her patrons' intellectual horizons. She was twenty-eight years old when Dell met her, a graduate of the University of Chicago and of the New York State Library School. Dell later described her as a "goddess," "an extraordinarily beautiful young woman, tall and slender, wide-browed, with soft dark hair, grey-blue eyes, a tender whimsical mouth, and a lovely voice—an idealist, and also a practical person, who immediately took charge of my destinies. I fell in love with her deeply."

Upon reading some of the verse Dell had begun to write, Marilla was convinced both of his talent and of his need to develop discipline as a writer. She introduced him to Charles Eugene Banks, a former Chicago newspaperman who for some years had devoted himself exclusively to writing plays, novels, and poetry. While Dell held himself aloof from his teachers and classmates at the Davenport high school, he warmed to Banks at once, displaying an awakening talent for intellectual apprenticeship and cooperation. Banks helped Floyd criticize and revise his poems, adding discipline to his youthful faith in self-expression.

Still, the poems remained overwhelmingly romantic in temper. In many of them Dell's feelings of alienation were allied to the conviction that his essential ties were to earlier figures, drawn from myth and the romantic tradition. Occasionally the tie was to political revolutionaries: "Nat Tyler, Jack Straw, Spartacus, and other famous rebels against enthroned injustice." Under Charles Banks's tutelage, Dell developed greater subtlety and range, and he learned to manage grand gestures and allusions with admirable compression. This was fully evident in a poem like "Tamburlaine," which Dell completed in the summer of 1908. Soon thereafter it was accepted for publication by *Harper's Magazine*:

> Shepherd of thoughts, by day and night
>> My watch upon the hills I keep.
> The Captains scorn me, passing by—
>> A simple tender of the sheep.
> But scorn for scorn I give them back,
>> And in my heart I think of this—
> They shall bow low, when I shall ride
>> In triumph through Persepolis.

How did a poem like this come from the pen of a working-class youth in turn-of-the-century Davenport? Marilla Freeman and Charles Banks must have asked themselves that question. Still, they did not hesitate to encourage Dell to submit the poem and others for publication, advice Dell dutifully followed. Other poems were accepted by *McClure's* and the *Century*. Dell gained local renown as a gifted poet, yet he claimed little satisfaction in being published. He held steadfastly to the belief that his poetry was too private to be

subjected to publication and impersonal scrutiny. He wanted it seen
by only a few persons, above all by the women he admired. Among
his many poems addressed to such women, some were chaste
celebrations of friendship between the sexes, such as the sonnet he
sent to a young socialist woman he met at a Socialist party state
convention in Iowa City in 1905, when he was eighteen. Franker
calls for intimacy occurred in poems Dell wrote for Marilla Freeman, the "maternal goddess" he also imagined as a lover. In still
other poems he aimed for a witty treatment of the relations between
men and women, as in this opening octave to a sonnet. In their
conversational air and worldly tone, the lines hint of John Donne's
influence, whose poetry Dell was discovering at the time:

> Dear, when you gave me your love, I signed no bond
> To be forever worthy of that trust;
> And if you think you have been overfond,
> Take back your darling favors, as you must.
> I will not bargain with you, knowing well
> How futile were the effort to make over
> Me, skeptic, vagabond, rebel and infidel,
> Into the pattern of a perfect lover.

"Skeptic, vagabond, rebel and infidel"—Dell tried all these identities on for size, satisfied that together they added up to conclusive
evidence of his perfect contempt for bourgeois society.

Strange, then, that it was precisely his rebellious, romantic poetry
that made possible Dell's belated entrance into bourgeois society.
Through Marilla he was introduced as a young poet into the homes
of upper- and upper-middle-class families. The people there who
interested themselves in literature and culture were almost always
women. Afternoons and evenings passed in such homes confirmed
Dell's conviction that his poetry should remain private—that it was a
trivial activity, and that it would never gain him the respect of other
men. At the same time he could not hide from himself the fact that
he enjoyed the company of these women, and that he fairly basked
in their admiration. He was ill at ease with girls his own age, but
with older women it was different. He relished sporadic forays into
sexually charged banter and innuendo. This atmosphere of harmless
flirtation suited bored married women and a shy, inexperienced boy.

One young married woman led Dell past the bounds of simple
flirtation. She was known to her friends as Maj, and her interests in

culture and modern ideas had spirited her away from the company of her respectable husband; she carried on her social and intellectual life quite apart from him. Dell met her at a dinner party hosted by Edward and Ellen Cook, prominent members of Davenport society and the parents of Dell's friend, George Cram ("Jig") Cook—poet, novelist, Nietzschean, and future founder of the Provincetown Players. The intimacies shared by Maj and Dell were by no means extraordinary, consisting "of a semi-possessive tenderness on her part, a few caresses, a very few light kisses." But they were ideal for Floyd, since there was no danger they would lead to any serious commitment between the two, and because they introduced him to "the small, light, gay ways of expressing affection, much needed by a youth so inclined to be desperately serious." With Maj, Dell suspected something later experience seemed to confirm: "that an older young woman often regarded it as a duty as well as a pleasure to initiate an inexperienced young man; she felt that she ought to give him not merely pleasure but a proper training in love-making." Still, his initiation under Maj's tutelage did not amount to much. She was a harmless rebel, a vaguely discontented woman who liked to ruffle the feathers of Davenport society by smoking cigarettes in public and adopting other "bohemian" habits. She encouraged Dell's rebellion against convention while never suggesting that the two of them might actually break free of society's constraints. In her company Dell saw plainly how bohemian and bourgeois society, purportedly irreconcilable foes, might find ways of settling into peaceful coexistence.

Dell was never quite comfortable with the feelings women like Maj harbored for him. He knew they enjoyed his exotic nature and interests, his artistic temperament and outlandish appearance. He had grown his hair long, flaunting his indifference to the clean-cut appearances of conventional youths, and he had taken to wearing a bohemianlike black silk scarf around his pale throat (what he never admitted to these women was that the scarf was really an affectation of convenience: he wore it mainly because he could not afford clean white collars). He realized that "cultured" women liked him for the ways in which he differed from their own husbands and sons, that he lent their staid lives an exotic flavor. But he also knew they had no stake in him or his work, and he deeply resented their wealth and comfort. Sitting in their parlors discussing poetry, he felt partly humiliated, partly furious as he pictured his mother's unglamorous poverty.

Clearly Dell needed friends other than the decorous ones Marilla Freeman managed to provide. These he was fortunate to find in the summer of 1904, a year after his family had arrived in Davenport. A few months earlier he had decided to drop out of high school without completing his final year so that he could work full time in a candy factory to help support his family. One evening that summer Dell heard two men arguing about socialism in a public park. The debate was typical of those dividing American socialists at the turn of the century, centering on the question of whether the Socialist party should be a revolutionary or a reform party. The first speaker was a local Socialist leader, Michael Kennedy, who proposed as a model for American socialism the German Social Democratic party, which he claimed was attuned to the revolutionary aspirations of the proletariat. Kennedy was interrupted by a confident, heavyset man who insisted that the German party was by no means revolutionary in character—that it was in fact a liberal party dedicated to peaceful, parliamentary reform. Kennedy stormed from the scene, furious to find his ideas challenged. Meanwhile, the other man steered his remarks toward an uncompromising attack on Marxist theory.

All at once the seventeen-year-old Dell began to speak out, firing angry questions at the speaker, then arguing with him outright. A romantic socialist and resentful working-class youth, Dell could tolerate neither the moderate measures advocated by the older man nor his dismissal of Marx's revolutionary aspirations. The man smiled contemptuously at this preposterous, upstart boy, refused to respond to Dell's points, and departed the scene.

Dell felt momentarily slighted by the man's condescension. But his embarrassment did not last. Immediately he was hailed by a rotund, middle-aged man who announced himself a determined socialist. He invited Dell, with several others, to join him for beer. Dell was enchanted by the men, the drinks, the conversation. Here was companionship of men of the world, utterly different from the genteel company he had met through Marilla Freeman. Above all he was delighted by the man who had first approached him, a German immigrant, postal worker, raconteur, and revolutionary socialist named Fred Feuchter, known to his friends as Fritz. The playwright Susan Glaspell later remembered Fritz's vociferous confidence. "No knowledge could disconcert him," she wrote, "for his personality was built around the idea that all knowledge was in him, and he was so big and ruddy and quenchless that his benign damnation did indeed seem to have the sanction of both heaven and hell." As for Dell, he was convinced that the friendship that instantly blossomed between him and Feuchter was "the most important thing that had happened in my life. I had found a man whom I truly admired, and wished to follow, a man who had wisdom and courage, a man—and the first man—whose advice I could ask about anything."

Feuchter eased Dell's induction into the Davenport Socialist party local, even though at seventeen Dell was officially too young to join. Fritz also arranged to have Dell appointed to the party's program committee, where he helped turn the weekly meetings (until then lackluster occasions) into more spirited and entertaining fare. Dell lived for Friday nights, when party meetings erupted into lively disputes. Soon he was passing out party leaflets at the factory where he worked and campaigning for the Socialist party presidential candidate, Eugene Debs. "In reaching out to Socialism," he wrote, "I was possessing myself of the greatest intellectual and imaginative stimulus which existed in the world. It [gave] me a guiding idea of my relation to the universe, and to society; and this was an idea that set free my capacities for study. It also set free some practical political capacities."

Friendship with Fritz provided a great deal more for Dell than entry into Socialist party ventures. Feuchter was an outsized, disreputable figure, boisterous and radical. He was also a warmhearted, pragmatic man who recognized Dell as a confused youth in need of the everyday knowledge and skills he had never received from his rudderless father. "What I learned from him were practical, sensible ways of dealing with the world," Dell wrote decades later, "attitudes, rather than specific things, and really but simple common-sense. . . . Under his influence I began to learn not to attach to situations emotional values which were not there for the other persons involved; to live as though the outside world were real, whether I liked it or not; and not to pre-judge life, but to take it as it came and see it as it was."

Whenever poetry seemed to push Dell dangerously far in the direction of self-congratulatory alienation, Fritz was always ready to haul him back with bracing humor and advice. In *Moon-Calf* Dell attributed much of his own Davenport poetry to Felix Fay, the young man clearly based on himself. In the same book Dell had Feuchter's stand-in, Franz Vogelsang, criticize Felix for writing "old maids' poetry." Vogelsang tells Felix straight out that he has come to him in order to be told some unpleasant truths: "You have been mooning about, writing verses about life, instead of living. You have been afraid to live. Most people are. Something stands between them and life. Not only economic conditions: something else—a shadow, a fear. Perhaps it is safer not to try, they think. So do you. These poems are your consolations for not living. That is why I called you an old maids' poet."

Feuchter reproached Dell in another way in which Vogelsang criticizes Felix—for confusing his romantic, escapist poetry with substantive opposition to capitalist society. Vogelsang reminds Felix that by withdrawing from society he cannot see it clearly. He charges Felix with a task that Feuchter frequently proposed to Dell: get rid of "romantic nonsense" ("Stop thinking of the middle ages," Vogelsang says impatiently) and find a way to live in "relation to your own time, which does not consist in lying down for it to walk over you." Vogelsang tells Felix to abandon the pose of a "romantic proletarian" —"working in a factory and writing bad verses"—and instead to live up to his responsibilities as a member of the modern "intellectual proletariat," searching for realistic ways to describe and influence modern society.

At the same time Feuchter warned Dell not to take the Socialist local meetings too seriously. Many of the regulars were eccentrics, he told his young friend; they had latched on to the Socialist movement simply because it promised change. Most valuable was Feuchter's advice that Dell find his work in the intellectual activities for which he had both a natural talent and bent. Fritz laid out the alternatives of mental and manual labor and assured Dell that he "would have less skilled competition in the [first] field than in the other."

IT WAS dumb luck, though, that finally landed him such a job. After the Christmas rush of 1904 Dell was among the workers fired from the candy factory where he had been cooking vast quantities of sugar and starch syrup for six months. A short stint at a print shop followed, mass-producing labels for beer bottles. Fritz urged him to quit. "Your family will not starve," he said. Dell was surprised by Feuchter's inspired common sense. He resigned at once.

Nonetheless, when he went to the offices of the *Davenport Times* that winter, Dell refused to believe he could ever convince anyone to hire him as a writer. His plan was to inquire after yet another printing-press job. But the city editor he spoke with thought he was applying for a job as a cub reporter (the position had been advertised in the paper, though Dell had no knowledge of it) and promptly gave it to him. Floyd was told to report early the next morning. He went home bewildered and elated, convinced that landing the job was in some mysterious way due to Fritz's benevolent genius.

At first he proved no success as a reporter. The paper's owner told him he had "no nose for the news," and he was fired in a month, with two weeks' notice. Determined to stay on, he hunted desperately for story material. What he came up with was a piece about an impoverished local woman who had died in the Davenport train station, where she was found with her tattered children. The article created a stir, and Dell soon found himself reinstated, assigned the task of writing more "human interest" pieces for the *Times*. It was hard work. Harry Hansen was working at the same paper; he described Dell's job as "capturing 'personal' items by watching the railway stations for arrivals and departures; chasing anything from a fire in a barn to a murder in a low resort, doing odds and ends of footwork in police courts, fire stations and steamboat offices from early till late."

All the same, it was better than factory work. Dell wrote easily, most of his articles were printed, and the work left him time for poetry and Socialist activities. It also introduced him to other intellectuals. Shortly after he began working for the *Davenport Times*, Dell was dispatched to a local synagogue in order to research a story on the Yom Kippur holidays. Rabbi Fineshriber, who was himself only twenty-seven, was impressed with the eighteen-year-old reporter who came to interview him: he had done his homework and asked good questions. Dell was also impressed. Despite his youth, Fineshriber struck Dell as "full of rabbinical wisdom; and the gracious affability of his manners did not hide from me his dignity and authority. I respected him at first sight." When Dell came to the synagogue a while later to do a story on Davenport's Jewish community, the rabbi invited him to his home for dinner. The two were soon fast friends. Dell became "one of the pagan members" of Fineshriber's congregation, which, he reported, "consisted to a considerable extent of Gentiles, Socialists, Atheists and other heretics."

Rabbi Fineshriber was a riveting speaker whose sermons were as

often on cultural and political matters as on religious topics. Sometimes Dell skipped the Friday night Socialist local meetings in order
to hear the rabbi's sermons. He also visited the Fineshribers in their
home, where regular gatherings of poets, journalists, and independent-minded persons took place. Marilla Freeman was often there,
as were young Davenport writers like Susan Glaspell, George Cram
Cook, and the poet Arthur Davison Ficke. The conversation bounded
from topic to topic, enlivened by high spirits and self-consciously
modern skepticism. For Dell this informal literary salon seemed the
center "of a broad and vital culture."

Yet even here he felt an urge to stifle his love of poetry and his
desire to write it. "I was on guard against falling into poetic trances,"
he recalled. "I was deliberately breaking off from my addiction to the
dangerous habit of poetry-writing." Only at odd moments did "the
old desire for a refuge from the world" break out in occasional verse.
Then in November 1905 he contributed a poem, "The Builders," to
the maiden issue of a new Socialist monthly published in Rock
Island, the *Tri-City Workers Magazine*. The poem—celebrating the
"slow subtle destiny" of world history, whose meaning stands clear
"at last to our maturer eyes"—makes plain in stiff, heavy-handed,
relentlessly didactic detail why Dell eventually had such a low
estimation of his "Socialist poems." Nevertheless, this first contribution to the new magazine initiated a crucial phase of Dell's career.
The magazine's unabashed endorsement of socialist principles ("In
all the world there are but two nations—a nation of producers and a
nation of exploiters") fit well with Dell's own rebellious inclinations.
He became an avid contributor to the magazine at once.

The *Tri-City Workers Magazine* allowed Dell to put political
passions into articles in a manner deemed inappropriate at the
Times. "As a reporter on a 'regular' paper... one had to be an eye
and an ear, an organizing memory, a pencil and a pad of paper and
two fingers above a typewriter, rather than a person; my own
opinions, feelings, convictions and tastes had to be shoved out of the
way." At times he hated his work at the newspaper, where he had to
assume a mask of detachment—"sans taste, sans guts, sans principles, sans feelings, sans damn near everything that made life worth
living." This masquerade of scrupulous objectivity was not required
at the *Tri-City Workers Magazine*. Here Dell was able to place his
blunt essays among others on unemployment, the trusts, Pinkerton
strike busters, and working-class conditions. Some of the magazine's

articles were almost scholarly, crammed with facts. Others were extravagantly angry: "Workingmen of the tri-cities," the magazine's editor-in-chief shouted in one, "the Plutocracy of America, drunken with power and crazed by greed . . . [has] robbed you legally and illegally. They have oppressed you, murdered your children, debauched your sons and driven your wives and daughters to prostitution."

Dell's contributions to the *Tri-City Workers Magazine* packed all the earnestness and passion his editors wanted. In a slew of muckraking articles, Dell, writing under pseudonyms to avoid angering his employers at the *Times*, took aim at corrupt institutions in the Tri-City area. He exposed the deplorable conditions in the candy factory where he had once worked. He railed in a series of essays against mismanagement by the library and public school boards. He lambasted the lack of modern sanitary precautions at Moline's garbage dump. Other essays contained general reflections on the working class in American society, mixing socialist theory with exhortations for class solidarity, political action, and "backbone" in standing up to the capitalists. One article accounted for the outbreak of a diphtheria epidemic in Davenport by attacking the city's—and the nation's—health-care policies: "In any sanely managed municipality," Dell declared, "medical service would be free as air."

In his most ambitious article Dell described a local Davenport dance hall that he claimed ushered poor girls into lives of prostitution. The happiness these girls experienced in Brick Monroe's Dance Hall was inauthentic, Dell was convinced; it was the product of a capitalist, patriarchal society that ruthlessly exploited women. The meaning of the dance hall was perfectly clear to a young socialist: "Under Capitalism the women of the working class are the prey of the men of the business and professional classes." The tragedy of the situation was that capitalist society led women to experience their degradation as a form of natural pleasure. "Incredible, amazing romanticists, at every stage of their helpless victimization, they cherished the illusion of free will." Dell exhorts these women, along with working-class men, to reject "the Profit System" that exploits sexual love and to fight for a world in which "the growing boy and girl and the young man and woman shall have amusement that is rational, pleasure that is lasting,—happiness."

This last appeal was typical of Dell's articles for the *Tri-City Workers Magazine*: often they closed with a socialist call to arms.

But this time exhortation failed to exhaust his feelings about the subject at hand. Dell never actually set foot in Brick Monroe's: his lifelong revulsion against prostitution and the economic exploitation of women was already fully developed by this time, and it served to keep him out of red-light-district dance halls. But he had stared anxiously past the hall's open doors for months, pausing before it during late-night walks through town. His essay was all purposeful radicalism and determined exhortation. But in a sonnet he wrote about the place, all his confidence disappeared, supplanted by an anxious, nightmare view of the hall where women are destroyed by forces they cannot comprehend:

> I watched last night; and watching there with me
> There stood two joyless shades, the ghost of mirth
> And the grey ghost of laughter; so we three
> Watched till the dawn lighted the shuddering earth,
> And all the music and the dancing ceased.
> And, as I went, I wondered: not, to find
> Each sorry forehead chartered to the beast—
> But still I wondered, seeing you so blind;
> Who make strange sounds and deem that it is laughter,
> Who weary hour by hour and call it joy,
> Who flee so fast before what follows after,
> You are not man and woman, girl and boy,
> But strange, sad creatures, dreary and dull-eyed,
> Wherein the light has flickered out and died.

This is an adolescent poem, with its lugubrious "shades" and "shuddering earth." Still, its view of human sexuality erased by depraved economic relations is powerfully pictured. Like the article, the sonnet suggests that love and sex are distorted by unjust economic relations. And yet the poem has a morbid atmosphere that is absent from the article: it has none of the reformer's zeal that is essential to the magazine piece.

At the same time Dell wrote a long poem that revealed another side to his view into Brick Monroe's Dance Hall: his private, compulsive fascination with the whole scene. What he does not mention in the article or the sonnet is that the forbidden, unabashed sexuality of the dance hall also attracted, even mesmerized, him. The women were victims, true, but part of him found them daring and thrilling; he was drawn irresistibly to their brash sexuality and militant joy. While Dell pitied these women, he also dimly sensed something splendidly resilient, even heroic, about them. The poem "Saturday Night" reveals these feelings. It is addressed to a nameless eighteen-year-old girl he sees in the hall: "imperious, wild, / spoiled, rude, affectionate,—a weary child." Yet while it is clear that this young woman is victimized by the men who patronize the hall, Dell admires her unwillingness to succumb to conventional morality by renouncing the pleasures the dance hall affords her. He sympathizes with her desire to "cut the gordian knot, / Pluck the irrevocable golden fruit." He concludes: "And who shall say / You were not right to ask for deeper breath, / For love and life, for laughter and for sin, / If thereby you might win / To freedom at last." Were the women essentially exploited members of the working class, or were they (as in this poem) heroic figures, remarkable for their courage, their disregard of conventional restraints? Dell did not know. For a moment, in any case, he gave vent to his dissatisfaction with the rigid morality of bourgeois society and radical socialism alike.

His impatience with socialism, though, never led him to reject it outright. In the summer of 1906, still at the *Times*, he became editor of the *Tri-City Workers Magazine* and piloted the magazine through several issues—an experience of immeasurable value to him. Putting together a magazine—shaping its contents, seeing it through production, recruiting authors, worrying over schedules and finances—prepared him for the important editorial jobs he later took on in Chicago and New York. He introduced sections on Socialist party news and reports on the Tri-City Socialist locals. He also added a cultural dimension to the magazine, inserting book reviews, remarks on such writers as George Bernard Shaw, Upton Sinclair, and Frank Norris, and even, in one issue, a bit of utterly incongruous verse about vagabond leisure from the bohemian poet Bliss Carmen.

To note the changes Dell made in his short tenure as editor of the magazine is to wonder what sort of journal he would ultimately have created: perhaps some volatile concoction of politics and culture like the *Masses*, where he went to work eight years later. But the *Tri-City Workers Magazine* was not destined for long-term success. It was destroyed in the early fall of 1906 as a result of controversies over the new radical labor union, the Industrial Workers of the World. What were by now familiar disputes over revolutionary and reform courses

for American socialism did the magazine in for good. Milo Mitchell
Clapp, in an article that appeared in the magazine's last issue,
argued that the radical principles of the IWW would ultimately
"clarify the political atmosphere surrounding the Socialist movement." But in fact the quarrels surrounding the IWW injected
uncontrollable confusion and anger into the Socialist party. Contributors to the magazine found themselves at loggerheads with one
another, unable to imagine a cooperative enterprise in which all
could participate.

At nineteen Dell was thoroughly perplexed by the controversy. He
had earlier tended to side with the revolutionary (IWW) faction, if
only because it better suited his own rebelliousness. But he was
unable to lend all his support to the radicals. Perhaps this was due to
the skepticism about radical fundamentalism that was to mark so
much of his adult life. In any case, in 1906, when controversy
rocked the Socialist party in the Tri-Cities, Dell was by no means
"conclusively dedicated to militant and intransigent politics." He left
the *Tri-City Workers Magazine* unsure of what to think about the
blowup that had led to its disintegration.

Not long afterward he was peremptorily fired from the *Times*. The
conservative editor at the newspaper had uneasily tolerated Dell's
socialism. But radical politics and poetry-making had distracted Dell
from his responsibilities at the *Times* too often, and he was cut loose
with no warning later that fall. At once Ralph Cram, editor of the
Times's chief rival, the *Davenport Democrat*, snatched Dell and
offered him work at a better salary.

The *Democrat* also expanded Dell's duties. He reported on a
series of lectures on modern urban problems given by Dr. Graham
Taylor, founder of the Chicago School of Civics and Philanthropy
and head of the Chicago Commons settlement house. The *Democrat*
also assigned Dell to write theater reviews, including some for plays
put on at Davenport's German theater. Dell confidently wrote these
reviews even though he did not understand the language and was
able to grasp only the barest outlines of the plots. Despite all the
doubts he harbored about his work as a mainstream journalist, Dell
exuded a winning arrogance that inspired confidence in his new
boss at the *Democrat*. Why let the mere fact of failing to understand German stand in the way of perfectly delightful work as the
Democrat's German drama critic?

*   *   *

APPREHENSIONS ABOUT THE balance between his public and private selves continued to trouble Dell. They surfaced most painfully in 1907 when he fell in love with a young woman (he named her "Joyce" in *Moon-Calf*) who belonged to Davenport's upper class. She was three years older than Dell, bold, confident, impulsive. And so it was she, more than Dell, who pushed them to become lovers. After months of growing intimacy, Dell realized that their relations had moved to a point where not to become lovers would have been regarded by both as an unpardonable failure on his part. Once they became lovers, though, what opened up to Dell was an unexpected realm of happiness: "It was a magical experience to take a girl utterly into my mind and heart and senses and imagination."

Several problems confronted the two lovers. First there were the conventions of American society, which prohibited sexual love between unmarried persons. For Dell these had the troubling effect of turning love into something diametrically opposed to respectable behavior. "In being true to our love," Dell felt, "we had to be, if only to protect it from instant destruction, liars and hypocrites to the world." The young woman found the situation unremarkable: "The secrecy of the affair was normal and natural to her; since when had daughters been what their mothers supposed them to be?" "Joyce" prodded the pair toward sex, even while she demanded that they acknowledge it was wrong. Dell insisted that the pair adopt a more enlightened view of their relations: "I was puritanically resolved not to do what she thought was wrong—she had to be intellectually free." "Joyce" would have none of his perverse idealism, however, and gradually Dell dropped his objections. He realized that to stick to his principles would mean to lose his lover and her respect forever.

Uneasily, Dell recognized inconsistencies in "Joyce" that were both dishonest and conventional. Her matter-of-fact acceptance of duplicitous behavior in the conduct of love disturbed her idealistic twenty-year-old lover:

> All this, though evidently a well-established part of American mores, was strange territory to me, who had got my ideas of love chiefly from advanced literature. I would have felt more comfortable in a situation in which my right, and the girl's right, to love without marriage could be frankly stated, sincerely defended, and courageously acted upon. But that was quite out of the question. I had no place to take her, no protection to offer her; and besides,

she wouldn't have gone. We had to take, and be satisfied with, the love we could get by lovers' cunning and lovers' lies and lovers' curiously innocent and shameless hypocrisy.

Still more troubling were the class differences that separated the two. The young woman recognized instantly that Dell would likely prove unable to support her should they decide to marry. Dell accepted the situation with a mix of feelings: relief, it is likely, but also the shame of a poor young man. He realized that poverty limited him in the conduct of his love life, even though American society pretended that such conduct was subject solely to free choice. Dell never blamed "Joyce" for her tough-minded view of such matters. But he felt resentment and surprise to discover that he was without options in this love affair they had chosen for themselves. "Certainly I could not support a wife and children, and I had no prospects which would warrant me in dreaming of becoming my sweetheart's husband; but these certainties were obscurely humiliating, never as frankly faced by me as by her." Theirs was a "holiday love," a "summer romance," as she was fond of calling it, and after a while it was the woman, not Dell, who forced both to admit that it had no future. In January 1908, only a half-year after they became lovers, she ended their relations by returning to a former suitor, a well-to-do young man whom she soon married. Dell was bitter about it, but shortly he accepted as inevitable this conclusion to their brief adventure.

Perhaps Dell's early taste for romantic poetry helped him accept his failure to maintain the affair; it may even have nudged him toward such failure. Romantic youths, after all, typically adore failure before they have had the chance to fail. Still, while he learned to accept the incompatibility of love and the world, he also began to grasp social causes for it—not in romantic choice and renunciation but in the tyranny of class distinctions. He took his "dismissal," as he termed it years later, as "Joyce" wished him to take it: "without scenes, and without my hating her." But deep down he felt the outcome of his first serious foray in love to be mortifying. Poverty and his failure to make a respectable living seemed to poison every corner of his life.

Worldly failure of a familiar sort made it impossible for Dell to protest his lover's decision to end their affair. In December 1907 he was fired from the *Democrat* "for insolence to the proprietor." His intellectual arrogance and determined preoccupation with matters apart from work had not boded well for his professional success, and in the winter of 1907–1908, Dell found himself without a job. He had also run out of newspapers in Davenport. The rebelliousness implicit in all his intellectual enthusiasms—socialism, nihilism, atheism—seemed to foretell what his work experience demonstrated: he was not likely to be a reliable employee. "Joyce" saw this as well. She pointed out to him that as a man unable to hold down a steady job, he would not be able to support her should she become his wife. Dell was in no position to argue. When she ended the affair a month later there were regrets and humiliation—but no serious objections—on his part.

BESIDES THE LOSS of love and his job, Dell had to contend with a nationwide depression in 1907. There were no jobs left in the Tri-Cities for him. So he did what made most sense at the time: in the spring of 1908 he headed for Buffalo, Iowa, nine miles upriver, to live and work on his friend George Cram Cook's farm.

Dell had met Cook not long after he came to Davenport. Marilla Freeman introduced the two men sometime in 1904 or 1905. They did not like each other much at first. Cook found Dell cold, overly intellectual, impersonal. Dell thought Cook a reactionary aristocrat averse to socialism and the cause of the working class.

True, George Cram Cook was no proletarian. The scion of one of Davenport's wealthiest families, he had studied at Harvard and Heidelberg and served on the faculty at the University of Iowa. He had also fought in the Spanish-American War and spent a few bohemian years in San Francisco. For Dell it was Cook's credentials as a social rebel that at last overrode his lack of working-class experience or sympathies. Despite class and age differences (Cook was fourteen years older than Dell), the two had become close friends by 1906, united by intellectual interests and their militant view of themselves as opponents of bourgeois respectability. They were boon companions with Fritz Feuchter, whom they affectionately named "the critic of the universe, discoverer of hidden poets."

In 1906 Dell and Cook had founded a radical "freethinkers" club, the Monist Society, which met on Sunday afternoons in a room above a tavern in Davenport. The society numbered Susan Glaspell and Rabbi Fineshriber among its members. In some ways an

extension of the gatherings already taking place at the Fineshribers'
house, the Monist Society was made up, as Susan Glaspell remarked,
of all "the queer fish of the town." "Get the queer fish in town into
one pond," Glaspell added, "and it's a queer pond—but it moves the
water around." Talk was of education, evolution, socialism, sex.
Then in 1907 Cook and his wife divorced, and he retreated to the
family farm in Buffalo. There he worried about his future as a writer
and pursued a most unpromising career as a truck farmer. Then
again, he did not really need the money. When Dell joined him,
Cook was awaiting the arrival of Mollie Price, a young, liberated
woman from an anarchist family he had met through Charles Banks
in Chicago. Mollie had agreed to marry him.

The friendship between Dell and Cook was close but unsteady.
Cook was a large, morose man, an adamant bohemian, but also
profoundly uncertain of himself in the winter of 1907–1908 when
Dell moved to the farm. His unfinished novels, coupled with the
failure of his first marriage, had left a man already inclined to
self-doubt still more thoroughly demoralized. Cook's low spirits
helped Dell gain the upper hand, at least some of the time, in their
friendship. In their endless discussions on literature and politics,
Dell managed to convert Cook to socialism. The result was Cook's
decision to begin a socialist novel, *The Chasm*, later that year.
Dell's quick intelligence and learning overwhelmed the older man.
"The cock-sure young Socialist," Susan Glaspell wrote decades later
of Dell, "kept biting at the Nietzschean, anarchist, profound and
lazy man of God, the way a terrier would worry a St. Bernard."
Glaspell remembered Dell in those days as "an inventive, soaring
young mind; an exasperating and quarrelsome young mind."

Cook sometimes found Dell's effusions irritating, flashy, superficial. He lacked Dell's incredible memory and mental agility; he
had instead a brooding intensity that impressed all his friends. But
generally the two were excellent company; their friendship was
sustained by literature and unmitigated contempt for the conventional folks in Davenport. Glaspell described Dell's presence on
Cook's farm as conducive to all sorts of productivity and excitement:
"In the whole history of Iowa there has probably not been so
stimulating a hired man [as Floyd Dell]; and perhaps since the
beginnings of growth seeds have not matured in so lively a stream of
intellectual life. Spraying the apple-trees with arguments about
Haeckel and Nietzsche and Marx, weeding potatoes and theories,

plowing the earth to its greatest poems!" Early summer mornings, Dell and Cook would ride their wagons into town, bringing crops to market, chanting in Greek stanzas from Sappho's "Ode to Aphrodite."

Not all the influence passed from Dell to Cook. For years Dell had been fascinated by bohemianism—not "disorderly, pig-sty, lunatic Bohemianism," to be sure, but a bohemianism that would mix quiet seclusion from society with high social ideals like those he associated with socialism. But the socialists he had known in the Tri-Cities had been decidedly "middle-class in their way of life," with the possible exception of Fritz Feuchter, "who combined the orderly habits of a civil-service employee with some mild Bohemian tendencies." In George Cram Cook, Dell met someone with a real bohemian past—a past in San Francisco, no less, a city whose bohemian reputation had long intrigued Dell. Cook's faith in sexual experience as redemptive and even sacred also impressed Dell, who only months before had struggled to convince "Joyce" of the wholesomeness of their sexual relations, no matter what conventional society might think.

Evenings were spent mainly in talk about literature and the books Cook and Dell would write. Both were scribbling away at novels. Dell had long wanted to write a novel but had felt he simply did not know enough about American life, or about human nature for that matter, to venture one. The novels of Frank Norris and Upton Sinclair had thrilled him, convincing him that his true ambition was to write fiction, not poetry. Dell had read Sinclair's *The Jungle* when it first appeared, serialized in the pages of *The Appeal to Reason*. He had been amazed by the scale of the novel—its portrayal of individual lives played out against a vast, oppressive social background. Now at Jig Cook's farm in Buffalo, Dell was trying one of his own, a largely autobiographical novel that he soon abandoned for reasons he had long anticipated: he was lost trying to make sense of his own life, lost among the formal and conceptual problems presented by novel-writing.

Dell met with more success in his efforts in early 1908 to hammer out a critical point of view. In a letter he wrote (but never sent) to George Bernard Shaw, Dell sketched out a theory of mid-nineteenth-century American literature that emphasized its relation to the politics of the era. The "Transcendental movement," he argued, should be understood in terms of "the impinging of the working class upon literature." He offered no explicit description of that relation. Instead

he emphasized how the writers he admired most from that period—
Whitman, Emerson, Poe, and Whittier—had refused to meet the
gentlemanly standard by which writers were prevented from speaking
openly about economic injustices, rather choosing vaguely scandalous literary and personal styles. In another draft of the letter
(addressed to "My Dear Doctor") Dell did offer a tentative explanation of the relation of working-class resentment to transcendentalism:
"What I mean is that the commercial class, as distinguished from
the new uprising manufacturing class, had passed from a stage of
activity into a stage of leisure, in which its best representatives, not
having any class-ideas of their own to blazon enduringly on the page
of the world's literature, had their minds open to receive the new
ideas brought to the surface of thought by the working class, and
gave them expression again, clothed sometimes—as in the case of
Emerson—in unforgettable beauty." This theory of a privileged
intellectual class alert to the political resentments of working people
is interesting, but it is plainly an insufficient account of the relation
between politics and transcendentalism. Even Dell seemed to recognize its shortcomings.

Both drafts of the letter are impressive, however, in their defense
of Whittier's poetry. Already at age twenty Dell was furious about
revisionist criticism in the late nineteenth and early twentieth
centuries that had erased all memory of Whittier's radicalism and
replaced it with the cozy image of a fireside poet. As with Whitman,
who had been domesticated into the image of "The Good Grey
Poet," Whittier had been misrepresented by a largely reactionary
literary establishment. Dell argued that Whittier had been an even
"fiercer iconoclast" than Whitman, a thoroughly "disreputable person," and that this had been "carefully suppressed by most writers on
American literature." Dell described Whittier as "a young Abolitionist editor in his shirt sleeves, raging over the latest news from
Congress." He pictured Whittier as the splendid figure of a poet: "a
man interested in vital things, loving life more than literature, and
transfigured by the grandeur of scorn and wrath into the accusing
spirit of an ignoble time—a spirit that, like Shelley's, walked into a
'flaming robe of verse.'"

Dell bitterly described the political climate within which Whittier
worked: an "American Union" founded on "slavery as an economic
institution," with "press and pulpit . . . gagged or intimidated," and
"literature poisoned by the infection of an enforced silence." "Exploi-

tation of the black worker," Dell wrote, had been regarded then as "in accord with the will of God." Dell portrayed Whittier as uniquely able to discern "the vital interrelations of the religion, politics and industrial system of his time." According to Dell, Whittier was remarkable for "the relentlessness with which he stripped away every veil from the face of things." Dell's theoretical positions were not yet thoroughly worked out, but he was already certain that literary judgments are often shaped by hidden political views and agendas.

In the midst of his literary work Dell was unsettled by the rapid succession of women who now entered his life. After breaking with "Joyce" he began a frequent correspondence with Marilla Freeman, who had since moved to another town and job. On a sudden impulse he sent her a love letter—precisely the kind of unabashed declaration he had always wanted to make to her. He immediately regretted sending it. And so he was flabbergasted when he received an instantaneous reply from her, telling him she had been delighted by his letter. Soon she arrived at Cook's farm for several weeks of summer vacation. She and Dell became "sweethearts," lying "out in the woods and pastures kissing."

Marilla remained in charge of the relationship. She refused to consummate relations with Dell, saying that the difference in their ages was too great for them to consider initiating a serious love affair. Still, their new relations amounted to a special triumph—a sort of coming of age—for Dell. Having been rejected by "Joyce" only months before, he now found himself welcomed by the woman he had always desired. "She had been to me at sixteen very much a goddess," he wrote fifty years later, "and at twenty-one I still felt somewhat in awe of her; and to lie in the woods with a goddess, to unbutton her shirt waist and fondle and kiss her beautiful breasts, to lift her skirt and see and caress her beautiful thighs—there was a touch of heroic impiety about it."

Opportunities for "heroic impiety" now seemed regularly to offer themselves to Dell. Cook brought Mollie, his second wife, home from Chicago, where they had been married that spring. Mollie was a perfect affront to the city of Davenport, a second-generation anarchist fond of overalls and bare feet. She had been a principled vegetarian and a member of an anarchist collective, an actress, a nude model for painters and sculptors, and an assistant at Emma Goldman's magazine *Mother Earth*. She was adventurous and high-spirited. She was also closer in age to Dell than to her new husband. Both had grown up in poor families; both were determined not to be confined by poverty. When Cook retreated to worry and work on *The Chasm*, Mollie and Dell became close companions—which irritated Cook even as he was beginning an affair with Susan Glaspell. On one occasion, when Cook was out of town, Mollie and Dell nearly became lovers. It was Dell, though, who pulled back, unwilling to follow through on his impulse to make love to Mollie. In fact he had reservations all along about Cook's self-indulgent ideas about love—"his romanticism made each new affair so wonderful that it justified him in his bad treatment of his former love." Now Dell decided not to emulate the older man by sleeping with his young, agreeable wife. As a result of this near encounter, and because he recognized the likelihood of a second tempting episode with Mollie, Dell left the farm in the fall of 1908. Briefly he returned to his family's house in town.

Davenport, though, could offer him little now. Both the city's newspapers had fired him, and he could imagine no other place in Davenport where he wanted to work. His attention shifted naturally to Chicago, especially now that he had met a woman from Evanston, just north of the city, who was encouraging him to go. Her name was Margery Currey, an English teacher at the high school in Davenport. She was friends with Mollie Cook, who had invited her to the farm and introduced her to Dell.

Margery Currey was roughly Marilla's age, eleven years older than Dell. But the difference in their ages seemed of no consequence. She was open and talkative, a small, dark-haired woman interested in new ideas and eager to expose him to the larger intellectual life of Chicago. She was extraordinarily well read, a graduate of Vassar College, a feminist who derided traditional sexual mores. Dell suggested that she read *Socialism, Utopian and Scientific* by Friedrich Engels. Margery told Dell that she would be able to introduce him to intellectuals in Chicago. She planned to be in Evanston for Thanksgiving, and she invited Dell to spend the holiday with her and her family. Dell accepted her plans for him, once again placing himself in the hands of a confident, older woman. He had no inkling of how she would figure in his future. With the quick resolve of youth, Dell made plans to leave for Chicago and began to imagine what might become of him there.

THREE

Literary Journalist

CHICAGO IN 1908 was infamous for its radicals and labor conflicts. The Haymarket Riot of 1886 and the Pullman Strike of 1894 had done nearly as much as skyscrapers and unprecedented population growth to create Chicago's reputation as a frighteningly modern place. The Industrial Workers of the World had been founded in Chicago in 1905. When Dell arrived a few years later, socialists and anarchists were in plentiful supply, as were radical magazines, publishers, meetings, and clubs.

Dell was an ideal prospect for the city's sundry radical enclaves. Yet from first to last he gave them slight notice. He found the Chicago Socialist party local meetings as boring, its membership as staid and middle class as their Davenport counterparts. Unlike in Davenport, though, he made no effort in Chicago to enliven the meetings. Instead he abandoned them altogether. He read the *Chicago Daily Socialist* and was introduced to radicals who had scandalized the city for decades. In November he even attended the annual memorial service for the anarchists who had been executed after the Haymarket Riot. But before long he was looking elsewhere for inspiration.

He did not find much of it among the writers who had challenged conventional literature in Chicago twenty years earlier. Starting around 1890, Henry Blake Fuller, Robert Herrick, and other authors began to reject sentimental ideals and civic boosterism as adequate bases for modern literature in Chicago. Instead they dedicated themselves to telling important, if unpleasant, truths about the modern city in which they lived. They had aimed—often with

impressive results—to write books that captured the city's impersonal, mercantile, violent nature. And yet, as with the socialists and
anarchists, Dell kept his distance from them. He attended several of
their social gatherings at the Little Room in the Fine Arts Building
after Chicago Symphony concerts but formed no close alliances with
any of them.

Many years later Dell insisted that he had admired these writers
while he was in Chicago. But his admiration appears to have been
lukewarm. Writers like Fuller and Herrick may have avoided conventional hypocrisies and superfluities—Fuller through ironic portraits
of the genteel class, Herrick through a closer look at the city's
violence and poverty—but to a young outsider like Dell, these two
older writers were also part of the city's outmoded literary past. For
all their rejection of saccharine images of the city, most of the older
writers were men whose cultural and moral values smacked of New
England tradition. Fuller and Herrick were ambivalent men, with
loyalties divided between genteel culture and morality on the one
hand, and distaste and impatience with genteel values on the other.
Dell may have been better able to appreciate these writers years later,
when he had come to recognize similar ambivalencies in himself.
But in his early days in Chicago he found them strangely detached
from a city that was extraordinarily vibrant. None of their writings
convinced him that these were men he needed to know intimately.

Other features of Chicago impressed Dell from the start. He was
struck by the city's dynamic life, by the great number of theaters,
libraries, concerts, and restaurants, and by the sheer diversity of its
peoples, activities, and opportunities. In Davenport he had anchored
his life and work in persons and institutions which, in one way or
another, lent the town a settled, old-world atmosphere. In Chicago
he was intrigued by the most modern and protean aspects of the city,
by everything that cleared free room for untrammeled intellectual
and personal freedom. What Dell found in Chicago, quite simply,
was a fine setting for experimental conduct in his life and work.

Part of this heightened emphasis on nonconformity was due to
having broken at last with his family and Davenport mentors; part
was due to being set loose in a large, impersonal city. But it was also
connected to the unique character of Chicago in those years.
Late-nineteenth-century Chicago may have labored to establish
intellectual and social institutions that would lend it a sense of
permanence and dignity—the Art Institute, the Symphony Orches-

tra, the Crerar and Newberry libraries, the University of Chicago—
but in a sense it had built these institutions too soon, before the city
had stopped growing and transforming itself in sudden and fundamental ways. To borrow a phrase from historian Asa Briggs, Chicago
around the turn of the century was a "shock city," a place astonishing for the way it exemplified a spirit of ceaseless change and
modernity. Signs of tradition and the past seemed strangely superfluous. The relentless newness of the place was crucial for Dell,
even if he was only vaguely aware of it. What impressed him most
were those things that resisted stability and permanence, those
features of the city that were thrillingly, splendidly in motion.

DELL ARRIVED BY train in early November, in the evening. He noted
some unremarkable first impressions of Chicago on a scrap of paper:
the city was dark, the buildings huge; anonymous crowds of people
were everywhere. He had delayed his departure from Davenport just
long enough to participate as a full adult in his first national
election. He voted "for the Future," as he imagined it at the
time—for Eugene Debs, the popular Socialist leader for whom he
had leafleted workers in front of Davenport factories four years
earlier. Upon arrival, Dell sensed that a different kind of "Future"
awaited him in Chicago.

He was met at the station by Dr. Graham Taylor, the sociologist
whose lectures Dell had attended in Davenport a few years back.
Not long before, Taylor had heard from Marilla Freeman, asking
him to look out for Dell when he got to town. Dell realized that
Marilla was back to her old habit of shepherding his career, provid-
ing him with contacts and letters of introduction he would need in
Chicago. Her brief affair with him had receded quickly; she was
again the older person who knew better than he exactly what he
needed.

He does not seem to have resented the help. To be met by a man
of Dr. Taylor's distinction was an honor, and Dell was relieved to
discover that the two of them had no trouble finding a lot to talk
about. Graham Taylor was still a relatively young man, but he was
already a well-known scholar and head of the Chicago Commons
settlement house. He was a commanding intellectual who was also a
man of action determined to remake the world around him. As
such, he was precisely the sort of man Dell was prepared to admire.

Dell stayed several days and nights at the Commons—"a gracious and homelike building"—then moved into rooms in a house owned by one of Mollie Cook's anarchist friends. Most of the anarchists and socialists he met in the coming weeks failed to impress him. Mollie's father, Dr. James Russell Price, was an exception. A kindhearted, elderly eccentric, Dr. Price was the perfect anarchist father for the anarchist daughter Dell had known back in Iowa. But most of the Chicago anarchists lacked Mollie's—and her father's—adventurous nature. Even their talk about "free love" seemed distressingly predictable. Faced with these uninspired rebels, Dell realized again that persons who pledged themselves to unconventional behavior could humorlessly standardize unconventionality itself.

Otherwise Chicago pleased him immensely. New acquaintances led him about town. He was stunned by the size and energy of the place. Chicago's population was now doubling every twenty years, with fully two million inhabitants when Dell arrived. Almost 40 percent of these people were recent immigrants, pouring in mainly from southern and central Europe, and so Chicago presented a volatile mix of people that shocked visitors and newcomers to the city. Cultivated European tourists were often dismayed by the chaos of the place, its blind commitment to expansion and its startling juxtaposition of poverty and wealth. The perturbed impressions recorded by an Englishman in 1893 were equally relevant fifteen years later when Dell arrived: Chicago "is in many respects a large cluster of incongruities. . . . The 'sky-scraper' and the shanty stand side by side." But for others Chicago seemed to offer opportunities not available in more settled places, including older American cities on the East Coast. The place seemed made altogether of ceaseless change, offering unprecedented opportunity to those who wished to place all their energies in the service of some revolutionary vision of the future. Settlement homes like that headed by Graham Taylor were not simply meant to accommodate the flood of homeless immigrants: they were charged with vision and optimism, idealism and purposeful, hard work. There were scattered signs that Chicago might have a worthy cultural future in store for it too. Dell had eagerly devoured the Chicago novels of Norris and Sinclair, written in the first years of the new century. Once in town, he began to sense that Chicago was indeed full of cultural promise—and not just as a setting for novels about corruption and the stockyards.

Soon Dell made his way to Hull House, where he heard Jane Addams speak. Inevitably he visited the Chicago Public Library and browsed through the town's big bookstores. A letter from Marilla Freeman introduced him to Elia W. Peattie, chief literary critic and editor at the *Chicago Tribune*. She invited Dell to her home and read one of J. M. Synge's recent plays to him. He was delighted by these hours spent in the company of a big-city literary editor. But he made no effort to get to know her better or to inquire after a job at the *Tribune*.

Another letter from Marilla got him in the front door at the *Chicago Evening Post*. There he met the newspaper's four editorial writers, among them Charles Thomas Hallinan, an old friend of Marilla's who lived at Hull House, and Francis Hackett, a young, aggressive, feisty Irishman who was committed, like Dell and Hallinan, to new political and cultural ideas. No job awaited Dell at the *Post*, but the editorial writers liked him immediately and invited him to hang around the office. Their irreverent energy appealed to Dell more than the conventional radicalism he had encountered elsewhere in town. He decided to make the *Post's* noisy editorial office home base for his intellectual life in Chicago.

In a few days Dell was uprooted again, this time heading to a large apartment on Indiana Avenue, where he moved in with Dr. Price and two middle-aged bohemians: one a trade magazine editor, the other a postal clerk who was researching a book on "some kind of more or less Socialist solution of all economic problems." The place was run, as Dell noted in his sketchy list of early impressions of the city, according to the "Bohemian plan," which is to say, on practically no plan at all. He was satisfied with the arrangement for a while. But he avoided serious intellectual relations with his new roommates. They aroused his amusement but also his pity: they seemed stranded and irrelevant in Chicago, where so much that was extraordinary was taking place. Dell made himself comfortable in a tiny room largely without furnishings. Harry Hansen, who had moved to Chicago some while before Dell, visited him in his new digs and noticed that there was little more than books in the room.

In all this there was little direction, little substance. Dell had been a bit scared to come to the city: the place had a reputation for violence and social chaos. Now, however, he encountered more kindness than he had thought possible, and he adapted himself effortlessly to everyone who was generous toward him. He was as likely to be pleased by radicals at the Haymarket memorial as by established, vaguely genteel literary figures like Elia Peattie. He was recruited to teach a literature class at Hull House, a task he gladly accepted. But he was no more a settlement house activist than he was an old-style anarchist. He was smart, handsome, and adaptable, but he was also formless, a bit lost in the big modern city where he had no job, no definite plans, no prospects. This is how Margery Currey found him when she arrived in town for Thanksgiving.

Dell and Currey had had time, between his arrival and hers, to exchange a flurry of letters. Hers turned out to be an inspiration for him. She was witty and lighthearted, able to convey her brilliant, ironic self in the most casual remarks. Dell was fascinated by her, both as a man and as a writer. He had spent little time with Margery in Davenport, so it was through her letters that he began to know her. She seemed extraordinarily worldly and kind, and her facility as a writer made him recognize the stiffness of his own prose. His earlier writings as a reporter, poet, and socialist had been unrelievedly earnest: he had not tried to capture in his writings the mixture of seriousness and comedy that surfaced naturally in his conversation. Now he found himself reading letter after letter addressed to him by a charming woman who effortlessly pulled off this delightful mixture. The experience led him to try writing a similar kind of prose in his letters back to her.

Once again, as so many times in Davenport, he maneuvered himself into something like an apprentice's relation to an older person. The spirit of the woman led him to reconsider his own character. He realized clearly now something he had always dimly sensed: that since childhood he had wished desperately to make sense of things, "to find order in the universe." His socialist enthusiasms in particular had been prompted by a desire to piece together a coherent account of his family's confusing, unhappy story.

Margery Currey was entirely different in this regard. "She was at home," he marveled, "on her terms of whimsical humor with an essentially chaotic universe." She seemed able to maintain balance and self-possession without resorting to untempered seriousness or the grand explanations Dell had sought. His fascination with her character seemed to remind him of the important place of humor, irreverence, and satire in his own personality. Together with the pleasure of her words and company, she seemed to lead him to a more worldly version of his own self—a self that might, in the end, prove a worthy literary identity.

At Thanksgiving dinner Dell met Margery's father, J. Seymour Currey, a man in his sixties who had put his decades as an accountant behind him in order to work full time on a remarkably ambitious project: a five-volume history of Chicago. The old man was as kind and intelligent as his daughter, a rather otherworldly gentleman but also a man of considerable cultivation. He and Margery were devoted to each other—she was helping him with his historical project—and soon the elderly man had recruited Dell to write several chapters of the Chicago opus: one on "The Railroad Riots of 1877," the other on "Socialism and Anarchism in Chicago" (this latter piece was to be concerned in particular with the Haymarket Riot). These were peculiar topics for a young man who felt himself detached from the anarchists and socialists he had met since coming to Chicago. But Dell gladly took up Seymour Currey's offer. The two men were instantly at ease with each other, pleased by their mutual enthusiasms. Only Mrs. Currey was a bit undone at the Thanksgiving meal, shocked both by her liberated daughter and by the preposterously young man she had brought home. No matter: Margery, her father, and Dell formed a fond little circle at once.

During her holiday in Evanston Margery devoted herself to Dell. They went to vegetarian and Chinese restaurants, attended concerts by the Chicago Symphony Orchestra and the Lyric Opera, went to the theater, and walked along Evanston's several miles of lakefront. When Margery returned to Davenport they resumed their correspondence, then resumed their time together when she returned at Christmastime. Their talk turned to marriage, which seemed natural enough. After all, Dell had spent most of his adolescence in the company of persons a decade or so older than himself, and Margery was by temperament and principle open to unconventional arrangements between men and women. "She was a girl of twenty-one in looks," Dell explained later, "and I was a man of thirty-one in mental powers, tastes and habits. We found no discrepancy to bother us in our friendship or in our love, and cared no more for that indicated by the calendar than we did for what anybody else might think about us."

They were married in August, in a small ceremony at the Currey home in Evanston. Rabbi Fineshriber performed the wedding. It was "a very beautiful old Jewish form," Dell remembered, "in which we drank one after another from a goblet of wine—an excellent burgundy selected with care by the bride's father." There was a bit of flaunting of tradition and convention about the wedding: the Jewish ceremony was intended, at least in part, as an affront to Evanston's proper Episcopalians, in whose midst Margery had always attended church. But the ceremony was perfectly genuine in reflecting the couple's fondness for Rabbi Fineshriber, whose presence lent the event unaffected warmth and happiness.

The couple moved into a new, good-sized apartment on Morse Avenue in Rogers Park, a residential district in the most northerly part of Chicago, several blocks west of the lake and just south of Evanston. Their first steps toward housekeeping were unimpeachably conventional. Dell was amazed to discover that he could get credit at Marshall Field's department store, and he and Margery wasted no time in buying furniture for the entire flat. All was in the current fashion, right down to the twin beds, which the clerk at Field's assured him were what all couples preferred in those days. Dell needled the clerk on this rather delicate matter of why modern couples chose this sleeping arrangement. "I asked if it was because American husbands and wives no longer enjoyed sleeping with one another; or whether it was the symptom of a growing sense of individuality, insomnia, or feminism; or whether it was just because two twin beds could be sold for more than the price of one." Dell's questions announced that he and Margery were not conventional newlyweds—not subject to fashionably puritanical sleeping arrangements, nor duped by the marketing strategies of capitalist enterprises like Marshall Field's. Still, the Dells do not seem to have felt strongly about the matter. They caved in to fashion and bought the twin beds.

Once settled on Morse Avenue, Margery and Floyd aimed consciously to create something other than a conventional marriage. They made an effort to be partners in their marriage—to divide tasks equally, and to handle financial matters and other decisions jointly. Margery was a feminist of long standing, and Floyd prided himself on being an outspoken champion of women's rights. The first years of their experiment turned out well, probably due more to Margery's patience than to her husband's scrupulous commitment to marital equality. "If my wife had, as school-teacher and home-maker too, a double burden, I was assistant cook and bottle-washer, expert in making a salad, lobster Newburg, and other dishes—I was assistant home-maker, and very much on the job." Floyd was in fact more an "assistant" around the house than he was an equally responsible homemaker and cook. In married life (as in his past relations with Marilla, Maj, and "Joyce") he was content to let an older woman lead the way. Still, the experiment suited both, and it was considered an extraordinary marriage by their acquaintances.

Equally extraordinary was the fact that both worked: Margery as a high school English teacher in Evanston, Floyd as assistant editor at the *Chicago Evening Post's* literary supplement, the *Friday Literary Review*. Opportunity for the job had fallen unexpectedly in his lap, and he had made the most of it. Hanging around the *Post's* editorial office, Dell was asked to dash off a few editorials for the newspaper. These tasks he acquitted with skill and alacrity. Then he was offered work as a reporter, racing about Chicago in search of human interest stories of predictable sorts. Inspired by Margery's letters and conversation, he was now imbuing his stories with a worldly tone that accorded nicely with the air of urbanity sought by the *Post's* editors.

Then Francis Hackett, the newspaper's new literary editor, asked Dell to write a book review. Hackett was impressed by the piece—it managed to sound both tough and fair—and by Dell's evident talent for getting the job done quickly and with a minimum of fuss. At the time the *Post* planned to start a literary supplement (until then, book reviews were integrated unobtrusively into the larger paper), and Hackett, it turned out, was to be the supplement's editor. He asked Dell to be his assistant, then painted a frankly unglamorous picture of the job: "That means that you will have a hell of a lot of books to review—unsigned stuff—all the dirty work. You will wash up the dishes in the kitchen, while I sit in the parlor and discourse enlightenment to the suburbs." Dell accepted without hesitation.

The *Evening Post* was an unlikely home for the *Friday Literary Review* that Hackett and Dell created. By no means was the *Post* a radical or even a liberal paper. It specialized, by Dell's own account, "in financial news, and the reading of it was an established habit among the best people." Still, like other Chicago newspapers, it was determined to extend its coverage beyond business and political news. Unlike other papers, however, it was determined not to cater to popular tastes. As Dell acknowledged, the *Post* had gained a well-deserved reputation for "intellectual brilliance." The paper was determinedly cosmopolitan—neither genteel nor tawdry. An afternoon paper, it had a dignified air and a reputation for a serious interest in culture.

This by no means meant that Hackett's desire to create a forward-looking literary supplement would prove an easy task. Fortunately, Hackett was a brilliant editor and forceful critic. He was twenty-five years old in 1909, only a few years older than Dell, an Irishman who had been a militant socialist since boyhood and who had immigrated to New York in 1902 after becoming convinced that the Irish would never run the British out of Ireland. After several years of desultory labor as a clerk in a New York law firm, Hackett had moved on to Chicago, where he worked first at Marshall Field's, advancing quickly as a result of his abundant talents as a salesman. But within a few years he had given up this position in favor of poverty and the writer's life. Soon he was writing editorials and reviews for the *Evening Post*.

When the editorship of the *Friday Literary Review* was offered to Hackett in 1909, he was peculiarly well suited for the thorny task of fashioning a progressive critical organ for a conservative newspaper intent upon maintaining a dignified reputation. There was serious-ness and sobriety about Hackett's intellectual character, qualities that carried over plainly into his work as a writer and editor. He was not a bohemian, nor was he enamored of the hyperbolic effusions in-dulged in by many young literary radicals. He was intensely earnest in his literary and political opinions, and he was determined that, in his effort to create a progressive literary supplement, he would make it solid and intellectually formidable. His emphasis on intellectual substance had telling effects on Dell as well. He fanned Dell's literary ambitions and appetite for hard work while impressing upon him the need for intellectual discipline and seriousness.

These qualities in Hackett's and Dell's work accounted in large measure for their success with the management at the *Chicago Evening Post*. The two also shared a skepticism about the protesta-tions of the literary left—skepticism that occasionally led them to praise conservative writers and institutions. This too must have pleased their superiors at the *Post*. Thus in an editorial on the "five-foot library" of canonized classics of Western (mainly British) literature proposed by Charles William Eliot, the former president of Harvard University, Hackett felt called upon to defend this tradi-tional selection from the jeers of literary radicals. These early-century canon-busters, he insisted, unfairly ridiculed Dr. Eliot for favoring any list at all, when they themselves would finally be compelled to substitute some equally confined list of their own making. "We agree with men of new ideas that the list is conventional," Hackett concluded. "But there is something to be said for the conventional. And we are not enthusiastic about the unconventional list that would come from the modern young materialist—literature selected for its proteid, fat and carbohydrate."

Some of Dell's articles must also have pleased the *Post's* management by poking fun at the literary and political left. He delighted in unmasking radical conformity and convention. In a brief review of *An Anarchist Woman*, a largely nonfictional work by Hutchins Hapgood about the anarchist community in Chicago, Dell gleefully turned Hapgood's argument on its head, praising the book for things Hapgood would have found deplorable. Hapgood had wished not only to offer a true picture of several anarchists but also to vindicate their courage and inspired rejection of social convention. Dell disingenuously praised the book while drawing exactly the opposite moral. Hapgood, he wrote, gave the reader an accurate impression of the anarchist "movement," particularly of its "futility and fatuity." The book, he remarked, "gives one the right to believe that cant and meanness of soul exist no less among these professed idealists than among the conventional people whom they so despise."

At the same time Hackett and Dell were able to temper or subtly disguise the radical opinions that the *Friday Literary Review* regularly espoused. In one essay (printed on the *Review's* front page, no less) Hackett praised Morris Hillquit's *Socialism in Theory and Practice*, a book by the left-wing New York lawyer that aimed both to explain and justify socialism to American readers. Hackett's sympathies must have been evident to the *Post's* well-heeled clientele. The book, he declared early on in his full-page review, provides "a definition of socialism, a diagnosis of our present disturbed social condition, a theory of social progress, and a report of the results that are coming from the proletarian acceptance of the socialist theory and ideal." Still, Hackett was careful to avoid an unambiguous endorsement of socialism in his review. He argued that, taken as a whole, the book "is not argumentative so much as expository. . . . In designating Mr. Hillquit's book admirable the demands of socialism are, in the famous phrase of the noncommittal, neither affirmed nor denied. What is affirmed, and positively, is the comprehension and lucidity of the work under consideration." Hackett made it clear that if his readers wanted to qualify as fully informed, up-to-date people, they needed to acquaint themselves with socialist theory.

Such reviews were the work of an inspired salesman, able to coax readers into entertaining ideas they may have otherwise considered abhorrent. Still, readers of the *Friday Literary Review* got more than long, serious articles on socialism, especially ones that insisted that "to understand socialism one must grant first of all that something's rotten in the state of society." The *Review* was a handsome tabloid insert, not unlike today's *New York Times Book Review*, with a photograph or drawing centered on page one of the author whose work was featured in the full-page "Book of the Week" column. From the outset Hackett and Dell managed to fulfill their plan that the *Review* would "cover all the affairs of the republic of letters, even to the small talk of the publishers and the personalia of authors." Weekly "Letters" from New York and London reported on life in the literary capitals, "Literary Small Talk" purveyed gossip. Short reviews of novels, critical works, plays, and collections of poetry were scattered throughout, as were occasional columns devoted to religious, historical, and biographical works. Occasional sections were devoted to children's literature. Snippets of poetry were sprinkled about the pages. A regular feature, "Magazine Critique," commented on other journals and their recent offerings.

The editors' strategy of mixing radical ideas with occasional conservative views allowed the *Review* to pass muster with the *Post's* management. The paper's owner, John Shaffer, sometimes complained about the scandalous ideas he detected in the literary supplement, but he was generally pacified by the *Post's* managing editor, Leigh Reilly, who assured him that Hackett and Dell were up to nothing harmful. The *Friday Literary Review*, in fact, turned out to be an unexpected success in Chicago and elsewhere, drawing new readers and advertisers to the paper. This too secured Shaffer's goodwill.

The *Review's* popularity was soon great enough to warrant selling the supplement separately, and it was not long before it was regarded as one of the nation's few important and genuinely influential literary publications. The *Post* proclaimed the *Friday Literary Review* "the sole literary supplement issued in connection with a daily newspaper outside of New York," and before long popular acclaim confirmed the *Review's* desire to prove itself "indispensable to the general reader who wished to keep abreast of current English and

American literature." In fact, the *Friday Literary Review* was one of the crucial publications of the early century that ushered in several decades of unprecedentedly brilliant literary magazines intended for general readers. Book publishers and sellers discovered still another reason for respecting the *Friday Literary Review*: it carried sufficient weight to influence book sales and authors' reputations.

A handful of themes emerged as the hallmarks of Hackett's literary essays and of the *Review* as a whole. Many were summarized in an early article on H. G. Wells's novel *Tono-Bungay*. Hackett described the book as "epochal" in that it "teems with ideas, seethes with opinions, writhes with self-consciousness." Also extraordinary was Wells's "dogged determination to reveal himself, whether his feeling be fine feeling or coarse, his breeding high or low." In an editorial from another issue of the *Friday Literary Review*, Hackett expanded on this aspect of *Tono-Bungay*: "The novel is near to sheer self-revelation. Although nominally vicarious and invented, the hero's experiences are suspiciously like autobiography. . . . They are intrinsically personal, a document of Mr. Wells's life." In reviews of books by other authors he admired—Shaw, Whitman, Ibsen, Galsworthy, among others—Hackett returned regularly to these themes: the importance of modern ideas; the crucial place of society as a theme within and influence upon literary works; the need for frank self-revelation by the author.

None of these points were new to Dell, but they were put across with such intensity and eloquence that they could not help but impress him. Even Dell's first essays for the *Friday Literary Review* reveal the influence of Hackett's imperious example. There is an aggressive worldliness in Dell's writing, along with a felt need to hammer out a mature critical position, that was lacking in anything he had written earlier. From his first essays for the *Review* he can be seen fashioning an impressive critical identity for himself: fair and yet never overly generous or sentimental; ranging over literary figures from many periods and from all over Europe and America; confidently passing judgment on all manner of literary and political topics, and on books about history, religion, science, and medicine.

The *Review*'s sense of its own importance was evident in Dell as well. He deliberately cultivated the appearance of a big-city literary editor: he kept his thin brown hair neatly trimmed, grew a faint mustache, wore dark suits and stiff collars. The urbane wit and grace he had detected in Margery Currey's letters to him—and that he had emulated in his own letters back—now surfaced in many of his writings for the *Review*. Beginning work as assistant editor when he was only twenty-one, Dell presented himself immediately as a masterful literary arbiter, willing to dismiss big reputations and laud unknown ones. He seems to have imagined himself—partly out of youthful arrogance, partly out of nervous will and determination—a full citizen of the literary republic, capable of taking on writers with global reputations.

If all this makes Dell sound preposterously brash, it is worth noting how poised were many of his critical judgments. In discussing *Egoists*, a collection of essays on modern literary heroes—Flaubert, Pater, Ibsen, Nietzsche, and others—by one of his earliest critical idols, James Huneker, Dell confidently identified the book's strengths and failings. *Egoists* served as a lively introduction to these important figures, Dell conceded, but it was marred by inaccuracies, exaggerations, and "journalistic" simplifications. The tone of Dell's review is refined, balanced, modern, learned. His impatience with Huneker's "journalistic" excesses announced plainly that Dell wrote as a journalist of a more distinguished sort. He seemed loath to gush about the book, however much he agreed with its critical sympathies. The review implies Dell's desire to contrast his own critical dexterity and balance to Huneker's elephantine, hyperbolic effusions. If Dell's point of view was plainly "radical," it was also determinedly sophisticated in a way that must have pleased the *Post's* management as well as his boss, Francis Hackett.

Along with other young critics at the time (Mencken and Van Wyck Brooks are two who come immediately to mind), Dell emerged in these years as a critic who was a pleasure to read. The tone of his pieces shifted between serious praise, lighthearted approval, and devastating critiques. He managed to handle these shifts in tone with aplomb, even grace. He created a literary persona that was varied and unpredictable but also identifiably that of a single dynamic critic. He was entirely capable of dispatching a writer's work with heartless wit. Of an egregious passage in Cale Young Rice's *Nirvana Days*, he wrote: "It is a matter of amazement that anyone should care to write lines like the following; they are entitled 'Written in Hell,' but that is not a sufficient excuse." He was also capable of sober praise for the Chicago novelist Robert Herrick as well as more enthusiastic encomiums for Frank Norris, who Dell insisted had died just before attaining the greatness that would have established him as "a towering figure among the great masters of literature."

Dell's astonishing capacity for work was evident not only in his many writings for the *Friday Literary Review* (he frequently wrote five or six reviews and essays per issue) but also in his more properly "editorial" duties for the magazine. Working with authors, editing copy, planning issues, assisting at numerous points along the supplement's production schedule—in these and other capacities Dell labored to lend the *Review* variety, intellectual energy, and entertainment value.

Within a year Hackett had made Dell "associate editor," placing his name, together with his own, on the *Review*'s masthead. Dell responded by churning out a prodigious number of essays on Emerson, Twain, Granville Barker, Shaw, Jack London, Hilaire Belloc, G. K. Chesterton, Ezra Pound, Tolstoy, Turgenev, William Blake, Arnold Bennett, Emma Goldman, Upton Sinclair, Arthur Schnitzler, Nietzsche, Aristophanes, and countless others, great and small, as well as pieces on everything from Chicago's libraries to books on science, psychology, and popular fiction. Working uninterruptedly for the *Review*, he transformed himself into an important public figure and literary man. Two years after he had arrived in Chicago, still a mere twenty-three years of age, Dell had established himself as one of the most powerful figures on the city's cultural scene.

NOT EVERYONE WAS impressed by Dell's sudden rise to literary influence. His old friend George Cram Cook, for one, found the Floyd Dell of the *Friday Literary Review* totally unsatisfactory. Jig abhorred Dell's efforts to be worldly. "Ten years ago," he wrote Dell in September 1909, "I began to learn that the disinterested and impersonal critical attitude was a failure. That way lies apathy— absence of feeling—the death of intellectual desire." Cook lambasted Dell without reservation, accusing him of being "inauthentic," of refusing to discover and write in his own voice. He forced upon Dell what was undoubtedly unwelcome advice: "If you wish to remain alive do not cease to be a partisan. Floyd Dell *was* egocentric. Now he aspires to write like everybody in general, nobody in particular, to be a literary ventriloquist, to have no color in his own soul, to let other men's light shine through him unstained, to have no bias, no preconceived opinion—to write *reviews*. Views? How crude!"

Cook's complaints may have disturbed Dell a few years later, but at first, in 1909 and 1910, they mainly confirmed his sense of how different were his own goals from those of his Davenport friend. Cook's criticisms seemed perverse, morose, and irrelevant to Dell in the summer and fall of 1909, when Cook appeared stranded on his farm in Buffalo and Dell was preoccupied with his new life as a big-city literary journalist. True, his job at the *Friday Literary Review* was primarily to write reviews of recent books and essays on current literary topics. Unlike Cook, though, Dell recognized the necessity of such work. As a critic and assistant editor, he was engaged in what he knew to be literary tasks of importance to readers and writers alike: hammering out aesthetic judgments and criteria; describing the relation between literature and society; encouraging new novelists, poets, playwrights, critics; defining ideas and tastes necessary to the creation of a literary movement.

At bottom, Dell, with Francis Hackett and a handful of others at the *Friday Literary Review*, was trying to make Chicago a place hospitable to new literary and critical developments, a place where adventurous writers might find the readers and artistic fellowship they needed. He insisted on the critic's responsibility to "discriminate between what is good and what is bad, between what is genuinely conceived and what is merely echoed, between what is honest and what is derivative." The critic, according to Dell, is a liaison between good writers and a curious public, but he is more as well: a leader who points writers and readers in the direction of a promising literary future. Already in 1909 Dell was impressed by the necessary, dignified place of serious criticism in a literary community, local, national, or global. Half a decade later he was able to look back with justifiable pride on his work at the *Friday Literary Review*, especially the way it had helped create formidable literary ideas and tastes among its many readers. "It is necessary to have clear thinking," he explained, and "not only about social and economic conditions and theories, but about books and painting and music and plays"; these were "the ideals of the old Friday Literary Review." If Cook failed to see that this was the important work Dell had set for himself in 1909, that was his problem.

Dell's feelings of estrangement from Cook were aggravated in the summer of 1910 when he and Margery took a brief holiday in Davenport and Buffalo, only to discover that Mollie was pregnant with the couple's second child and that Jig was frankly in love with Susan Glaspell. Mollie was putting a generous interpretation on Jig's affair. Dell realized that she "would really have been glad to settle down in respectable bourgeois monogamy with Jig for good and all," but she generously had "fallen back on her old Anarchist ideas, and was prepared to be tolerant of Jig's affair with Susan." By the time the Dells arrived in Buffalo, Cook and Glaspell had decided that this cheerful anarchist solution was unsatisfactory, that they preferred a full and exclusive attachment to each other.

All progressive pronouncements to the contrary, Mollie was crushed by this turn of events. In the presence of this desperately cheerful, pregnant young woman, Dell was disgusted again with his friend's unrelieved egotism, which allowed Cook to abandon wife, baby, and unborn child. It was, Dell bluntly pointed out, Cook's second failed marital experiment. In his private discussions with Cook, Dell was confronted with an even more morose, uncertain man than he had known before. Dell offered little sympathy this time in response to Jig's intermittent efforts to justify his failure as a husband and father with the old talk of freedom and ecstasy. That talk hardly fit with Dell's determined view of himself as a responsible married man.

DELL WAS NEVERTHELESS more susceptible to Jig's protestations than he liked to admit. In a letter that Mollie wrote to him shortly before he and Margery arrived at the farm, she had hinted at how Jig's affair with Susan Glaspell had made her reconsider all her anarchist principles: "I find myself growing Puritanical. I have little patience with my former deification of passion. I think the value of sexual love is very much over-estimated, and holds too consuming a place in the scheme of things. The old-fashioned God of Repression has a wise purpose behind him."

Dell undoubtedly read these remarks with sympathy for Mollie— and likely with some confusion. He remained adamant in his condemnation of Jig's romantic self-indulgence, particularly because children were involved. But in his own life in Chicago, without children to weigh him down, and almost in spite of himself, Dell was being drawn to the idea that the good life was spontaneous and passionate, properly governed not by any "old-fashioned God of Repression," as Mollie had suggested, but by that "deification of passion" that she, at least temporarily, had renounced. He may have watched the breakup of Jig and Mollie's marriage with sadness, but the spectacle was not sufficient to warn him away from a similar fascination with an unrepressed, extravagantly unconventional life.

At first this commitment to the unconventional was part of a joint effort with Margery to make a better marriage than those they saw around them. To establish equality as the hallmark of their married life was only part of what they had in mind. Another part—the desire for a frank, unembarrassed recognition of their sexual identities—was epitomized by a portrait hanging in their apartment in Rogers Park. Their friend Martha Baker, a miniaturist who had lived for some while in Paris and now was working in the less bohemian environs of Chicago, had complained to the Dells that she had not done a nude since her days in Europe. Margery and Floyd promptly offered to let her draw them together. Baker penciled in an earlier date and the word "Paris" at the bottom of the drawing so as to spare the couple embarrassment. But the Dells were determined to override local propriety and hung the portrait in their home. It symbolized for them, and for their many visitors and friends, their willingness to live outside the conventions of bourgeois American society.

More important was the circle of writers, critics, and artists who began to gather regularly at the couple's Rogers Park flat. Dell's inexhaustible enthusiasm for literary talk spurred the emergence of this amorphous group. Just as crucial to its success was Margery Dell, who had, as the poet Eunice Tietjens later wrote, "a genius for friendship." Those talents for conversation and humor which had first captivated Dell in the fall of 1908 now became instrumental in creating a circle of ambitious writers and artists who craved friendship with like-minded persons.

Guests came from different parts of Chicago's scattered cultural and intellectual life. There were Dell's colleagues at the *Friday Literary Review*—not Hackett, who kept to himself when he was not at the office, but other writers and editors from the *Post* who wanted literary company after working hours. Charles Hallinan, the *Post* editorial writer whom Dell had met through Marilla Freeman, had become a frequent contributor to the *Review* of essays on history and social issues. Hallinan was often at the Dells' in the evenings, as were Lucian and Augusta Cary, a married couple from Madison, Wisconsin, where Lucian had been a newspaperman. Both contributed essays to the *Review*.

Also present were Davenport friends, including George Cram Cook, who had left Buffalo in the spring of 1911 in order to wait for his divorce, after which he planned to join Susan Glaspell in New York. Dell was still disappointed by Cook's treatment of Mollie, but theirs was an old friendship, and the two men remained close. When he arrived in Chicago Cook spent a great deal of time at the Dells' home; for a while he worked for a publishing house that was compiling a dictionary. Another friend from Davenport was Arthur Davison Ficke, a wealthy young lawyer, art collector, and poet whom Dell had scarcely known when he lived in Davenport, but whom he had met again in Chicago through Maurice Browne, a young Englishman who was trying to establish an experimental theater in Chicago. Browne and his American wife, the actress Ellen Van Volkenburg, were soon friendly with the Dells and were occasional guests at their parties. But it was the Davenport mandarin, Arthur Ficke, who became especially close. Ficke continued to practice law in his father's firm in Davenport, but every chance possible he escaped to Chicago where he stayed with the Dells, discussing poetry and ideas, often through the night, with Floyd.

Others soon joined the Dells' parties. The artist Martha Baker was often present, as was Edna Kenton, an editor and writer from New York who had admired the *Friday Literary Review* from its start. Marjorie Jones, a photographer whom the Dells both liked, also became an intimate member of their circle. Margery's father was often at the couple's dinner parties, proud of his outlandish daughter and son-in-law and reveling in the company of talented young people who celebrated their estrangement from conventional Chicago society.

The evening gatherings were notable for literary discussions, poetry recitations, and, most of all, for a feeling of fellowship that prevailed among the guests and their hosts. Large parties were held in the spacious front parlor and adjacent dining room; more intimate groups met in the cozy back room, lined with books and comfortable furniture, that the Dells used as a study. In large groups or small, Dell was capable of conducting endless discussions on literary and political topics, even if he had little interest or talent for actually playing host to his guests. This latter task fell to Margery, who attended to practical details while making sure that the evenings flowered in natural, seemingly unplanned ways. Margaret Anderson, a later habitué of the Dells' circle, recalled in her memoirs that

Margery "relieved [Floyd] of all social responsibility and presented
him as an impersonal being whose only function in life was to talk."
In the first few years of this strictly divided arrangement, both Floyd
and Margery seemed happy with it.

There were problems within the Dells' marriage, however, even if
they were not evident to friends and families. Margery adored her
young husband, who had overnight become an influential literary
man. Without doubt Dell was fond of Margery too. But he was not
comfortable in a marriage in which he was worshiped by his wife
and in which so little was expected of him. Margery seemed willing
to make Floyd the center of attention in the marriage as in the
evening gatherings where his wit and erudition were allowed to
shine. For Floyd the arrangement felt confining, unnatural.

These problems were not dramatic. Dell was largely unable, in a
direct, explicit manner, to articulate his feelings of dissatisfaction as
they arose in 1910 and 1911. Only in several essays for the *Friday
Literary Review* did he address marriage and its discontents in ways
that might have reflected, if only half-consciously, his own marital
anxieties. In one piece he was able to maintain a light tone while
touching on matters that were potentially of the utmost significance
for him:

> If most European marriages are marriages of convenience, most
> American marriages are marriages of inconvenience—relative mis-
> alliances, mismatings of a thousand degrees of recklessness, experi-
> ments of which some are carried through triumphantly while
> others are proved failures in the divorce court. The way lads and
> lasses woo and wed is, despite the embroidery of our romancers, a
> simple matter; but the process of adjustment of mature men and
> women, of different breeding, different ideals, different notions as
> to what constitutes a joke—this is endlessly various, endlessly
> entertaining.

Despite the olympian, ironic tone, Dell was not able to think
clearly about the imperfections of his own marriage. There was little
for which he could blame himself or Margery. Still, that there were
problems became unavoidably apparent to Dell in the summer of
1911 when Margery encouraged him to take his annual trip to
Davenport alone. Decades later Dell guessed that Margery had
detected "some restlessness" on his part and that she had felt it "her
duty to give [him] a vacation from her wifely society." Whatever the

reason, Dell left for Davenport baffled by his wife's decision. Once there he stopped in at the Cooks' farm in Buffalo to see Mollie, who was living there alone with her two children. Mollie entertained him with stories and good cheer, then took him to bed. "I was afterward frightfully upset," Dell recalled decades later. That night, though, the experience came to him as a revelation, not unlike the one that had accompanied his first experience, several years earlier, of erotic love. Dell camouflaged the incident artfully when he recounted it in *Homecoming*, but he faithfully captured its overwhelming effect on him:

> There was a girl; and we kissed. And then, suddenly, I was in a realm more real to me than the world I had thought of as real—which had now become a shadow, a dream, something remote and dim. I was happy and free; not a literary editor; not a husband; only myself. All the values in my universe were suddenly transvalued. I felt like a wanderer, long absent in alien lands, who sets eyes again upon his native place. Why should I have ever imagined myself that stranger, worn that uniform? There need be no effort here to be what one was not, only infinite sincerity of oneself to another, in love and talk and laughter. We made love happily and solemnly.

Here is the self-conscious romantic poet-lover, a figure that would emerge more clearly as part of Dell's persona in the next few years. Yet the passage makes clear that the moment was for Dell spontaneous and surprising. What he discovered with Mollie that night in Davenport was a self altogether different from the professional, worldly self he had eagerly created in Chicago's literary milieu. It was also different from the pampered, youthful genius role that Margery had fashioned for him, growing as it did out of Margery's maternal mix of awe and condescension toward him. There was a formal, artificial character to their relations which Dell was beginning to deplore.

With Mollie things were different. She and Dell had always felt allied, from the days in which they first came to know each other in the spring of 1908, at Cook's farm. When Dell saw Mollie on his trip that summer, his feelings of pity for her, stemming from the bad treatment she had received at Jig's hands, quickly gave way to this earlier youthful kinship between the two. Their night together relieved both of the more constrained, unsatisfying relations they had seen develop between them and their older spouses. For Dell their lovemaking—spontaneous, illicit—had made it possible for him to forget, if only temporarily, the growing weight of convention and responsibility that marriage and professional life had forced upon him. When he left Davenport it was agreed that nothing would come of his night with Mollie, that they would go separate ways. But it is not surprising that once he returned to Chicago, and after weathering his initial feelings of awkwardness and guilt around Margery, he was quite willing to enter more fully into love affairs with other women.

"A New Era"

THE *Friday Literary Review* was essential to the creation of a literary avant-garde in Chicago. At the same time it was a supplement to a respectable paper, and in unmistakable ways its pages reflected the boundaries imposed by the *Post*'s watchful, demanding owner. Its editors and contributors were uncomfortably aware of the paper's management hovering over their shoulders, wary lest these young literary types try to promulgate ideas offensive to conservative readers. "There was always an implicit warning of 'The Bogey Man will get us if we don't watch out,'" Dell recalled. Within the *Review*'s inner circle there was "an earnest, unflagging effort to let no day pass without putting a fast one over on the Bogey Man." At first these cat-and-mouse maneuvers struck the young editors as a diverting test of wits. But as time wore on they began to feel like a nuisance, like an obstacle keeping the *Review* from becoming the unabashedly modern literary organ that the editors would have preferred.

This predicament became Dell's responsibility in July 1911, when Francis Hackett handed to him the editorship of the *Friday Literary Review* (the Irishman hoped to devote himself to his own writings, including a novel). In some ways Dell's contradictory tendencies made him the perfect radical literary editor of a solidly conservative newspaper. Fanny Butcher, who wrote reviews for Dell during his tenure as editor at the *Review* (and who eventually became literary editor at the *Chicago Tribune*), later remembered that "he was called 'the boy wonder.' He was brilliant, amusing, opinionated, and had all the yearnings of youth—to shock, to tell the world, and to lead it into the paths of his own righteousness, which was signposted freedom of thought and of action."

Dell was flattered by his reputation as an uncompromising literary rebel, but he never quite believed in it himself. Later he admitted that during his years at the *Review* he had been tempted to think of himself as a reckless journalist "working for some radical, incendiary sheet." Yet as an older man he realized that "the young editor seemed to some observers enough of a compromiser to succeed in the respectable world." The fact is that Dell enjoyed his success and knew how to ingratiate himself at dinners, teas, and parties hosted by the well-to-do. Added to professional compromises were Dell's reservations about inflexible critics of cultural and social convention. Even as he promoted socialism, new writers, and feminism in the pages of the *Review*, he was laughing in print at anarchists and indulging in fitful praise of conservative authors.

No wonder the *Post's* management never quite knew what to think of Floyd Dell. Certainly the owner and chief editors recognized his value as an industrious young man with a keen awareness of new trends in modern literature. According to Butcher, Dell had "a kind of prescience of what books and writing were headed for." The *Post's* affluent readers were anxious to appear up to date in cultural and intellectual matters, and Dell was undeniably qualified to supply them with guidance. In two short years Hackett and Dell had earned the *Review* a national reputation and an independent, nationwide circulation. Management was eager to maintain the supplement's prestige. But the matter of Dell's radical views could not be overlooked. Hackett had been constantly worried about his own standing with the paper's executives. Now he passed such worries on to his twenty-four-year-old associate.

Dell's opening salvo was meant to ease the concerns of management and readers alike. In his first issue as editor he led off the weekly editorial by praising his predecessor and assuring readers that "the standards for which the *Review* has been known in the past will be steadfastly maintained in the future." In fact, the *Review* under Dell's editorship continued as much the same journal it had been under Hackett. Its departments remained largely the same, and as editor and chief critic Dell carried on many of Hackett's themes: the stress on literature's relation to society; the discreet (and occasionally not so discreet) promotion of socialist politics; the praise of books that aimed to see society in all its parts, dynamic relations, and conflicts. Many of Dell's literary heroes—Shaw, Wells, Bennett, Butler, Ibsen, Synge, Galsworthy—were writers Hackett had already praised. The American authors Dell championed as editor at the *Friday Literary Review*—Norris, Twain, Sinclair, Emerson, Thoreau, Crane—he had already praised during Hackett's reign.

Nevertheless, the magazine evolved. The particular nature of that evolution showed that Dell was even more willing than Hackett to test and disconcert the *Post's* management. Margaret Anderson, later to be founder and publisher of the avant-garde *Little Review*, was struck by the changes Dell worked at the *Friday Literary Review*. Anderson had begun to contribute rather effusive reviews to the journal when Hackett was editor ("she wrote well," Dell recalled, "if more enthusiastically than anybody had ever written before in the whole history of book-reviewing"). Years later she remembered that Dell's "Friday book section was even more personal and brilliant than Francis Hackett's had been." Both her points are exactly right. The writing in the *Review* after Dell took over grew less sober and circumspect; Dell gave his writers more free rein, exhorting them to express themselves frankly and without hesitation. He also felt fewer compunctions to tone down essays and ideas so as to please respectable middle-class readers. He pushed his writers to be as remarkable and uncompromising—as "brilliant," to use Anderson's term—as they wished to be. She recalled a piece of advice Dell gave her that was typical of his practice as editor at the *Review*, advice that must have pleased a writer (and future editor) as independent-minded as she: "Floyd's injunctions to his reviewers were invariably interesting: Here is a book on China. Now don't send me an article about China but one about yourself."

Dell promoted the same gospel of individualism in the weekly editorials he wrote for the *Review*. Literature itself he described as an activity essentially opposed to the conventions of society. "Poets have always preached the gospel of disorder," he wrote in one editorial. "Novelists from Fielding to Galsworthy have spoken in behalf of the man at odds with society." The limitations of this platform are readily apparent. By making freedom and spontaneity central to literary work, Dell (like other literary radicals of his day) gave too little attention to the need for discipline and self-criticism. Similarly, he often ignored the ways in which productive literary work is related to the past.

In all fairness, Dell was well aware that a literary creed based exclusively on independence and individual expression was short-sighted. More than any of his contemporaries in Chicago (with the exception of Francis Hackett), Dell felt the power—the irresistible gravity—of the literary past. He knew that his own literary identity, including his most dearly held ideas about individual creativity and iconoclasm, was derived in large measure from writers he had absorbed in childhood and adolescence, and whose vitality he still felt in the most immediate way. But he was preoccupied with the challenge of creating an energetic literary community in Chicago, one that would gather its own momentum and resources rather than content itself with living off the cultural capital of New England and Europe. His stress on critical independence was to some extent a calculated risk, a bit of deliberate hyperbole needed to propel the Chicago literary scene into orbit. Little wonder that as an editor he counseled critical daring to his regular reviewers, going as far as to warn them not to worry about being confined by the plot or themes of the book under consideration. "In heaven's name," he exhorted them, "*don't* tell the story of the book! Bring to bear upon the book, in aesthetic terms, your attitude toward life."

The credo of self-expression also gained the upper hand in Dell's private life, though here it was mixed with misgivings that he was scarcely prepared to understand or resolve. Among Dell's closest friends and associates at the *Friday Literary Review* were Lucian and Augusta Cary. Lucian, a few years older than Dell, had worked as a college instructor, journalist, and most recently as a reporter for the *Chicago Tribune*. Augusta (or Gus, as she was known among friends), a stunning woman with luxurious, bright blonde hair, had as great an interest in and knowledge of books as her husband. The Carys shared Dell's literary enthusiasms, and the three often spent evenings together. Margery was ill at ease with the couple, so she encouraged her husband to spend his evenings with the Carys without her.

Dell's relations with the Carys reveal much about the awkward, even preposterous, way these embryonic Chicago bohemians tried to reorganize their lives along individualistic, "natural" principles. One evening in the winter of 1911–1912 Dell left the Carys' North Side apartment to return to his own place in Rogers Park. Gus walked him to the El stop, as Dell recalled many years later in a discreetly fictionalized account of the ensuing events:

On the way she told him that she was in love with him. She said that she had her husband's permission to have a love affair with him. But it would be necessary for him to have his wife's permission. Would he like to have a love affair with her, and if so would he ask his wife's permission? He was full of admiration for the heroic candor of this lovely Valkyr. But he said he wouldn't dream of asking his wife's permission.

Dell's refusal of this oddly principled request suggests how muddled were his ideas about marriage and love. He had betrayed Margery's trust earlier that summer by sleeping with Mollie. All the same he remained convinced of the rightness of married life. The apparent effect of his one-night affair with Mollie had been "to put me on my guard against becoming involved in any extramarital friendships with girls that might become serious." And yet he was flattered and intrigued by this brazen proposal from a beautiful young woman of whom he was already fond, and so his return home to Morse Avenue that night turned out rather differently than he anticipated. Once home he started chatting with Margery and soon began describing the startling episode to her, implicitly asking her (as Margery was quick to realize, even if Floyd refused to admit it to himself) for the permission Gus had required that he receive. Margery volunteered her permission that same night, all but pushing Dell into Gus's arms. Their affair, lasting no more than a few months, began the next morning, though only after Dell had dutifully satisfied Gus that Margery had lent her approval.

Even more incredible were the discussions about the matter between Dell and Lucian Cary. Lucian explained that "it is all right for there to be such love-affairs, so long as it is all open and above-board, with no hypocrisy or lies, and there are precautions against pregnancy." "So it was all very friendly," Dell remarked decades later. He added that the affair ended after "a few months because of hurt feelings." Still, "there were no harsh words," the ideals of openness and tolerance that had promoted the relationship in the first place now supplying a motive for renewed tolerance and friendship.

With so admirably open and principled an experience behind him, Dell proceeded to embark on love affairs with other young women in his circle of writers and artists. And he continued to discuss these relationships openly with Margery, who maintained a brave, tolerant view of her husband's derelictions. Dell later admitted that after his well-publicized affair with Augusta Cary, "it was now accepted as a fact about me that I fell in love with other girls, and taken, it would seem, by my wife as a fact that had to be adjusted to with tolerance—a tolerance so extreme in its generosity that I was before long in another and then another love affair." The reasons behind this peculiar tangle of relations were largely incomprehensible to Dell at the time. Only years later, after he had wed again and found happiness in a long marriage, was he able to see his youthful marriage to Margery Currey more clearly:

> I think that Margery, in marrying me, was conscious of how it looked from the outside, on account of my youth and her more mature years; and I think that she had a dramatic formula in her mind which in the first place assigned to me the privileges of youthful "genius" and in the second place assigned to her a role of infinitely maternal tolerance toward extra-marital love-affairs that were expected to occur. I, meanwhile, who had never accepted in my own mind the role of "genius," did not regard myself as entitled to these extraordinary privileges. . . . I was very earnestly resolved to maintain my marriage.

Later in life Dell had no desire to excuse the rapid succession of chaotic, confused affairs that followed the first episodes with Mollie Cook and Augusta Cary. But he also insisted that his conduct at the time "was not the behavior of an apostle of free love, nor was it the behavior of a person who delights in making new sexual conquests." He was fascinated by the idea of married love, as his articles in the *Friday Literary Review* clearly attest. But his failure as a husband shadowed all his enthusiasms. Somehow high ideals were not enough to make a marriage.

MEANWHILE DELL WAS gaining a reputation as Chicago's most brilliant literary editor and critic. In 1912 and 1913 the excitement in Chicago's literary community, centering in large part on Dell and the *Review*, reached its peak. Despite his worsening marriage, Dell was to remember 1912 as "a beautiful year, a year of poetry, and dreams, and of life renewed and abundant." John Butler Yeats, father of the poet and patron saint of the young intellectuals in New York, remarked that same year that "the fiddles are tuning as it were all over America." Fanny Butcher remembered 1912 as "the year when women first marched through Chicago asking for suffrage." Dell recalled the year's unprecedented cultural and political tumult:

> It was the year of the election of Wilson, a symptom of immense political discontent. It was a year of intense woman-suffragist activity. In the arts it marked a new era. Color was everywhere—even in neckties. The Lyric Year, published in New York, contained Edna St. Vincent Millay's "Renascence." In Chicago, Harriet Monroe founded Poetry. . . . The Irish Players came to America. It was then that plans were made for the Post-Impressionist Show, which revolutionized American ideas of art. In Chicago, Maurice Browne started the Little Theatre. One could go on with the evidence of a New Spirit come suddenly to birth in America. . . . And the Friday Literary Review, which had been thought rather "young," was in the middle of a movement.

Politics and literature—Dell's twin obsessions—were now regularly joined in his essays. In a series of articles published in early 1912 Dell described how evolving social and economic circumstances in Chicago had resulted in various efforts to portray the city in literature. The first essay was titled "Robert Herrick's Chicago." Dell summarized Herrick's view of Chicago as a place that exemplified the chaotic and appallingly ugly features of modern urban life. He identified Herrick's view of Chicago "as a muddy pathway down to hell" and stressed the way in which Herrick organized his Chicago novels around the tragic conflict between the city and isolated intellectuals and artists: Herrick "sees among the others a few clear-souled men and women who attempt to free themselves, to get out and away from it. And that effort, even though it be a weak and futile effort, he celebrates in novel after novel with passion and tears." Dell may have sympathized with Herrick's angry alienation from the vulgar spectacle presented by Chicago. But he also felt that Herrick failed to recognize much that was interesting, even wonderful, about the city. Dell's own version of the modern intellectual—ironic but basically optimistic—was dramatically different from what seemed the willfully anachronistic, oppressively disenchanted posture favored by Herrick. For Dell, Herrick was in essence a nineteenth-century literary man unable to recognize the beauties and human consolations of this bewilderingly modern metropolis.

In the humorous columns of Chicago journalist Finley Peter

Dunne, on the other hand, Dell discovered a writer who was open-minded enough to capture some of the city's humanity. His eloquent tribute to Dunne (and to Dunne's most famous creation, the garrulous barkeep Martin Dooley) shows how Dell, while a youthful radical, was also alert to authentic literary pleasures, no matter where he might find them. It also suggests that Dell, a child of the working class, was not entirely sympathetic to the elitist tastes and sensibility he discovered in Herrick. Dunne's Chicago, Dell wrote,

> is not a cruel place, as in Mr. Herrick's view, nor a romantic place, as plenty of other writers would make it. It is not ugly, because it is full of men and women and children. It is a place where people work hard in shops and factories and go home, not to an idyllic home, but a human one, and in the evening talk about the election or the neighbors. Mr. Dunne believes in those people. He does not despise their work, nor their homes, nor their conversation. He is an instinctive democrat.

To be sure, Dell felt that Dunne's work was limited by the absence of a comprehensive, conscious view of Chicago as a distinctively modern city. This he found in another writer: Theodore Dreiser, whom he considered sufficiently open- and broad-minded to recognize the larger significance of Chicago—its beauties as well as all that was deplorable about it. Dell praised Dreiser for capturing the "poetry" of this confusing place:

> The poetry of Chicago has been adequately rendered, so far, by only one writer, and in only one book. The book is, naturally enough, that one which Frank Harris declared in the London Academy to be "The best story on the whole that has yet come out of America," to wit: "Sister Carrie," by Theodore Dreiser. It is the most real, the most sincere, the most moving of all the books with which we have dealt, or are likely to deal, in this study of "Chicago Fiction." . . . [Dreiser] has not looked to see the badness of the city, nor its goodness; he has looked to see its beauty and ugliness, and he has seen a beauty even in its ugliness. And, in doing that, he has given us, there is little doubt, the Chicago of the whole middle west.

Dell's essay on Dreiser was the only one in the Chicago writers series in which he surrendered himself to uninhibited praise. Dreiser, he was certain, was the sole writer capable of capturing Chicago without the distortions that marred the work of city boosters and embittered mandarins alike. Dell's enthusiasm for Dreiser's work spilled over in this essay, so that he attributed an optimistic flavor to the older man's work that was not readily apparent to other readers (one gushy passage describes Dreiser's Chicago as "a place of splendor and joy and triumph, the place toward which the young faces turn and the end of the road along which young feet yearn to tread"). But such fervor was understandable in a young critic who wished to rescue Dreiser's reputation from the beatings it had taken in the preceding decade. There is no doubt that Dell's praise helped to build Dreiser a formidable reputation at last.

Still more important for Dell than changes in the modern city were those associated with women and the feminist movement. In scattered essays and reviews—and in a series of articles in 1912— Dell established a reputation as a vociferous champion of the Woman's Movement. In 1972 Fanny Butcher wagered that Dell "would have been patron saint to today's Women's Liberation for [the] series of articles he wrote about the Free Woman. . . . Floyd's articles caused a terrific uproar, especially those in which he advocated sexual freedom for women."

His articles on women were written in a mode typical of his work for the *Review*, that of the radical insider who aims to enlighten the benighted bourgeois masses. Dell had no trouble managing such essays as public performances: they were uniformly confident, worldly, witty, optimistic. But beneath their robust surfaces he was grappling with his own inconsistent attitudes toward women. A professed feminist, a public advocate of a woman's right to work, and a champion of equality within marriage, he nonetheless clung to earlier notions about woman's inescapable maternal and practical nature; he blithely referred to women as "girls"; and he relied upon his wife's selfless forbearance while he carried on affairs with other women. Perhaps unavoidably in light of these contradictions, his articles were only partially successful in accounting for the meaning that feminism held for women, society, and himself.

A representative article was Dell's December 1911 review of Ellen Key's *The Morality of Women, and Other Essays*. Key was a Swedish feminist who advocated the reformation of marriage in light of modern theories of human personality and sexuality. Dell emphasized that Key had no desire to undermine marriage as an institution; rather she wished to redefine marriage and monogamy in more realistic (and dignified) ways. Key, he maintained, was leading the way to a "newer ideal of marriage." For Dell, Key had an immediate, creative understanding of marriage and love that was inescapably feminine: "She treats of love and marriage not in an artificial isolation from the rest of the world, but with a complete consciousness of their endless interrelations with work, wages, education, the rearing of children, art, science, friendship. She is wise with a woman's wisdom;... Though she is weak in logic she has the woman's strong 'intuitive' grasp on vast multitudes of practical facts."

Such praise of female intuition veered dangerously close to the chauvinistic antifeminism Dell plainly wished to avoid. Also indicative of his state of mind was Dell's insistence that Key's views stood "in conflict with two other ideals—that of conventional morality and that of 'free love' or 'varietism.'" What he discovered in her writing was the promise of a "soulful and true devotion" between a man and a woman, a monogamous relation that would be personal and authentic, not something imposed upon an unwitting couple by an indifferent society. Dell complained that "so-called Bohemians" have demonstrated an unyielding, fanatical devotion to sexual freedom and "the right of the senses"—a fanaticism as great as that of "the zealots of traditional morality." "The extreme result of both would be retrogression to a lower degree of culture; in the one case to the ascetism [sic] of the Middle Ages, in the other to the promiscuity of the savage." Invoking Ellen Key, he rejected both and endorsed an ideal more in tune with "the reality of life":

> The new ideal of marriage, then, is neither the conventional one of a social duty or the romantic one of individual license. It is founded on a monistic conception of human nature which makes no attempt to separate the soul from the senses: it seeks to formulate a new erotic ethics which shall be in conformity with the whole civilized life of mankind: it would bring the loves of men and women into harmony with the demands of personality, as well as of the family and the state. Its form would be that complete and perfect union of one man and one woman which may be designated as the monogamic ideal.

Dell's emphasis on Key's determination to preserve monogamy appealed to the *Post's* conservative heart. It also clearly appealed to Dell. Yet his enthusiasm for her ideas about monogamy and marriage came at a time when his own marriage was beginning to fall apart. He may have come closest to touching on his own dilemma when he quoted Key's assertion "that love belongs not to the sphere of duty but only to that of freedom." Vaguely he seems to have felt that his marriage, for all its liberated gestures, was limited by the fact that his relations with Margery were more dutiful than they were heartfelt. Ellen Key's writings may have made him "dream of the perfect love of the one woman," but that woman, it was becoming clear, was not his generous, tolerant wife.

Whatever his contradictions and uncertainties, Dell was fascinated by feminism and the ways in which it was changing the world, and he was determined to invest good faith in it. In a series of front-page articles in the summer of 1912 he provided portraits of American and European leaders of the suffrage movement. In the spring of 1913 the essays were collected in a book titled *Women as World Builders*. Dell's introduction to the book accounted plainly for the method he enacted in the other essays. Rather than treat the feminist movement "as a sociological abstraction and [discuss it] at length in heavy monographs," Dell chose to present a series of biographical sketches of individual feminists, "a method," he insisted, "which preserves the individual flavor, the personal tone and color, which, after all, are the life of any movement." The portraits themselves—of Charlotte Perkins Gilman, Emmeline Pankhurst, Jane Addams, Olive Schreiner, Isadora Duncan, Beatrice Webb, Emma Goldman, Margaret Dreier Robins, Ellen Key, and Dora Marsden—may have been sketchy, fanciful, even misleading at times. But they accomplished their aim: to introduce the works and ideas of these women to an uninformed audience, and to present nearly unalloyed optimism and progress as the true spirit of the modern feminist movement.

The most personal portrait is the first one, a sketch of Charlotte Perkins Gilman. Rather than give a full account of Gilman's work as a public feminist and suffragist, Dell portrayed her as idiosyncratic and creative. She "is, first of all, a poet, an idealist," he wrote. Even her rejection of the home, according to Dell, stemmed from her aesthetic predilections, from her sense of the conventional home as vulgar: "In this 'home,' this private food-preparing and baby-rearing establishment, she sees a machine which breaks down all that is good and noble in women, which degrades and petrifies them." It was this exceptional artistic nature which Dell found decisive in

Gilman's character, and which he identified with her feminism. As such, hers was a type of feminism with which a rebellious, artistic young man could readily identify: a feminism founded not on any essential dispute with men but rather with conventional taste. Significantly, Dell's sole criticism was that Gilman "exaggerates the possibilities of independent work for women who have or intend to have children." Still, he described the "spirit" behind Gilman's writings as "one which cannot but be in the greatest degree stimulating and beneficent in its effect upon her sex." He praised her as "the most intransigent feminist of them all."

Dell also found praiseworthy qualities in feminists who were not artistic. He commended Emmeline Pankhurst, the British suffragist, for her militant politics—her willingness "to raid parliament and fight with policemen, to destroy property and go to prison." Dell found Olive Schreiner, the author of *Women and Labor*, admirable for her efforts to "send women into every field of economic activity." But it was for those feminists whose interests were expressly artistic or cultural that Dell reserved his greatest enthusiasm. While he admired Pankhurst's street-fighting politics, he clearly preferred Jane Addams, who, he noted, "has the gift of imaginative sympathy" (which he identified with her "passion of conciliation," another quality that made this particular feminist congenial to a male writer). Dell was even more impressed—and moved—by Isadora Duncan, whom he had first seen dance several years earlier in Chicago. "She has made us despise the frigid artifice of ballet, and taught us that in the natural movements of the body are contained the highest possibilities of choreographic beauty." In his discussion of Duncan, Dell abandoned practical feminist politics in favor of the cultural revolt that he felt Duncan embodied for men and women alike. Duncan's dancing, according to Dell, suggested that "the body is no longer to be separated in the thought of women from the soul." This observation led him to his fuzziest description of feminism yet: "if the woman's movement means anything, it means that women are demanding everything. . . . They will have a larger political life, a larger motherhood, and they will reconstruct or destroy institutions to that end as it becomes necessary. They will not be content with any concession or any triumph until they have conquered all experience."

Not all Dell's portraits were flattering. Nor were they free of remarks that some feminist readers likely found politically retrograde, sometimes even offensive. His sketch of Emma Goldman, the anarchist leader and publisher of the monthly magazine *Mother Earth*, was devoted mainly to relieving Goldman of her reputation as a dangerous, incendiary radical. Dell wrote that Goldman's work was like Henrik Ibsen's in its preoccupation with individual liberty; to a far lesser extent was it concerned with plotting the overthrow of capitalist governments. The problem, Dell insisted, was that Goldman was not as moving a writer as Ibsen. Comparing her work with the statistical writings of the British socialist Beatrice Webb, Dell "wonders if, after all, the prose [of revolution] is not that which women are best endowed to succeed in." Portraying women as more practical—and less poetic—than men, Dell argued that "a future more largely influenced by women [will] have more of the hard, matter-of-fact quality, the splendid realism characteristic of woman 'when she is herself.'" One can easily imagine feminists (very likely Goldman herself) reading Dell's confident dismissal of their poetic, imaginative powers, along with his rather patronizing references to women's "matter-of-fact" qualities, with irritation if not outright anger.

The women with whom Dell seemed most to identify were Ellen Key and Dora Marsden. This was not so much because they were feminists but because they were mavericks willing to break with conventions and formulas, including those of the feminist movement itself. His sympathy for Key, already noted, had much to do with the underlying conservatism he correctly identified in her work, a surviving attachment to monogamous marriage even as she rejected its conventional rules. Marsden, an iconoclastic British feminist who published (and single-handedly wrote) a lively magazine called the *Freewoman*, appealed to Dell for her insistence that each woman explore her own individuality. Dell admired Marsden's boldness and courage: she frankly discussed sexual relations in her journal and was fond of ridiculing "the cant of 'motherhood.'" But what he found most appealing was her rejection of feminist concessions to political expediency. This willingness to run afoul of orthodox feminists delighted Dell, who was himself eager to avoid doctrinaire positions of the left.

The most idiosyncratic (and outrageous) of Dell's remarks in *Women as World Builders* appeared toward the close of the book's introduction. Why, he imagined his readers asking, had a man written these essays? How was he qualified to comment on what was,

after all, a "woman's movement"? His answer was hardly predictable. "Men are tired of subservient women," he explained; they
wanted liberated, well-educated, worldly women because such women "promise to be more fun." "The motive behind the rebellion of
women," he insisted, was "an obscure rebellion of men." In a
statement that must have infuriated feminists, Dell insisted that it
was men, once again, who were the force behind this latest revolution in manners and politics:

> It is, then, as a phase of the great human renaissance inaugurated
> by men that the women's movement deserves to be considered.
> And what more fitting than that a man should sit in judgment
> upon the contemporary aspects of that movement, weighing out
> approval or disapproval! Such criticism is not a masculine imper-
> tinence but a masculine right, a right properly pertaining to those
> who are responsible for the movement, and whose demands it
> must ultimately fulfill.

Years later Dell would realize that this view of the feminist movement was shared by many young male radicals at the time, and that
it was profoundly wrongheaded, not to mention vain. The young
women struggling for emancipation and the vote, he came to
understand, had wanted to shed their traditional roles for reasons
quite different from those he had earlier claimed. They were
reaching toward greater autonomy and self-determination, not simply responding to the desire of masculine avant-gardists for more
interesting companions.

That *Women as World Builders* was a deeply flawed work is
beyond dispute. Just as surely, though, it had been written in an
experimental spirit, and it managed to introduce feminism to a large
number of readers. A reviewer for the *New York Times* called the
book "provocative" and "well worth the reading of any one who
wants to have his ideas on this subject well raked over and stirred
up." Elia Peattie of the *Chicago Tribune* described *Women as World
Builders* as "an exhilarating book, daring of youth, and as heartening
to the women actors in this new, vivid drama of unknown documents as the applause of many hands in a darkened theater." Even a
number of feminists praised Dell for having done feminism a public
service. Frances Maule Bjorkman, of the National American Woman
Suffrage Association, wrote Dell while the series was running in the
Friday Literary Review during the summer of 1912: "Your articles

have to me a quite unique quality. Psychological analysis in connection with the woman movement being very rare. I hope you will do some more along this line. Your point about the practical quality of the feminine mind is one that I was especially glad to see brought out."

The book, Dell soon realized, revealed as much about his own contradictory feelings as it did about feminism. In important ways it was sympathetic to the woman's movement. But it was also the work of a young man who was uncertain about private and public relations between men and women. This confusion was painfully clear in Dell's relations with his wife. A public champion of marriage, he was chronically unfaithful to Margery. Inspired more by regret than by passion, she eventually began to sleep with other men in their circle. By the time *Women as World Builders* appeared in the spring of 1913, the Dells' marriage was in shambles, and Floyd and Margery had decided that living together, at least for the present, no longer made sense.

South Side Bohemian

THE CRACK-UP OF the Dells' marriage occurred as the avant-garde surrounding their household grew increasingly vivid and productive. Together the Dells seemed indispensable to their community of friends—exemplars and catalysts of all that was modern in Chicago. Arthur Ficke described them in "Lines for Two Rebels": "Why does all of sharp and new / That our modern days can brew / Culminate in you?" Everyone knew that Dell was unfaithful to Margery, but the couple never aired their unhappiness or grievances in public. Friends were inclined to regard the happy relations between the two as a sign that they were above sexual jealousy. For Chicago's avant-gardists, the Dells' reasonable approach to Floyd's periodic infidelities had the paradoxical effect of making their marriage seem all the more impressive.

Beneath congenial appearances, however, things were beginning to spin out of control, and not only in the couple's marital life. By late 1912 Dell was becoming impatient with his work at the *Review*. The need for deference to the conservative tastes of management and his readership had led him to regard his editorial position as temporary. In his editorials and reviews appeared frequent signs of impatience: complaints about American provincialism and intolerance, mixed with ironic asides to the effect that he was not permitted, in so respectable a newspaper, to discuss certain topics in depth. In a review of William English Walling's *Socialism as It Is: A Survey of a World-Wide Revolutionary Movement*, Dell implied that his American readers would not know about developments and disputes in the international socialist movement. Even if these matters were patiently explained, he hinted, Americans would have a hard time grasping them. Conflicts between traditional socialists and radical syndicalists clearly interested Dell, but he was frustrated by editorial constraints that kept him from discussing those conflicts openly and thoroughly. "Well, it is very interesting," he concluded, "which is all that may decorously be said in a literary journal. But since Syndicalism is going to be one of the main topics of conversation at enlightened dinner tables during 1913, we cheerfully recommend Mr. Walling's pugnacious volume."

Sarcasm was also discernible in the headline of the 1912 Christmas issue recommending fifty books published during the year. In a literary supplement that included annual editorials deploring the capitalist zeal and moral hypocrisy surrounding Christmas, the headline's ironic tone was all the more conspicuous: "A Word With the Gentle Reader; Fifty Recommended Books—A Guide to the Season's Fiction—and much Candid Comment and Advice—Done With the Most Friendly Intention, and in the True Holiday Spirit." The list was a serious one, containing all the *Review's* regular heroes as well as books by authors not as predictably ones to be championed by Dell, Cook, and the *Review's* new associate editor, Lucian Cary. Chesterton and Kipling were recommended, as were the poems and plays of the late Chicago writer William Vaughn Moody. New continental iconoclasts and American rebels were also singled out. Henri Bergson's *Introduction to Metaphysics* was named a necessary philosophical work. *The Lyric Year,* a volume of modern verse that contained Edna St. Vincent Millay's "Renascence," was also recommended. Despite the occasional conservative or moderate volume, the overwhelmingly radical character of the list, together with the derisive headline, must have irritated the *Post's* owner, who was beginning to have serious doubts about the *Review's* propriety. Dell was aware of the owner's grumblings about the supplement, but he seems not to have worried about any unhappy consequences. In fact he seems to have been determined to pique his higher-ups whenever possible.

He was also tempted to return to his long-slumbering ambitions as a creative writer. Arnold Bennett came to Chicago in the winter of 1911–1912 to meet various of the city's literary luminaries. When Dell stopped by Bennett's rooms in the Blackstone Hotel, the talk turned soon to Dell's own work. Bennett encouraged the young editor to return to fiction-writing. Moreover, he advised Dell to focus as a novelist on his early days in towns along the Mississippi. This particular suggestion did not immediately suit Dell, who was eager at the time to prove his big-city credentials. But he filed it away, where it might kindle a project bigger than any he currently had in mind—a project not unlike the novel *Moon-Calf* that he was to publish nearly a decade later.

In the meantime, early in 1912 Dell published two short stories in the *International*, a small left-wing journal in New York. The stories were frail, unpolished works. One, "Mothers and Daughters," appeared in January. It is the story of June Poetl, a seventeen-year-old whose mother is pregnant and near her delivery date. It is clear to June that her mother dreads the birth—that she dreads the thought of bringing another child into the world. The story centers on June's efforts to arrive at some measure of happiness and youthful spontaneity while living in a household pervaded by her mother's despair.

June's dilemma becomes especially painful after she meets Philip Torrey, an employee of a religious publisher. The two young people fall instantly (and unconvincingly) in love, setting up the problem that really interests Dell: the fact that June is torn between her youthful love for Philip and her oppressive awareness of her mother's misery as a woman. As her mother enters labor, June runs out to the park across from her family's apartment to meet Philip. Just when she sees him, she hears her mother's screams behind her, hurled out into the evening air: "For a moment [June] was Woman, and felt in all her fibres a sympathetic dread of the doom of childbirth. . . . Vicariously she understood the supreme sacrifice of her sex. And then she was woman no more; she was Youth—knowing nothing, fearing nothing, desiring everything. For she saw her lover coming toward her across the moonlit grass." As her mother gives birth, June becomes oblivious to her misery and to the common fate she shares with her mother: "Another scream, more terrible than the first, floated across the street from the little upstairs flat. But the girl did not hear."

A hasty piece of work, "Mothers and Daughters" is weighed down by its young couple's wooden love affair and by June's susceptibility to equally wooden incarnations as "Youth" and "Woman." The story reveals more of Dell's preoccupation with the conflict of the generations than of his interest in aesthetic matters. Even the effort to evoke youthful sexuality seems overly intellectualized. Still, there is an eloquence to the final paragraphs that promised better things to come. Whatever its failings, the story (like others Dell wrote at the time) showed its author preoccupied with the tangled moral problems facing young people who attempt to extricate themselves from the tyranny of convention and the past.

A year later Dell published in the *Smart Set* "Jessica Screams," a far better story that made those dilemmas seem even more intractable. The story's main character, Murray Swift, is based largely on Ezra Pound, whose poetry Dell had praised in the *Friday Literary Review*, and with whom Dell had exchanged a few mutually flattering letters. Dell had been one of the very first American critics to praise Pound, insisting that the extravagantly modern features of his poetry—the "unconventional form, bizarre phraseology, catalectic or involved sentence structure and recondite meanings"—were employed by Pound in precise, fruitful ways. Pound responded by letter, praising Dell, in effect, as the only critic in America with sufficiently good sense to recognize his—Ezra Pound's—genius. Dell returned to the subject of Pound later, in April 1913, with another essay in the *Friday Literary Review*—a piece of unabashed homage: "Ezra Pound, we salute you! You are the most enchanting poet alive. Your poems in the April *Poetry* are so mockingly, so delicately, so unblushingly beautiful that you seem to have brought back into the world a grace which (probably) never existed, but which we discover by an imaginative process in Horatius and Catullus."

However great his admiration for Pound, Dell made sure in "Jessica Screams" that the character based on Pound, Murray Swift, was troubled by conflicts that were already typical of his characters. The story starts as the narrator, Jimmy Selden, prepares to leave Chicago for a weekend visit with his friend Murray Swift, a writer who has recently returned to the United States from Vienna. Swift is now reluctantly serving as high school principal in a small town, Hazelton, Indiana (these circumstances are patterned on Pound's brief, unhappy stint as a teacher at Wabash College in Indiana). He has written Selden, a writer clearly modeled on Dell, about the "unpublishable poem" he wrote in Vienna.

Once in Hazelton, Selden discovers that Swift is boarding in the house of Judge Wyman, one of the town's most respectable citizens. That evening the two young men go to a party at the high school, where they see the Judge's fifteen-year-old daughter, Jessica, dancing with conspicuous abandon. Later, as the three walk home, Jessica confesses that she finds Hazelton impossibly oppressive. " 'I want to

scream,' said Jessica. 'To scream!' she repeated in a fierce whisper."
Murray Swift identifies with her, pitying her for being "extraordinarily hedged in. And you happen to be the sort of girl," Swift half
praises, half lectures Jessica, "whose super-abundant energies demand unusual freedom."

The story resumes a year later with Swift and Selden strolling
through a Chicago amusement park. Swift has been fired from his
position in Hazelton and has returned to the more congenial
environment provided by a big, anonymous city. The two men enter
a tent to find burlesque dancing on stage. Before long they are
shocked to see Jessica strut onto the stage, dressed in "tawdry
Oriental finery, with a short skirt which showed the calves of her
legs." She is screaming happily. Selden notices that for all the
cheapness of the show and her outfit, Jessica enjoys the unfeigned
abandon permitted her here. The packed crowd of men and women
watches her with pleasure:

> She had a beautiful body, and she mixed the magic of sex with the
> abandon of youth. Her dance was an efulgent [sic] giving of
> herself to her audience. And when at last, in a sort of rhythmic
> paroxysm, she shook her torso with a violent motion that trans-
> mitted itself to her young breasts, she turned what should have
> seemed an ugliness into a symbol of sexuality that intoxicated the
> audience. She saw her triumph, and exulted in it—but exulted
> with a kind of wild sexless mirth, the sheer mad effrontery of youth.

Both men are mesmerized, and repelled, by the spectacle. Swift,
who had once pitied Jessica for her lack of freedom, now feels
uneasy. "In a way I'm responsible for this," he remarks.

The story ends with Jessica deprived of her freedom. In Dell's
original, it is Jimmy Selden who capitulates to convention by
telegraphing Jessica's father and informing him of his runaway
daughter's whereabouts, leading to her eventual removal to a religious school. In closing this way, Dell stressed the ambivalence of his
own double, Selden, torn between rebellion and conformity. But
Willard Huntington Wright, editor of the *Smart Set*, had a better
idea: that it be Swift, the outlandish champion of revolt, who betrays
Jessica to her father and Hazelton society. Dell saw that Wright's
ending was an improvement—one that perfectly suited his desire to
reveal conventional impulses in even the most militant of noncon-
formists—and so the editor's ending was retained.

"Jessica Screams" was published in the April 1913 number of the *Smart Set*. Readers responded in greater numbers than to any previous story in the magazine's history. Some were delighted, others outraged by the frank treatment of Jessica's youthful sexuality. For Dell, whatever scandal he had created through the story was a negligible matter compared with the fact that his work had for the first time attracted so much attention. "Jessica Screams" convinced him that he was indeed a promising young writer of fiction, and that he need not count on his job as editor at the *Friday Literary Review*.

"JESSICA SCREAMS" confirmed Dell's reputation, already widespread in Chicago, as a young man eager to offend respectable taste. That same spring he added to his standing as Chicago's most influential avant-garde literary figure by deciding, with his wife, to move to an artists' colony on Chicago's South Side. Both Floyd and Margery had for some while felt confined by their respectable apartment in Rogers Park. They wanted living quarters that would be an outward sign of their own inner, unconventional states of grace. What they wanted, quite simply, was to live in bohemia.

That Chicago had a bohemia of its own is perhaps the most remarkable fact of all. The city was still young in 1912—only three-quarters of a century old—and overwhelmingly preoccupied with practical matters. It was famously a city of hard, daily work. It was not falling dramatically into decay, nor conspicuously dotted with quiet, forgotten streets, nor filled with people oblivious to practical considerations—all usual conditions for the flowering of bohemian life. Chicago had a smattering of these features: some rickety buildings that might house an artists' settlement, and a handful of residents out of sympathy with the city's overwhelmingly industrious temper. But they were always in precariously short supply.

Much later in life, Dell reflected on the nature of bohemia and the conditions that make it possible: "It must be in a big city, with a university nearby and a good library. You've got to have an old section of town falling into decay, where the rents are low." He was thinking here of the Greenwich Village he came to know just after his years in Chicago—the prewar Village that turned out to be America's most famous and glamorous bohemian settlement. But Chicago had all these characteristics as well, even if it was never as congenial to bohemia as New York. The University of Chicago, established in 1890 with John D. Rockefeller's oil money and still something of an isolated intellectual outpost on the city's South Side, had begun to attract scholarly talent of considerable merit. And the libraries that the city had erected in the late nineteenth century—the public library downtown, along with the Newberry and Crerar libraries and the research libraries at the University of Chicago and Northwestern University—provided substantial sources of books and ideas for the city's ambitious young intellectuals. Most important, the city was vast and chaotic. There were bound to be places in the midst of all that urban space and energy where rebellious writers and artists could congregate and feel themselves at least a bit isolated from the city's relentlessly purposeful spirit.

Early in 1913 the Dells moved to the most promising of these places: a row of makeshift, one-story, boxlike dwellings at the corner of Stony Island Avenue and Fifty-Seventh Street, not far from Lake Michigan and directly across from Jackson Park. The buildings, which stretched for a block along both sides of Fifty-Seventh Street and around the corner for another block on Stony Island, had been built in 1893 to house shops in connection with the huge World's Fair—the Columbian Exposition—that Chicago mounted to commemorate the four hundredth anniversary of Columbus's arrival in America. Indigent artists moved into the buildings when the fair ended. By 1913 a continuous succession of bohemian artists and intellectuals had invaded these cheap, spartan quarters. Each consisted of little more than a single large room fronted by a large shop window. All were equipped with sinks; only a few had a bath or toilet. But for the Dells these unconventional dwellings, and their exotic tenants, made such inconveniences negligible matters. In April they rented two of the apartments—one for each—and moved in shortly thereafter. The Fifty-Seventh Street bohemia, they agreed, would provide the perfect solution to their marital problems: separate apartments, so that they need not live as husband and wife, but close enough that they might still enjoy each other's company.

For Floyd, life in the Fifty-Seventh Street colony amounted to a final, flamboyant phase in his brief career as a literary man in Chicago. Many people who lived in these quarters were formidable artists and intellectuals in their own right, and their presence pleased and inspired him. In the apartment on the corner of Stony Island and Fifty-Seventh—sandwiched, as it were, between the Dells' two apartments—lived the artist Bror Nordfeldt and his wife Margaret, a middle-aged couple who had been among the first to convert the Fifty-Seventh Street shops into living quarters. Nordfeldt, a small, gracious man of Swedish origin, was a postimpressionist painter of considerable accomplishment and a teacher at the Art Institute. He was also a set designer for Maurice Browne's Little Theater, the experimental troupe that was putting on stark, vivid productions of the ancients and modern European playwrights in a studio theater located on the fourth floor of the Fine Arts Building on Michigan Avenue. Margaret Nordfeldt, a psychiatrist, was also an important figure in the colony. For years the couple had been close friends with Thorstein Veblen, the scandalous University of Chicago economics professor, who had lived until 1906 in the apartment on Stony Island just south of theirs—the apartment into which Margery Dell moved in the spring of 1913.

The Fifty-Seventh Street community included artists of other sorts as well. There were a handful of actors, Little Theater members, who worked long hours for Browne and always for free. There were also several sculptors—Lou Wall Moore, Kathleen Wheeler, Mary Randolph—some of whom also worked at the Little Theater. Directly west of Dell's flat lived an etcher, Ralph Pearson; just south of Margery's was a metalcraft studio run by two University of Chicago students, Annette Covington and Blanche Manage. Raymond Johnson, a brilliant young artist who was creating spare, stunning sets for the Little Theater, lived in the colony as well. Marjorie Jones, the Dells' photographer friend, was another resident, as was Ernestine Evans, a recent graduate of the university and an aspiring writer. Oldtimers like the Nordfeldts had long lent the colony its bohemian flavor. But when the Dells arrived the small community gained a center of social activities and intellectual energy. In the next six months the Dells brought the bohemian colony to a level of excitement it had never before reached, and which it never fully regained after Floyd left six months later.

Dell flourished in his new quarters right from the start. Shortly after he moved into his bare, chilly flat in early May he wrote Arthur Ficke, describing the place in all its bohemian glamour:

> It is 11:30 P.M. I have just returned from the north side, where I have been seeing the Carys, to my ice-cold studio, where I have built a fire with scraps of linoleum, a piece of wainscoting, and

the contents of an elaborate filing system of four years creation. I am writing at a desk spattered with kalsomine, and lighted by four candles. The room contains one book case and nine Fels-Naptha soap boxes—full of books—counting the one full of books I am giving away to get rid of them—a typewriter stand, a fireless cooker, a patent coat and trousers hanger, and a couch with a mattress and a blanket. In this blanket I roll myself securely, and sleep till 5:30 A.M., when I am awakened by the flood of daylight, also by the fact that my shoulders are cold. I wrap myself tighter, and sleep till 8 o'clock, when I get up, take a sketchy bath at a faucet, and go around the corner for breakfast. In the window seat, along with my shirts, is a great bundle, containing a magnificent and very expensive bolt of beautiful cloth, for curtains for the windows. If I am ever able to pay for that, and for my new suit, I shall give a party, and you shall come and see the combination of luxury and asceticism which will be the charm of my studio. At present its only luxury consists in that same asceticism. I have been rather unhappy this evening, because of some trouble at the office, but as soon as I entered my studio, a balm descended upon my spirit. . . . After next Wednesday I shall sit at this desk and produce literature. Never was place so provocative of expression.

Ficke was pleased by the letter: "a prose still-life study of your studio in the soapbox stage" is what he called it by return mail. He also recognized the self-conscious tone of the letter, and he laughed in his next letter at his friend's evident determination to capture for all time the exotic flavor of his new life: "I suppose you wish me to preserve [the letter] for posterity."

Much of Dell's self-conscious pleasure in the Fifty-Seventh Street colony was due to the heightened sense of an avant-garde literary community that the place afforded. As during the years at their Morse Avenue apartment, Margery now became the prime social mover. She hosted frequent parties in her flat, which was larger than Dell's and, unlike his, equipped with a bath and toilet. Artists and intellectuals from all over the city and beyond arrived nearly every evening. Maurice Browne and Ellen Van Volkenburg came often, as did most of the regular cast members and crew from the Little Theater. Dell trumpeted the achievements of the Little Theater in the *Friday Literary Review* and the national press. In an article in

Harper's Weekly he accounted for the aims and early successes of the Little Theater, emphasizing Browne's efforts to produce "a more psychological, less objectively exciting sort of play than America has been accustomed to," and his desire to create "a more immediate relation between the players and their audience." The theater, Dell remarked, had found direct, intimate, barebones ways of recreating such works as Euripides' *Trojan Women*, Arthur Schnitzler's *Anatol*, and Yeats's *On Baile's Strand*. In his memoirs Browne recalled that "Floyd Dell went out of his way to publicize our little place; he more nearly than most of his colleagues understood what we were driving at."

Dell's closest colleagues at the *Friday Literary Review*—the Carys and Charles Hallinan—were often at the parties, as was a more recent friend, Michael Carmichael Carr, an outlandish, redheaded artist and set designer from the University of Missouri, who also collaborated with Browne at the Little Theater. A number of brilliant literary women appeared—Harriet Monroe, who had recently founded *Poetry*, and her assistant (and occasional contributor to the *Friday Literary Review*), Eunice Tietjens. Margaret Anderson also came regularly, just as she had at Morse Avenue. "I have always felt a horror, a fear and a complete lack of attraction for any group, of any kind, for any purpose," Anderson later protested. "But I was willing sometimes to see this one because Floyd Dell was in it—was it, rather. I liked Floyd—which means I liked his conversation. Liked it enormously." At one gathering Anderson announced her plans to start her own literary journal, the *Little Review* (the title was meant to echo the name of the Little Theater).

A number of fiercely independent writers started showing up at the Dells' parties as well. Among them were Carl Sandburg and Vachel Lindsay, poets in search of an audience—and of a critic, like Dell, who was leading his readers to an appreciation of new poems. Dell did not get to know Sandburg very well, but he did admire Sandburg's early impressionistic poems about the city. As Dell later recalled, Sandburg had not yet developed the forceful style that was soon to show up in poems like "Chicago" and make him famous. The two men interested one another, but there was little exchange of ideas between them.

Dell's relationship with Vachel Lindsay was closer. Lindsay was a strange fellow: a lanky, awkward young man who was part hobo, part romantic poet, part puritan, part mystic visionary. He had come across the *Friday Literary Review* soon after it commenced publication in 1909, at a time when he was living in his hometown of Springfield, Illinois. Lindsay contacted Dell first, thanking him for having said kind things about his poetry in the *Review*. "Nicholas Vachel Lindsay is something of an artist," Dell had written in October 1909; "after a fashion, a socialist; more certainly, a religious mystic; and for present purposes it must be added that he is indubitably a poet!" The two were soon avid correspondents, exchanging a great number of letters in 1910 and 1911. Lindsay complimented Dell on his work at the *Review*: "From time to time I improve my mind by reading the Friday Literary Review," he wrote in one letter. "It is beginning to tell on my brain cells, to their benefit." Dell also sent Lindsay copies of his poems—mainly those written in Davenport, for the simple reason that he had not found the time (or inclination) to write poetry in Chicago. Lindsay returned brief, impressionistic critiques, placing multiple hearts next to the names of poems he enjoyed. He could be critical of Dell's verse at times, finding its language a bit lacking in "color." But Lindsay was impressed by its purity and was generous in his praise: "You . . . are living in a high, beautiful spirit. I feel the aspiration, the delicacy, the life-worship that possesses you, the zest with which you eat your experiences, or rather breathe them. . . . I consider meeting you one of the fine adventures of my life, especially meeting you in rhyme."

In 1911 Lindsay came to Chicago, largely in order to meet Dell. Soon he had been taken in as a friend by Floyd and Margery. Dell had always loved reading poetry to others. At a party that ended up on the Lake Michigan beach, Dell chanted some verse by Yeats, thereby inspiring Lindsay to write some verse of his own that might be chanted. The experience had a great effect on Lindsay, who began writing verse—including most of the poems that eventually made him famous—in this style. For Dell and the other bohemians, Lindsay was an eccentric figure who mixed his own bizarre, idiosyncratic nature with a prudishness much out of keeping with their own unconventional behavior. He was accepted by most of the Fifty-Seventh Street bohemians as a preposterous original, an innocent, otherworldly stranger.

An even more extraordinary figure who showed up at Margery's parties was Theodore Dreiser, whom Dell had acclaimed so loudly in the pages of the *Review*. Dreiser was now in Chicago working on the second installment of his fictional account of the life of Charles Yerkes, *The Titan.* He had met Dell in December 1912 during a visit to Chicago: Dell had gone to meet him at the Sherman Hotel. Not until 1913 did the two become well acquainted. Dreiser returned Dell's public praise by referring to him on several occasions as the best critic in America. Dreiser made an eccentric addition to the Fifty-Seventh Street parties, nervously folding and unfolding his handkerchief and making sudden interjections into the conversation. Margery was also much impressed by Dreiser's writings, and she went to considerable pains to make him feel appreciated and at home whenever he came to her place.

Dell and Dreiser had another reason for taking notice of each other in 1913: both had fallen in love with one of the principal actresses at the Little Theater, Elaine Hyman, who was now using her stage name Kirah Markham. A tall, dark-haired woman, Elaine had appeared to great acclaim in the Little Theater's productions of *Trojan Women* (in which she played Andromache) and Yeats's *On Baile's Strand.* She made a riveting impression on stage, contributing much to the company's success. Dell later described her as "an artist with an extraordinary gift for the expression of beautiful and romantic emotions in design and color, and her voice in the singing of old ballads was as moving as in her speaking on the stage; as an actress she was perfectly fitted to the poetic drama."

Dell was the first to be captivated by her, and in the winter of 1912–1913 the two had begun an affair which entirely absorbed his imagination. Elaine was equally obsessed with him. Besides being impressed by Dell's important, influential position in Chicago's literary scene, she was captivated by his learning, intelligence, and charm. They were seen everywhere together. Elaine drew the attention of any crowd, but Dell was also a memorable figure, with the cane and cigarette holder that were now regular features of his public image. Dell later insisted that until he met Elaine Hyman he had been intent upon saving his marriage—that his affairs had never moved him to wish to leave Margery for good. But Elaine stirred in him a desire to end his marriage and marry this stunning, brilliant actress.

Dreiser, however, was also attracted to Elaine, and by early spring she had shifted her loyalties from Dell to the older man. That same spring she left Chicago to be with Dreiser in New York, devoting herself to him with a selflessness that surprised everyone who had

known her as an uncompromisingly independent woman in Chicago. Dell sensed early on why she had left him: Dreiser was a man
who knew his own mind and his place in the world, a man of solid
achievement who had suffered great disappointment and humiliation
as a result of the reception of his shocking early novel, *Sister Carrie*.
Next to so impressive a figure, Dell—though brilliant, precocious,
and successful—seemed innocent and half-formed. He was devastated by the loss of Elaine, especially when a large envelope
containing the letters he had sent her in New York—all of them still
unopened—arrived in early June. Dell was certain that Dreiser had
made Elaine put on this dramatic display of loyalty to himself.

In a series of letters to Arthur Ficke, Dell provided a detailed
account of the breakup of his affair with Elaine. One, dated June
19, summarized his feelings about the turn of events: "I learned a
great deal in the smash-up. . . . It has hurt like hell: but now that I
am convalescent I don't regret it, for it leaves me with certain
convictions that I might have taken a much longer time to reach.
. . . It is better to surrender oneself utterly, and to get smashed up,
than to fool around on the edge." The feeling that it is best
wholeheartedly to embrace experience, no matter how painful,
rather than to live cautiously—this youthful credo of the young
Chicago bohemians was one Dell relied on to weather the despon-
dency he felt after his affair with Elaine Hyman fell through. It also
contributed to his ability to bounce back, as did the fact that he soon
fell in love with another woman: Marjorie Jones, a woman once
again several years older than Dell.

Even as Dell was nursing his battered ego after the debacle of
Elaine, parties and literary activity at the colony were reaching their
peak. The management at the *Evening Post* had finally decided that
the supplement should be terminated—that the *Review*'s editorial
posture had become too radical, and that the literary section should
be reduced, as it had been in the years before 1909, to a few pages
buried in the body of the paper. The change convinced Dell that his
days in Chicago were over. In the summer of 1913, with fewer
editorial responsibilities at the paper and no prospects for work
elsewhere, he devoted himself to the bohemian life on Fifty-Seventh
Street. Now there were nightly parties in Margery Currey's place,
with evening excursions to Jackson Park and the beach.

More artists were showing up at the parties. Lawyer and poet
Edgar Lee Masters came occasionally, as did the English novelist

and critic John Cowper Powys and Masters's former mistress, Tennessee Mitchell, a sculptor. Most significant, perhaps, was the
arrival of Sherwood Anderson early that summer. Anderson was
working at an advertising agency in Chicago at the time, but he was
also devoting many hours each day to his novels and stories. His
brother Karl, an artist, was in Chicago at the time and an occasional
visitor at the Dells' parties. Karl had shown Floyd and Margery a
manuscript copy of his brother's first novel, *Windy McPherson's Son.*
Both were impressed by this unsettled, questing work, and they
asked Karl to bring Sherwood to one of their evening gatherings.
Karl encouraged his brother to come, assuring him that there at last
he would find like-minded writers with whom he could feel at
home.

Anderson, though, was too nervous to introduce himself to the
bohemians on Fifty-Seventh Street, convinced they would dismiss
him as a conventional businessman. One evening he actually
walked up to Margery's studio but could not bring himself to go in
and introduce himself to the twenty or so people plainly visible
through the open door, sprawled casually about the room. "A man I
later knew to be Floyd Dell, was holding forth," Anderson remembered. Dell's animated talk about literature and ideas was clearly
discernible. Anderson was fascinated. Margery Currey was moving
about the room, serving food and drinks. "In some way," Anderson
remembered, "I sensed the fact that she was carrying the tone of the
party, making it go." Certain that he would be out of place in that
"gloriously happy group," Anderson slipped away.

On a second trip he mustered sufficient courage to speak with
Margery, whom he happened to see leaving the flat alone. She
invited Anderson to walk with her in Jackson Park, across the street
from her home, and spoke to him about *Windy McPherson's Son.*
Anderson was easily won over: "She was one who had an extraordinarily sharp and sensitive feeling for people and perhaps even at
the beginning of our acquaintance she felt something of the struggle
going on in me and wanted to help build belief in myself. She spoke
of the world of the arts, the world that had seemed such a shadowy,
dim, faraway place to me, as having a real existence. I could find
comrades there. I could find friends." Soon afterward Margery
introduced him to the entire company.

Anderson fast felt himself at home among them, entering intimately into the lives of several of the regular members of the

community. With Currey he was to have a brief, unhappy affair in the summer after her final separation from Dell. Anderson also fell in love with Tennessee Mitchell, who eventually became his second wife. Anderson's estranged first wife, Cornelia, showed up that summer, moving with her children from Elyria, Ohio, in one last desperate effort to salvage her marriage to Sherwood. Cornelia was neither an artist nor a bohemian, but she was an open-minded woman who was liked by most of the Fifty-Seventh Street regulars. She became a frequent visitor to the colony, though she never was able to reconcile with her husband. To Dell she was "a slender, delicate, self-contained, warm and understanding person; she wore, I remember, what someone called 'her sole recognition of evening dress,' a Dante wreath about her hair; she talked to me of her three children."

It was with Dell that Anderson had his closest artistic relationship. Later he was to refer to Dell as "my literary father," a label that Dell, more than a decade Anderson's junior, was reluctant to accept. In extolling Anderson's work, Dell convinced him that his years of thankless labor on literary manuscripts had not been in vain. That praise seemed a godsend to the older man, giving Anderson the push he needed to continue writing, bolstering his often wavering conviction that the peculiar novels and stories he had already written were in fact respectable literary works. Never stingy with praise or encouragement, Dell gave both to Anderson at a time when Anderson was starved for productive contact with another writer. Anderson regarded Dell as an immensely respected, influential critic, and was mesmerized by his impassioned, unashamed talk about books:

> Floyd walked up and down before us. At the time he was wearing a stock and looked I thought like pictures I had seen of Poe. When he was on the subject of literature he talked, I thought, brilliantly. I had never before heard such talk. How it flowed from him. What vast fields of literature he covered. He became excited. He shouted. The intense little figure became more and more erect.

Anderson was not a bad talker either. Margaret Anderson described him as talking all night long—"Sherwood and Floyd would talk to chairs if they had no other audience," is how she put it—though Sherwood Anderson's conversation was not as intellectual as Dell's: it consisted mainly of anecdotes and stories.

For all the excitement they shared, Dell and Anderson would later remember the Fifty-Seventh Street bohemia in different ways. According to Anderson the summer of 1913 was "a gay happy time, the gayest and happiest I have ever known, a feeling of brotherhood and sisterhood with men and women whose interests were my own." Of that summer and the next, Anderson had the tenderest of memories:

> So there was that summer, to be always remembered, the days got through in the advertising place and then the summer evenings, the walks in the Park, the gatherings in one of the little rooms. Arthur Davison Ficke, already itching to throw all of that over and to devote himself to poetry, coming to town to give us a blowout. Wine, whiskey, and beer brought in. Some singing. Ben Hecht trying out a play in a tiny theater arranged in one of the rooms.
>
> The week ends at some little town on the lake shore, six or eight of us men and women sleeping perhaps, or at least trying to sleep, under one blanket by a low fire built on the shore of the lake, even perhaps going off in the darkness to some secluded spot to bathe, all of us in the nude, it all quite innocent enough, but such a wonderful feeling in us of leading a new, free, bold life, defying what seemed to us the terribly stodgy life out of which we had all come.

Dell's recollections of those days were also tender, but they were mixed with irony and regret. "Candor was more in fashion," he recalled; "only that didn't solve everything. It didn't solve anything. It didn't heal the cruelties of love." His own life at the time he remembered as "bewildered and inconsistent." For the bohemian crowd, Dell's memories were warm but clear-sighted:

> I don't think any of us quite knew what we believed about love and 'freedom.' We were in love with life, and willing to believe almost any modern theory which gave us a chance to live our lives more fully. We were incredibly well meaning. We were confused, miserable, gay, and robustly happy, all at once. Perhaps we were groping hot-bloodedly toward friendship; perhaps we were in a desperate scramble after a lifetime's happiness; we hardly knew, and would never know.

Much of Dell's melancholy had to do with the state of his marriage. It was Dell, not Margery, who was responsible for their crumbling relations. Part of him continued to crave the stability and permanence provided by marriage—qualities that had been so fragile in his family's home because of years of economic distress. Nevertheless, as the youngest child, Floyd had been loved and cherished, particularly by his mother, and he had always retained the desire to recreate (if on a sounder economic basis) that framework provided by family in which love has the chance to endure and flourish.

His discontent was also due to accumulating impatience with the demands of his life as a journalist. Even with reduced editorial responsibilities at the *Post*, Dell had little time for creative writing. He constantly promised himself stories, plays, poems, even an autobiographical novel about his early years in the rural Midwest. But apart from a few short pieces and fragments, he was not able to produce much. His time was spent at the *Post*, at parties on Fifty-Seventh Street, in pubs and restaurants with friends. There was laughter but also a nagging sense of lost time.

He had cultivated an elaborate public image by 1913. One day he was having lunch with Michael Carmichael Carr, the artist and Little Theater set designer, and Charlotte Perkins Gilman, the feminist whose poetry he had praised in the *Review*. Gilman and Carr urged him to "wear a high collar and black stock, and carry a stick and gloves." Dell followed their advice and was soon known around town for his outlandish European attire. The small-town boy had come a long way indeed. That same spring Bror Nordfeldt painted Dell in his aristocratic getup, capturing both his youth and determined sophistication.

Even this sartorial affectation caused Dell to doubt himself, as became evident in a story he wrote in early 1913, "The Portrait of Murray Swift." He employed the same character as in "Jessica Screams," but here Murray Swift was clearly patterned on himself, not on Ezra Pound. As the story opens, Murray Swift is seen pausing at an impressionist exhibition at Chicago's Art Institute, speaking to Jimmy Selden of his admiration for the art on display, and particularly for the work of the Chicago artist Nordberg (based on Bror Nordfeldt). Swift decides he wants his own portrait done by Nordberg, even as Selden warns him, "You'll be sorry." When they arrive at Nordberg's studio on the South Side, the artist offers a similar warning. "He will make a very interesting picture," Nordberg remarks to Selden and Swift, "but perhaps not just what you have in mind." For all his sophistication, Swift cannot imagine what Selden and Nordberg mean.

Nordberg works quickly, and Swift conjures up the image Nordberg must be laboring to capture: "He realized he was in a characteristic attitude, pausing with one knee bent, his body slightly inclined forward, his stick hanging from the crook of his left arm, a cigarette in his other hand, his head twisted at a slightly critical angle to face the painter. His face, as he figured it in imagination, must express some of his habitual curiosity, his eagerness, his detachment." A woman enters the studio—a sculptor who lives in one of the neighboring apartments. She seems aloof but also interested in him. Swift recognizes her as the woman he had seen in one of Nordberg's portraits, and he asks himself if he would be so interested in her had he not seen her painted image first. Nordberg, he realizes, had emphasized "her vitality—hits you between the eyes with it." Swift tries to assure himself that he too is alert to life and not just to art. "I hope I can recognize vitality without the assistance of art," he lamely remarks to himself. Determined to prove his own vitality, he proposes to meet the woman later. She agrees, without any fuss, to meet him that same evening.

The story is destined to end unhappily. Late that afternoon Nordberg finishes the portrait, then says he wants to wait an hour or so before showing it to Murray Swift. In the meantime Swift walks out to Lake Michigan with the woman. It is stormy at the lakefront, and the woman seems absorbed in the outdoors scene. Swift realizes that in contrast he "preferred that conversation which subsists in a room filled with men and women, all in comfortable attitudes, himself most comfortable of all in a large chair with one leg thrown over the arm; under those circumstances a staccato eloquence, attuned delicately to the moment, was at his command. He disliked this wild lakefront, where already the civilization that lay a block behind them was almost forgotten." Swift chatters on as the woman sits silently beside him. Finally she speaks, telling him he will not come to her that night. "It was not a command," Dell writes, "it was a statement, with the faintest touch of sadness to color its indifference." When Swift asks her what she means she smiles and says, "Go and look at your portrait!"

If all this reflected Dell's own insecurities—his worries that he was a superficial newspaper critic, a salon raconteur not capable of sustained literary work or romantic love—the final passage, in which Murray Swift sees his portrait, represents the apotheosis of Dell's self-doubt. The portrait is as disturbing as Selden and Nordberg had said it might be: "He saw himself, drawn with an exquisite and mordant irony, with stick and cigarette, the face curious and evasive, with something that was almost boldness in the eyes, something that was almost courage in the chin. Murray Swift, observant, indecisive, inadequate, against a rose-colored background. Then he understood. The girl was right. He would not be there."

This damning self-portrait had been a long time coming. Dell rehearsed all his doubts about himself in "The Portrait of Murray Swift": that he was an idle talker and unproductive, detached aesthete, lacking in passion or any vital connection with other persons. His life was stimulating and busy, but it was also disjointed and aimless. At last it was Margery, not Dell, who gathered sufficient resolve to end their hopeless marriage. In a letter she wrote Dell that spring, she acquitted herself in a forthright manner that must have humbled him and won again his admiration. Coming after a discussion in which they had considered the possibility of divorce, and in the course of which Dell had complained that he was disgusted with himself, Margery wrote him a bracingly sensible letter:

> I guess I mean what I said, Floyd. There seems no other way but to drag it up by the roots. I'd rather do that than let it do the poetic *trash* flowers are accustomed to—such as withering slowly, becoming distorted, breaking, being choked by weeds, etc. etc.
>
> I don't know much about the techniques of morality—but I do feel that one should not continue to annoy a man when he doesn't care and never will. I'd like to be in your presence—I found the whole of you so delicious—but it wouldn't be fair to you to let me love you when you knew you couldn't.
>
> I rather resented your saying you are spiritually sick—you're not a bit. You're in fine health. Spiritually, I think. To know oneself— to admit it—that's good digestion; oh it's so much better than hoodwinking your own wisdom. You just didn't hit the right woman (confound my meagerness!) but that's not saying you haven't the sagacity to find her and the capacity to feel her sufficient. I think you have. . . .
>
> I wish you all the joy and completeness you'll one day know and which I'll dream of for you.

The letter must have reminded Dell why he had fallen in love with Margery in the first place. His response seems to have been mixed:

he was saddened, relieved, ashamed. In any case, he put up little fight, resigning himself to what they both now felt was inevitable. The couple continued to live next door to each other all summer and into the fall. But they had firmly agreed to divorce. They spent their evenings together at Margery's parties, rarely complaining to friends about the unhappy fate of their marriage. In this, as in Margery's letter, they were guided by the ideal of relations free of the pettiness, bitterness, and possessiveness of more traditional marriages. Margery was capable of admitting that deep down she had wanted a more dependable marriage from the start. Her husband was uncertain about what he wanted at all.

His marriage in shambles and his editorial job reduced in scope and freedom, Dell was aware of little in Chicago that might keep him there. Cook, Susan Glaspell, Elaine Hyman—these and others of his more ambitious Chicago friends had already left for New York. By the late summer of 1913 Dell was resolved to move there too. Every fall since he had become the *Post*'s literary editor, Dell had gone to New York to meet with publishers and gather news of their forthcoming books. Earlier he and Margery had gone together, both pleased to be in touch with New York's literary and publishing worlds. In late August 1913 Dell went alone, and not primarily in his capacity as the *Post*'s literary editor. Rather he spent his time in New York looking for a job. None came to hand.

But other things happened to him in New York that convinced him he should move there. He visited Dreiser and Elaine Hyman and was at last reconciled to Elaine's decision to stay with Dreiser. He also went out to Provincetown, Massachusetts, on the tip of Cape Cod, where he visited with Jig Cook and Susan Glaspell. The bohemian life he encountered there—even more exotic and removed from ordinary life than the little bohemia he had known in Chicago—reawakened enthusiasms that had been stifled of late in Chicago. "The life at Provincetown," he wrote Ficke, "is the life for me. . . . I'm going back to Chicago for a few days, maybe ten, and then coming back to New York."

One last event sealed this decision. While in New York he heard from colleagues back at the *Post* that John Shaffer, the newspaper's owner, had finally erupted about the radical contents of the literary pages and, after abandoning his initial impulse to fire Dell, had fired a number of the subsidiary editors on Dell's staff. Leigh Reilly, the managing editor who for four years had successfully mollified

Shaffer's grievances, was unwilling to carry on in the face of these dismissals. He resigned immediately, as did Dell's friend and close colleague at the paper, Charles Hallinan. On hearing the news Dell was again filled with mixed emotions. He was partly outraged but also relieved to be handed an opportunity to sever himself from the paper. He wired in his resignation and returned to Chicago a few days later, planning to leave for good in a week or so.

He ended up staying in Chicago long enough to ease the transition of editorial responsibilities at the *Post*: Lucian Cary became the new literary editor, Augusta his assistant. Dell also wrapped things up amicably with Margery and her father and said goodbye to all his Chicago friends. Shortly before he left there was a final dinner at Fifty-Seventh Street, at which Margery, who had already quit her teaching post, announced that she would soon be going to work full-time as a reporter for the *Chicago Daily News*. Dell, meanwhile, continued his romance with Marjorie Jones. By the time he left for New York in late October, she too was talking about leaving and joining him in Greenwich Village.

On the train to New York he wrote his old Davenport mentor, Rabbi William Fineshriber, straining to make sense of the years he had spent in Chicago and what he had learned from them. As he acknowledged years later, he had loved Chicago and enjoyed his years there. To Fineshriber, though, he wanted to talk about his chaotic private life. He weakly implied that his failed marriage and fleeting love affairs might be seen as necessary stages in his progress toward maturity and self-understanding. But he was also inclined to be hard on himself. He had lived exclusively for ideas in Davenport and Chicago, he wrote, and this exclusive faith in "reason and logic" had made him "callous," "hypocritical in my relations with women," "unsatisfactory as a lover," "intolerable as a husband." He was particularly harsh about his Chicago days: "I suppose that during those five years I have inflicted upon everyone who has cared for me, every variety of cruelty which an arrogant and ignorant idealism can unconsciously devise." The ideals that had led him to disregard convention and indulge his desires—even if it meant the ruin of his marriage—now struck him as more vicious than liberating. "I now care a great deal for people and damned little for ideas," he insisted. He vowed never to "hurt anybody's feelings to prove the most beautiful theory ever invented."

Dell no longer wished to think of himself as a member of the intellectual elite, no longer wished to present himself as a haughty literary man. Life in Chicago had made him "an ordinary person"; it had made him crave common pleasures. As he traveled to New York and the extraordinary literary, political, and bohemian worlds that were converging there, Dell was determined never to be an innocent, blindly idealistic rebel again. To a considerable degree he was to make good on this resolve. Skepticism and irony were already beginning to temper the ruthless idealism of his youth, and they were leading him to view his contemporaries with a saving measure of detachment. Henceforth he would always stand a step apart from the radical cultural and political worlds where he would continue to make his home.

"Revolutionaries Without a Revolution"

EVERY WAVE OF Greenwich Village rebels has looked back to an earlier, ostensibly more authentic generation of Village radicals. When the writer Malcolm Cowley, who was born in 1898, arrived in Greenwich Village soon after World War I, he and his contemporaries felt they were less remarkable in every regard than the bohemians (among them Floyd Dell) who had dominated Village life during the half-decade before America's entrance into the war in 1917. According to Cowley, there were two distinctly different generations of Villagers in the years just after the war: the authentic radicals of the prewar era, and the less adventurous younger crowd which started to pour into the Village in 1919: " 'They' had been rebels: they wanted to change the world, be leaders in the fight for justice and art, help to create a society in which individuals could express themselves. 'We' were convinced at the time that society could never be changed by an effort of the will." For Cowley and others of his generation, the prewar Villagers had been romantic rebels: a passionate, vivid group of cultural and political radicals. Compared with them, Cowley's own generation seemed pale, insubstantial, humble in its dreams and aspirations.

Cowley's generational tableau, published in 1934, has survived in the writings of cultural historians for sixty years. Surely it describes a great deal about Greenwich Village life in the years just after the war. But in his exalted view of the prewar Villagers, Cowley missed the fact that many of the earlier bohemians also felt like latecomers to a place where genuine radicalism was already a thing of the past. In a memoir of Greenwich Village that he wrote in 1947, Floyd Dell stressed how belated and ephemeral he and his contemporaries had felt when they arrived in the Village in the early 1910s. Dell looked back to two earlier generations of Village inhabitants: the bohemians of the late nineteenth century and the serious-minded progressive reformers who set the tone for Village life in the first decade of the new century. The "authentic bohemian glories [of the 1880s and 1890s] had faded out before I came there," he wrote. "Its best people were now seriously interested in social reform, votes for women, the labor movement—and, of course, in art and literature, especially the kinds devoted to social progress. . . . As for the artists and writers who then lived in the Village—such as John Sloan and Art Young, Mary Heaton Vorse, Inez Haynes Gillmore, Susan Glaspell, Theodore Dreiser—they already had positions of importance in the realm of art and letters." The new Villagers, Dell wrote, had little of the substance of the older inhabitants. "This [new] Village bohemia was composed in part of young people, economically insecure and with uncertain or unproved talents—or with perhaps no real talents, but only artistic temperaments." Village chronicler Allen Churchill also noted a lack of artistic substance among many of Dell's generation: "For a time at least, it seemed that members of the younger generation traveling to Greenwich Village did so as much from an urge for general emancipation, as from a desire to express themselves artistically."

Dell was like Cowley in believing that "authentic bohemian glories" belonged to an earlier Village era than his own, but he still found more to like in his own crowd than Cowley did in the postwar Village denizens. His generation of Villagers, Dell noted, took shape between 1913 and 1917, years mainly shadowed by the war in Europe. Bohemia seemed to billow out in a brief surge of hectic, unconstrained idealism. The result was a more chaotic scene: greater delirium and uncertainty, but also a touching, desperate idealism. Dell was probably right when he said that the distant, ominous war had made his own Village so rash and disorderly: "The wartime years turned the Village into a melting-pot in which all group boundaries were dissolved. Artists, writers, intellectuals, liberals, radicals, IWWs, bohemians, well-to-do patrons, onlookers—all were hurled into a miscellaneous social melee in which earnestness and frivolity were thoroughly intermingled. The 'real' Greenwich Village [of the preceding generation] was swept away in the flood."

Dell knew that this atmosphere had little of the social or artistic seriousness of the Village's preceding decade; nor did it offer the rarefied bohemian isolation of the eighties and nineties. But the new Villagers were possessed by a strangely persistent conviction that the moment belonged to them. Older Villagers seemed to reflect a more settled world. The younger crowd was part of a new world in the midst of profound political and cultural turmoil. Its members tended to see in their own lives signs of the general crisis of modernity. They were arrogant enough to discern a wider crisis of political and cultural meaning in their own restless (and often incoherent) search for new social, cultural, and personal values. Not surprisingly, then, the prewar Village was a fascinating place. To mix culture and politics, social and sexual rebellion, bohemia and socialism—these efforts may have been mad and doomed to failure, but for the new Villagers they seemed necessary responses to the combination of crisis and possibility in the world and in their own lives.

Dell arrived in October 1913, just as the new Village's main social and cultural institutions were taking shape. Earlier that year Mabel Dodge had initiated her "evenings" at 23 Fifth Avenue, gatherings that quickly metamorphosed into a nightly salon for all sorts of New York artists and intellectuals. In February and March the International Exhibition of Modern Art at the Sixty-Ninth Regiment Armory—the Armory Show, as it has been called ever since—jolted the Villagers, as it did many other New Yorkers, with its presentation of literally hundreds of disconcertingly modern works by artists from Europe and America. And in June, John Reed, with other Village leftists and striking workers from Paterson, New Jersey, had staged "The Pageant of the Paterson Strike" at Madison Square Garden, merging the radical politics of the IWW with the avant-garde theatrics of the Village. All these events and enterprises inspired the new Villagers with the feeling that they were participants in an important, if rather chaotic, awakening of radicalism in America. The Paterson Strike Pageant in particular suggested an unprecedented coalescence of radical politics and culture. It seemed to promise not just a new episode in labor politics but a broad radical movement that might eventually remake all American life.

The precise day on which Dell arrived in New York promised nothing quite so grand. He was escorted to a boisterous Village gathering and taken from there to the apartment of "a beautiful girl dancer who kept a pet alligator in her bathtub." He recalled that the young woman "bade me let it bite my finger, saying it wouldn't hurt me; I obeyed her trustfully, but offered the alligator the little finger of my left hand, just in case—; and the amiable reptile nipped it very gently."

The next morning Dell met Henrietta Rodman, who asked him to write "a play to produce at the housewarming of the Liberal Club." Rodman taught English literature in one of the city high schools, but her greatest talent was as a social catalyst among the new Village intellectuals. A champion of every radical cause from women's suffrage to labor rights to free love, she tended, like others among the new Village rebels, to make up in enthusiasm what she lacked in intellectual rigor. Dell described her as "incredibly naive, preposterously reckless, believing wistfully in beauty and goodness, a Candide in petticoats and sandals. . . . She was especially in touch with the university crowd and the social settlement crowd, and the Socialist crowd; and it was these, many of whom never actually lived in the Village, who, mixing with the literary and artist crowds in the Liberal Club, gave the Village a new character entirely."

For all her causes, Rodman's favorite was likely the Liberal Club itself. This she was intent upon transforming from a stodgy intellectual parlor into the young Village's most hyperbolic and up-to-date meeting place. She sensed the way in which Village rebels were searching for an inclusive form of radical identity and community. So eclectic a community needed institutions—social, political, journalistic—that could embrace all the forms of rebellion that the new Villagers wanted to try on for size. What Rodman had in mind was an intellectual and social center beholden to no particular party or platform, where members could drink, dance, and gossip, and where they might participate in impromptu discussions of the newest fashions in literature and politics. Far more than Mabel Dodge's self-consciously elite salon, Rodman's Liberal Club was a chaotic, unpretentious institution perfectly suited to the new bohemians' undisciplined tastes.

When Dell arrived in New York in the fall of 1913, Rodman had only recently relocated the Liberal Club from its uptown quarters to 137 MacDougal Street, just a half-block southwest of Washington Square, in the very heart of Greenwich Village. Downstairs was Polly Holladay's restaurant where Villagers could find cheap meals.

Next door was the Washington Square Bookshop, owned by Charles and Albert Boni. (Several years later, with Charles Liveright, Albert Boni founded Boni & Liveright, one of the most adventurous publishing houses in postwar New York.) Members of the Liberal Club soon included Villagers of several generations. Dell and the writers Max Eastman, John Reed, and Alfred Kreymborg were among those still in their twenties and early thirties; Theodore Dreiser, Hutchins Hapgood, and Upton Sinclair were among the older crowd. But it was generally the younger bohemians who set the club's unconventional tone. In a letter to Dreiser, H. L. Mencken warned the novelist whose cause he had championed for years about the lack of substance at the youth-dominated Liberal Club. The organization was made up, he insisted, "of all the tin pot revolutionaries and sophomoric advanced thinkers in New York." Mencken was correct about the pretensions of many of the club's members. But he was also too harsh, missing much of the club's purpose. The Liberal Club was not intended to nurture older talents like Dreiser and Sinclair; rather, it aimed to give bohemia (always in danger of dissolving into factions, solipsism, and general incoherence) a lighthearted intellectual and social home. In this, if not in any more serious sense, the club was a success.

Likely Rodman had heard of Dell when he had visited New York the summer before. Then he had come as a worldly literary man whose reputation had long since spread from Chicago to New York. When he moved to the Village that fall, she latched onto him as a writer who might provide the club with an initiatory piece of theater. Dell was happy to oblige. Back in Chicago he and Arthur Davison Ficke had collaborated on a brief sketch of a play, "St. George of the Minute," which poked fun at modern ideas and the pretensions of young people like themselves. Now, in no more than a few weeks, Dell filled out the original idea, arriving at a short play that he called *St. George in Greenwich Village*—"a satire on the earnest Bohemianism of our little world." The play laughed at every Village cause, from woman's suffrage to anarchism to Montessori schools ("What! You've never heard of the Montessori System?" exclaims one character. "Why, my dear, it's simply a lot of things. And you put the baby down among the things—and you never have to bother about it again!"). Dell starred in the title role at the first Liberal Club production that November, with other Villagers, Helen Westley, and Sherwood Anderson (also recently arrived from Chicago) in the supporting cast. The play was presented, as Dell wrote Ficke shortly thereafter, "to immense applause." Later he recalled that it was produced " 'in the Chinese manner,' without scenery—also without a stage, curtains or footlights. The Village enjoyed being satirized, and this was a satire upon everything in which the Village believed." The new Greenwich Village "wanted its most serious beliefs mocked at; it enjoyed laughing at its own convictions."

Dell found himself in demand after the play's premiere, with Rodman and Liberal Club regulars clamoring for more self-reflective theatricals. "For a while," he accurately recalled, "I was the satirist of the Village." In the next year and a half he produced a string of plays, all dashed off in no time and all received with delight at Liberal Club performances. *The Perfect Husband,* which Dell very likely wrote with his affair with Augusta Cary in mind, made fun of that absurd species of bohemian idealism that demanded that a husband remain friendly with his wife's lover. *Enigma* was more a dyspeptic than comic look at the new rebels' idealization of excessively independent men and women. In the play a young couple (played in the first performance, appropriately enough, by Dell and Elaine Hyman) are unable to save their relationship from collapse for the simple reason that neither is willing to confess his or her desire *not* to split up. *Ibsen Revisited* (which Dell accurately subtitled "A Piece of Foolishness") presented Hedda Gabler and Lövborg, both still alive after the conclusion of *Hedda Gabler* and devoted not to "divine adventurousness" but rather to stultifying, bourgeois "reform" and the belief that "We must all learn to function socially." Another play, *The Idealist,* Dell remembered as "a mocking footnote upon the behavior of myself and various of my friends, who in our search for 'eternal love' went from one wife and sweetheart to another."

All these plays were transparently autobiographical; most were graced by the playwright's light, ironic touch. Performances featured the widely varying histrionic talents of such Villagers as Helen Westley, Ida Rauh, Marjorie Jones (Dell's lover from Fifty-Seventh Street, recently arrived in New York), Maurice Becker, Clement Wood, Jo Gotsch, and numerous others. Dell's light dramatic exercises were soon among the most prized features of Liberal Club life, and the actors were frequently referred to collectively as Dell's Players.

For his own part, Dell never took the Liberal Club plays seriously.

They were fun to write, and he took special pleasure in the communal exercise of staging them—starring in many of them with other Villagers, and presenting them in informal settings without much scenery or finery and with an enthusiastic audience always on hand. He never aimed at anything other than local and transient theatrical pleasures, deftly assembled vignettes that were unimaginable apart from the community that staged and attended them. Certainly there was no money to be made from them. What little money he did make at the time came from writing for a handful of national magazines. Abridged versions of some of the articles he had written for the *Friday Literary Review* on Chicago fiction appeared in November and December in the *Bookman.* An enthusiastic account of the work being done at the Chicago Little Theater appeared in *Harper's Weekly,* as did a review of H. G. Wells's *The Passionate Friends.*

Dell sold another piece to *Harper's* that finally appeared in July 1914: "Mona Lisa and the Wheelbarrow," a clever piece of cultural criticism that described feminism and the mechanization of modern life as "the two great riddles of the world to-day." A fitting culmination to his work at the *Friday Literary Review,* "Mona Lisa and the Wheelbarrow" reveals Dell looking (with notable aplomb, though not without a measure of bewilderment) toward the American future in which his own life and career will be played out. Liberated women and modern technology—those two awakening forces that Dell gladly welcomed—seemed also to baffle and disconcert him at the time.

Dell's real work in Greenwich Village began in December when he returned to the business of running a radical cultural magazine. One day in late fall he was walking along Greenwich Avenue when he was hailed by Horatio Winslow, a tall, affable young man and frequent contributor to the satiric journal *Puck.* Winslow asked Dell to come with him into Gallup's Restaurant, where editors and contributors to the *Masses*—Max Eastman, John Reed, Berkeley Tobey, and Winslow himself—had been sitting over lunch, trying to figure out how to bring editorial discipline to their woefully haphazard journalistic enterprise. Tobey, who had left the respectable business world in order to become the *Masses'* business manager, had become close friends with Dell since the latter's arrival several months earlier in the Village.

"There goes your associate editor," Tobey told his companions in

Gallup's, pointing at a slender, bohemian figure. "That's Floyd Dell." In the time it took Dell to walk by, the group resolved to make him associate editor—right-hand man to editor Max Eastman—provided he could be convinced to take the job.

Dell was not a complete stranger to the men he sat down with at Gallup's. He had met Eastman and Reed at the *Masses'* disorderly offices at 91 Greenwich Avenue earlier that fall, when he had offered them a story, "A Perfectly Good Cat," to publish. That meeting had ended with the usual *Masses* agreement that he, the author, would receive no money for his contribution. "The magazine didn't pay for anything," Dell remembered, "but it was a great honor to have the privilege of contributing to it."

Editors at the *Masses* were accustomed to transacting business in an abrupt, peremptory fashion. Little more than a year before, Eastman, until then an academic philosopher with no real journalistic experience, had been recruited to be the magazine's editor in a preposterously blunt way. Opening his mail one morning, he discovered a note from the journal's artistic director, John Sloan, confined to the following choice words: "You are elected editor of *The Masses.* No pay." Now Dell found himself confronted by Eastman and several of his associates and presented with a similar offer. John Reed, who was eager to go to Mexico to cover the revolution there for the *Masses* and other magazines, went to work on Dell as soon as he sat down at the table.

"Floyd, you are going to help edit the *Masses,*" Reed insisted. "You know about make-up and such things. You will attend to all that, while Max writes the editorials. Your title will be associate editor." Dell was flabbergasted by this unsolicited overture from the most flamboyantly radical journal in the Village.

He also maintained enough self-possession to make certain stipulations. "Bohemian ways are all right in some respects," he began, "but not, in my view, when it comes to money matters. I know how it is over at the *Masses* office. Sometimes the office force doesn't get paid because there isn't any money. But I expect to be paid whether there is any money or not. The first time I don't get paid, I won't say anything. The next time I don't get paid, I won't say anything, either, but I won't be there any more."

He began work at once. Immediately the magazine reflected his influence, becoming more diverse than before and fleshing out its literary and cultural dimensions. In this he was contributing to

developments already under way. The *Masses* under Eastman's
editorship had become a vastly different publication than the more
or less conventional socialist magazine it had been during its first
year, from January 1911 to August 1912. A former lecturer and
doctoral candidate at Columbia University, Eastman had no interest
in publishing dry socialist exposés, theoretical diatribes, or run-of-
the-mill propaganda. Instead he brought to the *Masses* a more
eclectic, artistic temperament. When he arrived he was completing
his first book, an idiosyncratic piece of literary criticism called *The
Enjoyment of Poetry*. Tall, strikingly handsome, articulate, confident,
he was already assembling a glamorous reputation as a political
radical, feminist, poet, and lady-killer. Bringing diverse cultural and
political interests to the nearly defunct monthly, he started instantly
to transform it into an attention-grabbing hodgepodge of radical
politics and culture, with criticism, fiction, and artwork, much of it
shot through with irreverence and an irascible, satiric spirit.

"We plan a radical change of policy for The Masses," Eastman
announced in an editorial in the December 1912 issue, his first as
editor. "We are going to make The Masses a *popular* Socialist
magazine—a magazine of pictures and lively writing." He went on
to suggest more precisely what he had in mind:

> There are no magazines in America which measure up in radical
> art and freedom of expression to the foreign satirical journals. We
> think we can produce one, and we have on our staff eight of the
> best known artists and illustrators in the country ready to contri-
> bute to it their most individual work. . . . We shall produce with
> the best technique the best magazine pictures at command in
> New York.
>
> But we go beyond this. For with that pictorial policy we
> combine a literary policy equally radical and definite. We are a
> Socialist magazine. We shall print every month a page of illus-
> trated editorials reflecting life as a whole from a Socialist stand-
> point. . . . In our contributed columns we shall incline towards
> literature of especial interest to Socialists, but we shall be hospit-
> able to free and spiritual expressions of every kind—in fiction,
> satire, poetry and essay. Only we shall no longer compete in any
> degree with the more heavy and academic reviews.

Two months later Eastman (with John Reed's assistance) spelled
out the *Masses'* eclectic, nondoctrinaire principles and priorities in
even clearer, more obstreperous, terms:

This magazine is owned and published co-operatively by its editors. It has no dividends to pay, and nobody is trying to make money out of it. A revolutionary and not a reform magazine; a magazine with a sense of humor and no respect for the respectable; frank, arrogant, impertinent, searching for the true causes; a magazine directed against rigidity and dogma wherever it is found; printing what is too naked or true for a money-making press; a magazine whose final policy is to do as it pleases and conciliate nobody, not even its readers—there is a field for this publication in America.

The magazine's rebellious, uncompromising temper was in full flower by the time Dell arrived in December 1913. Nowhere was that temper more fully evident than in the magazine's artwork. John Sloan, the magazine's art editor, had assembled a remarkable throng of artists whose works reflected to varying degrees the gritty realism of the so-called Ashcan School. Frequent contributors included Maurice Becker, George Bellows, Kenneth Russell Chamberlain, Glenn Coleman, Stuart Davis, Henry Glintenkamp, and Boardman Robinson. All seemed to strive to outdo the others in making their works brash and irreverent. Another regular at the *Masses* was Art Young, a political cartoonist whose artistic goals were even more pointedly political than those of the other artists. A typical cartoon by Young portrays a villainous-looking man labeled "The Associated Press" who is poisoning a pool labeled "The News" with vials of "Lies," "Slander," "Prejudice," "Suppressed Facts," and "Hatred of Labor Organization." The cartoon, which appeared in the July 1913 issue of the *Masses*, precipitated a number of libel suits by the Associated Press (the charges were later dropped).

In the midst of all this talent there was a desperate need for editorial and journalistic expertise. Dell supplied both. He brought invaluable experience in planning, designing, and producing a magazine. Eastman wanted to concentrate on writing editorials for the *Masses*, shaping its general policies, and raising money. Dell's presence allowed him to do this. He was, Eastman recalled, "the most perfect example of an associate editor that nature's evolution has produced." Dell read submissions, worked with contributors, assembled issues, and oversaw production. Eastman prized Dell as his one indispensable associate:

I never knew a more reasonable or dependable person, more variously intelligent, more agile in combining sociability with industry, and I never knew a writer who had his talents in such complete command. When we would be down at the printer's correcting page proofs and revising our make-up at the last moment, as we always did, and would find some unfilled space staring at us, all I had to do was give Floyd its dimensions. He would sit down in the midst of all the ear-and-cortex-splitting roar and riot of a press room, where I could barely retain the faculty to measure a space, and write a shapely verse or paragraph, timely, witty, true, acute, and perfectly designed to fit it.

Dell also brought to the *Masses* his interests in literature, feminism, and other cultural and political topics. He wrote Ficke in Davenport and described his new position, as well as his plans for improving the *Masses*: "I am the managing editor of The Masses, which contains the best art in the U.S.A. and will presently contain the best prose." From the start he contributed a great many reviews and essays and recruited a remarkable collection of literary and critical contributors. The poets eventually included Dell and Eastman themselves, as well as Louis Untermeyer, Arthur Ficke, Jean Starr Untermeyer, Carl Sandburg, Jean Toomer, Mark Van Doren, Edna St. Vincent Millay, Witter Bynner, Amy Lowell, William Carlos Williams, Vachel Lindsay, Eunice Tietjens, John Reed, Joel Elias Spingarn, William Rose Benet, Edmund Wilson, Babette Deutsch, Elinor Wylie, Upton Sinclair, Dorothy Day, Josephine Bell, Helen Hoyt, James Oppenheim, and e. e. cummings. Stories came from, among others, Dell, Reed, Djuna Barnes, Susan Glaspell, John Dos Passos, and Sherwood Anderson, who published several of the *Winesburg, Ohio* stories he was then writing. Dell contributed by far the greatest number of reviews and essays; others came from Randolph Bourne, Bertrand Russell, Arthur B. Davies, and John Sloan. Years later Eastman wrote that "Floyd brought to *The Masses* a gift of literary criticism as fine as we had in the country. I thought, and still think, that he wrote the most charming and judicious book reviews of the whole period." The literary and cultural contributions, overseen (and often written) by Dell, added as much as any other pages in the magazine to the air of brilliance and untrammeled variety that were hallmarks of the *Masses*.

Dell also led the *Masses'* monthly meetings, generally held in an artist's studio somewhere in the Village, where potential contributions were discussed by the magazine's editors and assorted hangers-on. As many as twenty or thirty people were typically present; the room was invariably filled with tobacco smoke and unconstrained talk. Usually on hand were the *Masses'* main editors and contributors. Among the so-called "literature" editors were Dell, Eastman, sometimes Reed, Louis Untermeyer, Mary Heaton Vorse, Howard Brubaker, Robert Carlton Brown, and William English Walling. Also present were the art editors: the artistic director John Sloan, the genial radical Art Young, Stuart Davis, Cornelia Barns, Glenn Coleman, Maurice Becker, Alice Beach Winter, Charles A. Winter, Henry Glintenkamp, Kenneth Russell Chamberlain, and George Bellows. Berkeley Tobey was also a regular participant. Other writers, editors, and artists would show up on a less regular basis, and everyone would be allowed to vote on each work under consideration—these being meetings, after all, held by radical socialists and democrats who professed to despise any sign of editorial hierarchy.

Dell, standing or sitting before the rabble and smoking one cigarette after another, would read a poem or essay and then lead a discussion on the work's merits. What would follow, more often than not, was chaos, shouting, laughter, and irresolvable disagreement. The artists were especially merciless in their denunciations. "Oh my God, Max," one would call out in the middle of a reading, "do we have to listen to this tripe?" The feminist and labor journalist Mary Heaton Vorse recalled that the artists contributed disproportionately to the atmosphere of unconstrained judgment. "Nothing more horrible can be imagined than having one's piece torn to bits by the artists at a *Masses* meeting," Vorse wrote in her memoirs. "On the other hand, there was no greater reward than having them stop their groans and catcalls and give close attention; then laughter if the piece was funny, finally applause."

Others present added to the general hullabaloo. According to Dell, "Louis Untermeyer, the poet and critic, beamed through his glasses and set off puns like bunches of fire crackers." Polly Holladay's anarchist lover and fellow restaurateur, Hippolyte Havel, ridiculed the editors' willingness to vote on the merits of art. "Bourgeois!" he yelled out one night, "Voting! Voting on poetry! Poetry is something from the soul! You can't vote on poetry!" Dell responded that anarchists also had to make decisions. "Sure—sure," Havel fired back, "we anarchists make decisions. But we don't abide by them." John Sloan, famous for harsh critiques of what he deemed unsatisfactory illustrations, would lead similarly chaotic discussions on the proposed artwork.

Frequently arguments broke out along party lines—which most commonly meant between writers and artists. Eastman later described the disputes as "a war of the Bohemian art-rebels against the socialists who loved art." Eastman and Dell clearly placed themselves among the socialists. Despite their leadership of the Village's favorite magazine, both men remained skeptical about what Eastman once called "the puny, artificial, sex-conscious simmering in perpetual puberty of the grey-haired Bacchantes of Greenwich Village." Years later he insisted that "hardly a month passed that I did not take some action designed to hold the propaganda of revolutionary class struggle clear of the mere rebel moods of those who mistake the delights of a venturesome life, or of creative art itself, for the effort toward world transformation."

The artists were uncowed by such pronunciamentos. They accused Dell and Eastman of holding too much control of the magazine, shaping it in the image of their own literary and political interests and relegating the artwork to a subordinate role. Dell responded to this objection at several meetings, pointing out that editorial leadership was needed in order to give the magazine a semblance of coherence. In fact, once the meetings ended, Dell and Eastman frequently revised the contents that had just been agreed upon in order to give the issues "some kind of unity, or balance":

> So we went about and got new contributions; we wrote things ourselves; we received unexpected treasures in the mails. Sometimes a literary masterpiece or drawing would be taken out of a desk-drawer where it had accidentally got left. Some of the artists thought there was some shenanigan about those features which turned up at the last minute, and which were printed without having to run the gauntlet of a meeting where they might have been voted down. Max Eastman and I were literary guys, and they didn't think that literary guys could be trusted an inch.

All rivalries between artists and writers aside, the magazine was, for a while, a happy and productive enterprise. Its monthly circulation hovered around fourteen thousand, with individual issues sometimes selling as many as 25,000 copies. These were by no means negligible sales figures for a radical literary and political magazine, but they were still not enough to pay the bills. The *Masses* was a stunning journal, with two-color lithographs for covers and excellent reproductions of artwork scattered throughout its pages. Producing such a magazine cost a great deal of money. Much came from wealthy liberal patrons, whose contributions Max Eastman spent a great deal of time soliciting. These benefactors—Howard Brubaker, Mabel Dodge, Alva Belmont, E. W. Scripps, Adolph Lewisohn—Dell called "the Rebel Rich." "Our getting money from the rich was a sort of skeleton in our proletarian revolutionary closet," he later wrote. "It was kind of hushed up." The benefactors, like those who were soon to support other leftist journals—the *New Republic*, the *Seven Arts*, the *Dial*, and the *Freeman*—were "reformers, liberals, progressives." They tolerated the *Masses'* frivolous excesses, giving money instead for the magazine's more serious attacks on political corruption, oppression, and intolerance. This association of wealth with radicals and bohemians may have seemed incongruous in 1914 and 1915, when the styles and spirit of avant-garde culture had not yet permeated middle- and upper-class American life. In retrospect it is clear that this association at the *Masses* was an early instance of a relationship that was later to become a permanent, crucial feature of twentieth-century American life: that awkward coalescence of well-meaning benefactors and a radical, alienated intelligentsia.

DELL FLOURISHED AT the Liberal Club and the *Masses*, but his life was by no means confined to these two highly visible venues. When he arrived in the Village in the fall of 1913 he was determined to work—not to fritter away his time at parties and in an exhausting succession of love affairs. That he should be waylaid by Greenwich Village's noisy new bohemians had certainly not been his intention. Despite his reputation as one of the Village's exemplary bohemians, he never felt at ease with that characterization of himself. He always harbored misgivings and suspicion about the bohemian community of which he was so prominent a member.

When he had visited the Village in the late summer of 1913, at a time when he was still editor of the *Friday Literary Review*, he had stayed in a boarding house frequented by other writers and artists at 45 Washington Square South. He returned to the same house that fall when he moved to New York, settling down to the literary work—stories, essays, plays, poems—that he had planned to accomplish once he arrived. Not long afterward he moved down the street to another large old building filled with bohemians, this one at 61 Washington Square South. Writers had roomed there for decades, lending the house a local reputation: it had come to be known as the "House of Genius." Several of Dell's literary heroes from his days in Davenport and Chicago—Stephen Crane, Theodore Dreiser, Frank Norris—had lived in the house at one time or another, as had Willa Cather and the muckraking journalist Lincoln Steffens. The poet Orrick Johns, who was rooming there when Dell arrived, remembered the place—and the proprietress, Madame Katarina Branchard—as enchantingly eccentric:

> My room was big and bare, with a cot, a kitchen table and chair, a coal grate, and a chipped plaster cast of the Venus of Milo. The maiden lady who ran the establishment lived in a studio that was like a decayed museum. She kept parrots, canaries and cats, and some of her dead pets were stuffed and mounted on the shelves. It was the most bewildering room I had ever seen, itself seeming to be stuffed and dead, and buried under paintings, plaster statues, old bottles, boxes, knick-knacks and *objets d'art*. But the old girl herself was lively enough, full of talk, which included intimate reminiscences of her former tenants, and even gossip about our fellow tenants.

Johns remembered Dell as an uncommonly serious young man. In the weeks after he arrived from Chicago, Dell worked "like a dock laborer. I think he must have spent twenty hours a day writing, for his typewriter could always be heard."

Dell moved another time or two before settling at last, in early 1914, into a stable relationship with Marjorie Jones, the photographer he had known in the Fifty-Seventh Street bohemia in Chicago, and with whom he had had a brief romance in the spring and summer of 1913. Marjorie—or M.J., as Dell called her—had been an unabashed bohemian for years. Before falling in love with Dell she had had fleeting affairs with Arthur Ficke and Jig Cook. She was several years older than Dell, slender, with strong, regular features and short dark brown hair. She had followed him to New York, slipping easily into the pattern of Village life, acting in Liberal Club plays, and pursuing her work as a photographer. After a while she moved with Dell to a large apartment near Washington Square where they lived "like a true married pair." "In the Village," Dell wrote of his time with M.J., "there were to be rented, for thirty dollars a month, whole floors in old houses, each with two enormous rooms—high-ceilinged rooms, with deep-embrasured windows, and fireplaces—and a hall bedroom, a kitchen with a gas-range, and a bathroom. In one of these apartments I lived very happily for several years with a girl with whom I was deeply in love. It was a companionship of two artists, which we knew might not last long, but which we hoped would last forever. Those were beautiful and serene years."

This domestic arrangement proved fruitful for Dell in several ways. Theirs was a self-consciously modern relation, dispensing with the formality of marriage, both names proudly displayed on the downstairs mailbox. "We held the same views of literature and art," Dell recalled a decade later, "we agreed in hating capitalism and war. And, incidentally, we agreed in disbelieving in marriage. We considered it a stupid relic of the barbaric past, a ridiculous and tyrannical convention." It was essential that both earn a living and that each be permitted to cultivate separate friendships and, should things so develop, to pursue love affairs with others.

As things turned out, their relationship was, for several years at least, deeply satisfying to both. Dell and M.J. were among the Village's most prominent couples—members of the bohemian elite, as it were, essential participants in the round of Village activities. Neither led a scattered, wasteful life. Both attended with seriousness and perseverance to their respective artistic pursuits. For all their Village celebrity, theirs was a notably quiet, purposeful life. Despite their willingness to imagine outside love affairs for each, they maintained, at least for a while, a monogamous relation with each other. Rather than reject marriage outright, they wished (much in the spirit of Ellen Key) to create a more perfect (if not officially sanctioned) marriage together: "The laws of the land, we knew, permitted within marriage a degree of selfishness, of brutality, of cruelty even, which we as civilized lovers would never for a moment tolerate. We were going to behave *better* than any husband and wife." Their companionship reminds one that, for many Villagers, life there was not a relentless scouting out of wild, extravagant experiences but rather a search for a simple, productive existence that would suit the purposes of serious, hard-working people.

This sober side of Dell's personal and intellectual character led him at times to feel out of sympathy with such projects as the *Masses*. In his first months at the magazine the position felt temporary, and sometimes unsatisfactory, to him. In a letter to Arthur Ficke in March 1914 he hinted that the *Masses* was hardly the kind of journal to which he wished to devote himself. What he wanted, he claimed, was to start a magazine devoted more exclusively and rigorously to "ideas":

> I want to be an editor. I want to edit a real magazine. A weekly. A weekly carrying out the ideals of the old Friday Literary Review. . . . I believe that the business of spreading the gospel of clear thinking is more important than any other at the present time. It is necessary to have clear thinking not only about social and economic conditions and theories, but about books and painting and music and plays. . . . On the one hand we have in general an unintelligible hurrah about these new ideas; and on the other a stupid hostility toward them. The world needs criticism.

Without mentioning the magazine by name, Dell hinted that the *Masses* was excessively dogmatic. What he had in mind as an alternative was an independent publication patterned after the British weeklies. Most of all, "it ought to have at its service a group of active intelligences, who are sufficiently free from the bonds of party or creed or clicque [sic] allegiance as to be under no obligation to lie about anything. In particular, I am tired of the lying that is being done on behalf of Socialism, of feminism, of sexual freedom, of political democracy. I want the truth told about all these things."

Dell was groping toward an ideal of the modern intellectual as an individual whose primary responsibility is to examine, clarify, and create ideas. He realized that young intellectuals are too often tempted to abandon this responsibility to intellectual precision and honesty and instead to take up a cause—more often than not, a revolutionary one—that distracts them from their sterner, truer calling. Dell suggested to Ficke that young intellectuals in 1914 had inherited the revolutionary ardor of earlier generations without inheriting the world that gave birth to such ardor.

Put another way, Dell realized that young intellectuals are tempted to adopt the mantle of revolutionary virtue without asking themselves whether their cause is not already an anachronism. Dell sensed that his own generation was primarily concerned not with revolutionary political action (as it sometimes pretended) but with a broad revaluation of American social, cultural, and ethical values. This kind of rebellion required clear thinking and definitions, not revolutionary sloganeering and posturing. But what Dell tended to recognize among his contemporaries (not least among those at the

Masses) was a revolutionary fervor notable for its insupportable pretensions. To Dell the new rebels were hopelessly out of date and fuzzy-minded:

> We have inherited the revolutionary tradition of the last century. We have the feeling that we want to go out and fight on the barricade. But there is no barricade. We are revolutionaries without a revolution. Some time, perhaps within our lifetime, there may be a revolution, and a visible enemy through whose head we can put a bullet. It will be a great relief to pick up a musket to go out to shoot. It is so much easier to shoot than to think. But just now we have the infinitely harder task of thinking.

This conclusion followed inevitably from Dell's prescient, pitiless reading of his own generation of political rebels. "I am not interested in any sort of future which is not based on a general spread of critical intelligence," he wrote Ficke. "The world is only to be set free by thinking. Like everybody else, I want to fight every now and then. But I know perfectly well that my real business is to help the world to think."

Some of this serious commitment to intellectual work is apparent in Dell's decision to contribute to the *New Review*, a journal that proclaimed itself "A Critical Survey of International Socialism." The journal had been started by Max Eastman and several other radical journalists in January 1913—"in the same exciting winter," Eastman later wrote, "that saw the rebirth of *The Masses*." All clearly hoped that the *New Review* would serve as an expression of "highbrow" intellectual interests and writings, in contrast to the more eclectic, often humorous and lighthearted contents of the *Masses*. Dell became an editor of the *New Review* in May 1914, two months after he had indicated his frustrations with the *Masses* to Ficke. What in March had amounted to a clandestine revolt on Dell's part against the *Masses* and Eastman's leadership was now resolved (if only in part) by joining Eastman in a second, more exclusively intellectual, journalistic enterprise. The *New Review*'s other editors—Walter Lippmann, William English Walling, W. E. B. DuBois, and the radical syndicalist Arturo Giovannitti—were exemplary instances of that new breed of radicals, the intellectuals, who patterned themselves at least in part on Russian and continental European models. Many of them provided highbrow companionship of a sort that was not to be found, at least in so unmixed a form, at the *Masses*.

Nevertheless, Dell was unable to bring himself to write dry, theoretical socialist criticism, and his essays for the *New Review*, while often more sober and self-consciously "intellectual" than those he published in the *Masses*, were still similar to them in subject matter and point of view. His subjects—socialism and feminism, for example, or birth control, Walt Whitman, and still controversial "modern" novelists like Dostoevsky and Dreiser—were of sorts he had taken on before in the pages of the *Masses* and the *Friday Literary Review*. Sometimes his writings for the *New Review* seemed as casual as anything he contributed to the *Masses*.

But there were also pieces in the *New Review* which showed Dell striving for a serious criticism of literature and society. In "Change in American Life and Fiction," published in May 1915, he briefly examined the works of several recent novelists—Robert Herrick, Frank Norris, Ernest Poole, Jack London, Upton Sinclair, Edith Wharton, Theodore Dreiser—who in one way or another reflected what Dell described as an important development in American fiction: the tendency to develop character and plot in connection with the larger political and economic transformation of American life. Earlier American writers, Dell suggested, "had mainly regarded America as a set of picturesque backgrounds in front of which might be placed a woman and two men and some supers, reciting lines in appropriate dialect, and acting out a carefully censored love-drama." More recent novelists had begun to see character and story as inextricably implicated in the evolving facts of the American scene. Dell conveyed how differently his various novelists accomplished this new principle of novel-writing: from Robert Herrick's effort to show the dilemmas faced by intellectuals in an increasingly cynical, violent world; to Upton Sinclair's unprecedented effort to convey "the condition of working-class misery which creates revolt"; to what Dell felt was Dreiser's largely unconscious revelation of the new America. Dreiser, Dell pointed out, was determined in his works to portray "life-forces that have always existed since the beginning of the world." But Dell was most impressed by Dreiser's apparently unintentional ability to capture with lifelike precision the features of his American characters and settings. According to Dell, Dreiser may have fancied himself a writer of universal insights, but his genius lay in his ability to understand ordinary, humble characters in terms of their connection with the facts and details of the new American scene.

Because of articles like "Change in American Life and Fiction," many young readers at the time regarded Dell as the critic most worth reading. For these readers—in New York and Greenwich Village, and scattered around the country—Dell represented, better than any other American critic, the effort to understand culture in relation to society. He was unsystematic in essays like this one, a fact that partially undermined any reputation he wished to cultivate for himself as a highbrow, theoretical critic. But that lack of systematic rigor was, for many of his young readers, a second great virtue of his work. His essays possessed a judicious flexibility that was a refreshing antidote to the doctrinaire work of other critics. To many readers Dell exemplified the ideal of a critic who approached each work without debilitating political or theoretical commitments.

One young reader who admired Dell's essays for the *New Review* and the *Masses* was Joseph Freeman, later to gain renown himself as a critic, novelist, and editor. Freeman, a Ukrainian-born immigrant who had been raised from the age of seven in a Jewish ghetto in Brooklyn, was nearly twenty when he first came across Dell's writings in the mid-1910s. He was drawn especially to Dell's "social approach to books." Dell's honesty and directness—his willingness to transgress all manner of literary and political shibboleths in order to record his immediate response to literature and ideas—also caught Freeman's attention: "I was impressed by an acuteness of insight which did not preclude generosity of spirit. Few contemporary writers were so free of needless awe for the great or needless contempt for the unknown. Dell had the courage to damn acknowledged masters like George Moore, and to hail the early efforts of Sherwood Anderson as the work of one who wrote 'like a great novelist.'"

The reasons why Freeman admired Dell's criticism—his sociological slant and unconstrained honesty—certainly reflected Dell's own critical goals at the time. More than Freeman and many other young radicals, however, Dell realized that the second of these goals was threatened as much by the left as by the right. In his letter to Ficke, Dell had envisioned a "critical journalism" that would be, above all else, thoroughly nondoctrinaire. Certainly critical honesty was threatened by the genteel literary establishment, which had rigidly canonized a select group of American and British writers, and which recognized only a narrow collection of literary principles and values. But Dell could also see (and more clearly than any of his contemporaries at the *Masses* and in Greenwich Village) that the goals of "critical journalism" and "critical intelligence" were threatened by the extravagant, instantly conventionalized political and cultural enthusiasms of the avant-garde. Young writers in search of an exemplary radical critic may have made Dell their favorite literary arbiter because of his seeming immunity to traditional literary wisdom, but Dell was pointedly aware by this time that his critical independence was also endangered by orthodoxies on the left.

DELL'S LIFE DURING his first few years in Greenwich Village fluctuated erratically between these sober and bohemian, reflective and frivolous, enthusiastic and skeptical, extremes. Here was Floyd Dell, the well-known Village bohemian, seen about town in fashionably working-class flannel shirts and rough pants (although even in this getup he allowed himself certain flourishes, including a necktie for a belt and silk underwear). At other times, as Allen Churchill reports, he decked himself out in "white pants, orange-colored ties, and Byronic collars." He was a central, dominant figure at the *Masses*, the Liberal Club, and at bohemian restaurants and parties. It was the bohemian Dell who in 1914 proposed the first *Masses* Ball and then went out and reserved Webster Hall, on Eleventh Street near the intersection with Third Avenue, in order to put it on. The ball was originally envisioned by Dell and the other editors at the *Masses* as a onetime fund-raising costume party to boost the chronically underfinanced magazine. What followed was a series of uninhibited parties in which Villagers aimed constantly to outdo one another in creating outrageous costumes and partying until dawn. Dell suggested that the balls be called "Pagan Routs"—the name by which they were known thereafter. Other Villagers called Webster Hall the Devil's Playhouse. Dell remembered being "shy and unsocial" at the time, and he claimed not to care for raucous parties. He went anyway, enjoying the opportunity for conversation and occasionally drinking enough to shed his inhibitions and dance with congenial Village women. At one of the balls he actually climbed up an iron pillar in the middle of Webster Hall, cheered on by a crowd of enthusiastic Villagers, only to unscrew "a pocketful of electric light bulbs" once he arrived at the top.

At the same time there was the Floyd Dell who impressed many of his friends and colleagues as an acutely serious young man: as the

Villager most plainly devoted to literary work—and most likely to make it a serious career for himself. Looking back at his early days in the Village, Dell insisted that, contrary to his reputation as a "Bohemian," he was "actually quiet, sober, hard-working, faithful to [his] love, and one who [paid] his debts as a matter of course." He was writing constantly and devoting himself without pause to editorial duties at the *Masses*. Writing was easy for him. He was able to churn out fiction and nonfiction manuscripts without perceptible blocks or crises. He later noted that the three novels he worked on during his first years in the Village were appallingly unsuccessful. But he was becoming increasingly serious about his literary endeavors, and a number of New York publishers were encouraging him to submit a novel.

One of his stories for the *Masses*, "The Beating," gained widespread attention and praise. A harrowing account of life in a girls' reform school, it vividly evokes the atmosphere of terror created by the whippings regularly meted out by two of the school's matrons, Miss Hampton and Miss Carter. In the story a sixteen-year-old girl, Minnie, anxiously awaits a whipping while she listens to the beating administered to her friend Jeanette in the adjacent dormitory. Straining to pull herself up and peer through the small, high window that separates the two long rooms, Minnie watches Miss Hampton and Miss Carter take turns beating Jeanette with a rubber hose. Jeanette, lying naked and face down on the bed with her arms and legs pinned down by other girls, refuses to cry out. Minnie, made desperate by the endless spectacle, eventually drops from her window perch and runs along the aisle of her own dormitory, striking out at the iron bedsteads on either side. When she stops before the sign that reads "God is Love" and cries out in despair, the beating stops and the matrons appear at the door, ready to give Minnie her own whipping. The story, accompanied by a graphic drawing by John Sloan of Jeanette being whipped, appeared in the August 1914 issue of the *Masses*. It revealed Dell's growing abilities as a realistic fiction writer and his even more impressive talent for rendering the thoughts and emotions of his characters.

He was also writing poetry again, after several years in which he had largely given it up. Rather than a vehicle for his growing seriousness and determination as a writer, however, Dell's poetry remained a largely casual activity in which he indulged various of his contradictory inclinations. Inspired briefly by the new rage for free verse, he wrote a faintly free-verse poem, "Apologia," for Harriet Monroe's *Poetry*. In it he presented himself as the infinitely curious bohemian, fascinated by the characters—the "dolls"—which he fashioned for his stories. Another poem, titled "On First Seeing Isadora Duncan's School" and written at roughly the same time, was even more evocative of the bohemian spirit (though it clung to traditional sonnet form). Dell later described it as "a feminist poem." Whether truly feminist or not, it conveys much of the idealistic spirit that survived—and actually flourished—in the Village in the years just before America's entrance into the war. Dell had seen Duncan dance for the first time shortly after his arrival in Chicago in 1909: "I remember the revelation it was of the full glory of the human body," he wrote in the *Masses* of that first exposure to Duncan. His poem preserved formal constraints while conjuring up the unprecedented spontaneity of Duncan's dance:

This is the morning of the world, and these
Stars from the burning hand of God outflung
In lovely constellations; goddesses,
The first-born of the heavens, strong-limbed and young,
Walking beside the amaranthine streams—
Touching our hearts with terrible loveliness;
Or figures seen within the bower of dreams,
Whose meaning the waked mind dare never guess.
    This is a poem and a prophecy—
A glimpse across the forward gulf of time,
To show our dazzled souls what life can be
Upon the sunlit heights toward which we climb:
A flaming challenge to a world benighted—
A lamp of daring in our darkness lighted.

Other poems revealed a sterner temper. A few even managed with some success to address political issues—something Dell had hoped to achieve in his poetry since his days as a teenage poet-socialist in Davenport. In one Dell found words for his growing—and increasingly outraged—opposition to the European war. The occasion for the poem was the recent death of the English poet Rupert Brooke, who had briefly glorified the war as an escape from "a world grown old and cold and weary," peopled with "half-men, and their dirty songs and dreary, / And all the little emptiness of love!" Repulsed by these sentiments, Dell felt that Brooke's miserable death in battle was a peculiarly bitter and ironic comment on what he referred to as Brooke's "British young-gentlemanly patriotism." He furiously dashed off a sonnet upon hearing of Brooke's death:

Poor pretty little fool, to whom so early
An ending came in answer to your cry,
How does it feel, now your bright locks and curly
Are laid to rest under a tropic sky?
Is this peace better than the life you tired of,
Or thought you tired of, though you were not thirty,
The worms' lips than the lips you were admired of,
This silence, than the "dreary songs and dirty"?

Such poems were isolated events, though, not part of a coherent poetic program. Dell's accumulating seriousness showed up more clearly in his determination to write an autobiographical novel about his childhood and adolescence. By late 1915 or early 1916 he was at work on the early chapters of a novel that would eventually become *Moon-Calf*. In discussions and letters with Sherwood Anderson, Dell insisted that the novel he was slowly putting together should be a realistic one, faithful in spirit and detail to his ordinary working-class boyhood, and not couched in elitist, avant-garde literary techniques. Rejecting Anderson's advice that he valorize the alienation from society and ordinary life felt by Felix Fay (the book's autobiographical hero), Dell insisted that he wanted to emphasize the character's ordinariness. Pushed by Anderson to adopt a more self-consciously avant-garde approach to Felix's character, Dell responded with a firm view of his novel as a sympathetic representation of normal life—not as an alienated artist's grouse against it.

This long-lasting debate with Anderson over his novel was actually part of a growing estrangement between the two men. In Chicago Dell had been Anderson's chief mentor and champion. Once in New York the two men discovered that their literary tastes and ambitions were actually quite different. In Chicago Dell had been an accomplished literary man who encouraged Anderson to leave the business world behind and take up his work as a novelist full time. Dell had actually brought the manuscript of Anderson's first novel, *Windy McPherson's Son*, with him when he moved from Chicago to New York in 1913, and then spent a number of months looking assiduously for a publisher for it. At last he had found one: John Lane, a London publisher who operated a branch out of New York. Lane was swayed by Dell's insistence (which he had already trumpeted in the *Friday Literary Review*) that *Windy* was a brilliant first book. In the confident manner that marked all his early relations with Anderson, Dell took it upon himself to make a few changes to the book. Without even consulting Anderson he deleted most of several paragraphs from the book's ending, which he felt was overdone. Only then had he handed the manuscript over to Lane.

Anderson came to visit Dell several times during Dell's first months in New York, staying with him on at least one occasion in Dell's cramped quarters in one of the Washington Square boarding houses. The two started to fall out at once. Dell had affected his proletarian flannel shirts by this time, while Anderson was beginning to adopt the elaborate dress of a literary dandy—not unlike the sartorial excesses Dell had indulged in Chicago. The clash in styles was mirrored by their evolving literary opinions. Dell was now championing socialist journalism and literary realism; Anderson was moving toward a more experimental, modernist literary style. As Dell recalled later, Anderson "was writing a semi-mystical prose-poem about himself": the *Mid-American Chants* that he later published to decidedly mixed reviews in 1918. Dell found Anderson's quasi-Whitmanian celebrations of himself and the Midwestern landscape a deplorable falling off from the greater simplicity and realism of *Windy*. Anderson, according to Dell, "had suddenly become an admirer of Gertrude Stein's unintelligible prose. And there were qualities I did not like in his latest stories—the beginnings of a new manner which was to gain him fame, but which I never liked, because it seemed to me an abandonment of simple truth." Dell's dislike of these stories (the *Winesburg, Ohio* stories that did in fact soon make Anderson's reputation) anticipated the friction that would later develop between the two men when Dell, as managing editor of the *Masses*, was reluctant to publish some of them in the magazine.

It would be too simple, nonetheless, to describe Dell's dissatisfaction with Anderson as founded exclusively on his own growing faith in literary realism and Anderson's increasing mysticism and unconventional aesthetic tastes. Dell clearly recognized much of himself in Anderson (just as he did in Dreiser). Both were products of a largely rural Midwestern world. Both came from working-class backgrounds that had been profoundly disrupted in the social and economic upheavals of those years that transformed America from an essentially rural to an urban society. For Dell, what united him and Anderson were their complex, even fractured identities, which these disruptive historical, economic, and geographic circumstances had done much to create. By abandoning the rural-Midwesterner and advertising-man sides of his identity, Anderson, Dell felt, was turning away from the complex fate which the two men, in important if not identical ways, shared.

In a letter written several years later, Dell encouraged Anderson to acknowledge the complexity of his own character, just as he set himself the task of doing justice to his own contradictory inclinations. Anderson, Dell wrote, should not deny the businessman in himself, just as he, Dell, should not suppress the poet—that which was "supernormal" or "queer"—in himself:

> I'll tell you, Sherwood, I can believe we're both wrong. I can believe we would be better artists if we weren't afraid of anything— you not afraid of being commonplace, I not afraid of being queer—but I won't regard art as *another* side of life, making up for a want or a need. It can have that aspect of it, but I want it to stand alone. If I am partly a damn fool, I've no right to pose as a wholly reasonable person in my writing. If you're partly a clever business man, I want to see that too. We're entitled to get from each other all he has to give—the whole man, not what he regards as the best of himself.

His insistence that art not stand in as *"another* side of life" shows how suspicious Dell had become by the late 1910s of any theory that posed artistic experience as essentially opposed in spirit to the quotidian world. Perhaps Dell misread Anderson in this regard, exaggerating Anderson's literary elitism in the effort to define his own—Floyd Dell's—view of culture as inseparable from society and everyday life. In any case, by the time he and Anderson began to fall out in 1914 and 1915, Dell was already fashioning a literary credo for himself that would assiduously avoid anything smacking of the aesthete's determined alienation from ordinary life.

Dell's consolidating literary opinions also appeared in his evolving relations with Dreiser. Dell had been greatly moved when he first read *Sister Carrie* years before. He had been similarly impressed by *Jennie Gerhardt*, which appeared in 1911, and which Dell praised exorbitantly in the *Friday Literary Review*. It had been Dell's praise, along with H. L. Mencken's, which had established *Jennie*'s reputation among young intellectuals as a ground-breaking book. Dell had admired "the long-sustained simplicity of the narrative" and had proclaimed Dreiser a giant among contemporary American writers.

Now Dell was beginning to feel impatient with several elements in Dreiser's work. While still in Chicago Dell was asked by Dreiser to read a manuscript copy of The "Genius." Much to Dell's surprise, he found the book considerably below the standards established by the earlier novels. It was too long, he felt, and clumsily executed. He wrote Dreiser, "I have put off writing to you about 'The Genius' because of a natural hesitation to tell a writer whom I tremendously admire and respect that he has written a very bad book." Dell's prognosis: "No amount of cutting could improve it—it would have to be rewritten from first to last." A year later Dreiser asked him to edit the book into publishable form. Dell worked hard during free evenings, cutting whole portions of the "mountainous manuscript." But Dreiser could abide few of his editorial deletions. "When I returned for more [portions of the manuscript]," Dell recalled, "there sat Dreiser, with a large eraser, rescuing from oblivion such pages, paragraphs and sentences as he felt could not be spared."

When The "Genius" was finally published in 1915 (to more than a few bad notices, including some from others among Dreiser's early admirers), Dell published a review which revealed as much about his own literary opinions as it did about Dreiser's cumbersome, disappointing work. Appearing in December in the New Review, Dell's essay was actually quite generous. He praised The "Genius" for qualities he had always admired in Dreiser: for its detailed portrayal of character and for the similarly dense portrait of the social setting in which that character's story is enacted. Dell insisted that "the result shows that Mr. Dreiser possesses superhuman energy, if not superhuman taste. He has written a great and splendid book which contains many dull pages." Dell graciously added that in light of the book's realism, "one forgets these imperfections."

Despite his generosity to Dreiser, however, it was Dell's criticisms that were most significant. He suggested that Dreiser was unable to recognize his hero Eugene Witla's flaws because he was "too immersed" in the character and his story. This exaggerated identification with Witla, according to Dell, was associated with a second flaw: Dreiser's unwillingness to judge the character. Dell suggested that Dreiser paradoxically limited himself by telling "all the facts about his hero. He suppresses nothing." This was for Dell the book's most serious failing: Dreiser's inability to develop a clear view of his character—a view that would necessarily involve judgments, criticisms, and even humor. "The case needs more than candor; it needs as heightened a sensibility on the part of Mr. Dreiser to comic fact as he has to tragic fact. Mr. Dreiser lacks that sensibility." Missing from *The "Genius"* was the fully developed perspective needed to lend the characters and story a moral dimension and meaning.

Dreiser's effort to view life in an impersonal, fatalistic manner was beginning to erode Dell's admiration for his work. In an essay published in the *Masses*, titled "Mr. Dreiser and the Dodo," Dell described Dreiser as an instance of "an intellectual species that is fast becoming extinct"—the species of intellectual that placed little faith in human will and intelligence. Like Darwin, Dreiser made "people think of change as something outside human effort." Like others at the time, Dell had come to identify Dreiser with Darwin, who "with the chill of his doctrine froze the blood of revolution for a generation." By 1914 Dell was beginning to respond impatiently to this fatalism in Dreiser's work. In "Mr. Dreiser and the Dodo" he countered with an idealistic, revolutionary pronunciamento more in line with the *Masses'* platform: "We can have any kind of bloody world we bloody want." He exhorted Dreiser and others to note the ways in which the world was yielding—and had always yielded—to the constructive power of human volition. "Look, this world is changing," he once remarked to Dreiser during these years. "You might as well point to the clouds and say they will remain as they are forever. It's changing before your eyes—changing because of human effort."

Here Dell spoke for many of the youthful radicals in the Village. Yet these were remarks that no other *Masses* critic was quite prepared to make. They reflected Dell's willingness to take on a new literary idol and scold him. They also revealed how far Dell had gone toward developing a persuasive point of view in literary matters. No other literary critic for the *Masses* possessed a similarly forceful and coherent perspective.

Such criticisms could only have come from Dell for another reason as well: their undercurrent of conservatism which Dell fully recognized. He may have taken Dreiser to task for his outmoded pessimism, but Dell must also have realized that his own literary preferences—a strong narrative voice and an interest in plot as the record of a character's conscious, developing will—were largely traditional ones. In a letter he wrote Arthur Ficke two days after his article on *The "Genius"* appeared in the *New Review*, Dell frankly acknowledged the conservatism which coursed through his—and the *Masses'*—literary opinions:

> I believe the Masses has the opinion of itself that it cannot be shocked: I know better. And you know that poor old Floyd, with his classical standards still fluttering in the cyclone of modernism, is very capable of it. . . . About nine-tenths of the new art, in painting, sculpture and poetry, seems to me to have no aesthetic values at all. When people write the kind of free verse that Matthew Arnold, Heine, Southey, Henley, and other forgotten poets whom I read in my childhood wrote, I can tell whether it is good or bad. In regard to most of the new things, I am in a mood of skeptical sympathy. Bring em on, I say, and I'll see what happens to me. Mostly nothing happens.

Above all, the letter to Ficke reflected Dell's uneasiness about his position within the cultural avant-garde. He realized that his effort as a literary editor and critic to define modern culture and ideas was a problematic endeavor. Already Dell had begun to wonder whether any of the causes with which he was widely identified—bohemianism, literary modernism, and the politics of the avant-garde—were really his causes at all.

Love in Greenwich Village

AN ENTRY IN one of Dell's notebooks from the early 1950s sums up the problems that faced him during his Greenwich Village years:

> On two important subjects—perhaps three—the young poet (if I may keep on calling him so) has a divided mind. He is now heartily interested in reforming the world—or changing this sorry scheme of things entire—and again he wants to take refuge from the world in an Epicurean garden of some kind and let the world rush to destruction (or be somehow miraculously saved) without his lifting a finger. . . . He veers from complete despair about the meaningless chaos of existence to a complete belief in the meaningfulness of life—his own life and the vast historical life of mankind.

In the daily conduct of his life and literary career, Dell gave plentiful evidence of confusion. Often he was willing to entertain an unmanageably wide range of opinions—a fact that alternately pleased, worried, and perplexed many readers and friends. Max Eastman later commented on how receptive Dell was at this time to greatly varying, if not actually contradictory, ideas. Eastman remained undecided, even decades later, whether this feature of Dell's youthful intellectual character should be regarded as a flaw or virtue. To Eastman, Dell seemed at the time to lack "stability of opinion." But he also acknowledged Dell's frequent skepticism about socialism, which was otherwise embraced by the *Masses* radicals with devotion. "Floyd was free of any limiting fixation on this doctrine, freer than I was, or at least more pliant in his welcome to other ideas and attitudes."

Healthy skepticism allowed Dell insight into one contradiction that he shared with other Village radicals: the conflict between political radicalism and a Henri Murger–style bohemianism that retreats from social responsibilities. (Murger's *Scènes de la Vie de Bohème*, a collection of fictionalized sketches of bohemians in mid-nineteenth-century Paris, was required reading among Villagers.) Much like New Leftists of the 1960s, prewar Villagers were fond of arguing that radical politics and bohemianism—or socialism and the cultural avant-garde—were essentially compatible. The Paterson Pageant, in which Villagers had joined forces momentarily with striking workers, seemed to point toward a future in which radicals and artists would work closely together. Dell placed less confidence in this alliance than did many of his friends. He recognized both tendencies in himself—that much is undeniable. But he differed from other Villagers in that he perceived the relation between these diverse cultural and political tendencies as problematic. He had little confidence that the two might ever function in tandem.

Avid readers like Joe Freeman recognized both strains in Dell's writings for the *Masses* but were unable to say which one Dell favored. Nor could they guess how he might reconcile the two. At times, according to Freeman, Dell "made it clear that a writer could not escape his social responsibilities by hiding behind the skirts of art." For Freeman and others, this was the Dell who proved himself a man of political principle in response to the war in Europe—a public figure who "lashed Anatole France and H. G. Wells for supporting the war, and praised Romain Rolland and Gilbert Cannan for opposing it." At other times Dell gave Freeman "the impression that rebellion had implications which were personal rather than political. He described the individual in revolt against conventions from which he could escape now, before America established the socialist society. The solution for certain contemporary evils seemed to lie in the cult of vagabondage, and in the cult of love."

Perhaps it was in response to this state of affairs that Dell began to fashion an ironic identity that allowed him both to cultivate and to distance himself from his contradictions. In fact, Dell was beginning to feel that irony was essential to his identity as a modern intellectual. In this he was allied with Randolph Bourne, the radical critic whose work had appeared for some years in the *Atlantic*

Monthly and *New Republic,* and who in 1917 was to become the dominant critic at another left-wing journal, the *Seven Arts.* Much like Bourne, Dell was coming to believe in the middle years of the decade that the future of radicalism lay in a "life of irony" rather than in an orthodox set of political and intellectual principles. Both Dell and Bourne identified their radicalism with the cultivation of an ironic, preternaturally alert sensibility capable of embracing all their contradictory, fluctuating sympathies. Such irony involved the ability to recognize one's own shortcomings. Dell would certainly have agreed with Bourne's assertion that the radical ironist "sees his own foibles and humiliations in the light of those of other people. He acquires a more tolerant, half-amused, half-earnest attitude toward himself."

Each man wished to distinguish his radicalism not only from the sober, straight-faced views of genteel conservatives but also from the humorless positions of old-fashioned socialists and middle-class progressives. Neither Dell nor Bourne was content to endorse traditional radical causes or institutions. Dell may have been a socialist from adolescence, but he had always felt impatient with the doctrinaire positions of old-time socialists. By 1915 he was looking for a radicalism whose essence lay not in a predictable set of radical opinions but in a complex, volatile sensibility. This preference for sensibility over doctrine led him, years later, to remember Bourne for "his beautiful mind." The two became close friends in the years between 1916 and 1918, Dell noted, because "each of us had a good deal of sardonic wit, which we heartily enjoyed in each other."

But Bourne likely took the goal of creating a radical life of irony more seriously than Dell. For Bourne the matter was one to be addressed at length and in more than one essay. For Dell irony was a style that he cultivated with great care but little explicit comment. Equally telling is the fact that Dell, more than Bourne, resorted to irony not so much because he wished to exalt the ironic life, but because he felt that the behavior and ideas of his generation of young rebels was, sadly enough, best treated ironically. His irony seemed balanced between the effort to create a new radical point of view and a desire to deflate the insubstantial radical pretensions of the Villagers.

Dell's ambivalent feelings about the Village were apparent in discussions he had with friends at the time about "what the Village meant." It was not, he felt, a place where serious people would choose to live forever; nor was it a place where much important work was likely to be accomplished. He likened the Village and its often specious radicalism to a "mountain health-resort":

> A moral-health resort—that was what it was. Work and love were both concerned. People who found in themselves inadequate emotional motives for sticking to their jobs or their marriages in the outside world, and were cracking under the strain, dropped everything and came here, found peace and tolerance, and a chance to discover what they were like and could do. . . . But it was not, except for some, a permanent refuge. One hoped to find out what one was like, what one could do happily in the way of work, and straighten out one's love life. Being free to have all the love affairs that one might wish, was a means to the end of finding one love affair that suited, that could be permanent.

Some people had encamped in the Village for good: "Already we could see them settling down to be the Swiss innkeepers and Tyrolese bell-ringers of our mountain health-resort." By 1916 Dell knew he was not one of them.

HIS SKEPTICISM ABOUT Greenwich Village was fueled by the type of love he found there. Domestic harmony with Marjorie Jones had lasted for several years, but it began to crumble in the summer of 1916. Dell had long speculated upon the ways in which economic constraints had limited his romantic attachments. Now he was forced to admit that his own self-absorption had helped to undermine every serious relation he had entered with a woman. Dell knew that the decisive element in the collapse of his earlier marriage had been his own selfishness—what he was beginning to call, under the influence of the new Freudian psychology, his untempered narcissism. In 1916 he recognized that same narcissism as the destructive agent in his deteriorating relation with Marjorie Jones.

In December 1915 Dell had heard in a roundabout way that his divorce from Margery Currey had finally come through. One day while walking through the Village he ran into Lucy Hufaker, an old friend from Chicago now living in New York. She relayed news from Edna Kenton that Margery had successfully wrapped up the divorce proceedings in Chicago. Dell conveyed these tidings in cavalier fashion to Arthur Ficke. "The news of the village is that everybody is getting married," he wrote Ficke. "As for me, I met Lucy on the street yesterday morning, and she told me that I was divorced." Hints of uneasiness crept into his letter. What Dell had gleaned from Hufaker was an impression of the distress—and dignity—displayed by Margery and her father in the divorce court. Old Seymour Currey had clearly been confused at the trial, testifying (contrary to instructions given him earlier) that the separation had not been a surprise to him, an admission that might have made the divorce more difficult to obtain. Margery ably patched things up once she took the stand, convincing the judge that the grounds for divorce were quite sufficient. "According to Edna," Dell wrote Ficke, "my father-in-law showed great grief during the proceedings, apparently not so much over his daughter's troubles as over the loss of a son. Which should prove to you, if you have not learned it before, that this is a beautiful and absurd world, in which none of us, luckily, get our deserts."

By this time Dell and Marjorie Jones had moved toward the outer rim of Greenwich Village, living comfortably in a large apartment at 106 West 13th Street. Earlier in 1915 Dell had bought a cottage in Ridgefield, New Jersey, "back of the Palisades" on "the edge of a ravine-like valley with a stream at the bottom, where summer visitors bathed." One visitor in the summer of 1916 had been a beautiful schoolteacher named Margot, twenty-two years old, "with light brown hair and blue eyes, and, apparently, a sunny disposition." Dell glimpsed her bathing in the stream below the cabin one day and immediately wrote a bright, impressionistic poem about her: "Who shall stir the peace / Of that unstirred bosom?" he wondered. "Who is he, / The lucky youth / Who shall take the kisses / Of her laughing mouth?"

As it turned out, it was Dell who soon afterward became Margot's lover. Their affair signaled the beginning of the end of his long romance with M.J. The new affair was far from idyllic. Failing to believe that Dell was serious about her, Margot entered the affair with no plans to make it last. "Only two or three days together," Dell recalled, "she left me—without explanation—for another lover, in whose arms I miserably watched her dancing happily at a Village Ball." The new lover was in fact Margot's old one—a drunken vagabond who some years later burned to death when he fell asleep while smoking in bed. Soon she returned to Dell, only to leave him again several times. The laughing girl he had spied down at the river, Dell realized, was perfectly confused and miserable.

This was a peculiarly pointless episode that shattered Dell's household with Marjorie Jones. He and M.J. remained a couple for some months, but by November they had split for good, he remaining only a brief while longer at the apartment on West 13th, she staying with friends and at her studio on West 11th. Dell sent Ficke a "Special and Private Bulletin" detailing the split: "M.J. and I, having become too good friends to be lovers anymore, are going to separate. . . . Reflect that it is better to become friends than enemies, which is the more usual result of living together." The two did remain close friends for many years to come: Dell's ex-lovers seemed never to dislike him afterward. But the breakup, he knew, was his fault, and the loss of M.J. left him cut off to a degree he could never have imagined—more bereft than he had felt after the breakup of his marriage to Margery Currey.

The end of the affair left him isolated in another regard as well. The community in which Dell and M.J. had found their home in Greenwich Village was badly disappointed by the dissolution of the couple's relationship. A new Village had come into being in 1913, and Dell and M.J. had been "among its first families." That Village may have prided itself on its carefree ways, but in fact it was a social group much like any other, with certain couples and households serving as pillars of the community. "The breaking-up of a settled though illegal domesticity in Greenwich Village," Dell wrote, "appeared to be as great a shock to the community as the breaking-up of a home in any other part of the United States. A social centre which had been a gathering-place for our friends had been suddenly destroyed; and its destruction was resented."

His Village friends and colleagues were not prepared to accept Margot as one of their intimates. Gradually it dawned on Dell that there were social—or cultural—classes in Greenwich Village, and that Margot indisputably belonged to a less desirable one. The essential Village class division was between "highbrow" and "lowbrow." Those Villagers who had arrived around 1913, and who had established the modern Village's leading institutions had come quickly to regard themselves as highbrows of a distinctive sort—as members of an elite *intelligentsia*. This last word, along with the less exotic *intellectual*, had potent connotations for them. The historian Henry May has pointed out that such words "associated one with Europe, and particularly with the young heroes of novels from

Stendhal to Joyce: the young man from the provinces who had come to the capitals in search of experience and a role in the movement of their time." For Dell and others at the *Masses* and the *New Review*, the words *intellectual* and *intelligentsia* epitomized the new life that they were forging in Greenwich Village.

Nevertheless, they felt that their transformation of the Village had had, among many good consequences, at least one bad one: it had attracted the attention of many people throughout New York City and the country generally. Now an unexpectedly large number of these were eager to come to the Village and sample the bohemian life. Dell's generation of Villagers was quick to disown this new generation, even though the latecomers had been drawn to the place by the older crowd's well-publicized antics and productions: Webster Hall "Pagan Routs," Liberal Club plays, the *Masses*, a pervasive atmosphere of sexual freedom and revelry. The fact that few of these things actually qualified Dell's circle as authentic intellectuals and rebels mattered not at all. They maintained an arrogant, unapproach- able posture vis-à-vis the newcomers.

Once Dell discovered that Margot was not welcome in his old circle of friends, he resolved to ingratiate himself as much as possible among the younger Villagers. Further disappointments awaited him:

> I found that I was regarded by these younger people as one of the pillars of a hated Village orthodoxy. The Masses, and subse- quently the Liberator, though regarded by the rest of America (wherever it was known at all) as daringly modern in its pictures and poetry, was thought of by the younger Villagers as tame, old-fogey, stupidly conservative. . . . From their point of view, they had good reason to think of me as a moss-backed conservative, since the Cubist and Futurist pictures they produced under the influence of the Post-Impressionist Show were, to my mind, too often only ugly and silly and their modernist prose and verse too often incompetent, unintelligible, and uninteresting.

The younger crowd resented Dell as a salaried, influential editor on a successful literary and political magazine in which many of them had tried, unsuccessfully, to publish their work. They had found Dell's trademark rejection notice—"Sorry, F.D."—written in green ink on slips enclosed with their manuscripts. Added to this was their impression of Dell's circle as comprised of arrogant elitists. He was forced to agree with one young woman who told him that Green-wich Village was "an extraordinarily snobbish and sanctimonious place."

As if this were not trouble enough, Dell was also forced to admit that, in the case of he and Margot, the highbrow / lowbrow distinction was largely accurate. He saw that he and she were not "intellectually compatible," that their affair amounted to little more than a sexual infatuation. It had been unpromising from the start. "While she was in musical matters quite sophisticated," Dell sneered, "she had intellectually no brains at all." Early on "I decided not to go on with the affair, and I neglected her on purpose, and she found herself another lover."

The pattern of brief, inconsequential affairs was reestablished with Margot. With M.J., Dell had again reached for the ideal of a monogamous relation: the ideal he had imagined with Margery Currey and which he had sketched out in his essays on Ellen Key. Now, after the episode with Margot and several similarly unsatisfying affairs, Dell began to revolt against what he perceived as a certain "disposition" in himself: the tendency "to get into love affairs of a kind that inevitably brought disillusionment—a revolt against a determinism located psychically in myself and not economically in the outward world—a revolt that was an effort to become simpler, more inwardly harmonious: to become, as I would soon learn to call it, less neurotic in this matter of love."

He had already learned to label problems of this sort "neurotic." In Chicago he had led the Fifty-Seventh Street bohemians into a shared fascination with Freudian ideas, which had only in 1909 begun to gain general circulation in America. As Sherwood Anderson recalled, "All the young intellectuals [in Chicago in 1913] were busy analyzing each other and everyone they met. Floyd Dell was hot at it." Relying on a hasty and rudimentary understanding of Freud's work, Dell and his Chicago friends had searched for clues to their own personalities in ticks, habits, psychological obsessions and disturbances. "It was a time," wrote Anderson, "when it was well for a man to be somewhat guarded in the remarks he made, what he did with his hands."

In New York Dell proved himself a facile explainer of Freud. "Everybody in the Village had been talking the jargon of psycho-analysis ever since I came," he recalled in the early 1930s. "We had played at parlor games of 'associating' to lists of words, and had tried

to unravel dreams by what we supposed to be the Freudian formula."
In December 1915 he published an informal primer on Freudianism
in *Vanity Fair*, to which he gave the lighthearted title "Speaking of
Psychoanalysis: The New Boon for Dinner Table Conversational-
ists." The article presented psychoanalysis in the optimistic fashion
of Village Freudians. It discerned in Freud's theory a technique for
relieving oneself of crippling internal contradictions and taboos. It
also suggested that psychoanalysis offered a method for getting "at
grips with the realities of life." For Dell, Freudianism was like
socialism in that it provided him with a map for crossing over from
his inner confusions to productive contacts with the ordinary world.

Dell's slant on psychological theories became more apparent in an
essay for the July issue of the *Masses* on Carl Jung's *Psychology of the
Unconscious*. Relying on his reading of Jung, Dell wrote that life was
characterized by "the necessity not merely to accept new realities but
to impose one's own will upon them." He added that "it is from that
necessity that the too-sensitive soul recoils into a dream which is an
imaginative restoration of the conditions of infantile irresponsibility
and peace." Jung's most valuable insight, according to Dell, was that
the individual's retreat from contact with the world is a highly
ambiguous matter, for it can lead either to failure or to worldly
success:

> For rest, the return, the retiring into oneself for the obscure
> nourishment of dreams, is a preliminary to all great effort. But in
> that return lies the danger. If one's Life Force comes out again to
> the real world it is with renewed power; but it may become
> beguiled by the dream and not come out. *The dream thus
> possesses the double quality of savior and destroyer*, and the
> greatest problem of any man's life is to determine, if such a thing
> is possible, which it shall be. Such is the contribution of Jung.

In late 1916, when Dell found himself passing through a series of
trivial love affairs, his interest in psychoanalysis became urgent. This
was joined by a growing dissatisfaction with his literary output, made
up of such ephemeral projects as reviews, stories, and one-act plays.
For all his productivity, he felt he had been wasting his time. "I
wasn't living up to my expectations. . . . I wasn't achieving anything.
I had been fiddling along for five years." Dell hoped to find in
psychoanalysis answers to his most pressing problems. "I wanted to
be set free to love deeply enough to get married and have children;

and I wanted to find in myself the powers necessary for completing my novel."

When M.J. encouraged him to go ahead with his plan to see a psychoanalyst, Dell made an appointment with Dr. Samuel Tannen- baum, at the time a rather strict Freudian. Tannenbaum was happy to have so curious and brilliant a patient; he assured Dell that his therapy would cost no more than the little he was able to afford. After years of advocating Freudian analysis and playing parlor psychoanalytic games, Dell threw himself into his own therapy with unbridled enthusiasm. Tannenbaum seems to have been largely an innocent bystander during Dell's sessions: "My psychoanalyst gave me no interpretation of my dreams, but let me interpret them myself; nor did he tell me I had a terrific mother-complex, and was narcissistic, had a great deal of unconscious homosexuality, and a variety of other frightful-sounding traits; I found all that out myself, and told him." With no prompting from Tannenbaum, Dell decided to forgo love affairs for the time being. "This decision," he later admitted, "was not carried out with complete consistency."

It was unavoidable that Dell should work through his therapy not solely as a man intent on resolving his problems but also as an intellectual exploring a new way of understanding the world: "These psychoanalytic ideas affected literature, criticism, education, love, family life, child-rearing, and provided a basis for a new view of history, not supplanting the Marxian one but supplementing it. Here was an idea of the same importance as the Copernican idea, the Darwinian idea, the Marxian idea—destined, like them, to revolu- tionize human thought in a thousand ways. My mind leaped to grasp the multiform significance of this new truth."

Psychoanalysis scarcely swept away all of Dell's confusions. In contrast to socialism, which he always associated with the effort to discover his place within large political and economic developments, psychoanalysis at times seemed to draw him into further self- absorption. Nevertheless, psychoanalysis provided a framework that Dell needed for thinking about his past and for understanding the problems that confronted him now as a man and as a writer. Under its influence he began to feel that he might eventually make sense of his life and thereby find his way to the work he really wanted to do. In 1917, as his analysis with Dr. Tannenbaum continued, he began to work more determinedly on the autobiographical novel he had planned for nearly a decade.

* * *

HIS LITERARY RESOLVE stiffened, Dell managed to convince Eastman that he needed an assistant—a plan designed to clear time for him to retreat to his apartment or the cottage in New Jersey and devote himself to his novel. Eastman came up with a small sum—$10 a week—to pay for the assistant, should one ever turn up.

One did, and soon, in the person of Dorothy Day, later to become one of the great Christian radicals of the century. In 1917 Day was little more than a child, a twenty-year-old who had worked as an assistant and then as a reporter at a New York socialist paper, the *Call*. Having quit the *Call* in the early spring of 1917, Day was looking for work at precisely the time when Charles Wood, a drama critic for the *Masses*, invited her to meet Floyd Dell.

Wood and Day met Dell at a German restaurant in the Village, where he was eating lunch alone. In the novel Day later based on her life in Greenwich Village, *The Eleventh Virgin*, she provided a vivid portrait of Dell on the day she encountered him. The description of "Hugh Brace" is clearly modeled on Dell:

> There was a look of great delicacy about him, an appearance of living in the night-hours and sleeping during the day. As a matter of fact, most of his work was done at night, not only his own writing, but his editorial work on the Flame, a monthly magazine.
>
> . . . During the course of the lunch, June noticed that his clothes as well as his manners had the same awkwardness. It came, she thought, from extreme shyness, and remained with him even when he forgot himself in the heat of discussion.

Day was soon to notice that Dell was most confident as a writer and editor, that when he was "behind his writing desk, he had poise. With a pen in his hand, he was gracious as well as graceful." She noticed more as well. "In back of his apparent softness," she wrote, "there was a streak of iron."

Dell was equally impressed with Dorothy. She struck him as "an awkward and charming young enthusiast, with beautiful slanting eyes." Immediately he encouraged her to write a book review for the *Masses*. A week later he telephoned and asked her to have lunch with him at another restaurant, this one closer to the *Masses'* office. At lunch he offered her the job as his assistant. She was to read literary submissions and help with various phases in the production of the magazine.

Day proved a godsend for Dell during the next six months. She helped him in innumerable ways with his editorial work and sometimes filled in for him entirely when he took off for New Jersey and work on his novel. The two became part of a foursome that shared an apartment perched above the Provincetown Playhouse at 139 MacDougal Street during the late spring and early summer of 1917. Their roommates were David Karb, the *Masses'* advertising manager, and Merrill Rogers, the magazine's business manager. Day called it a "menage au quatre." All spent hours at the bright orange kitchen table, with its fresh-painted black chairs; all ate with newspapers and journals open in front of them. It was a bohemian flat, with Japanese prints and brass candlesticks scattered about the largely empty rooms. Dell later remarked that the arrangement had been a "delightful" one. But he soon tired of it. After only a few months he moved into a basement apartment on Charlton Street, where he was able to work on his book and other writing projects in greater privacy.

Day recognized Dell's unsteadiness at the time, even while she deferred to him as the dominant intellectual figure in their household. For a while he was vaguely interested in her; he wooed her with theoretical discourses on the need for women to respond without shame or hesitation to their sexual impulses. Day brushed him off. She was not impressed by what she took to be Dell's credo: that it is "a supremely right thing to do—to take a lover or as many lovers as you want." He struck her as an exotic, unpredictable, even opportunistic figure. Spinning off from one woman to another, interrupted only by fitful resolutions to avoid romantic entanglements altogether until he had worked fully through his psychoanalysis, Dell was more likely to exasperate a serious young woman like Dorothy Day than to awaken her interest. His love affairs, she felt, "should really [have taken] place on the stage of the Hippodrome before a packed house."

DELL'S LIFE WAS interrupted also by the summer weeks he spent in Provincetown, Massachusetts. He had first visited the town at the tip of Cape Cod in the summer of 1913, staying with old friend George Cram Cook and Cook's third wife, Susan Glaspell. Since then Dell had passed through Provincetown each summer. Life there was even more exclusive than in the Village. Peopled with the Village's most prominent couples (Cook and Glaspell, Dell and M.J., John Reed and Louise Bryant, Max Eastman and Ida Rauh, Hutchins Hapgood and Neith Boyce) and with a great number of other Villagers (Elaine Hyman, Robert Edmond Jones, Charles Demuth, Mary Heaton Vorse, Hippolyte Havel, Mabel Dodge, Alfred Kreymborg, Harry Kemp), Provincetown offered further escape for people whose ordinary lives came close to unqualified rejection of the respectable world.

Dell had been in Provincetown in August 1914 when World War I broke out. Holiday life on the beach made the war seem strange and distant to him. In 1915 Villagers summering in Provincetown informally staged four plays in the main room of a cottage rented by Hutchins Hapgood and Neith Boyce. The plays were Neith Boyce's *Constancy*, Cook and Glaspell's *Suppressed Desires*, Cook's *Change Your Style*, and Wilbur Daniel Steele's *Contemporaries*. All were one-acts about the lives of rebellious people bearing a suspicious resemblance to themselves. All were inspired to some extent by Dell's Liberal Club plays which had satirized the Villagers in 1914 and 1915. Cook's contributions in particular reflected the influence of his Davenport friend. *Change Your Style* mocked the cultural avant-garde, especially trendy modern artists. *Suppressed Desires* made fun of the popular fascination with psychoanalysis; it focused on the unfortunate effects of psychoanalytic wisdom on the relations between a young husband and wife.

Throughout the winter of 1915–1916 Cook became obsessed with what everyone else generally regarded as the casual success of the 1915 Provincetown performances. Returning to Provincetown in the summer of 1916, he convinced the assembled Villagers to put on a handful of new plays. They hammered together a rough little theater inside a dilapidated fish shed owned by the radical journalist and *Masses* editor Mary Heaton Vorse. Cook, Hapgood, Reed, Bror Nordfeldt, and William Zorach built the playhouse, soon christened the Wharf Theater; they installed bench seats for ninety people. Short plays were provided by Reed, Cook, and Boyce. Later that summer the Wharf Theater crew became acquainted with an unknown twenty-seven-year-old seaman-turned-playwright, Eugene O'Neill, and persuaded him to show them some of his work. In July they staged his powerful one-act play *Bound East for Cardiff*, which astonished everyone who worked on the production and those who saw it. According to Glaspell, once the Provincetowners discovered O'Neill, "then we knew what we were for."

The idea of a serious avant-garde theater was born that summer. The main motivating factor was Jig Cook's ambition to create it, but there was also the community's recognition that a serious playwright was now in their midst. Before they left Provincetown that summer, twenty-nine members of the avant-garde community, including Dell, decided to pursue their theatrical venture once they returned to New York. They agreed that "during the winter season active members must either write, produce, act, or donate labor." They resolved to go on calling themselves the Provincetown Players. Only O'Neill held out for another name: The Playwright's Theater.

Once back in New York, the newly formed Players rented an apartment at 139 MacDougal Street and transformed it into an idiosyncratic, intimate theater. The Provincetown Playhouse opened in November with a trio of one-act plays: O'Neill's *Bound East for Cardiff*, Louise Bryant's *The Game*, and Dell's *King Arthur's Socks*. O'Neill's play was clearly the important one, inspiring the actors (among them Elaine Hyman, Harry Kemp, Bror Nordfeldt, George Cram Cook, and O'Neill himself) and audience members alike.

Dell's play was also warmly received. Much in the tradition of his earlier Liberal Club productions, *King Arthur's Socks* was a gentle satire about a young male artist (played in the original production by Max Eastman) and a married woman (played by Edna James), in love with each other but unwilling to act upon their amorous inclinations. The play focused on the paradox that had always troubled and delighted Dell: that the rebellious generation of which he was a part was also traditional in its underlying desires and principles. In this play as in other works Dell was writing at the time, marital faithfulness and stability, not amorous spontaneity, wins the hearts of its self-consciously sophisticated characters.

Dell's part in the first performances by the Provincetown Players was not an entirely happy one. Unwilling to devote a great deal of time to the play that fall, Dell had granted responsibility for the production to Edward J. Ballantine, a professional actor, who did a reasonably competent job staging it. In January Dell handed over another of his plays—*A Long Time Ago*, written during his last months in Chicago, and largely out of frustration over his unhappy courtship with Elaine Hyman—to the Provincetown troupe. This

Anthony Dell served in the Union Army during the Civil War, then settled in Barry, Illinois. His butcher shop failed in the aftermath of the Panic of 1873; thereafter he worked fitfully as a laborer. *(Floyd Dell Papers, Newberry Library)*

Kate Crone, a schoolteacher, married Anthony Dell in 1870. She passed her love of literature on to Floyd, the youngest of the couple's four children. *(Floyd Dell Papers, Newberry Library)*

Floyd Dell at twenty-one was already an experienced newspaperman and radical socalist. During his years in Davenport he avidly pursued his literary and political ambitions. *(Floyd Dell Papers, Newberry Library)*

Dell drew this fanciful self-portrait in 1911, when he was twenty-four. Already he was literary editor of the *Chicago Evening Post* and a leading figure among Chicago's awakening avant-garde. *(Floyd Dell Papers, Newberry Library)*

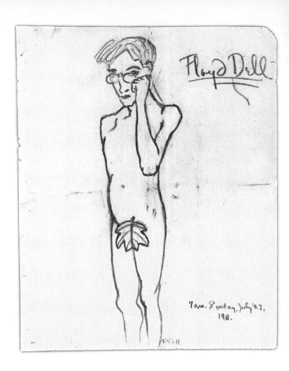

The Chicago artist Bror Nordf painted this portrait of Dell d the young literary editor's last in the city. The painting inspi Dell's ironic story "The Portra Murray Swift." *(Floyd Dell Pa Newberry Library)*

Margery Currey married Dell in August 1909. She and Dell hosted a lively salon for Chicago's avant-garde, first at their Rogers Park apartment, then at their studios on the city's South Side. *(Eunice Tietjens Papers, Newberry Library)*

B. Marie Gage, a feminist and pacifist from Pasadena, California, married Dell in February 1919. Friends predicted their marriage would meet the same fate as Dell's other fleeting romantic liaisons, but the couple remained married for fifty years. *(Floyd Dell Papers, Newberry Library)*

The poet Edna St. Vincent Millay in a photo taken in the 1920s, when Millay was enjoying her greatest fame. Dell and Millay had a brief, turbulent affair in 1918. *(Floyd Dell Papers, Newberry Library)*

In April 1918 Dell, Max Eastman, Art Young, and Merrill Rogers were tried under the Espionage Act for printing antiwar essays and drawings in the *Masses*. Left to right: Crystal Eastman, Young, Max Eastman, attorney Morris Hillquit, Rogers, and Dell. *(National Archives)*

Sherwood Anderson on Lake Chateaugay, upstate New York, 1917. In 1913 Dell encouraged Anderson's literary aspirations, then found a publisher for his first novel. Anderson acknowledged his debt by calling Dell his "literary father." *(Sherwood Anderson Papers, Newberry Library)*

Theodore Dreiser sitting in his Greenwich Village apartment in the late 1910s. In Chicago Dell wrote influential reviews commending Dreiser's early novels. Dreiser later praised Dell's first novel, *Moon-Calf*, as "an intimate & faithful picture of middle west American life." *(Theodore Dreiser Papers, Van Pelt Library, University of Pennsylvania)*

The Provincetown Players began staging plays in Greenwich Village in 1916. Among those preparing the set for Eugene O'Neill's *Bound East for Cardiff* are O'Neill (on ladder), Hippolyte Havel (seated), set designer Bror Nordfeldt (right, above), and the troupe's founder, George Cram Cook (far right). *(Museum of the City of New York)*

Dell in 1920, the year in which he published *Moon-Calf*. This photo, taken by Marjorie Jones, captures his self-conscious persona as literary artist and bohemian. *(Floyd Dell Papers, Newberry Library)*

Dell in 1928, when he was a well-known novelist, critic, and lecturer. That same year his comedy *Little Accident* was a Broadway hit, eventually playing for 289 performances at the Morosco Theatre. *(Floyd Dell Papers, Newberry Library)*

Edna St.Vincent Millay and Arthur Davison Ficke at Ficke's home in Santa Fe, New Mexico, in the 1920s. Ficke, a lawyer and poet from Davenport, was one of Dell's closest lifelong friends. *(Floyd Dell Papers, Newberry Library)*

Upton Sinclair in the 1920s. Dell befriended Sinclair in Greenwich Village during the 1910s and wrote a critical biography of him in 1926 and 1927. *(Floyd Dell Papers, Newberry Library)*

Nearly a decade younger than Dell, Joseph Freeman became one of his most cherished friends in the early 1920s. During the 1950s they corresponded voluminously on literature and politics. *(Floyd Dell Papers, Newberry Library)*

Dell in the early 1950s, after he had retired from government work. He continued to write stories and poems and carry on an extensive correspondence nearly up to the time of his death in 1969. *(Floyd Dell Papers, Newberry Library)*

Dell in the late 1930s, when he was working as a writer and editor for the Works Progress Administration. Dell later wrote: "I am still as proud of my governmental reports as of anything I have ever written." *(Floyd Dell Papers, Newberry Library)*

production was not nearly so successful in Dell's eyes. He was probably uneasy with the play to begin with, it being a decidedly lugubrious tragedy that was very likely patterned on Yeats's short tragedies. If the play embarrassed Dell, the production disgusted him. The director was Allan Macdougall, who put the players (including the massive Jig Cook and the preternaturally serious Ida Rauh) on stilts, perhaps to emphasize the artificiality of their relations. Dell was furious. Shortly thereafter he resigned from the Players, vowing not to offer the company the two unproduced comedies he had written for them.

Dell had other problems with the Provincetown Players as well. Some had to do with other productions, which Dell found erratic, even fatuous. "Nothing was too mad or silly to do in the Provincetown Theatre," he later complained, "and I suffered some of the most excruciating hours of painful and exasperating boredom there as a member of the audience that I have ever experienced in my life." He was also irritated with Cook, who had always relished the idea of his own greatness, and of his consequent exemption from the rules of ordinary decency observed by other people. This tendency seemed to Dell to reach absurd heights during the early years of the Provincetown experiment, when Cook was convinced that his genius had finally been vindicated by the creation of a ground-breaking theater. At parties Cook would drain the punch bowl by himself. "Give it all to me," he reportedly would say, "and I guarantee to intoxicate all the rest of you." To many Cook seemed frantic, possessed, out of control; to Dell this seemed a preposterous affectation. "I did not like George Cook during this period," he later remarked; "he was a Great Man, in dishabille; and Great Men, whether on pedestals or in dishabille, tended to provoke only irreverence from me."

Dell was also appalled by the naked ambitions set loose by the Provincetown venture. He had been present at the birth of the American little theater experiment in Chicago, cheering on Maurice Browne's troupe in 1912 and 1913 and writing heartfelt essays on their work for the Chicago and national press. This had been a happy experience, as had been his own little theater productions at the Liberal Club, where he had been "playwright, stage designer, scene painter, stage manager and actor." But Dell was painfully disillusioned and chagrined by the infighting and unscrupulous behavior that soon became common practice at the Provincetown Playhouse. He lamented

> the ruthless egotisms which ran rampant in the Provincetown Players. I saw new talent rebuffed—though less by George than by the others—its fingers brutally stepped on by the members of the original group, who were anxious to do the acting whether they could or not—and usually they could not; but I need not have wasted my sympathy, for the new talent, more robust than I supposed, clawed its way up on the raft, and stepped on other fingers, kicked other new faces as fast as they appeared. It was all that one had ever heard about Broadway, in miniature; but nobody seemed to mind.

Cook, often drunk and tyrannical, presided over this maelstrom of "jealousy, hatred and self-glorification." Dell began to view the Players as a "Walpurgis-night mob." The original resolve for a communal theater seemed to disappear almost as soon as the Players returned from the Cape at the fall of 1916.

Dell's resolve to quit the Provincetown Players lasted a year, until the fall of 1917, when Cook persuaded him to let the Players produce those two comedies he had earlier promised and then retracted. This time, however, Dell was determined to oversee production of the plays himself. The first, *The Angel Intrudes*, had already been published by *Vanity Fair* in the summer. Dell was eager, despite the time and hard work he was then devoting to his novel, to see it successfully staged. A lighthearted comedy, *The Angel Intrudes* presents a pair of young lovers about to elope when the young man's guardian angel intrudes and falls in love with the girl himself. Like earlier Dell plays, *The Angel Intrudes* was a satiric spoof on the transience of youthful love and idealism. Dell was determined that it would be handled with grace.

That December he sacrificed much of his time to directing *The Angel Intrudes*. At the casting sessions early in December, a slender young woman tried out for the female lead, Annabelle. "She had a beautiful voice," Dell remembered thinking, strangely deep and resonant. "She looked her frivolous part to perfection, and read the lines so winningly that she was at once engaged—at a salary of nothing at all, that being our artistic custom." Only after she had been awarded the part and left the theater did Dell and the other Provincetown regulars notice her full name, written on a slip of

paper she had filled out and left behind at their request. She was
Edna St. Vincent Millay, a twenty-five-year-old poet who had
already earned a reputation among Villagers for her poem "Renascence." She was not yet well acquainted with the Villagers, but her
reputation among them was already considerable. On the basis of
that one poem she had established herself as a writer whom many
Villagers regarded with awe.

Dell later said that he was pleased early that December "to have
Millay acting in my play. But I was not in the least under the Millay
spell." He was determined not to think of her romantically. He had
resolved once again to stay out of love affairs until he had finished
his psychoanalytic treatment with Dr. Tannenbaum. And his attention was also taken up by a pending trial: with Max Eastman and
several other editors at the *Masses*, Dell had been indicted under the
Espionage Act, mainly for inciting others to resist the draft. The
magazine itself had been shut down for good in November, and Dell
and the other editors under indictment were to be tried sometime in
the next few months. Preoccupied with other things—the play, his
novel, his ongoing psychoanalysis—Dell managed not to worry
about the upcoming trial obsessively. In fact, the nightmarish quality
of the situation (to think that he, an author, was to be tried for
espionage in a matter of months!) made him wish to forget it
altogether. Yet he knew that the trial was coming soon and that it
threatened to remove him altogether from the accustomed round of
life in Greenwich Village.

Although he was resolved to stay out of romantic entanglements,
he was impressed by Millay. She responded with alacrity and
precision to his directions. "Without demur or delay she did whatever she was asked to do," Dell noticed. "She was eager to please;
and it appeared that she especially wished to please me." He had the
distinct impression that she was enthusiastic about all his directorial
decisions. Even the simple backdrop that he had painted for the
production—little more than a fence, covered with snow, and with
"misty shapes in the background"—received her praise. "The others
were at first doubtful of my Washington Square backdrop, but she
instantly pronounced it beautiful." Members of the company were
certain they recognized another Floyd Dell love affair in the making
and joked about it among themselves. Dell was certain that this time
they were wrong.

By Christmas, though, he realized that his feelings toward Millay

were changing. When Dell stepped in from the bitter cold one
winter evening he discovered a Christmas party put on by the
Provincetown Players. Mistletoe had been hung in a corner of
the room, and men and women cast members were playing at the
pastime of kissing beneath it. Sensing that he did not want to see
Millay kissing anyone, he hurried off. Her power over him became
more distinct once the production opened after Christmas and
through the first few weeks of January. The play was a hit, as was
Edna St. Vincent Millay. Dell was entranced by the charm which she
brought out in Annabelle. In Millay's intriguing person the character
took on a vitality that even Dell had not discerned in the script.

Early that same January he asked her to take a part in the second
of the comedies he was preparing for the Provincetown Players,
Sweet-and-Twenty. Millay was flattered by the request; she asked
Dell if he would read the play to her. They agreed that this would be
best accomplished after dinner at a neighborhood restaurant. On the
agreed-upon evening Dell went to Millay's apartment on East 52nd
Street. There he was made to wait outside in the cold for her while
she took an exasperatingly long time to dress. When she finally did
appear, Dell was surprised to see her waylaid by her landlady, who
complained loudly about unpaid rent. She demanded that Millay
pay up at once. Dell presented himself to the importunate woman
and paid the back rent himself, ignoring Millay's objections. This
incident behind them, they proceeded happily with their original
plan, heading to the restaurant in the basement of the Brevoort Hotel,
"a place," as Dell recalled, "much frequented by the New York
intelligentsia." Afterward they returned to Millay's room where Dell
was to read her the play.

Dell later recalled the simplicity of the room. "There was a big
iron-framed bed, a small fireplace, and among other furniture a
battered old sofa." He was sure that the night before he had dreamed
of this same room, though he had never seen it before. He seemed
to have dreamed that he and Millay were sitting together in the
room in much the same way they were sitting there now. In his
dream he had suddenly seized her hand, then kissed her. Now,
having promised to read Millay the play he had brought with him,
and suddenly made awkward by being alone with her, he remembered this dream and felt how it seemed to mock his present lack of
resolve. Just as quickly, he overcame his irresolution, and they
kissed. "In a husky, vibrant violin-tone voice that I had never heard

before," Dell remembered, she said how glad she was that he had summoned up the courage to kiss her.

The romance that ensued, lasting off and on for much of the next year, had drastically different meanings for Dell and Millay. Both entered it with a mixture of eagerness and reluctance. Dell knew that in falling in love with Edna Millay he was breaking the restriction he had set himself to wait until he had finished psycho-analysis to resume his love life in earnest. But he was fascinated by this brilliant, lovely woman whose interests and views seemed so much like his own. Millay was equally intrigued by Dell. Of all the Villagers he seemed most likely to share her literary passions. For years Dell had enjoyed a reputation as the Village's most promising literary talent. Millay seems to have taken that reputation as a sign of his kinship with her.

She too partly dreaded romantic entanglements. In 1917 she had not yet had a serious affair with a man. And yet she had already imagined with perfect clarity how thoroughly she would resent the intimate knowledge and interest—the appalling lack of privacy and mystery—that comes with love:

> This door you might not open, and you did;
> So enter now, and see for what slight thing
> You are betrayed. . . . Here is no treasure hid,
> No cauldron, no clear crystal mirroring
> The sought-for Truth, no heads of women slain
> For greed like yours, no writhings of distress;
> But only what you see. . . . Look yet again;
> An empty room, cobwebbed and comfortless.
> Yet this alone out of my life I kept
> Unto myself, lest any know me quite;
> And you did so profane me when you crept
> Unto the threshold of this room tonight
> That I must never more behold your face.
> This now is yours. I seek another place.

Millay published this sonnet, "Bluebeard," a full year before she met Dell. Still, the poem did not bode well for their eventual happiness together. That was not clear, though, on the January night when Dell first went to Millay's room on 52nd Street. Millay insisted that Dell read *Sweet-and-Twenty* to her. Another light play satirizing young love, this one brought a serious young man together with a carefree young woman. They fall effortlessly in love, only to discover they have practically nothing in common. Dell had started the play in 1916, on a weekend alone at his cabin in New Jersey. He had been waiting for Margot to arrive. When she failed to show up, he had decided to write a play based partly on the incongruity of their relationship: that of an overly serious young man in love with a young woman with few intellectual interests. The couple in *Sweet-and-Twenty*, interested only in each other, become recipients of the unasked-for wisdom of a real estate agent, who informs them that marriage is "an iniquitous arrangement devised by the Devil himself for driving all the love out of the hearts of lovers." He generously advises them to avoid the institution and escape society itself: "If you are wise, you will build yourselves a little nest secretly in the woods, away from civilization, and you will run away together to that nest whenever you are in the mood. A nest so small that it will hold only two beings and one thought—the thought of love. And then you will come back refreshed to civilization . . . and forget each other, and do your own work in peace."

Beneath these lighthearted sentiments lay a surprising, barely acknowledged irony. Dell had been in precisely such "a little nest" when he wrote these words in 1916. Yet this distance from the civilized world had only added to his distance from Margot, his worldly American lover. Rather than provide him with a proper setting for romance, his hideaway cabin had seemed to separate him as much from human love as from hypocrite civilization. Dell could hardly have missed this final paradox as he composed *Sweet-and-Twenty* in his solitary retreat. Could the desire to abandon the world ever really be reconciled with the desire for love?

Questions like this had been at work in Dell's mind in 1916, even while he toyed with the theme of romantic escape. He had been scrupulous in *Sweet-and-Twenty*, as in other plays, to treat the subject with both affection and irony. Millay was delighted with the play and accepted the part of Helen, the young woman, as her own. She had heard much of Dell's love affairs, and she had decided, she told him that first night in her cold, bare room on 52nd Street, that his fickleness and inconstancy were much like her own. "We are birds of a feather," she told him. Dell halfheartedly resisted Millay's desire to idolize him as an unscrupulous lover. He insisted that he was really not polygamous; he pointed out that he was being psychoanalyzed largely to find stability in his love life.

"You wish to become a paragon of fidelity," Millay teased him. "If you want to put it that way," he replied, "yes." Edna insisted that fidelity would only make him "dull and stodgy," which would be too bad: "You would not talk so well," she insisted. "And you might not write so well. Your sympathies might become narrow. Loving your lawful wedded wife with an inflexible constancy might make you withdraw your sympathies from all the rest of us sinful and suffering creatures." But Dell insisted that at age thirty he had already had enough love affairs. Sexual fidelity, he hoped, would not rob him of a writer's imaginative understanding of others.

Eventually Millay suggested that they go to bed together, where they might warm up and continue their conversation. But she insisted, as she did for some while afterward, that they keep their relations "platonic." Dell's idealism helped him weather this disappointment. It seemed reasonable to him "that a girl, in taking a lover, should delay for a while the final intimacies of love until they knew more about their feelings for each other."

In the weeks that followed, their relations seemed to Dell to be made up of an unsettling mix of worldly and otherworldly matters. Their love seemed "an adventure out of space and time," he later wrote. "But our talk had dealt with some of the world's harshest realities. We were two rebellious young artists, very much akin, yet not entirely agreed in our ideals, not even in the realm of love, for she thought my Freudian ideal of marriage too stuffy, and I thought her ideal of feminist freedom too rash." Both were comfortable assuming an ironic, carefree tone with the other. Dell knew he was falling in love with Millay and was unhappy with her unwillingness to give herself fully to him, emotionally and physically. She struck him as strangely changeable, shifting from irreverence to moments of arresting seriousness. One evening when he gave her a feminist medallion that Dorothy Day had left at his place—"one of those given to the militant women suffragists who had chained themselves to the White House fence and, when taken to jail, had gone on a hunger strike and been forcibly fed"—Millay was visibly moved. No possession, she whispered, could possibly honor her more. Dell was moved, and slightly intimidated, by her unaffected seriousness.

Dell also impressed Millay, particularly his ability to see into her work and character. Once, when they were speaking about "Renascence," Millay admitted that the poem had been written during two different periods of time. She was certain that no one could ever disentangle the two parts. The next evening Dell correctly identified both parts. Then he added this surprise: "These first two lines of the second part were written later than all the rest of the poem, and replace some lines by which the two parts were originally joined together." His conjecture was exactly right, and for some while Millay retained her shock at Dell's keenness. According to Dell, she was equally astonished when a few weeks later he guessed at the reason behind her continued insistence that their bedtime relations remain "platonic": that she was in fact still a virgin, her previous sexual relations having been lesbian relations with fellow students during her undergraduate years at Vassar. Again Millay was disarmed by Dell's inspired conjecture. "She was awed by my deductive powers," he later remembered, though she was also defensive about her wish to keep their relations platonic. Dell, however, "refused to take any further part in the 'platonic' performances. I lectured her, instructively, affectionately, scornfully. I felt that it was my duty to rescue her from her psychological captivity."

Some weeks later Millay abandoned her resistance, and for a while their intimacy deepened. Spurred on by the Village's cult of authentic, spontaneous experience, Dell and Millay seemed briefly to become entirely absorbed in one another, perfectly content with the intellectual and physical intimacy they discovered in each other's presence. For Dell this seemed a fulfillment of his old dream of a perfect—and perfectly isolated—union with a woman. For a short while—perhaps no longer than a few weeks—Dell gave himself over to the desire for a lasting relation with Edna Millay.

Yet there were signs that this sort of relation was not likely to work out. Immediately after they first made love, Millay said, with fresh self-absorption, as if an entirely unpremeditated idea had just struck her, "I shall have many lovers." Dell later confessed he found the remark "frightfully disconcerting." Soon she discovered other ways to disconcert him. Sometimes she intimated that their sexual relations robbed her of her privacy. Dell pressed her on this belief, so antithetical to his own desire for perfect intimacy between himself and a woman: "Did you feel that you had been faithless to the god of poetry when you were no longer a virgin priestess?" Millay resented the question: it seemed to slight the privacy and solitary devotion to poetry which in fact she took entirely seriously. "You ask too many questions, Floyd," she told him. "You know that our happiness cannot last very long, anyway. And it will end all the sooner if you try to analyze me. There are doors in my mind that you must not try to open. Am I to have no self that is mine alone?" Dell insisted that she commit herself more thoroughly—more permanently and with greater seriousness—to their relationship. She brushed off his insistence. He pressed her with questions about her feelings and with theories (many from Freud) about her confusions. She fended these off with ever greater irritation.

In the months that followed their relationship became more uneasy. Playing upon the name Vincent, which Millay's closest friends were accustomed to calling her, Dell began to call her Vixen, a half-affectionate, half-irritable nickname that Millay found wonderful. She posed problems for him that had never arisen in his earlier relations with women. "In my previous love affairs," he wrote decades later, "I had always been more narcissistic than the girl; sometimes I was adored and put up with patiently just because I was so much of a narcissist." But with Millay, Dell realized, "I had a girl whose narcissism was to my narcissism as the Himalayas are to a hillock. I yielded her the palm without a struggle. I adored her, I put up with her patiently—but I could not keep it up."

Dell talked to her about marriage but found that she did not take him seriously. Then in February, Arthur Ficke, now a major in the army and recently arrived from France, came to visit Dell before returning to Europe. Ficke stopped for only a few days in New York. His support of the war effort and Dell's opposition to it hardly affected relations between the two friends. But Ficke had not come to New York solely to see Dell. He and Millay had been writing one another for years, since Ficke, upon first reading "Renascence" in 1913, had dashed off an adulatory letter to the young poet. They had written each other often about poetry. Ficke was eager to meet Millay; Dell arranged a party for the occasion. The company consisted in its entirety of himself, Millay, and Ficke, together with Millay's sister (and roommate) Norma and Norma's sweetheart, the painter Charlie Ellis.

Ficke, Dell recalled later, "was a very attractive figure—tall, handsome, elegant, rich, a distinguished poet, intelligent, kind, gentle." He had an unmistakably aristocratic bearing. Everyone, particularly Edna, was impressed by his ability to improvise poems on the spot. When the company shared a large pickle, each member taking a bite and then passing it on, Norma intoned with mock seriousness, "This pickle is a loving cup." Ficke laughed, delighted by Norma's conceit, and spun off a quatrain: "This pickle is a little loving cup / I raise it to my lips, and where you kissed / There lurks a certain sting that I have missed / In nectars more laboriously put up." Edna recognized the poet she had corresponded with for years. She and Ficke, long acquainted with each other through their letters and poems, seemed to fall in love before the eyes of everyone present. In the next few days, before Ficke headed back to Europe, he and Millay fell seriously in love, surprising and discomforting Dell, even though he and Millay were going through one of the periods in which they spent little time together. "This girl poet," he had begun to realize, "would always be falling in love with someone else."

Later that spring Millay told him she had slept with still another man, "the Angel" in the play they had put on a few months back. Soon Millay tried out for a part in a play to be put on by the Washington Square Players, a company that had grown out of the Liberal Club but that was less experimental in its theatrical productions than the Provincetown Players. Without any plan or direct statement, the two drifted apart into quite different worlds. Millay was fast absorbed in her work and circle of friends at the Washington Square theater; Dell was the more outwardly disappointed by the outcome of their affair. He returned to work on his novel, more determined than ever to write about his boyhood and adolescence in which he was certain he would discover the sources of his present discontent. And he awaited the *Masses* trial, now scheduled to begin in April. It promised to disrupt his life even more thoroughly than Edna Millay.

Then in the spring, not long before his trial, Dell met Millay on a Village street. She told him that her part in the Washington Square production had fallen through and that she was miserable. He consoled her and brought her home to his basement apartment on Charlton Street. Millay was moved by his unaffected generosity, just as he was moved by her unhappiness and by the vulnerability she had often tried to conceal from him. Again he realized what had often struck him earlier: that she was "at moments a scared little girl from Maine, and at other moments an austere immortal." It was a mix, he realized, that "drove everybody who knew her to writing poetry in the attempt to express that recognition of her lovely strangeness." Briefly he accepted her as she was. That spring they resumed their romance as both prepared themselves for the trial that was taking shape in the hysterical atmosphere of a nation now wholeheartedly at war.

E I G H T

Wartime

For the radicals in Greenwich Village, the war in Europe was only partly real. Certainly they cared about the widening conflict from its inception in 1914; many regarded it as the nightmarish death throes of a politically and morally corrupt civilization. But in April 1917, when America abandoned its isolationist posture and entered the war with gusto, the Villagers felt the war in more immediate ways. For Dell it was vividly present as the source of a "sinister psychology of fear and hate, of hysterical, far-fetched, and utterly humorless suspicion, which is invariably directed against minorities, independent thinkers, extreme idealists, candid and truth-telling persons, all who do not run and shout with the crowd." In the summer of 1917 he scrawled "Conscientious objector against this war" across his draft card, a token of his sense of alienation from the great mass of war supporters. As a socialist and bohemian, he knew himself to be a perfect target for the nation's accumulated fury.

Like many of his friends, though, Dell had trouble seeing the war plainly. When hostilities broke out in August 1914 he had been at Provincetown. "George Cook and I tried to apprehend what it might mean," he wrote. "I recalled H. G. Wells's stories of such a war. I couldn't envisage this one. . . . Nobody knew what to think, what to hope for, or what to fear." It was a shock that August when the German Socialists capitulated without a struggle to the kaiser's nationalist battle cry. Then news of the war's unprecedented carnage began to spread. Hutchins Hapgood claimed that within a year the war had caused widespread moral confusion among the Villagers: "All existing theories had been shown to be impotent. . . . Individuals had stopped their spiritual existence. All were waiting. Lives were vacant."

The *Masses* devoted much space to the war, publishing John Reed's frontline reportage and editorials by Max Eastman and others condemning the war effort. But most of the Villagers, including those at the *Masses*, appeared at times strangely oblivious to the fighting in Europe, a fact Dell later acknowledged: "The world was plunging through the horrors of war, and I was writing lighthearted little plays about young lovers. . . . The future, for all of us, was uncertain; and the more darkly uncertain it became, the higher rose the tide of gaiety in Greenwich Village."

The atmosphere of uncertainty was not due solely to the war but also to the basic instability of life in Greenwich Village. Nowhere was this instability more evident than at the *Masses*, where conflicts among the writers and artists had always disrupted the magazine's equilibrium. In March 1916 one such dispute actually resulted in an outright battle, prompting several contributors—all of them artists— to leave the *Masses* for good. The rebellious faction had been led by the art editor, John Sloan, and included Glenn Coleman, Henry Glintenkamp, Maurice Becker, and Stuart Davis. All complained about the practice of adding captions to their drawings—an imperti- nence, they contended, no self-respecting artist ought to endure. More generally they objected to the control exercised by Eastman and Dell over the magazine and its contents. At the March 1916 meeting, a grim, sober affair much in contrast to the usual monthly free-for-alls, Sloan demanded that Eastman's and Dell's command- ing editorial positions be abolished. The *Masses*, he said, was "no longer the resultant of the ideas and art of a number of personal- ities." Rather, Sloan complained, it "seems to have developed a 'policy.'" He proposed that the editors "get back to the idea of producing a magazine which will be of more interest to the contribu- tors than to anyone else."

Dell and Eastman regarded the whole proposal as a childish charade put on by incorrigibly bohemian artists. Sloan too, if not the other artists, seemed to realize deep down that the suggestion of a more perfectly democratic, and anarchic, *Masses* was impracti- cable. When the assembled editors finally voted on the matter the result was a tie, with the gang of five, led by Sloan, lined up against Eastman, Dell, Mary Heaton Vorse, Kenneth Chamberlain, and Art Young. Everyone agreed the issue should be put to a second ballot in a few weeks, with a fuller representation of *Masses* editors and contributors on hand to vote.

At the second meeting, held April 6, seventeen people voted, and the matter was decided decisively: Eastman and Dell won easily, garnering eleven votes to six for Sloan and his crew. Still, there was rancor enough now between the two factions to prevent the matter from ending there. Eastman recalled that immediately after the vote, Dell seized the floor and proposed

> that Sloan, Davis, Coleman, Brown, and Glintenkamp be dropped from the magazine. The motion was seconded, to everyone's astonishment, by Art Young—the most genial and easygoing, most tolerant-hearted, and also most loved of all the contributing editors. That really was a bombshell. . . . Maurice Becker leapt from his seat, as though exploded out of a gun, and demanded that his name be added to those to be dropped.
>
> "I accept the amendment," Floyd said sharply.
>
> "I also accept it," Art stated, his face set and his mild eyes burning as no one there had seen them burn before. "To me this magazine exists for socialism. That's why I give my drawings to it, and anybody who doesn't believe in a socialist policy, so far as I go, can get out!"

Afterward everyone pulled back from this outright antagonism. Amidst conciliatory gestures, all the artists were reinstated. But the next day the core of the rebellious faction—Sloan, Davis, Coleman, Becker, and Robert Carlton Brown, a writer who had been swept up in the artists' uprising—resigned.

Young's angry words indicate how frayed the nerves of all involved had become, but they only partially suggest the nature of the problem that had broken out at the *Masses*. To varying degrees Young, Dell, and Eastman all insisted that the magazine was essentially a radical publication with a basic commitment to socialism and political rebellion. All three men discerned in the seceding artists self-absorbed aesthetes with little interest in this political dimension. In fact, though, most of the artists, especially Sloan, were political radicals of one sort or another, their artistic work reflecting the social interests and commitments of the "Ashcan" school. Their radicalism was not much more impressionistic than that of Eastman, Dell, and Young. The real source of the dispute lay at the very heart of the *Masses* enterprise: in the impractical

enthusiasm for unbridled individualism and self-expression that was
nearly as typical of Dell and Eastman as it was of the artists. Rather
than a dispute between socialists and aesthetes, the *Masses* revolt
had been more a symptom of the magazine's permanent state of
chaos and division. The *Masses* may have gained its spirited flavor
from this condition, but it was also always imperiled by it.

THE DEPARTURE OF Sloan and the other artists had surprisingly little
effect on the magazine. Brilliant artists were still on board—George
Bellows, Boardman Robinson, Robert Minor, Henry Glintenkamp
(who never followed through with the rebellion of which he had
initially been a member), Arthur B. Davies—to provide the magazine with drawings and cartoons. But the magazine's contributors
remained divided on many issues, including the war. Resistance to a
unified, rational, coherent "policy" for the magazine continued to
be typical of editors and contributors alike. Eastman, whose interests
were overwhelmingly political, found this editorial incoherence
terribly irritating. With his finely tuned awareness of his own
contradictions, Dell was more inclined to accept it with irony,
warmheartedness, laughter, and regret.

In March 1917, only weeks before America entered the war,
Eastman asked the editors to commit themselves to a unified policy
opposing American intervention. As usual he encountered resistance. George Bellows, one of the *Masses'* finest artists and a man by
no means devoid of social conscience, responded to Eastman by
echoing John Sloan's complaint of a year earlier, insisting that *"The
Masses* has no business with a 'policy.' It is not a political paper and
will do better without any platforms. Its 'policy' is the expression of
its contributors. They have the right to change their minds con-
tinually, looking at things from all angles." Perhaps tipping his hand
more than he wished, Bellows suggested that his feelings in this
regard were the product of political incoherence and inconstancy.
"In the presence of great, ultimate, and universal questions like these
[about the war]," he wrote Eastman, "it is impossible, at least for
me, to know quite where I stand." Fuzzy convictions like these
butted up uncomfortably against radical sentiments like those proclaimed in the July 1917 issue by Arturo Giovannitti: "This paper
belongs to the proletariat. It is the recording secretary of the
Revolution in the making. It is NOT meant as a foray of unruly

truant children trying to sneak into the rich orchards of literature and art."

For Dell all this political and artistic confusion was understandable. If he was strongly possessed at times by his long-held socialist principles, he also recognized full well that socialism could never account for all his interests and objectives. Probably the real source of his exasperation with the artists at the March 1916 revolt had been their suggestion that the magazine might be produced in a purely democratic way, with no governing editors in sight. Having worked at papers and edited political and literary magazines for years, Dell knew better than that. But the idea that the magazine must center itself exclusively on the socialist gospel was one he only intermittently endorsed. More often he stuck to the view that the *Masses* should try to present a very great range of subjects, from politics to feminism to art.

Once the United States joined the war in April 1917 the *Masses* entered its most brilliant stage. Much of that brilliance had direct reference to the war itself, as the magazine moved at last toward something resembling a consistent focus in its opposition to the war. The peculiar intensity of its pages in the months following the declaration of war also came from nonpolitical contributions. In his autobiography Dell described these last months of the *Masses*, its idealism heightened by the atmosphere of emergency and impending ruin spread by the war:

> The "Renaissance" that had been predicted in 1911, that had begun in 1912, was still—fantastically!—going on. The war only made it bloom more intensely. And The Masses became, against that war background, a thing of more vivid beauty. Pictures and poetry poured in—as if this were the last spark of civilization left in America. And with an incredible joyousness, the spirit of man laughed and sang in its pages.

Many of the magazine's pages continued to be filled with poems, drawings, stories, and literary essays, even as the war tempted the editors to make it more exclusively political. Dell remarked years later that "It is strange to look through the files [of the magazine]. So much good humor, sweetness, happiness is there! A few of us could be sane in a mad world."

Still, much of the *Masses* was devoted to the war; the magazine played a significant role in this peculiarly desperate chapter in

American history. Other journals, too, contributed materially to the domestic debates surrounding the war. The *New Republic* and the *Seven Arts* tended to focus on the role of intellectuals in response to the war. John Dewey led the *New Republic* in its efforts to convince progressive intellectuals that they must work to control and direct the war effort rather than run away from it; for the *New Republic* writers, the war presented intellectuals with an unprecedented opportunity to seize the reins of American policy. Writers for the *Seven Arts*, particularly Randolph Bourne, set themselves in direct opposition to the *New Republic*. Bourne argued that to endorse and cooperate with the war effort was to lose the independence and critical spirit essential to radical intellectual life. In one of his *Seven Arts* essays Bourne described the dilemma facing intellectuals during wartime: one could "either support what is going on, in which case you count for nothing because you are swallowed in the mass and great incalculable forces bear you on; or remain aloof, passively resistant, in which case you count for nothing because you are outside the machinery of reality." Bourne counseled holding oneself apart from the great mass of war supporters, all the while developing ideas that might one day rescue society from its worst instincts.

The *Masses* contributors tended to share the views of Bourne and the *Seven Arts* writers. But on the whole there was less agonizing in the *Masses* over the intellectuals' dilemma and more direct outrage at the war effort itself. According to Dell, the *Masses* writers and editors agreed that "there was something to be said about war profiteering; something to be said in defense of pacifists and conscientious objectors; and, increasingly, something to be said about the blind, blundering ferocity with which the government was undertaking to silence all minority opinion under the Espionage Act."

The magazine's most regular contributors of essays on the war were Eastman and John Reed. Reed's reports from the front in Europe were among the best journalistic pieces he ever wrote, vivid pieces of unsentimental observation mixed with undisguised indignation at a war that was turning out to be unprecedentedly vast and gruesome. Eastman editorialized incessantly on the war, deploring everything from the way in which disputes surrounding the war had divided the international (and American) socialist community to the fuzzy motives underpinning the American decision to join the slaughter. He railed against the wave of passionate intolerance, violence against dissenters, and frank censorship that had been unleashed by the war in the United States.

Dell devoted himself largely during these months to the literary pages, which he tended to value even more now that the war had pushed the country to such apparent indifference to the cause of culture and beauty. But he also spoke out against the war. In an essay in the July 1917 issue he gently decried the *New Republic's* support of the war effort, describing its desire to support both the rights of the individual and a war effort marked by unmitigated contempt for such rights. In another piece, this one unsigned and published in the August issue, Dell defended the rights of conscientious objectors. He echoed earlier American writers who had championed the unencumbered individual conscience: "There are some laws that the individual feels he *cannot obey*, and which he will suffer any punishment, even that of death, rather than recognize as having authority over him. This fundamental stubbornness of the free soul, against which all the powers of the state are helpless, constitutes a conscientious objection, whatever its original sources may be in political or social opinion."

Despite its unmistakable American provenance, this remark proved to be among those that infuriated United States postal authorities, who decided that the August issue of the *Masses* ought not be distributed through the mails. On July 5, 1917, the postmaster of New York City informed the editors that the August issue of the magazine would not be mailed because it violated the Espionage Act, which had been passed a month earlier in an effort to extinguish antiwar sentiment. Besides Dell's piece, the postmaster cited statements by Eastman, cartoons by Art Young, Boardman Robinson, and Henry Glintenkamp, and several other seditious items. One of Glintenkamp's drawings in particular—titled "Conscription," and showing two naked men and a woman chained to a cannon—evoked special outrage among the authorities. The *Masses* protested the action, and on July 21 Federal District Judge Learned Hand ruled that the magazine should indeed have access to the mails since the essays and cartoons fell "within the scope of that right to criticize, either by temperate reasoning or by immoderate and indecent invective, which is normally the privilege of the individual in countries dependent upon the free expression of opinion as the ultimate source of authority."

For a brief moment all seemed well. But when the New York

postmaster appealed Justice Hand's ruling, the August issue was again denied access to the mails, as were several subsequent issues that contained still more antiwar cartoons and statements. In October the *Masses* ran a particularly shocking picture by Glintenkamp. Titled "Physically Fit," it shows a skeleton measuring a naked young man, with a coffin ready at his feet and a great many more propped against the wall behind him. Glintenkamp (apparently with the help of Dorothy Day) had managed to slip the drawing into the issue without the knowledge of Eastman and Dell. Both men saw the drawing for the first time when the issue appeared for sale.

The *Masses* seemed more vibrant, more combative than ever before. Issues were sold primarily at newsstands in New York; but the inability to mail issues placed the magazine's survival in jeopardy, since it drastically reduced the number of issues sold. Short of funds, the editors barely managed to print a November-December issue. When a circuit court overruled Hand's ruling, the *Masses* shut down for good. That same November Dell, Eastman, Reed, Young, Glintenkamp, business manager Merrill Rogers, and a young poet named Josephine Bell were formally indicted under the Espionage Act, charged with "conspiring to cause mutiny and refusal of duty in the military and naval forces, and to obstruct recruiting and enlistment to the injury of the service."

By the time the trial was held in April 1918, the indictment had attracted much public attention, and the defendants had gained a large measure of notoriety. The presiding judge was Augustus Hand, cousin of the same Learned Hand who had overruled the first decision to suppress the *Masses*. The defendants had severe doubts that this outcome would be as favorable as that earlier ruling. The fighting in Europe was intense and grim during the spring of 1918: Germany embarked on its last offensive in France, and sentiment against dissenters was running high. It seemed unlikely that jury members could be found who would not share the country's violent antipathy to critics of the war effort. When the defendants, accompanied by their attorneys Morris Hillquit and Dudley Field Malone, filed into the courtroom on the morning of April 15, 1918, they expected to be found guilty and sentenced to jail for as many as twenty years.

Neither Reed nor Glintenkamp was present for the trial: Reed was in Russia reporting on the Revolution, while Glintenkamp had fled to Mexico. On the first day of the trial Judge Hand threw out the indictment against Josephine Bell, who had never even met the other defendants. Bell had been indicted on the basis of a poem celebrating the anarchists Emma Goldman and Alexander Berkman, who had been jailed for their antiwar activities. Judge Hand also dismissed the charge that the defendants had conspired "to cause mutiny and refusal of duty in the armed forces." But the judge clearly regarded the second charge—that the defendants had conspired to obstruct the draft—with complete seriousness.

Judge Hand was not amused by the behavior of one of the defendants on the first morning of the trial. A brass band played in the park across from the courtroom, which was on the third floor of the New York City post office. As prospective jury members were questioned and, without exception, rejected by the defense, the band frequently broke out into renditions of "The Star Spangled Banner." Each time the anthem began, Merrill Rogers would jump to attention, impishly shaming the judge, jury candidates, and gallery full of onlookers; all felt compelled each time to follow his lead and drag themselves out of their chairs to attention. At last the judge put a halt to such behavior and irritably pushed the proceedings forward.

The two defense lawyers lent their clients a solid respectability which they might otherwise have lacked. Morris Hillquit had just concluded his race as the Socialist candidate for mayor of New York, an election in which he had won a surprising number of votes. Hillquit had long been a prominent figure in the socialist movement (he had a nationwide reputation as a respectable reformer, not a raving radical). Now the *Masses* defendants and their supporters had persuaded Hillquit to lend his talents as an orator and legal strategist to their cause. Dell recognized Hillquit as a serious man with little sympathy for the *Masses* but who saw the trial as a fit occasion to present a public case for freedom of speech and opposition to the war.

Hillquit's coattorney was Dudley Field Malone, once a confidant of President Wilson and the former collector of the Port of New York. Malone was a generous, idealistic man. He gladly took up the cause of young rebels who, he felt, were victims of a government that had veered dangerously far from its democratic origins. In characteristically impulsive fashion, Malone, as Eastman recalled, had not long before the trial "fallen in love with Doris Stevens, a militant suffragette, at the very moment when she was engaged in getting arrested and locked up in jail for picketing the White House. Outraged by this violation of the principles of civil liberty and political chivalry, Dudley resigned his position and broke off his very close and very valuable friendship with the head of the nation."

Hillquit and Malone built their defense on two related strategies. The first recalled the principle invoked by Judge Learned Hand in his July ruling, namely, the right of all citizens to criticize the government in a society that cherishes free speech. The second strategy responded more specifically to the charge that the defendants had conspired to obstruct the draft. Hillquit and Malone set out to prove that there had been no general agreement to publish the essays or cartoons named in the indictment—general agreement being essential to any proper conspiracy—and that no one had wished specifically to obstruct the draft. The defendants agreed that this was the soundest possible defense. They also agreed that the mood in the courtroom and in the nation at large did not bode well for them. Such apprehensions seemed confirmed as Hillquit and Malone examined one prospective juror after another, only to be told by each one that he was prejudiced against socialists and conscientious objectors. Dell and the other defendants listened as the same litany was repeated by each jury candidate: "Are you prejudiced?" "Yes." "Can you set aside that prejudice?" "Yes." After failing to accept a single candidate on the first day, Hillquit and Malone finally resolved to weed out the least prejudiced of the candidates and, after a long second day, a jury had been selected and the trial commenced.

THE APRIL TRIAL was complicated for several of the defendants by changes in the world since the indictment had been handed down in late 1917. While the *Masses* had been, with the *Seven Arts*, chief among the magazines opposing the war during most of 1917, some of its editors had had an unexpected change of heart in the months after November. The October revolution in Russia, which seemed to the *Masses* editors—particularly Eastman and Dell—to promise so much for the cause of world socialism, now appeared to be threatened by the German army. The war which had earlier seemed a senseless contest of reactionary, imperialist parties was suddenly redefined by the need to preserve the socialist experiment in Russia. When Germany and Russia signed a peace treaty in early March at

Brest-Litovsk, forcing Russia to abandon a great deal of territory—
and not entirely removing the threat of future German aggression—
various radicals became convinced that it would be necessary for the
allies to defeat Germany in order to assure the survival of socialist
Russia. By the time their trial opened in April, both Dell and
Eastman had spoken out in favor of the American war effort. But
they were unwilling to play up their newfound support of the war in
order to win favor with the jury. They claimed the trial was ultimately
about the right to free speech, and they decided to base their defense
upon that right.

For Dell the trial was a confusing, grotesque, sometimes entertaining, often absurd experience:

> It was with the oddest feelings that we sat there, waiting. This, we
> knew, was a serious matter. And yet it seemed strange, and rather
> funny, and not quite credible. It was hard to believe that this
> court-room, that judge, these expert prosecutors, and those rows
> of tired men behind us, should be concerned with our destinies. It
> took an effort to realize that we were truly the centre of these
> elaborate proceedings.
>
> It was in the nature of a grim joke. The Government of the
> United States was going to devote its energies, its time, and its
> money to the task of sending us to prison for the next twenty
> years. For a moment it seemed fantastic, grotesque, in the mood
> of a queer dream or a sombre and morbid farce.

Dell watched passively as the trial unfolded: jury selection; the
prosecution's laborious presentation of facts proving the *Masses'*
existence and the printing of the allegedly conspiratorial essays and
drawings; Max Eastman's clever defense of the magazine, which
alone lasted three full days. All the while Dell felt he was out of
place in these proceedings, that he would rather be back in his
basement apartment at work on his novel. He came to the trial every
day with Millay—once even arriving late with her, striding awk-
wardly to his seat beside the other defendants, certain that every
respectable person in the courtroom was imagining how he and she,
unmarried poets indifferent to the U.S. government's righteous
concern in this matter of espionage during wartime, had remained
in bed even as his own trial was under way. Millay walked through
the hallways with Dell during recesses, reciting poems to distract
him in the intervals between the proceedings.

Not that Dell was cowed or rendered speechless by the trial.
When it was his time to testify, he spoke with full confidence, fairly
basking in the attention he now received. He was eager to explain
his ideas and their evolution. As he joked in the pages of the radical
Liberator after the trial, "I had always secretly felt that my opinions
were of a certain importance. It appeared that the government
agreed with me. . . . It was naturally a pleasure to tell the government what I thought about war, militarism, conscientious objectors
and related subjects."

The jury—even chief prosecutor Earl Barnes—listened with interest as Dell explained his earlier view of the war as a pointless
struggle between equally illiberal adversaries. Again he defended the
rights of conscientious objectors. All present in the courtroom were
disconcerted to discover that Dell now supported the effort to defeat
Germany in the interests of preserving the revolutionary society now
taking shape in Soviet Russia. By April 1918 Dell was eager to see
Germany defeated, not only to eliminate the threat of a renewed
German attack on Russia but also to set the German working classes
free to push forward their own revolutionary government. Dell told
the court he was now prepared to fight in the war—a declaration
that surprised jurors and prosecutors alike, not only because they
had expected him to speak out for pacifism but also, as Eastman
later wrote, because these prowar sentiments seemed entirely incongruous coming from "so slight and pale-skinned and delicate a
poet—a sort of Shelley or John Keats in appearance."

Dell also enjoyed the volleys of questions and answers exchanged
between him and prosecutor Barnes. "I found in cross-examination
the distinct excitement of a primitive sort of game of wits," he
reported afterward. Barnes made no secret of his admiration for Dell
and for the other defendants. He argued to the jury that these men
had conspired to obstruct the draft, and that they should be sent to
jail. But he also praised the defendants. Clearly he was intrigued by
these writers and editors who had adopted such unconventional
attitudes toward the war. Dell later pasted together a mock free-verse
poem made up of phrases used by Barnes in his final statement to
the jury. "These men / Are men of extraordinary intelligence," it
read in part. "Eastman is one of the brainiest men of our / time— / A
college professor, a writer of remarkable / poetry, a brilliant orator,
and a keen analyst / of social conditions. / Rogers is a graduate of
Harvard University / and a hustling / Man of business. / Dell, / A

trained journalist, a writer of / Exquisite English, / Keenly ironical, bitingly sarcastic."

Dell realized that much of Barnes's admiration for him and the other defendants came from the recognition that they were all articulate Americans. Their comments may have seemed unconventional and radical to Barnes and the jury, but there was no mistaking these thoughtful, well-spoken journalists for working-class rebels or immigrants. In the year preceding his own trial, Dell had attended trials of other persons who allegedly opposed the war. In these other tribunals,

> the defendants were not treated with such courteous consideration. No, for in these war-time trials the defendants were often both poor and of foreign origin—and as such not entitled by American custom to the civilities which we reserve for our peers. These "foreigners" were here to do our dirty work and take our orders, with no right to criticize. But we, as it appeared, were American-born and bred, obviously well educated, belonging by prescriptive right among those who give rather than among those who take orders; and if we were found on the "wrong" side of such a controversy, along with discontented foreign-born workers, it would naturally be inquired how the devil we came to be there, and our reply would meet with a respectful, if puzzled, hearing.

The congenial relation between prosecutor, jurors, and defendants remained largely unacknowledged among the *Masses* defendants, who preferred not to face up to their own underlying cultural and social affinities with the society that had placed them on trial. Only Dell faced it squarely.

For all his confidence on the stand and the sympathetic treatment he received during his own testimony, Dell knew that the verdict might well be *guilty*, and that he and the others might soon join other antiwar protesters in prison. His newfound enthusiasm for the war may have baffled the jurors, but it was also likely in the long run to alienate them, since most Americans already regarded the latest Russian Revolution with suspicion, if not outright hostility. And the defendants' behavior at the trial—their boldness and occasional irreverence, Rogers's mock patriotism, Dell's late arrival with Millay, Art Young falling conspicuously asleep in his chair during the trial itself—was scarcely likely to win the sympathy of respectable jurors. Hillquit summed up with admirable force, urging that no real case of conspiracy had been brought against the defendants. Malone, in his closing remarks, invoked the figure of Tom Paine, a champion of free speech likely to stir the sympathies of any patriotic jury. The decisive principle in the jury's deliberations, Malone said, was "that opinion in a democracy like ours, must be free, freely spoken, freely written." But when the jury was sent out to decide the case, war hysteria still seemed likely to carry the day.

The jury members argued for two days and nights, returning several times for further instructions from Judge Hand, who pressed them to come to agreement. Afterward it was reported that the debate had fluctuated from six to six at one point early in the deliberations, to eleven to one for conviction much later on. Eastman later claimed to have learned from prosecutor Barnes that their lone supporter had been Henry C. Fredericks, a man of Austrian descent whom the other jurors threatened to lynch "as a pro-German when they got him outside of the courthouse." Fredericks stood his ground, reportedly winning over two other jurors, only to lose one again to the other side. After two days of deliberations, Judge Hand decided that the jury was hopelessly deadlocked and dismissed it. Dell and his colleagues had been saved, if only by a mistrial.

During the trial Dell sometimes had been consumed not by the case and the impending announcement of his fate but by his sense that the trial was superfluous to his life—that his real destiny lay elsewhere. Literature, not politics, seemed central to his identity. He concluded an essay on the trial in a way certain to unnerve those ready to venerate him for his political courage: "I am not ashamed to say that to me art is more important than the destinies of nations, and the artist a more exalted figure than the prophet."

Even as the jury members were thrashing things out, Dell awaited the verdict not with intense concentration on what was going on in the jury room but with the feeling that all that commotion was strangely irrelevant to him. On the second night of jury deliberations the defendants were able to see, in the reflection of windows of the building opposite the post office, an image of the jury debating angrily. As Dell and the others watched, the men gesticulated wildly, pacing up and down the room. For Dell the debate appeared slightly ridiculous and finally uninteresting: "The whole thing seemed as dim and as unreal as that ghostly reflection in the window." As he awaited judgment, Dell's imaginings turned elsewhere. "I thought about stars and flowers and ideas and beautiful women."

NOT LONG AFTER the trial concluded, and before any date for a retrial had been set, Dell was called to military service by his draft board. For several months after the trial he had helped edit the *Liberator*, the magazine Max Eastman had started as a successor to the *Masses*. A more earnestly political magazine than its predecessor (though one that did not oppose the war effort), the *Liberator* still found space for Dell's essays on literary figures as diverse as Vachel Lindsay and G.K. Chesterton. Eager as ever to disrupt the comfortable assumptions of complacent radicals, Dell cast aside Chesterton's reputation as a reactionary and praised him instead for his antistatism—for his liberating faith in the principle of free will in human affairs. In another piece Dell recounted his experience of the trial, making no pretense to having been possessed during the proceedings by unswerving radical zeal. Instead he emphasized his bewilderment and persistent sense of detachment during the most dramatic confrontation between radicals and the U.S. government that Greenwich Village had yet seen. Dell's self-deprecating irony may have been out of keeping with the more serious political content of the *Liberator*. But his frank depiction of his own uncertainties appealed to many Greenwich Village readers.

The July evening before he was to leave for boot camp, Dell had dinner with Edna Millay at the home she now shared with her mother and two sisters on Charlton Street. The two had resumed and abandoned their affair several times in the months after the trial, and there seemed little reason to hope their romance would endure. Millay was given to dramatic gestures, and she arranged a special meal for him as a send-off from New York. The two sat in the garden behind her house, Edna carefully orchestrating their last hours together: "When it grew dark she put candles on the stumps of the sawed-off leafless branches of a tree that, no longer a living tree, was now used for a clothesline. The candles dripped in the breeze, and these lighted candles looked like flowers of flame with icicles hanging from them." The eerie scene seemed to Dell, then as later, to stand for much that he had discovered in Millay and in their relationship. There was without doubt something intoxicatingly beautiful in the atmosphere that she created. Yet it also struck Dell as cold, unwholesome, inhuman.

He was happy to leave his fitful, disturbing relations with Millay behind and to report to army camp in Spartanburg, South Carolina. He later claimed to have relished every aspect of his military training: taking orders, the camaraderie with the other recruits, life in the barracks and mess hall, even the food. Drill reminded him pleasurably of the mock drills he had practiced with his father as a boy in Barry. He freely admitted the irony of his position: preparing happily for participation in a war that he had earlier deplored, redeemed for him now by the wish to defeat a Germany that threatened Soviet Russia. But his willingness to go to war proved insufficient. Once the military authorities discovered that Dell had recently been tried for espionage in New York (and that a retrial was likely in the near future), he was honorably discharged. Ten days after arriving in Spartanburg, he boarded another train and returned to New York.

Back in the Village, Dell found himself without money or prospects for a job. The affair with Edna seemed finished for good. He rented an apartment on the ground floor of a narrow wooden house at 11 Christopher Street. Before long he was back at work at the *Liberator*, serving as the magazine's associate editor and contributing, among other things, a series of articles on progressive education. Separated from Millay, he passed from one romantic liaison to another, placing little faith in any of them. He remained morbidly fascinated with Millay, though also determined to rid himself of his obsession with her.

Part of that effort was enacted in several sonnets he wrote at the time. One, published in *Pearson's Magazine*, recalled their dinner the night before he left for Spartanburg:

> The sunny magic of a tree in flower
> Some day perhaps shall allure me as of old;
> But now the blossoms of your garden bower,
> That never drew their sustenance from the mould,
> So haunt me that I cannot even lift
> My eyes to look, walking the orchard through:
> Cherry-bloom, apple-bloom, all the season's gift
> Is worthless now in my eyes because of you—
> Who lit three candles on a windy night

And hung them like three blossoms in a tree:
Three frost-flowers, each with icy stalactite
Drip-dripping into the darkness. Foolish me,
That in my petal-dripping orchard close
Must shut my eyes and think of flowers like those!

Millay seemed to occupy a realm divorced from sunny nature and ordinary pleasures. Other times Dell acknowledged her childlike vulnerability, which made her extraordinarily sympathetic, and which he associated with her intermittent talent for friendship and affection. In a poem he had written earlier in the spring, Dell captured both her imperious nature and the sudden vulnerability which had surprised him so often:

Child of the lightning, alien to our dust,
We seek you in the tempest—you are there,
Drenched with the storm of beauty, gust on gust
Of poignant sweetness only you can bear.
Startled, you vanish in the darkness, fleeing
The too-close human handclasp; you are fain
Of the caresses native to your being—
Strange joys that wound intolerably with pain.
But all in vain your hands to touch the sky
Reach up, in vain your bosom to the thunders
Bared—there is only you and mayhap I
And the old commonplace authentic wonders
Of food and fire and bed. There's no use trying.
So back you come, and yet—Why, you are crying!

Dell published the poem in the May 1918 issue of the *Liberator* under the title "On Reading the Poems of Edna St. Vincent Millay." Ostensibly a review of the volume *Renascence* (1917), the poem granted Dell a public occasion on which to make sense of his feelings for Millay. The opening octave, with its conventional, if sharply etched, portrait of the solitary romantic poet, is ably handled. But it is the sestet, where Dell names the features of life that matter to him most—"the old commonplace authentic wonders / Of food and fire and bed"—that is most vivid. This timeless domestic setting, to which his inconstant lover returns, has a solidity that the child of lightning lacks. And yet the poem is full of tenderness for Millay, in whom he recognizes a vulnerability that cannot be

consoled by "commonplace authentic wonders." The poem is memorable not for its language or formal qualities: in these it is utterly
conventional, relying, as do other Dell poems, on the poetic diction
of his cherished English romantics. Its virtues lie instead in its
tender view of Millay and in its quiet affirmation of the speaker's
own values. What the poem captures is the unbridgeable gap
separating two lovers with vastly different temperaments. Like the
other poems he wrote for Millay in the spring and summer of 1918,
it celebrates her beauty and genius. But it is also a poem charged
with failure and regret.

MILLAY RETURNED to Dell again in September when he, together with
the other defendants from the April trial and Jack Reed (who had
since returned from Russia), was tried a second time for conspiring
to obstruct the draft. Much of the trial repeated the pattern of the
first one. The chief prosecutor was Earl Barnes, again torn between
his firm conviction that the defendants should go to jail and his
stubborn admiration for them. The defendants repeated their earlier
testimonies that there had been no conspiracy and that their views
on the war had changed considerably in light of the evolving
political situation in Russia. This time, though, there was a new
judge, Martin Manton, who was even less sympathetic to the
defendants than had been Augustus Hand. And Hillquit and Malone were unable to serve in this second trial as defense attorneys.
The attorney this time was Seymour Stedman, who had just days
before finished defending Eugene Debs in Cleveland, also for
speaking out against the war. There Stedman had lost the case and
Debs was sentenced to ten years in jail. Now in New York Stedman
was ill, unable to attend most of the trial's five days of testimony.
The *Masses* defendants sat through the second trial with little proper
legal representation, doubting once again their chances of escaping
fines and prison terms.

The atmosphere of the trial, however, was rather different this
time. The war was heading unmistakably to its conclusion, and war
hysteria was abating from the fever pitch it had reached the previous
spring. This development boded well for the defendants; but their
support for Soviet Russia was less likely to meet with sympathetic
hearings in September. By then American troops had joined the
Allied counterrevolutionary forces in Russia, the United States

having decided that the Bolsheviks were as much America's enemies as were the Germans. Barnes argued in this second trial that the Bolsheviks were Germany's allies, and therefore that the defendants' support of the Russian revolutionaries was tantamount to support of the Germans. The defendants' sympathy for the Soviets, which they had presented in April as evidence of their opposition to the Germans, now was described by the prosecution as further evidence of conspiracy against the American war effort.

It was left primarily to Max Eastman to rebut this charge. In a three-hour summation that Eastman, in Stedman's absence, made for the defense, he argued that the international socialist movement spearheaded by Lenin and the Bolsheviks was fundamentally opposed to German militarism—that to conflate the two was thoroughly to misrepresent the revolutionary socialist position. The enthusiasm felt by the *Masses* defendants for the Soviet revolutionary experiment had been central to their opposition to Germany; by no means was it (as Barnes suggested) a sign of a conspiracy to obstruct America's war effort against the Germans. Eastman's fellow defendants were impressed by his eloquence, but all were uncertain that his remarks would secure their liberty.

Eastman admitted afterward that Judge Manton's advice to the jury was remarkably evenhanded: Manton "declared that anyone in the United States could say that the war was not a 'war of democracy,' that it was an imperialist war, that the government of the United States was hypocritical—in sum, he reminded the jury that even under the Espionage Act, every American had the right to criticize his government and oppose its policies, so long as he did not intend to discourage enlistment and recruiting or cause mutiny and disobedience in the armed forces." Charged with this straightforward advice, the jury retired and proceeded to debate the case, returning a day later with the news that, like the last jury, it was deadlocked. There was no likelihood that further deliberations would result in a guilty verdict, since eight of the twelve men declared themselves firmly in favor of acquittal. Judge Manton dismissed the jury and declared a second mistrial. Afterward the government dropped the indictment against the *Masses* editors and contributors for good.

Like the other defendants, Dell was much relieved at the conclusion of the second trial, but his confusions were by no means diminished as he returned to everyday life. His opinions on the war had shifted wildly in the course of the past year. Now in the early fall of 1918, even while he lamented the deployment of American troops against Soviet Russia, he remained convinced that Germany must be defeated. And while as a socialist and supporter of the Soviets he felt alienated from the American majority, he nonetheless was impressed by the fact that he had been set free—twice—by American juries. He continued to regard himself as a Greenwich Village bohemian, separated from ordinary American life. Yet what he hoped for, now more than ever, was a stable, productive life that would take him far away from the inconstant pleasures and consolations of bohemia.

Soon after the trial Dell and Millay, with John Reed, spent an evening riding the Staten Island ferry and walking along the Staten Island beach, celebrating the news of the coming armistice that Reed had received from one of his inside sources. In the months before the second trial Dell and Reed had worked more closely with each other than ever before. With Frank Harris, the editor of *Pearson's,* they had laid plans for a journal of modern literature to be called *These States.* Potential contributors included Randolph Bourne, Sherwood Anderson, and Van Wyck Brooks—writers who had been associated with the *Seven Arts,* which had also been a casualty of the war. Almost immediately, though, the project began to come unglued. The three editors were unable to agree on what they meant by "modernist literature," with Reed and Dell favoring realistic writings and Harris leaning toward more experimental works. When Harris stiffly refused to consider the poetry of Carl Sandburg for inclusion in the magazine, all three editors knew there was little chance of their ever agreeing on editorial policy. Soon all the potential financial backers had withdrawn their support from the venture, and the magazine was quickly forgotten.

Now in October, as Dell and Reed stood with Millay aboard the Staten Island ferry, the two men felt little in common. Dell watched uneasily as Millay encouraged Reed to recount his adventures. Reed had become a nearly mythic figure on the left, having written gripping accounts of the Ludlow massacre in Colorado, the war in Europe, and the Mexican and Russian revolutions. With *Ten Days That Shook the World* about to be published, Reed was "very much the Richard Harding Davis reporter hero" that Dorothy Day recalled in her autobiography. "Wherever there was excitement, wherever life was lived at high tension, there he was, writing, speaking, recording the moment, and heightening its intensity for everyone else." On the ferry Millay reveled in Reed's portrayal of himself as a man of incomprehensibly vast experience. Dell later recalled that, after listening for hours to Reed, Millay "cried, Desdamonaishly, 'I love you for the dangers you have passed.'" Dell suffered through the night, determined to end the relationship forever.

But Millay returned a last time, pregnant and inconsolable. Dell offered to arrange an abortion; the dilemma vanished when she miscarried shortly thereafter. Dell asked her, as he had before, to marry him. She said yes this time, agreeing when he remarked, "It looks as though we can't give each other up." She wished to preserve some degree of unconventionality in their relations, though, and insisted that she give him a ring rather than the other way around. She slipped a ring she had received from her mother on his little finger. The gesture, so individual and heartfelt, led him to hope, if only for a few days, that this time they might find lasting happiness together.

But within a few weeks Dell realized that the marriage should not take place. Millay told him she had gone to bed with a prizefighter, but that she had not made love to the man, resolved as she now was to remain faithful to Dell. Dell was shocked by her admission, though this time he hid his feelings from her. Afterward he returned the ring, offering no comment. She accepted its return without requiring an explanation.

It was October. The *Masses* trials were behind him now, the future more uncertain than it had been since his last days in Chicago. Dell admitted that his relations with Millay had brought him little happiness. As he faced a life without Edna Millay, without the *Masses*, Dell was desperate to find some new course that would bring him satisfaction as a writer and as a man.

Postwar Novelist

GREENWICH VILLAGE was a changed place in the fall of 1918. Even in the years between 1913 and 1917, when the Village was notorious as a hotbed of bohemianism, it had begun to lose its separateness from mainstream America. Middle-class Americans viewed the Village bohemians with growing fascination. Soon that same middle class was venturing into the Village, eating at its restaurants, aping its manners and styles of dress, reading its stories, attending its plays, buying its artworks.

There was money to be made catering to the curiosity of these middle-class interlopers. Villagers liked to claim they were appalled by the invading hordes of bourgeoisie. It would be more accurate to say that they reacted with a confusion of feelings. They were flattered to be regarded by so many as extraordinary creatures; but they were also inclined to respond with militant snobbishness and withdrawal into what were still inviolate bohemian circles. In any case, there were always people on hand willing to sell the Village and its unconventional atmosphere to whomever had the money. Restaurants like Grace Godwin's Garret, tearooms like the Mad Hatter, sightseeing tours through the streets, shops, and studios—all catered to the multiplying hordes of tourists. Dell described afterward how things changed:

> Greenwich Village had become commercialized during the war. The little basement and garret restaurants, decorated according to our own taste, proved a lure to up-towners, who came into the Village with their pockets full of money and their hearts full of

a pathetic eagerness to participate in the celebrated joys of Bohemian life. The restaurants responded by laying on Village quaintness in thick daubs, to tickle the fancy of the visiting bourgeoisie; and every month new restaurants sprang up underfoot and overhead to meet the demands of this new clientele.

For Dell the Village of 1918 was "a show-place, where there was no longer any privacy from the vulgar stares of an up-town rabble." Village institutions—restaurants, pubs, the Provincetown Playhouse—filled up with pleasure-seekers for whom the Village was an entertainment venue. One night, sitting over a cup of coffee in a restaurant, Dell was confronted by a gaggle of tourists who asked, "Are you a merry Villager?" He swore at them and stormed out, appalled to discover that his Village could disappear so fast.

Still, the relation between the Villagers and the invading middle class was not a simple one, as Dell vaguely and uneasily realized. From the start, Villagers like Dell and the *Masses* crew had aimed for more, in their relations with the mainstream, than merely *épater la bourgeoisie.* They had preferred to imagine themselves prophets, political activists, cultural revolutionaries. Perhaps they were reluctant to conciliate anyone, as the *Masses* bragged, but they certainly aimed to win converts to their sundry causes. They had wished to remake America, to effect a vast cultural and political transformation of the national landscape. Now their first wave of converts was flooding into the Village, eager to sample the liberation from cultural and personal constraints that magazines like the *Masses* had long promised.

In fact the arrival of the "up-towners" in Greenwich Village signaled that bohemia had actually begun to transform the nation. The problem was that this transformation was not proving especially pleasant. That many established Villagers were repulsed by the newcomers may have been due partly to the fact that these intruders had vulgarized their bohemian example. But some members of the avant-garde realized that the "bohemianization" of America might have unfortunate consequences—that converts to bohemia might pick up on the Village's devotion to spontaneity, pleasure, and ecstasy without taking notice of the Village's more serious political and cultural ideas. Dell had long found some of the Village's features vulgar and specious. Now he watched as those features proved irresistible to outsiders.

There was a special irony in this situation for Dell in 1918, since at precisely that moment he wished to leave bohemia and live a more conventional life. Bohemia seemed inevitably marked by fleeting pleasures. Now that he craved something more substantial, Dell was surprised to discover middle-class America lining up at Greenwich Village's gate.

PART OF THE Village's growing appeal for the middle class, as Dell vaguely realized at the time, had to do with the changes that took place in bohemia itself during the final year of World War I and the years just afterward—in its turn to cultural and "personal" issues that, far more than radical political causes, seemed to answer to the interests of the American people. Historians have argued that as the war drew to a close, the volatile mix of political and cultural radicalism that characterized the American avant-garde in the years between 1910 and 1917 began to fall apart, resulting in tiny enclaves of hard-core political radicals and a much greater number of cultural rebels. Malcolm Cowley provided the classic statement of this theory when he wrote that the prewar Village's heady brew of *"bohemianism* and *radicalism"* dissolved under the pressure exerted by war hysteria and the draft: "People were suddenly forced to decide what kind of rebels they were: if they were merely rebels against puritanism they could continue to exist safely in Mr. Wilson's world. The political rebels had no place in it." Meanwhile, Cowley claimed, the cultural vanguard flourished. "The bohemian tendency triumphed in the Village, and talk about revolution gave way to talk about psychoanalysis."

Dell regretted the fact that the exhilarating mix of radical politics and cultural ambitions epitomized by the prewar Village was never entirely recovered afterward. But the situation was complicated in Dell's case by his own growing reluctance, in 1917 and 1918, to devote all his time and imagination to political causes. Years later he speculated that he had begun to write about education and Freudianism because he sensed the eventual disillusionment he would feel about the Bolsheviks and American radicalism: "It now occurs to me that I was developing various interests which would occupy my mind after the subsequent collapse of post-war Communist hopes." Yet Dell was also determined to sharpen his understanding of the political and economic dimensions of culture. In this regard his career during the 1920s poses a notable exception to Cowley's portrait of a postwar literary scene devoid of political consciousness. In his continuing efforts to understand the relation between literature and politics, Dell attempted to perpetuate—and improve upon—the earlier Village practice.

Early glimmers of this effort were evident in the articles on education that he published in the *Liberator* in the summer and fall of 1918. The book he eventually compiled from the essays, *Were You Ever a Child?* (published in 1919), is informal, conversational, ironic. Its chapters devoted to delineating the ideals, conditions, and failures of American education are punctuated by fictionalized dialogues with children, citizens, artists, and philosophers. In dramatized colloquies between educational reformers and skeptics, Dell permitted himself to layer on jokes and hyperbole. There was a ready insight into the experience of children in classrooms: their frustrations with the instruction they encountered, the stultifying textbooks they were forced to read, the rigid course of study they found mapped out for them beforehand. Dell's sympathy was for the imaginative child, whom he described as stymied rather than liberated by the education he or she received. His aim, he announced halfway through *Were You Ever a Child?*, was to imagine an educational system fully adequate to the needs of such a child—adequate, moreover, to the closely related needs of a democratic culture and society.

Much of Dell's argument was based on the pragmatic theory of education that had been developed by John Dewey and implemented by William Wirt in the Gary, Indiana, schools. Dell insisted that the essence of traditional education in the United States had been its dissociation from "reality"—from the world outside the classroom where the student would eventually have to live and work. In classic pragmatic style, he argued that "truth is reality brought into vital contact with the mind. . . . For truth does not reside in something outside the child's mind; reality becomes truth only when it is made a part of his living." Remembering his own school days and the subsequent shock of trying to find his way in the world, Dell wrote that "the values which had obtained there did not exist outside. One could not cram for a job as if it were an examination; one could not get in the good graces of a machine as if it were a teacher; the docility which won high 'marks' in school was called lack of enterprise in the business world, dulness in social life, stupidity in the realm of love. The values of real life were new and different."

Often Dell reformulated progressive ideas in strikingly original fashion. In one such passage, questions about the child's artistic nature led to the larger question of art's relation to the world. Dell paused before the dilemma that had perplexed him for years: whether to commit himself to worldly tasks and aspirations, or to remain apart and devote himself to the appreciation and creation of artistic works. The artist-child, he wrote, "is content to live in that little corner of life in which he can play undisturbed by worldly interests." Dell claimed that modern adult artists had accepted this essential division between art and "the world," asserting their own radical separation from all other interests. Indeed, modern writers had affirmed their separation from the world by exerting irresistible pressure on one another not to write clearly about recognizable human problems and aspirations: " 'The artist must not be a propagandist,' it is declared indignantly. And finally it comes to such a pass that it is not artistic good-form for the artist to tell stories which the public can understand—the painter is prohibited from making images which the common man is able to recognize—the musician scorns to compose tunes which anybody could dance to or whistle!" Dell then proceeded to a formulation which he had been seeking for more than a decade:

> But the artist cannot get along without the world. His art springs from the commonest impulses of the human race, and those impulses are utilitarian at root;... When art becomes divorced from the aspirations of the common man, all its technical perfection will not keep it alive; it revolts against its own technical perfection, and goes off into quaint and austere quests for new truths upon which to nourish itself; and only when it discovers the common man and fulfils his unfulfilled desires, does it flourish again. Art must concern itself with the world, or perish.

His focus on education and art was enriched by passages of shrewd political analysis. He related the authoritarian educational programs of the late nineteenth and early twentieth centuries to the capitalist desire for an efficient work force. What he recognized in American public education was a deliberate effort to prepare young people for lives as obedient wage slaves. Nor were the social relations that interested Dell in these articles confined to those between labor and capital: they also included the social and economic relations between the sexes. What Dell described as particularly unfortunate in traditional education was the preparation of boys and girls for vastly different lives: boys for work in the public world, girls for domestic tasks. As such, education had figured as an essential element in a social system committed to perpetuating inequalities between the sexes. In the end, Dell claimed, both men and women suffered: all were prevented from cultivating talents that the educational system fostered only in members of the opposite sex.

Dell argued that in the modern world—characterized by heightened economic pressures—women were placed in a peculiarly vulnerable position. Educated for home life, they now found themselves thrown into the workplace. One of the few places where women were able to find work, he noted, was in the schools. But since women had not been prepared by their educations for a life in the public realm, they were unable to impart such knowledge to their students. Faced with youngsters in need of educations that would bring them into productive contact with the world, Dell wrote, society had handed them over to a class of women ill prepared to facilitate that contact.

Other champions of progressive education emphasized the need for contact with reality. What Dell was uniquely alert to was how modern educational dilemmas were part of larger social ills. Still, he had no desire to write a despairing book. For all its emphasis on the underlying sources of cultural and educational failure, *Were You Ever a Child?* was infused with the conviction that America could reform its schools and thereby revitalize society as a whole. In addition, the book pointed toward a solution to a problem that had troubled Dell for years. In his blunt assertion that the artist's work was essentially connected to the world, rather than a refuge from it, Dell was already moving beyond the bohemian gospel which he had begun to find less than satisfactory in Greenwich Village. More than a book on education, *Were You Ever a Child?* was an essential step in Dell's progress as a critic and novelist.

THE HOPEFUL FLAVOR of *Were You Ever a Child?* makes it easy to forget that Dell was enmeshed during much of its composition in the final months of his unhappy love affair with Edna Millay. An effervescence about the book—not to mention a robust interest in children,

family life, and love—seems strange coming from a man unhappy in
his love life. The book's optimism suggests that Dell was not entirely
devastated by that turn of events.

For some while he had wanted to break with Millay. Even in the
midst of their romance he had begun to imagine a different kind of
woman with whom he might have a better chance for lasting
happiness. His requirements, as he later described them with self-
deprecating irony, suggest a mix of radical and conservative impulses
as well as growing skepticism about the compatibility of unqualified
feminism and domestic happiness: "She must have had, like me, a
socialist background. She must be capable of supporting herself for a
while. She must want to have children. She must be well educated.
She must have good taste in literature. She must not have any
fanatical ambition to be a writer, a painter, an actress, a musician.
She must be truthful and courageous. She must have a sense of
humor."

Little more than a month after returning Millay's ring and
breaking with her for good, Dell met another woman and fell in love
again. This new romantic liaison was made possible by Alex Gumberg, a close friend who had immigrated to the United States from
Russia in 1903, at age sixteen. Gumberg returned to Russia in June
1917 as a representative for a group of American businesses interested in plying their trades abroad. He stayed long enough to
witness the Bolshevik Revolution in October. After he returned to
the United States in June 1918 he regaled Dell with tales of the
Revolution and of the new Soviet society. Gumberg was seeing an
independent-minded young woman named Frances Adams, known
to everyone as Frankie. Dell frequently accompanied Gumberg to
Frankie Adams's Greenwich Village apartment, where the talk
ranged from Gumberg's adventures in Russia to Adams's work in the
free-speech movement.

Her roommate was Berta Marie Gage, a twenty-four-year-old
newcomer to the Village. Dell was smitten at once. Born in
Minnesota, B. Marie had moved as a child to Pasadena, California,
where as an adolescent she took up all manner of radical causes:
socialism, feminism, pacifism, free speech. Like Dell she had been
tried under the Espionage Act—in her case, for distributing antiwar
literature during the war. She too had managed to elude government
conviction. Dell was later to acknowledge the role her defense
attorney, John Beardsley, played in winning her freedom at the trial.

But he mainly attributed her successful defense to B. Marie herself: "her youth and courage and candor—and without doubt her good looks, too, her blue eyes, golden hair and peaches-and-cream complexion—were much in her favor, and she heard with astonishment the Prosecutor plead her case for her." How could anyone, Dell wondered, fail to fall in love with this remarkable young woman?

The two were also quite different. B. Marie was outgoing and robust, with untamed blond hair and expressive features. Dell was slender, bordering on frail; unlike B. Marie, he was inclined to be nervous, introspective, moody. B. Marie was eager to devote herself wholeheartedly to political causes, much in contrast to Dell's increasingly diffident attitude toward time-consuming political commitments.

As a student at the University of Wisconsin, B. Marie had organized a free-speech movement during the war. She was an unyielding proponent of women's suffrage. Upon her arrival in Greenwich Village she had gone to work for the Woman's party and, soon afterward, for the Near East Relief foundation. In public and in private life she was confident and straightforward—a forceful young woman who knew her mind and had no reluctance expressing it. Unhappy with her first name, she had simply rechristened herself B. Marie. She formed political and personal convictions with similarly unambiguous resolve. When she met Dell's occasional housekeeper, a black woman from Georgia named Mamie Golden, the two formed an instantaneous bond. B. Marie even helped Mamie Golden overcome her alcoholism in 1918 and 1919.

Dell was fascinated by B. Marie's forthright manner and confidence. He had always admired women, trusting their judgment and steadiness of purpose. One result of this had been his willingness since adolescence to attach himself to older women. Now he had met a woman seven years younger than he who impressed him equally much. "I fell in love with B. Marie at once, recognizing her as the most splendid young woman I had ever seen; and we were everywhere together from that moment."

Dell was by no means inclined to let bohemian principle stand in the way of his desire to marry B. Marie. On only their third meeting he proposed marriage. Wisely, she refused. She had already heard much about his reputation as a bohemian and inconstant lover. Something of Dorothy Day's view of Dell in 1917—that he should have carried on his love affairs "on the stage of the Hippodrome before a packed house"—still clung to him in late 1918. B. Marie was not so vain as to regard herself as somehow different from Dell's earlier lovers.

She was also reluctant to enter into so disreputable, so conventional an arrangement as marriage. She preferred to remain unattached, to devote herself to political causes. But Dell persisted, telling B. Marie all about his Village life—about his romances, certainly, but also about his growing dissatisfaction with transient affairs. He gave her chapters of his unfinished autobiographical novel to read. Still she refused and talked about returning to her home in California.

Ten weeks passed. Both lovers had bouts of uncertainty about the other. There was also undeniable rapport between them. Radical politics, bohemian tastes, feminist convictions, but also underlying desires for a monogamous sexual relation and family life—all these drew them together. Much time was spent at Dell's Christopher Street apartment. A preposterously narrow wooden house nestled between more robust stone buildings, 11 Christopher Street seemed to epitomize the out-of-the-way glamour of Greenwich Village that was disappearing in the very days when Floyd and B. Marie were falling in love.

When B. Marie dropped her objections in early February, they decided to marry at once. That weekend, accompanied by Alex Gumberg and Frankie Adams, they headed for City Hall in New York, where they spoke with an official who insisted that Dell present documentary proof of his divorce—a requirement that the official soon conceded was not strictly necessary by law, but that so infuriated Dell that he refused to pursue the matter further. B. Marie was surprised by Dell's fury: she had never seen him so righteously angry before. They were both nervous and agreed they should get married at a more hospitable place. The four proceeded to Jersey City, a ferry ride from New York, where they encountered more obstacles, including the very real restriction that they could only be married twenty-four hours after applying for a license. They headed back to New York.

Once in the city, Dell recalled that he and B. Marie had been invited to visit Jane Burr, a writer who ran a lodge called the Drowsy Saint Inn in Croton-on-Hudson, a suburb north of the city in Westchester County. The couple took off for Croton in the hope that a justice of the peace would marry them there. When they arrived, Jane Burr was happy to discover they had taken up her invitation but shocked by their plan to marry. She was, she informed them, opposed to marriage in principle. She also doubted that Dell, whom she had known for years in the Village, was suited for married life. Shortly she gave in, phoning the town clerk and asking him to prepare a marriage license, then arranging for a Judge Decker to marry them. The couple asked for the simplest ceremony possible (Dell worried that B. Marie would raise feminist objections to any number of passages and vows along the way). Afterward B. Marie said she did not want a marriage certificate. But the wedding was satisfactory to everyone involved. Years later Jane Burr remembered how they had walked home afterward through the snowy streets, B. Marie racing up and down Croton's icy hills, shouting to Burr not to worry about falling down. At ten o'clock that evening, as they sat down with Jane Burr to a home-cooked meal and impromptu wedding cake (donated by a neighbor, who had intended it for her own family's Sunday luncheon), Dell realized that the new life he had been imagining for some while was suddenly upon him.

AFTER THEIR MARRIAGE Dell and B. Marie lived in the house on Christopher Street, moving into the upstairs apartment and settling into an intimate, productive life. The place was a mixture of bohemian intimacy, glamour, and inconveniences: "outside toilet; baths in the kitchen sink; candlelight and kerosene lamps, wood for the little fireplace brought in a sack by Nick from around the corner." The rooms were large with high ceilings, the windows hung with bright-orange curtains. Nordfeldt's portrait of Dell as a fin-de-siècle aesthete hung on the wall along with Japanese prints that Dell had received from Arthur Ficke.

The Dells' happiness, though, was not likely to last long in their Christopher Street abode. For all its intimate, bohemian ambience, it remained a rented apartment in the midst of an increasingly commercialized Village. What Floyd yearned for was a home. B. Marie was less certain that she wanted a house of their own: to her it smacked too much of premature domesticity. But Floyd was adamant. For years he had used his cabin in the New Jersey hinterlands as a refuge from urban distractions, as a place where he could devote himself to his myriad writing projects. Now he wanted a home where they could settle permanently. He wanted a place where he could work on his novel.

These literary and domestic concerns did not altogether supplant political passions. Floyd and B. Marie were central participants at a March 1919 suffrage rally in New York that turned violent. In a protest aimed at President Wilson, a group of suffragists (the Dells among them) confronted a mob of men—"soldiers, seamen and citizens," in the words of the *New York Tribune*—and a general melee ensued. The riot continued all the way back to suffrage headquarters on East Forty-first Street. According to the *Tribune*, "a man dressed in overalls wrestled with Mrs. Bertha Dell to take a banner from her, and when her husband, Floyd, went to her assistance he was assaulted. He fought back with vigor, but was badly handled and sustained a cut lip in the fracas. The women formed a flying football wedge and rescued him." Afterward, when Floyd and B. Marie boarded a Fifth Avenue bus, a mob of more than a hundred men came after them again. The *Tribune* reported that "several attempts were made to drag Dell from the motor bus, and a man in overalls, who was active in the earlier fighting, tried to climb up the steps." Another suffragist, Rhoda Hunt, knocked the man to the pavement by poking him in the chest with a banner pole. Only then did policemen rein in the crowd and allow the bus, the Dells safely on board, to depart the scene.

At other times the couple seemed to retreat entirely from public concerns into private happiness. B. Marie's birthday came in April 1919, and Dell gave her a birthday sonnet that testified to the first flush of pleasure he had found in marriage. Yet for all the poem's romantic language and mood, it is B. Marie's will and independence—not her union with him—that Dell emphasizes:

> Not only that I love you—that in you
> I find old dreams incredibly come true,
> And you in every dream, world without end,
> Goddess and girl-child, lover and guest and friend:
> Not only that I love you, seeking still
> To bend and break the guarding of your will,
> And find, behind your stubbornness, the splendor
> Of body and soul in triumph of surrender:
> But that, deep under deep, in you I find
> Something to my caresses deaf and blind—

Something not mine to take nor yours to give,
But only by whose light our love may live.
Lovelier in you than all your laughing youth
Is that which holds love lightly beside truth.

That same day they took the train to Croton-on-Hudson to visit friends. Besides Jane Burr there were other transplanted Villagers living in Croton: John Reed, Louise Bryant, Max Eastman, the radical journalist Albert Rhys Williams, the *Masses* artist Boardman Robinson, and others. When Floyd and B. Marie arrived they came across a troupe of friends walking down Mount Airy Road, where Eastman and several others from Greenwich Village had already bought homes. Among the crowd walking toward them was John Reed, who proclaimed: "This is the Mount Airy Soviet, and we have decided that you two are to live here in Croton. And this is the house you are to live in!" The house was small but for sale. Dell wanted it immediately. B. Marie was not as enthusiastic about buying the place. But Floyd insisted, handing over ten dollars as down payment. Later that month he was able to finance the transaction, and the house became their own.

When Floyd and B. Marie returned to Croton on May 1 they went to work at once on the house. They tore down rotten woodwork, weeded and replanted the garden, painted the entire house. They spent most of their time in Croton that summer, renovating the house while Dell continued to work on his writing projects. Evenings were spent in endless talk with friends. That fall the Dells returned to the Village, spending only weekends in Croton.

All the while Dell worried about his novel which remained, despite intermittent bursts of productivity, unfinishable. Other projects seemed always to take precedence. Alfred A. Knopf, a young New York publisher eager to bring the writings of young American novelists and social critics into print, pressed Dell that summer to turn his articles on education into a book—encouragement that flattered Dell and that he readily took up, adding chapters and shaping all into an engaging whole.

Were You Ever a Child? was published to good notices in September 1919. A review for the *Dial* noted that Dell's "studied audacity and his pleasing conversational prose should be sufficiently stimulating to awaken reflection in the minds of those who have never been forced by experience to examine the debris of what has been called an education." The *Chicago Tribune*'s Elia W. Peattie described *Child?* as alternately "exhilarating" and "absurd." "At least he is not hackneyed," she concluded, "though he does to an extent follow trails which have already been blazed if not much trodden."

Dell was flattered by the attention and excited by news that the book was soon to be translated and published in the Soviet Union. (It was in fact translated into Russian, but the Soviets decided at last not to publish the book: Dell's arguments for liberating each individual child's mind, they apparently realized, in no way suited their own agenda.) But he remained unsatisfied even with the success of this book. He was regarded by friends and the public at large as an author, but he did not yet feel himself to be a true author—not without a novel to his credit. As the year 1919 ran out, he felt desperate to turn his half-formed chapters into a book. That winter, back at Christopher Street, he began to realize that he would need to cut back on other projects if he was to accomplish the large-scale literary tasks he had imagined for himself for more than a decade.

IN EARLY FALL he and B. Marie had taken their first real holiday together, a hiking trip through the Vermont countryside. They spent a week alone together—"carrying packs on our backs, with blankets and simple cooking utensils, cooking our meals at a fire built by the roadside, and sleeping usually in the woods or fields." Even here, work was not absent from Dell's mind. That week he imagined the outline of an ambitious book, a critical study spanning the period from the early eighteenth century to the present and focusing on the fate of the literary intelligentsia in Europe and the United States during the era of industrialization. Even in embryonic form the book presented itself to Dell as something unprecedented in American criticism: an effort to understand the evolution of significant literary ideas in connection with the economic, technological, and political features of the modern world. When the couple returned to New York, Dell sketched out the book and began to write portions of it.

But he found too little time to devote to the book. Dell was as swamped with editorial duties at the *Liberator* as he had been at the *Masses*. He contributed several essays, sometimes more, each month. In the December 1919 issue alone he contributed reviews on a daunting array of books: one by Louis Untermeyer on recent American poetry; a collection of poems by Babette Deutsch; Albert

Rhys Williams's *Lenin: The Man and His Work*; H. L. Mencken's *Prejudices: First Series*; and several others. In January there were reviews of Joseph Conrad's *The Arrow of Gold* and Waldo Frank's *Our America*. Dell was as much in the middle of the literary scene as he had been in Chicago and at the *Masses*. But there was less satisfaction for him now than before. By January 1920 he was desperate to get away from the *Liberator*, at least for a while.

That January he made arrangements with Max Eastman for a three-month leave of absence from the *Liberator*. It was to begin February 1—but when the day arrived Eastman pleaded with him to stay a while longer, at least until the next issue was finished. Dell reluctantly agreed: the men had always worked easily together, and Dell was unwilling to leave Eastman in the lurch. But the postponement of his leave reduced Dell to something like despair. He began having terrible headaches; a doctor diagnosed them as due to a sinus inflammation, but Dell suspected they were psychological in origin. "I 'associated' to the subject for an hour," Dell recalled, "and the headaches disappeared completely. I knew why I had them; the fact was that I was homesick for work on my novel, and unwilling to postpone it." With new resolve he insisted that his leave begin at once. Eastman reluctantly agreed.

Dell went to work day and night on the novel he had struggled with for more than half a decade. The chapters he had already accumulated were good ones in many regards, he thought, but years of constant, obsessive revision had made them "too polished, too much like a prose poem." Something more natural was what he now wanted.

After years as a literary journalist he had developed a deceptively simple writing style: clear and straightforward, emphasizing content and ideas, rarely calling attention to itself, eschewing anything resembling modernist or obscurantist techniques. A scent of irony could be found in his writings, mixed with an effort to illuminate the matter at hand. These features of his work were overwhelmed in the unfinished chapters of his novel which had become too self-conscious for Dell's taste. Working in the Christopher Street apartment (with occasional weekends in Croton), Dell began to rewrite these chapters in what he later called "a simpler and more flexible narrative style. . . . I had come to detest tricks of style," he noted, "and I wished to write a prose that was clear as air, through which life itself could be seen without the distortion of the writer's temperament, which had sufficiently exercised its prerogative in the selection of the facts to be viewed." As he rewrote the book it seemed to grow effortlessly. All at once the novel that had eluded him for years began to take on an impressive shape.

The book that Dell finished in May 1920 and handed over to Knopf for publication was a vivid reimagining of his own early years in the Midwest. Nothing in Dell's earlier writings suggested that he was capable of a book as original and deeply felt as *Moon-Calf*. Before he had often been limited by the need to make a polemical or satiric point. Character and plot tended to be subordinated to other things—the desire to lampoon conventional society or to examine modern ideas and the avant-garde.

In *Moon-Calf*, on the other hand, Dell was able to put his usual polemical interests aside and concentrate in convincing detail on his young protagonist's unfolding life. Telling the story of Felix Fay, based on his own younger self, Dell painted fictional portraits of his parents and siblings and of his family's trek from Barry to Quincy to Davenport (in *Moon-Calf* the towns are renamed Maple, Vickley, and Port Royal). Much of the novel's detail was drawn directly from Dell's past. Other details were altered or invented. Most important in this regard was Dell's treatment of Felix's character. "I left out of the story, or 'played down,' my hero's energies," Dell noted; "I was actually unaware of, or completely forgetful of, when writing the story, his social capacities, thinking of him as being always a shy, lonely, sensitive youth, and not as a bumptious, aggressive fellow, which he was at times; and I emphasized and, to my present view, somewhat sentimentalized him as a dreamer, easily hurt by the world."

A good portion of Dell's interest in *Moon-Calf* centers on how Felix Fay's character is shaped by the evolving circumstances in which he lives. Crucial is the Fay family's worsening poverty during the years when Felix is growing up. Dell drew liberally on his own family's history: the collapse of his father's butcher business; his mother's anguish about the family's loss of a respectable place in society; his older siblings' early entrapment in unfulfilling industrial jobs; the family's migration from town to town in search of better jobs.

But Dell had no desire to present Felix's story solely as a function of economic circumstances. He may earlier have praised Dreiser's *Sister Carrie* for its portrayal of men and women in the grip of circumstances beyond their control, but he was determined not to repeat this approach in his own novel. His portrait of Felix Fay in

Moon-Calf stressed Felix's own responsibility for his failures. As the book progresses it becomes apparent that Felix is frustrated as much by his own carefully nourished alienation from respectable society as by impersonal economic conditions. His early absorption in books and dreams, the romantic-poet persona that he adopts as an adolescent, his perverse reluctance to succeed at school and as a cub reporter in Port Royal—all demonstrate Felix's willful alienation from the respectable world.

Dell was able to regard Felix's withdrawal both with sympathy and detachment. "I should define a 'moon-calf,' briefly, as an awkward young man with a touch of intellectual lunacy," he explained in a piece published at the time in the *New York Tribune*. He seems to have picked up the term from H. G. Wells, who had used it some years before in his story "The First Men in the Moon." There Wells had described certain laborers among the creatures living on the moon as "mooncalf-herdsmen": stunted, largely formless beings that performed the same simple tasks day after day. If Dell's use of the term "moon-calf" called up the popular usage—that is, of an innocent youth, dreamy and moonstruck—it also echoed Wells's usage, evoking an indistinct, largely undifferentiated creature. For all Felix's willful character, there is something half-formed about him. He is chronically uncertain, confused, aimless. The novel traces his effort to overcome that crippling uncertainty, to arrive at a sturdy perspective and distinctive, forceful personality. An ironic Bildungsroman, *Moon-Calf* at last reveals this effort to be no more than partially successful. In the end Felix confronts nothing so clearly as his own perverse failure to pursue wholeheartedly any tangible success in the world.

Personal failure is overwhelmingly present in *Moon-Calf*'s closing pages, when Felix's love affair with Joyce Tennant ends with Joyce's decision to marry another man. Their affair, patterned on Dell's real-life affair during his last year in Davenport, is presented as passionate but secret, divorced from the public world where Felix and Joyce otherwise live. Felix urges Joyce to think of their love as utterly private, even otherworldly. Their romantic trysts take place outdoors, often at a solitary cabin on an island in the Mississippi. For Felix, "he and Joyce were somehow not mere anxious lovers, but beings suspended in space, between sky and water, where nothing mattered except truth, and that beauty which is the same as truth." Felix tells her that he will never offer her "ordinary happiness." " 'I

don't want it for myself, and I don't offer it to *you*.'" When Joyce
asks him what he means, he explains that he rejects the notion of
"conventional marriage"—the "'conventional idea of how people
who are in love with each other ought to behave. They are supposed
to own each other. And belong, both of them, to a home.'"

Joyce is confused by Felix's opposition to marriage and home life.
For a while she dismisses her apprehensions, enjoying their evenings
together, amused by her unworldly poet-lover. At last, though, she
realizes that their romance is inevitably temporary. When she
decides to marry the respectable young man who has been courting
her for months, Felix is unable to talk her out of it. Until this
moment it had been Felix who had provided them with an understanding of their relations. Now it is Joyce who defines their love and
the reasons for its failure. Their romance, she explains, "'was an
outdoor, holiday sort of love. It was an adventure—for both of us.'"
Love, she says, was in the end not enough for her. "'I had my fling,
as you call it; and then I discovered I wanted something else.'" Her
desire for marriage and family—for love in the world, rather than as
an escape from it—finally overcomes her attachment to Felix. Her
decision baffles and demoralizes him. Mixed with great unhappiness
at losing her is his dim recognition that her decision is right. He
realizes that the end of their affair represents his own failure to play
out his ambitions—romantic, literary, professional—in the contingent, human world.

Finishing the manuscript that spring, Dell suspected he had
achieved something like the personal and artistic maturity that Felix
would have found incomprehensible and terrifying. Married, and
with his long-anticipated novel finally completed, Dell had reason to
feel he had at last become the sort of productive citizen of the world
that Felix Fay half envied, half despised.

Moon-Calf WAS published that October. For a few weeks it attracted
little attention. Then enthusiastic reviews began to surface. One, by
Heywood Broun, appeared in the *New York Tribune*: "Drop whatever
you are doing and read Floyd Dell's *Moon-Calf*. Yes, *Main Street*
can wait. . . . No writer of our day has gone so fully or so deeply into
the heart of a child." People began buying the book in great
numbers, and a series of printings followed in rapid succession.
Favorable reviews appeared in newspapers and magazines across the

country. *Moon-Calf* emerged as a minor sensation, appearing on best-seller lists and becoming the object of a great deal of critical and casual discussion. Harry Hansen announced in the *Chicago Daily News* that *Moon-Calf* is "the clearest and most promising note struck in American literature in our day and generation." H. L. Mencken, who had counted Dell among the "red-ink" crowd that he generally despised, commended the book's "very competent writing" and its lack of political propaganda. Placing the book among the best of 1920, the *Chicago Tribune*'s Fanny Butcher described *Moon-Calf* as "a fine, free, honest, sincerely beautiful piece of work." Suddenly Dell, whose reputation had hitherto been confined chiefly to the literary vanguard, was a novelist known to mainstream readers across the country.

Most satisfying to Dell was the praise that came from novelists whose work he admired. Sherwood Anderson, whom Dell had championed nearly a decade earlier in Chicago, but with whom Dell had more recently fallen out, wrote a letter of undisguised praise and affection. "The book makes me love and understand you as I never have before," Anderson wrote. "What a very sensitive fine figure you have been. And this book—clean straight writing—. . . everything a fine novel should have." Upton Sinclair, whose novel *The Jungle* had been among the first fictional works to impress Dell as a teenager, and whom Dell had come to know in Greenwich Village, wrote, "I have called you the best reviewer in the country, and now I'll add *one* of the best novelists!" Most gratifying of all was a letter from Theodore Dreiser. He praised *Moon-Calf* as "an intimate and faithful picture of middle west American life." Then he closed: "You spoke of yourself as a follower of mine. More flattering. I ask nothing more of life as a testimony than that it honor me with a few such. Yes, I will be content with you alone."

Years later Dell modestly attributed *Moon-Calf*'s success as much to popular misperceptions of the book as to widespread recognition of its virtues. All modesty aside, Dell had a point. Shortly before *Moon-Calf* was published in October 1920, Sinclair Lewis's *Main Street* and Zona Gale's *Miss Lulu Bett* had appeared, both attacking Midwestern, small-town conformity and intolerance. Dell described these books as "the best sellers of that year, marking a revulsion of feeling against the mob-hysteria of the war period; and my novel, which was usually referred to in all the reviews along with 'Main Street,' was carried along with it to a considerable sale." In 1920 and afterward Dell found this a preposterous basis for *Moon-Calf*'s success. "It was often described in reviews as an exposé of the Middle West," he noted, "which was ridiculously untrue." Rather, he had intended the book as "an exposé of 'Felix Fay.'" He even claimed initially to have believed that "Sinclair Lewis's novel was intended as an exposé of Carol Kennicott, not of Main Street."

Dell had infused a great deal of tenderness toward Midwestern life throughout *Moon-Calf*; little in the book resembled the satiric venom of Lewis's portrait of Gopher Prairie. Most of Dell's satire had been persistently directed at Felix himself. "I knew better than to think of him as a model or ideal personage," Dell remembered. Felix "had a great deal to learn about life, and it had taken me ten years and much pain to learn it." Still the fact that so many young people identified with Felix was sufficient to give Dell pause. He was surprised to discover how many people accepted Felix as a perfectly sympathetic American youth, understandably uncertain about himself and his place in the world. "I was said to have described what was going on among the young people of America as a result of their disillusionment by the war. And, oddly enough, there seemed to be some truth in that. Post-war youth wrote letters to me confirming that notion."

Although Dell was willing to concede that Felix Fay might stand for the confusions and rebelliousness of modern youth, he was certain he was aiming at something altogether different from younger novelists like F. Scott Fitzgerald, with whom he was often compared. Dell had little taste for Fitzgerald's glamorous portrayal of confusion and despair in *This Side of Paradise*, published that same year. Certainly he did not share Fitzgerald's fascination with reckless, wealthy types. Dell was happy to discover that so many young readers were moved by Felix's story, but he was determined to preserve the meaning of that story for himself. For Dell, Felix was a failure as a man and as an artist; he had failed to achieve those forms of success—marriage and solid literary work—that would have been the proper outcome of his striving. For readers who failed to grasp this meaning behind Felix's story, Dell resolved to write a second book, a sequel in which the meaning of Felix's story would become unmistakable. That story he began in the fall of 1920, as *Moon-Calf* was earning Dell his first taste of the kind of literary fame he had dreamed of—in his own moon-calfish way—since the days of his own Midwestern boyhood.

"Literature and the Machine Age"

DELL WORKED ON *The Briary-Bush*, the sequel to *Moon-Calf*, through the fall of 1920 and into the following winter. Responsibilities at the *Liberator*, to which he had returned full time in the late spring of 1920, again made his progress difficult. Perhaps it was the commercial and critical success of *Moon-Calf* that emboldened Dell to take a second extended leave from the *Liberator* to work on his account of Felix Fay. Whatever the case, in the early months of 1921 he again left his desk at the magazine and holed up in New York and Croton, working long days and nights on his novel.

The Briary-Bush is set in Chicago, the scene of Dell's own youthful triumphs as a journalist and literary man. Felix Fay's life in the city echoes Dell's adventures. Felix arrives in Chicago at age twenty-one, eager to put his moon-calf tendencies behind him. Like Dell, Felix lives briefly at a settlement house, works as a reporter and critic at a respectable newspaper, and takes up with an assortment of earnest aesthetes, radical intellectuals, and drunken bohemians. Dell describes these barely fictionalized personages and scenes in a clear, unobtrusive prose that suggests a sincere desire to bring his old Chicago days vividly back to life. And yet these early pages also betray an easy detachment on Dell's part, as if these characters and incidents did not seize his imagination with the same intensity that had been evident in *Moon-Calf*.

The book's imperturbable air largely vanishes, though, when Felix

falls in love with Rose-Ann Prentiss, an independent young woman
from Springfield. Their marriage, performed in a country town
outside Chicago, is clearly drawn from Dell's marriage to B. Marie.
But the aftermath to their wedding—their uneasiness with domesticity, Felix's rise as a theater critic and well-known intellectual in
Chicago, their decision to move into a flat in a bohemian colony on
the city's South Side—all this is loosely inspired not by Dell's life
with B. Marie but rather by his first marriage, to Margery Currey. As
in the case of that unsatisfactory marriage, Felix and Rose-Ann are
soon miserable with each other. Both wish to avoid the usual traps of
matrimony: they agree not to let domestic concerns thwart their
careers, and each is reluctant to impinge on the other's freedom. At
the same time their renunciation of traditional forms and responsibilities seems to fill both (particularly Felix) with uneasiness. Again
as in Dell's first marriage, crisis in Felix and Rose-Ann's marriage
arises as a result of Felix's infidelities. When he embarks on several
indecisive liaisons with other women, Rose-Ann responds much as
Margery Currey had: she is hurt by Felix's unfaithfulness but
unwilling to criticize him for it. Instead she leaves for California to
pursue a career and life of her own.

Felix's decision to follow Rose-Ann to California and try to salvage
their marriage indicates how different were Dell's aims in this novel
than in the one before it. In *Moon-Calf* Dell had recorded Felix's
failures with a delicate, often poignant mix of sympathy and irony.
In *The Briary-Bush* he aimed for something more emphatic: to trace
Felix's triumph (even if it is no more than a momentary triumph)
over his own self-imposed alienation from life. It becomes clear to
Felix at the end of *The Briary-Bush* that his desire to rescue his
marriage is allied to his desire to renounce the self-consciously
marginal, bohemian intellectual pursuits he had cultivated in Chicago. When he asks Rose-Ann to return to him, Felix speaks also of
his desire for a fully engaged intellectual life. "I'd like to live in a
world where ideas counted for something—where people might put
you in jail if you disagreed with them. . . . I want the feeling of other
minds resisting the impact of my own."

Felix realizes that he and Rose-Ann had failed at marriage in
much the same way he had failed as an intellectual: " 'We were
afraid of life,' he said. 'We were cowards.' " As they decide to give
their marriage a second try, the two barely regret the loss of those
ideals of untrammeled individuality that had doomed their first

marital experiment. Dell notes that Felix's "mind, as by a shadowy wing, was touched with a faint regret... for what?... for an old dream, beautiful in its way—a dream of freedom; but a dream only—and worthy only the farewell tribute of a faint and shadowy regret."

With so unambiguous a statement, Dell plainly wished to dispatch the moon-calf forever. But was that really possible? The sheer, almost desperate vehemence with which Felix bids adieu to the temptations of alienation and uninhibited individuality suggest that those temptations—both for Felix and for Dell—were not yet gone for good.

The Briary-Bush COMPLETED, Dell decided in May 1921 to take a respite from literary work. He and B. Marie embarked by train for points west on a trip that would last all summer. They visited Marjorie Jones, now married and mother to a baby boy, in Detroit (M.J. had remained friends with Dell after their breakup; she had even encouraged B. Marie to marry him). Later Floyd and B. Marie rode on to Chicago where they visited friends from Dell's years there. Next came a week or so with Floyd's parents on their small farm in Pike County, where the old people had gladly returned after years of hardship in Davenport. Earlier the farm had been owned by Mrs. Dell's two unmarried sisters. One had recently died, and the surviving sister now threatened to sell the place unless the Dells could pay her one-third its total value. The needed sum was $1,500—money that Dell's elderly parents did not have. When Floyd and B. Marie arrived, he had already resolved to pay the money himself, drawing in part on royalties from *Moon-Calf* and making up the rest with a loan from Arthur Ficke. Kate Dell, who had always encouraged her youngest son's literary talents, was delighted to find him willing and able—and precisely because of his literary success—to help. Dell too was pleased by this turn of events: "I was happy to be able to give my mother this fairy-tale ending to her life, a life in which so many hopes had been centered in a son who must have seemed, to all the world but herself, unworthy of such faith."

Dell found his parents unexpectedly old on this last brief visit. He had not seen them for years. They were relieved to be back in the country, where both felt at home. Years of searching for a decent life

in Mississippi River towns had brought them little happiness. Kate
Dell was content to tend her vegetable garden. Anthony Dell was
now in his eighties, a man who had failed as a businessman and
laborer but who was still full of high spirits and tales of his glory days
as a soldier. With his chest-length snow-white beard the old man
had shed all vestiges of the respectable business class to which he
had briefly belonged. That both approved of B. Marie, pregnant now
with what would be their first grandchild, was heartening (Dell's
mother had never taken to Margery Currey, apparently because she
thought Margery too old for her boyish son). Still, Dell was
overcome with pity for his parents; their lives, he recalled thinking,
"had always seemed to me tragic examples of unsuccessful struggle."
Now he marveled at their optimism, at their undaunted belief that
the years of struggle had ended in triumph.

Dell and B. Marie visited her relatives in Minnesota, then
journeyed on to Pasadena where they visited more of her family, and
to San Francisco, a city Dell had fantasized about as a child. The
couple traveled a week in California with the artist Lydia Gibson
and her first husband, Pat Mestre, staying for a while at the ranch of
Lloyd Osbourne, the stepson of Robert Louis Stevenson. Dell
remembered their time on the ranch as gloriously lazy days, with
barbecues, literary talk, and nude swimming parties. The greatest
thrill for Dell came when they hiked out to the mountain where
Frank Norris had sat at a packingbox he used as a writing desk. Dell
was amazed to find the box still there, as if Norris had just stepped
away from his work. "Like a pilgrim approaching a sacred relic,"
Dell wrote, "I touched with my own hands the surface which the
writing hand of Frank Norris had touched."

On the return trip the Dells stopped again in Chicago and
Detroit, returning to Croton in September. They were glad to be
home, particularly Floyd, who had never enjoyed traveling and
who, apart from occasional happy interludes along the way, had
been homesick for Croton and long days of literary work. That fall
he returned to his editorial duties at the *Liberator*. In October Knopf
brought out *The Briary-Bush*. From the start the book sold well in
New York and elsewhere throughout the country.

Coloring the whole fall for Floyd and B. Marie, however, was
their anticipation of the coming birth. On New Year's Eve B. Marie
entered the hospital in New York. Several days later she gave birth to
a son. At her suggestion they named the baby Anthony, after Dell's

father. She was exhausted but happy. Dell was in decidedly worse shape. Having spent three days and nights in the hospital waiting room, followed by several days of celebrating with friends in New York, he collapsed and remained in bed for several days. B. Marie tolerated his inopportune breakdown. (Dell sheepishly compared it to the tradition in Brittany whereby "it is the father who goes to bed after a child is born.") But she was not without impatience with her fragile husband's timing. When he recovered they repaired to the house in Croton, where they now settled for good.

Meanwhile reviews were flooding in on *The Briary-Bush*, reviews that were altogether more mixed than those for *Moon-Calf* a year earlier. Some notices were wildly enthusiastic. In a piece titled "Approaching Mastery" that appeared in the *Chicago Daily News*, Harry Hansen praised Dell for his concentration on the relations between liberated young men and women, and for forging a literary style that resisted the cheap, popular idiom of the new decade. *The Briary-Bush*, Hansen wrote, is "the most important novel of marriage between two persons of literary and artistic impulses that has ever been written in the United States." He called Dell "one of the few Americans who have shaken loose from journalism and developed an artistic attitude toward their work, who have not been influenced by the prevailing mode and 'jazzed' their style." Carl Van Doren, literary editor at the *Nation*, lauded the book's depiction of its protagonist's conflicted psyche. *The Briary-Bush*, he wrote, "hovers over the dark waters of the unconscious on perhaps the surest wings an American novelist has ever used."

Others were not so fervent. Many readers who had identified closely with Felix Fay in *Moon-Calf* had turned to *The Briary-Bush* with expectations that it too would conclude with Felix unable to reconcile himself to worldly success or responsibilities. When the second novel closed with Felix committing himself, with Rose-Ann, to conventional marriage and family life, many felt betrayed by Dell. He had believed it necessary, on the book's final page, to have his characters turn away from the "old dream, beautiful in its way, the dream of freedom." Many readers, not to mention friends from Greenwich Village, could hardly believe that Dell, who had once seemed the archetypal Village rebel, would conclude his book in this fashion.

Reviewers complained about other aspects of the novel as well. For some the book seemed more prosaic—less intensely imagined—

than its predecessor. John Peale Bishop, who had earlier praised Dell as a postwar novelist who rejected "the silliness and complacency of commercialized literature," detected in *The Briary-Bush* an unfortunate "mood of sentimental reminiscence." Francis Hackett, Dell's old boss at the *Friday Literary Review* and now literary editor at the *New Republic*, compared *The Briary-Bush* to William Dean Howells's *A Hazard of New Fortunes*. Hackett implied that the two books were alike in their focus on conventional protagonists who confront thoroughly unconventional circumstances. Both books, Hackett suggested, revealed their authors' underlying sympathy for traditional values and institutions. Hackett insisted that Dell, as much as Howells, was "decidedly genteel."

It was a new (and not terribly pleasant) experience for Dell to be criticized in print by old friends like Hackett. Nonetheless, he met head on the charge that he was conventional. While writing *The Briary-Bush* Dell had begun to feel that his central preoccupation as a novelist was with what he later called "the break-up of the old patriarchal family institution in contemporary America." Now Dell announced to his detractors that he was far from wishing to affirm that earlier patriarchal society. Rather, he insisted he was tracing its collapse and the emergence of new paradigms for marriage and family life. Prompted by a wide range of sources (his readings of Marx and modern feminists among them), he had come to view the patriarchal family as an essential part of capitalist society. It had served, Dell believed, as an institution for preserving and transmitting private property, for upholding social classes and patterns of legitimacy and illegitimacy, and for oppressing and degrading women. This traditional family form, Dell felt, had been a bulwark of aristocratic, and then of bourgeois, society. At the same time, he insisted,

> there was a non-aristocratic kind of marriage, of plebeian origin, having nothing to do with the conservation of property, a love-marriage, which was instinctively human, and which arose whenever and wherever property considerations were removed; it was the instinctive arrangement by which in our species the nurture of children was ensured—and this natural marriage and natural family, which had already begun to exist in a modern form under capitalism, was, with certain legal reforms, what would exist in the Socialist state: not irresponsible 'freedom' and not Platonic public nurseries.

Many of Dell's critics remained unconvinced by this effort to redefine marriage and the family so as to make them, as Dell put it, "part and parcel of our revolutionary ideals." With *The Briary-Bush* and his insistent journalistic defense of marriage and family, Dell became the center of controversy at the *Liberator.* "We had debates to help support the Liberator," Dell recalled, "and the most popular and crowded debates were those in which I defended Marriage and the Family. . . . I once debated with Michael Gold on Freedom vs. Marriage; and Michael Gold upheld what he fondly believed to be the true revolutionary position of Freedom. I afterward debated with V. F. Calverton, who upheld the same vague Anarchist ideal of Freedom in the belief that it was revolutionary. No young 'radical' was surprised at their views; but mine seemed strange and fantastic." Joe Freeman remembered just how strange and fantastic Dell's views on marriage had seemed in 1922: It was "almost as if [Communist party leader] William Z. Foster had come out openly in favor of private profit. It meant practically the sexual counterrevolution."

The substance of these debates, as with so much that went on among the Village radicals, was often wildly unsystematic. Dell claimed that in working out his ideas on the subject of the family he was trying "to co-ordinate the Marxian social-economic and the Freudian psychoanalytic points of view." This suggests greater theoretical rigor than in fact could be found in many of his remarks. All the same he was wrestling with issues that were important. Besides the specific matters of marriage and family, he was aiming to fashion a clear picture of an alternative society and culture. However uncertain and unsystematic he may have been, Dell wanted to create in both his fiction and nonfiction radical ideals for the future. What alarmed him were signs that the literary and political vanguard was now heading toward the renunciation of any such ideals—that it was now inclined to celebrate only alienation, nihilism, and its own powerlessness.

Already by 1921 Dell guessed that the avant-garde's zeal for purely negative political and intellectual virtues might create an inhospitable atmosphere for his work. He suspected that the postwar world—both the avant-garde and the growing middle-class audience that was eagerly following it—was cultivating a disturbing

taste for chaos, romantic disillusionment and despair; James Joyce and James Branch Cabell and Eugene O'Neill were portents. Sinclair Lewis was said to have cut out from his 'Main Street,' on the advice of Cabell, the one sensible character in the book, through whom his own constructive views were to have been expressed. Middle-class morale had been shattered by the war; people knew they had been lied to, fooled, betrayed; they would not want to believe anything, or think hard about anything. It would be a period of cynicism—already it was, under President Harding, a period of tolerance for the grossest corruption. The era was unfavorable for me as a novelist, I felt; this accidental popularity of mine would not endure.

TO TRACE DELL'S career through the 1920s is to discern a counter-motion to the celebrated cultural trends of that extraordinary decade. The picture of the twenties that has coalesced around figures like Hemingway and Fitzgerald—of a decade with epic quantities of cynicism, disillusion, gaiety, jazz, and excess—has become so omnipresent that it has obscured many other cultural tendencies of those years. Perhaps most pernicious of all has been the suggestion that the decade was devoid of political consciousness or idealism—a sentiment famously summarized in Fitzgerald's remark, early in the following decade, that "It was characteristic of the Jazz Age that it had no interest in politics at all." For Floyd Dell and many other writers, this statement was profoundly misleading.

Not that Dell found it easy to fashion a political stance for himself in those hectic years. At times he wavered between political and apolitical—committed and alienated—extremes. His role in certain controversies within the radical community toward the end of the war revealed just how uncertain Dell was in his political views. In 1917 his close friend Randolph Bourne had concluded that the most compelling course open to opponents of the war was to retreat from direct political confrontation and instead to cultivate their discontent. "A more skeptical, malicious, desperate, ironical mood may actually be the sign of more vivid and more stirring life fermenting in America today," Bourne wrote. "It may be a sign of hope."

Not long after Bourne died of influenza (only weeks after the Armistice), leftist intellectuals began debating the meaning of his legacy. In a review of Bourne's collected war essays that appeared in May 1920 in the *Freeman*, Harold J. Laski defined Bourne's position as an identifiably liberal one, allied in temper to William Godwin's protest "against the encroachment of political power" and "deeply influ-

enced by the attractive anarchism of Tolstoy and Kropotkin." Laski
praised Bourne for his fearless stand in the name of conscience
against a coercive government. But Laski also argued that Bourne
had allowed his principles to overcome his good sense. He launched
several penetrating criticisms of Bourne's unyielding pacifism: "Neutrality in the modern conflict of nations is an unthinkable attitude.
The business of the world is the business of the world. We can not
stay at Armageddon to philosophize upon the abstract injustice of
war. Bourne's attitude, I think, comes perilously near to that
manoeuvre." Laski identified a second problem as well. "The
individualism he preaches is one in which the single person stands
as an Athanasius against the world. . . . Mr. Bourne's freedom is the
freedom of a lonely vagabond whose soul does not dwell in the
common haunts of men."

A week after Laski's article appeared in the *Freeman*, the magazine printed a letter from Dell that objected to every part of Laski's
argument. "Where does Mr. Laski get the idea," Dell erupts,
". . . that Bourne was a liberal?" Dell goes on to argue that "Bourne's
own description of his attitude is to be found in the phrase, 'creative
scepticism'—an attitude which is throughout its pages set in contrast
with the *'naivete'* of the liberal. The book is an attack on liberalism—an expose of liberalism, a calm and ironic and thorough
showing-up of its preferences and performances with reference to the
late war." All this is a little surprising coming from a man who had
himself come to distrust a purely skeptical and ironic understanding
of the war—who had in fact come to support the war in the name of
Soviet socialism. Now Dell asserted that "the war was an opportunity
in which the positive effort of Bourne's personality, his creative
scepticism, magnificently flowered." Dell quoted one of Bourne's
characteristic remarks to the effect that alienation and skepticism
might "be made a shelter" for developing constructive ideals for
American culture and politics. Could Dell actually be suggesting
that the war, in driving intellectuals from pragmatic liberalism to
irreconcilable alienation, had been a blessing for American radicalism? He seemed to come perilously close to making that point.

Dell went on to dismiss Laski's suggestion that Bourne's essays, in
recommending isolation and detachment, posed no coherent alternative to purposeful public action. Laski had argued that Bourne's
essays advocated solipsistic withdrawal from all public debates about
national policy. "A liberty that is not shared with one's fellows,"

Laski insisted, "is at its best a puny thing and, at its worst, a vicious form of self-indulgence." Dell responded with olympian assurance: "Yes, intellectual courage was ever a puny thing, in comparison with the huge and sociable mechanics of mass prejudice; and candour has ever been, from the point of view of those who lack it, a vicious form of self-indulgence." Dell seemed to echo Bourne's own assertion, made in late 1917, that the war had left intellectuals with only two possible choices: either support the war effort and be swallowed up in mass hysteria, or withdraw to a bitter, powerless spot on the margins of American society.

These were surprising sentiments coming from Dell—and not solely because he had avoided this sort of obstinate alienation during the war. Dell's letter to the *Freeman* was written in May 1920, at the very time he was finishing *Moon-Calf*. That novel about an alienated young writer had been intended—according to Dell's own testimony—as a satire on such writers themselves, *not* on the society to which they could not reconcile themselves. Now Dell reaffirmed all the pent-up alienation and discontent harbored by America's literary radicals. Clearly *Moon-Calf* had not laid all his earlier tendencies to rest.

Dell acknowledged the survival of some of his earlier contradictions in an essay for the *Liberator* that he wrote at roughly the same time, "A Psycho-Analytic Confession." He had embarked upon psychoanalytic treatment several years earlier in an effort to overcome what he guessed were buried reasons for his inability to find sustained productivity in his literary work and permanence in his love life. By the spring of 1920, with *Moon-Calf* nearly complete and his marriage to B. Marie entering its second year, Dell had reason to believe the treatment had been a success. In the *Liberator* essay, however, he "confessed" to a potent nostalgia for selfish pleasures preferred by his Unconscious—pleasures rejected by his earnest public self.

"A Psycho-Analytic Confession" is in fact a lighthearted dialogue between Dell's conscious and unconscious selves. The irrepressible Unconscious is perfectly happy with Dell's literary and marital pursuits—these seem to him the kinds of private, selfish pleasures that an Unconscious naturally craves. What the Unconscious rejects (and what Dell's conscious self desperately affirms) is the wish to commit himself actively to the creation of a new political order—a Cooperative Commonwealth much like the infant Soviet state in

Russia. The "I" in the *Liberator* essay—Dell's tentative and easily confused political-activist persona—defends the Soviets and the industrial program being pushed into place by "Comrade Lenin." But the Unconscious knows that Dell's tottering "I" would rather leave all that political earnestness behind and indulge himself in the private consolations of literary work and family happiness. The "I" insists that "'we are going to have a revolution because of—well, you wouldn't understand if I told you. But it's all in the Communist Manifesto.'"

"It's true, I never could understand that book," said my Unconscious. "I seem to take more readily to poetry."

"You're a Utopian," I said.

"Of course," said my Unconscious. "And between us, I think you are, too. I think you are a Socialist simply because you want a different kind of world, one you can be happy in. . . . But the dream which you want to see come true is my dream—not Lenin's seven hundred million electric bulbs, but a houseboat and a happy family living in a state of moderately advanced and semi-nude savagery!"

In part Dell intended "A Psycho-Analytic Confession" as a satiric affront to the humorless political radicals at the *Liberator.* He strongly suggested (though only through the mouth of his icono-clastic Unconscious) that Marxism and the Bolsheviks posed no genuine alternatives to capitalist society—that like the capitalists before them, the Soviets were devoted to an industrial civilization that ignored the spiritual health and happiness of the individual. The "I" discerns the Unconscious's radical renunciation of politics toward the end of their dialogue when he complains that "'It's impossible to argue with you. . . . You seem to think civilization is a disease that people are going to get over after a while.'" The Unconscious agrees, rejecting both bourgeois and revolutionary political platforms. Dell seemed to suggest to his readers that their radical sympathies were thoroughly conventional, that their enthu-siasm for the Soviets was a betrayal of their desire for freedom from political and economic regimentation.

Dell found the form of "A Psycho-Analytic Confession"—a con-versation between two sides of his own divided self—a suitable one for highlighting his own divergent allegiances to literature and politics. It also allowed him to dramatize the split between his earnest political passions and his equally great tendency toward humor and self-deprecation. The essay's form was perfectly suited to the division between commitment and irony that he detected not only in himself but in literary radicals generally.

He was determined, however, to push on toward a more decisive formulation. In July 1920 he published another article on psycho-analysis—called "Psychanalysis and Recent Fiction"—which aimed to account for the social position of modern artists in a less ambiguous light. Dell started this sober, scholarly essay by asking "why, toward the end of the XIX century, a literature so crowded with 'raw' and fairly unassimilable fantasy-creations of the Unconscious should so suddenly burst upon an astonished and bewildered public." The answer, he suggested, was to be found "in the social position and function of the writer, or indeed of the artist, literary or other, in that period."

Dell argued that in centuries before the nineteenth, the artist had held a respected position in society. As figures of considerable public stature and influence, artists had gladly discarded "wilful" and "infantile" and utterly "private" fantasies from their works, knowing that to give voice to those fantasies would be to undermine their public eminence. This changed with "the advent of modern commercialism" in the nineteenth century. Artists overwhelmingly found that commercialism repugnant and alien. What's more, the insistent rationalism and cynicism of commercial civilization, Dell claimed, rendered the imaginative powers of the artist irrelevant. As a result, "the arts begin to decay, in direct proportion to the spread of modern commercialism." In England, where commercialism emerged most strongly at first, poets fled to the continent—particularly to Italy—where they could discern the vestiges of precommercial civilizations. Those poets who remained in England, such as Tennyson, turned their attention increasingly to medieval topics.

Dell argued that as the century progressed, artists had the choice of following one of two paths: either surrender to commercialism and celebrate business and the entrepreneur; or retreat into arcane and irrelevant topics. Those who chose the second option struggled briefly against society's repression of their genuine artistic impulses, then "burst forth" with disturbing and "infantile" artistic works. Such works, Dell claimed, represented in several ways their irrelevance to society at large: they emerged out of society's repression of the artist's instincts and as a furious cry against a populace with no need for them. Once commercial capitalism destroyed the reciprocal relation between artist and society—the "compromise effected between the individual need of fantasy-production and the social gratification of finding these fantasy-productions understood and shared by others"—the artist flew off into an imaginative world reflecting both his irrelevance and childish rage.

Dell insisted in this essay, however, that in the decade or so prior to 1920 artists had begun to recover their social role. "As capitalism began to involve itself in economic predicaments which led down to disaster, and as the spirit of the age became more tolerant of criticism, the artists, sensitive to this change, began to speak out once more. . . . The novel, as a critical study of the disintegration of commercial society, became once more a significant art-form." The recent revolution in Russia, Dell added, had created a climate in which the artist's discontent with commercial society was more likely to receive an interested hearing than had been the case in the decades around the turn of the century. At a time marked by general "perceptions of social disintegration and change," Dell felt that society again would turn to artists for significant and meaningful accounts of the world they lived in: "The artist is once more beginning to fulfill his social function and that social function appears now very clearly to consist in elucidating and justifying the discontent of the common man with a state of society in which his best instincts are stifled, in searching out and emphasizing the significance and the promise of all those instincts, in expressing for him aspirations which have been too long repressed for a free and more adventurous and more beautiful and more creative life."

The most impressive passages in "Psychanalysis and Recent Fiction" were those that attempted to sketch out a modern literary history based on the interrelation between political developments and literary movements. Dell's essay came at a time when American writers were looking for overarching interpretations of American and European culture. Van Wyck Brooks had only five years earlier published *America's Coming-of-Age*, in which he described American culture as the unsatisfactory product of a society that had never managed to combine its highbrow and lowbrow elements. In the early 1920s T. S. Eliot speculated on how a "dissociation of sensibility" had disrupted and diminished English literature sometime in the late seventeenth century—a rather mysterious condition that was only now being rectified, Eliot hinted, due in large measure to his own poetic and critical efforts. At the same time Dell was fashioning his own comprehensive view of European and American culture of the past century and a half. More than Brooks or Eliot, however, he identified specific political and economic developments as key elements in the history of literature.

Still, "Psychanalysis and Recent Fiction" was no more than a partial sketch of ideas Dell was developing. In the years following the essay's publication, he worked intermittently on a series of articles that presented a more detailed and refined account of those ideas. Those essays, which he had first formulated on his Vermont hiking trip in 1919, and which he eventually published in the *Liberator* in monthly installments in 1923 and 1924, Dell called "Literature and the Machine Age." In 1933 he looked back at the series as "a kind of Marxian essay in literary criticism"; it was, he insisted, "the first attempt in America to apply a particular principle of historical criticism to any wide range of literary productions." The left-wing literary historian Bernard Smith went further when he claimed (in 1939) that in these essays Dell "raised socialist criticism to a plane that would entitle him to be called the true precursor of Marxist critical writing in America."

In fact, as Dell himself was quick to point out, it is inaccurate to describe the essays first published as "Literature and the Machine Age" as strictly "Marxist." They make scarcely any reference to Marx, nor do their analyses of literary and intellectual trends ever amount to a rigorous Marxist reading of culture. Already Dell found much Marxist thought excessively systematic and reductive. Yet something of Marx's influence—if only in the vaguest sense—does permeate these essays. In their discursive, nondoctrinaire way, they add up to a coherent, materialist reading of Western culture since the middle of the eighteenth century. As such they were every bit as original as Smith and others later claimed. What interested Dell in these essays is the way in which political, economic, and technological developments that had transformed the West since around 1750 had resulted in particular literary and intellectual styles. He examined how these developments had driven literary intellectuals to adopt peculiarly alienated identities, making them content to stand passively on the sidelines of mainstream society.

"Psychanalysis and Recent Fiction" had looked at a smattering of recent European and American writers—among them D. H. Lawrence, J. D. Beresford, Sherwood Anderson, and James Joyce—

in connection with social transformations that had pushed these and other writers toward the creation of new types of literary works. "Literature and the Machine Age" now attempted a more ambitious survey, offering brief, incisive readings of dozens of authors and nearly as many literary movements. Dell opened with Defoe, Rousseau, and Voltaire, then proceeded rapidly through Byron and the romantics; Tennyson, Browning, George Eliot, Dickens, and other Victorians; the Pre-Raphaelite movement, Ruskin, Swinburne, Arnold, William Morris, and the rage for medievalism. He then embarked upon "A Spiritual Autobiography of My Own Generation in Its Literary and Social Aspects." This absorbing survey included glances at a wide range of intellectuals and writers who had influenced Dell's generation: Jules Verne, Robert Ingersoll, Ibsen, Whitman, Nietzsche, Edward Bellamy, Wells, Shaw, and a great many others. The essays provided an overview of a literary tradition that extended right up to America's newest and most disillusioned young writers of the postwar era.

The articles were as much an improvement over Dell's earlier literary essays as *Moon-Calf* had been over his youthful stories and plays. Dell had always managed a graceful, urbane critical style, full of learning but never stiff or overbearing; his essays had long since established him as one of the most accomplished and original critics of his generation. But "Literature and the Machine Age" was more brilliant in every regard. Read as a single continuous work, the essays presented an original view of the less-than-satisfactory progress of Western literature since the simultaneous rise of industrial society and the modern bourgeoisie. For all its individual parts, it was the whole of Dell's analysis that mattered most: a full indictment of literary and critical ideas that Dell felt had been designed to justify the writer's contempt and powerlessness before the protean modern world.

Most impressive was Dell's ability to relate his unfolding literary history to the developing social history of the period. Dell was acutely interested in how literary rebels aligned themselves against the new commercial and industrial enterprises promoted by the emergent bourgeoisie of the eighteenth and early nineteenth centuries. But he also recognized how these same literary rebels—from Rousseau and Voltaire to Byron, Coleridge, and the other romantics—were products of the new middle class's ideology of individualism and untrammeled self-assertion. Nevertheless, Dell argued, by the second decade of the nineteenth century whatever optimism the literary figures had gleaned from the bourgeoisie had been supplanted by the angry satire and embittered escapism epitomized by Byron. The Napoleonic wars, the filth and despair of modern urban and industrial life, the rapacious tendencies of capitalism—these seemed to dissociate young, idealistic writers from the society in which they lived. The writers themselves cultivated and eventually celebrated their own alienation. It is the mood of bitterness and disenchantment that Dell finds most typical of Western writers since the early 1800s. In his own generation's wild swings from pseudoscientific utopianism to free love to unrestrained bohemianism to equally unrestrained aestheticism to the shell-shocked disillusionment of the postwar era, Dell detected a recurring tendency to retreat from serious engagement with society and to console oneself instead with private dreams and the conviction of one's own superiority.

When Dell collected his "Literature and the Machine Age" essays several years later and published them under the title *Intellectual Vagabondage*, he subtitled the book "An Apology for the Intelligentsia." In a sense the book could claim to be exactly that: a work full of sympathy for his own literary generation and the ones before it. But readers were baffled by the word "apology" in the subtitle. In many ways *Intellectual Vagabondage* seemed more an attack on a literary tradition that had consistently opted for powerlessness in a world it professed to despise, and that had just as consistently found ways to justify its retreat into private self-absorption, abstruse aesthetic pastimes, and intellectual chaos. Dell described the book as "a plea in defense of that generation of intelligent, sensitive and more or less creative young people to which I and most of my friends belong." But, he added, "it is a candid defense, and so it may appear to be actually an attack."

Dell's impatience with the full span of modern literary trends inspired fervent passages of a sort that had never appeared in his writing before:

> It will be by this time apparent that the literature upon which we grew up had thus far failed in the task of enabling us to face realistically the world in which we lived. It failed, because its efforts to interpret that world to us, to give us such conceptions of it and of our relation to it as would make life worth living, had not borne the test of experience. It succeeded only in its other

function, that of enabling us to blink the full import of realities, to accept without shame the indignities of life, and to evade with undiminished self-respect our responsibilities toward a world in which such indignities were inflicted.

So much for the romanticism, aestheticism, medievalism, and fin-de-siècle detachment that the nineteenth century had bequeathed young literary intellectuals of Dell's generation. So much even for the utopianism inspired by H. G. Wells, which Dell realized had always been eccentric and undisciplined, appealing to elitists who had little taste for down-to-earth reform. Wells's heroes, Dell insisted, had appealed not to his own generation's desire to rebuild society but rather to its barely hidden ardor for wrecking the old world. "Querulous and ignorant, in spite of our gospel of 'love and fine thinking,' we represented a generation which had endured a misbuilt civilization so long that we were destructive in all our instincts. We talked of order, but it was only as a justification for throwing more monkey-wrenches into the machinery of the existing system."

Although Dell seemed to regret his youthful enthusiasm for Wells in "Literature and the Machine Age," he retained all his earlier esteem for George Bernard Shaw. He especially admired Shaw's satiric insights into the vanities of the intelligentsia. Shaw seemed to toss a challenging question in the face of smug literary rebels: "Can you create a new civilization upon the ruins of the old? Can you even get along in such a new civilization if some one else creates it for you?" Dell pitilessly looked back on his own experience as a literary bohemian as he faced this rebuff to elitist radicalism. If some of the withdrawal from social engagement and idealism had been forced on writers, much of the blame deserved to be placed on the writers themselves.

In the postwar literary scene Dell discovered the apotheosis of the cynicism and alienation that had been refining itself for the better part of two centuries. He conceded how disillusioning had been the war and its aftermath at Versailles. "The future," Dell wrote with appalling prescience, "can be envisaged only as a lull of temporary exhaustion and of preparation for further and more gigantic and more destructive and more futile wars to come." There is undisguised sympathy in Dell's writing for the fears of the intelligentsia as it faces this unpromising postwar world. "Facing an ironic doom which it feels powerless to avert," Dell wrote, "the intelligentsia of our time has for the most part put aside with a kind of shame its broken and shattered ideals, and has confessed its hopelessness by the very nature of its new esthetic and intellectual interests." These included "such harmlessly esthetical pastimes and intellectual cross-word puzzles as will serve to pass the time," but also a disturbing tendency to celebrate "the ugliness and chaos of life."

This last development particularly worried Dell in the early 1920s. Writers, he claimed, had always sensed the chaos and meaninglessness of life, but they had earlier responded to such premonitions by laboring to create human order and meanings for themselves and their readers. Contemporary writers alarmed Dell with their determination to preserve disorder and meaninglessness in their works. For Dell this celebration of chaos was a frankly reactionary political gesture: an unsubtle strategy for justifying their own unwillingness to speak out against injustice and human suffering. "It is evident that we, at this moment in history, do *not* want life to seem capable of being interpreted and understood, because that would be a reproach to us for our own failure to undertake the task of reconstructing our social, political and economic theories, and in general, and in consonance with these, our ideals of a good life." Dell wrote that this "view of life which sincerely denies validity to almost the whole scheme of civilized life is a view natural enough to what we may call spiritual vagabonds—to those who, whatever their actual position in the worldly scheme of things, have withdrawn from it altogether or in great part their loyalty and belief and consent."

At the end of his long essay Dell posed the example of the Russian Revolution and the incentive it might offer American intellectuals. He complained that "the intelligentsia has for the most part become indifferent to the new order in Russia—an indifference which masks a secret temperamental antipathy." After all, the Soviets were busily transforming a vast nation—hardly the sort of work likely to appeal to American intellectuals with, as Dell put it with admirable satire, "a deep sentimental attachment to barbarism and savagery, preferably of a nomadic sort." Still, he hoped that the coming generation of intellectuals "will take themselves and their responsibilities more seriously" than had *Wasteland* poets and Jazz Age cynics. In a breathless peroration he anticipated a revitalized literary scene:

It may not be impossible for a younger generation to begin to formulate and erect into socially acceptable *conventions*, and where possible into laws, some healthy modern ideals of courtship, marriage, divorce, and the relations of the sexes in general. It may not be so difficult for them to find the political terms upon which they can accept and serve and use a machine civilization. It may be quite natural for them to think of the arts as means of communication rather than merely opportunities for irresponsible self-expression.

Dell's study of the long tradition of intellectual vagabondage ended not with an attack on the uncompromising despair of the lost generation but with the hope that vagabondage might soon cease to be the predominant cultural style. He was terrifically apprehensive about the literary scene he saw springing up around him during the early 1920s. But he was too great an optimist to end his account of literary vagabondage without some glimmer of hope for an emergent literary movement that would address itself once again to history, politics, and ordinary humanity.

E L E V E N

Under Fire

THE YEARS BETWEEN 1922 and 1925, when Dell was at work on "Literature and the Machine Age" and other politically charged writings, were astonishingly productive for him. In 1922 Knopf brought out *King Arthur's Socks and Other Village Plays*, containing most of the plays Dell had written for the Liberal Club and the Provincetown Players. The next year Knopf issued *Janet March*, Dell's first novel since *The Briary-Bush*. That same year Dell contributed a series of essays to the *Liberator* called "The Outline of Marriage," an unsystematic overview that focused on the dilemmas posed by modern industrial society to the marital institution. Later that year and through most of the following one, Dell published his "Literature and the Machine Age" articles in the *Liberator*. In 1924 Knopf put out *Looking at Life*, a collection of Dell's essays that had originally appeared in the *Masses*, the *Liberator*, and other magazines. Dell published two more novels in 1925, *This Mad Ideal* and *Runaway*, the first with Knopf, the second with George H. Doran. Besides a large number of reviews and essays that he also published during this handful of years, he found time to edit and write introductions to collections of poems by William Blake, Robert Herrick, and Wilfrid Scawen Blunt.

The sustained literary purpose and productivity that had eluded Dell in the prewar years were now established features of his life. Working every day (and often through the night) in the house on Mount Airy Road in Croton, he eagerly took up the life of a versatile man of letters. Dell knew that his work ran counter to the literary fashions of the moment. Understandably he worried that literary tastes would desert him altogether, and that he would lose his ability to make a living for himself and his family. But he never doubted the general tenor of his work. The course he had taken consistently impressed him as the fulfillment of all he had struggled to achieve during the preceding decade.

He had friends in Croton—old ones from the *Masses* like Max Eastman and Boardman Robinson, both of whom lived in the town, and younger visitors like Joseph Freeman. Coming of age in the postwar world, Freeman was among the young writers and journalists who rejected the "lost generation" ethos espoused by many of their contemporaries and aimed to carry on the prewar tradition of literary radicalism. He admired Dell as a representative of the old *Masses*-style radicalism that combined culture and politics, and that seemed so different from the apolitical concerns of the emergent avant-garde. After nearly a decade spent poring over Dell's writings, he had introduced himself to the older man in a Greenwich Village restaurant one evening in January 1922 (the very week, as it turned out, when Dell's first son, Anthony, was born). Freeman was grateful for Dell's willingness to entertain the ideas and conversation of a younger, unproven writer: "Something in Dell's personality broke down all barriers at once. I felt at home, convinced that there was nothing you could not say to this man." Dell was sympathetic to Freeman's worries about his antithetical loyalties to literature and politics. Such conflicts, Dell assured the younger man, were typical of the intelligentsia. Freeman remembered Dell saying "that as a citizen he would always be interested in the political destinies of mankind; as an artist he would find in his political hopes a stimulus to creative effort."

Freeman became a frequent weekend visitor at the Dells' place in Croton, where he found uninhibited conversation and the warmth of a bohemian home. "Ideas flowed without reserve, false shame, class or racial prejudice," Freeman recalled. "We fancied ourselves disinterested devotees of art, revolution and psychoanalysis. All of these seemed indiscriminately to point the way to universal human freedom from external oppression and internal chaos." For Freeman, Dell's house was the center of an intellectual community in whose midst he felt more at home than among the conscientiously disillusioned types of his own generation. He described the house as "a magic little world retaining all that was best in the tradition of Greenwich Village. That tradition shone from the orange curtains at the windows, Nordfeldt's portrait of Dell as a young man, the walls lined from floor to ceiling with books."

Dell struck Freeman as uncommonly eager to bridge the gap between the two generations. Satisfied at last in his private and intellectual life, Dell was now prepared to take an interest in young, uncertain intellectuals. Freeman experienced it as an unprecedented "genius for friendship with younger people. In literature the poet of the moon-calf, in life he was father confessor to dozens of moon-calves to whom he opened his house, gave time and energy, literary and material help, to whom he talked with that profusion of ideas, that wealth of information, that brilliance for which he was famous in the prewar village."

Smoking one Richmond Straight after another, Dell would sound out the ideas of others, listening intently. Then he would seize the floor. Once he began speaking, his face—pale and framed by long sideburns that were holdovers from his Village years—would become wonderfully animated. He was accustomed since his days in Chicago to speaking to rooms of attentive listeners. Now, among friends and young admirers in Croton, he would embark on eloquent, lively monologues on a staggering range of topics. Debate often followed. These discussions would have gone on forever had B. Marie not been on hand to rouse the group from its stupor of talk, cigarettes, and coffee, and push everyone outdoors for brisk walks down Mount Airy Road into the village of Croton. Freeman recalled B. Marie as "blond, husky, genial and imperious." She evidently knew how to keep her husband (who often seemed inclined to live exclusively for ideas, books, and intellectual talk) in contact with the daily family life that he claimed was his greatest pleasure.

Still, these were not entirely happy years for Dell. By general agreement his critical writings were more impressive and influential than ever. But his novels—following the initial enthusiasm for *Moon-Calf* and the more modest success of *The Briary-Bush*—received uneven reviews. When the collection of his Village plays was published in 1922, few reviewers took the volume seriously. Light, passing spoofs of Village life, they had seemed entertaining and timely when they were written. Now many readers found them dated and irrelevant. In his introduction to the book, Dell tried to head off such criticisms by calling the plays "souvenirs of an intellectual play-time"—a time which he ventured to guess was now "dead." But the impatient, offhand reviews of the book, which largely confirmed

Dell's disclaimer, must have added to his worries that he was no longer attuned to the tastes of the new decade. "This is not what one expects of a man said to possess an active and astringent mind with a radical trend," wrote one reviewer. The notices that greeted his next few novels only added to his apprehensions. Even admirers like Freeman worried that Dell's books were becoming "progressively weaker as he drifted from the essay to the novel, [and] as he prolonged his absence from the city and from the revolutionary movement."

As an opponent of much that was new and acclaimed in literary work during the 1920s, Dell was faced with a difficult task in fashioning a consistent—and commercially and artistically success-ful—literary path. His job as a critic was somewhat easier. Taking aim at the new literary fashions from his left-wing vantage, Dell was able to develop a well-honed point of view built on his impatience with literary styles that exalted alienation and powerlessness. The result was a vigorous dissident criticism.

But this adversarial mode was not a sufficient foundation for fiction. Here Dell needed an equally sharp alternative to prevailing fashions. Hammering out that alternative proved no easy task. The result was an uneven succession of novels. Several were lively, original works; most were redeemed in part by their author's deter-mination to fashion an affirmative literature for postwar America. But reviewers understandably complained that some of the books seemed conventional and at times sentimental. Dell sought a hope-ful view of the coming era—a view he found lacking in writers as different as Lewis, James Branch Cabell, Fitzgerald, Hemingway, and T. S. Eliot. In presenting that view, though, Dell too often seemed a throwback to an innocent, bygone time. Hope was anathema to a generation that took its disillusion and ennui rather seriously.

It would be a mistake, though, to suggest that all of Dell's novels after *The Briary-Bush* were harmless and conventional. *Janet March*, which appeared in October 1923, stirred controversy throughout the United States for its frank account of the sexual coming of age of two young people, Janet March and Roger Leland. Dell later wrote that his portrait of Janet represented "an attempt to present a character-istic modern girl truly against her social-historical background." He aimed to offer Janet—the smart but vaguely discontented child of a successful Midwestern family—as representative of the most recent generation of young American adults. These young people, Dell felt, had grown up in an America which had lost its earlier, patriarchal framework but which had also failed to create a new social order that might help young people gain a sufficient sense of identity and direction.

Sex was at the heart of Janet March's struggle for maturity. This shocked a great number of readers and reviewers in 1923, many of whom denounced the book as obscene. Dell was certainly writing well beyond the boundaries of convention. Janet's adventures include impersonal sexual encounters with respectable boys and several illicit love affairs. One of these leads to pregnancy and an abortion performed by an independent woman doctor in Chicago. The ordeal unsettles Janet, but she stoutly refuses to regard herself as in the wrong. In fact, while she recovers from her abortion Janet happily recalls the afternoon of lovemaking with Vincent Blatch, a young, irresponsible artist, that had led to the pregnancy. She had felt at the time that their sexual love was an uncomplicated matter—"Not strange, not terrible, not mysterious, its romance lay in its very simplicity." If Dell's writing in such passages was sometimes stiff, it also represented an effort to capture thoughts that had earlier been off limits for writers—the thoughts, in this case, of a young woman who goes to bed with a man she scarcely knows.

Later in the same passage Dell tried to evoke Janet's memories of sex still more directly:

Strange, that it should be so many different things, such a melange. Play, a frolic, as of romping kittens, silly laughing childishness, a release from all the sober constraints of everyday life, a discovery of an Arcadian realm in which the only reality was play. Strange, too, that Arcadian realm was but a single step from the world of commonplace—and another step might bring one into this world of bewildered wondering in the dark! But it hadn't been merely play, there had been something antique and noble in its very naturalness, it was a rite that took one back out of civilization into some earlier world, it was a solemn and sacred ceremonial of the worship of nature. And it was the satisfying of some deep impersonal need, like hunger, like thirst, like the wish for sleep; it was rest, healing, quietness after tumult; . . . And it was finding hints, through one's body, of something that might be one's soul; it was a taking of wings and soaring into perilous heights of ecstasy, alone.

This is uneven writing, part description, part bohemian sermonizing, part poeticized, artificial language. In our own jaded age its description of sex seems remarkably demure. What is unmistakable, in any case, is Dell's determination to capture the confused mix of loneliness, independence, adventurousness, innocence, and curiosity that make up Janet's discovery of sex.

Taken in light of the literary and social conventions of the early 1920s, *Janet March* displayed both shocking and conventional bents. Janet's rites of passage may have outraged many readers, but there was also, as some reviewers suggested, a conventional pattern to her development into a mature young woman: childhood with her tolerant but uncertain parents; the confusions and aspirations of her adolescence; her sexual awakening as a teenager; her discovery that she is pregnant a second time (this time by Roger Leland, the man whose restlessness and idealism best matches her own); and finally her realization that she wants to marry Roger. The conclusion to Janet's story was much like that of *The Briary-Bush*, and readers who had found the earlier book disappointingly conventional felt the same about this one. For the Greenwich Village crowd and the emerging postwar generation, *Janet March* confirmed their growing impression of Dell as an apostate to the cause of free love and rebellion.

Yet it was the shocking side of the novel that received the greatest attention in the months after Knopf published the book in October 1923. Upton Sinclair, Dell's literary hero of nearly twenty years back and now a friend, led the critical and popular clamor against *Janet March*, reviling the book in an article that appeared in Hearst newspapers across the United States. Sinclair was a radical when it came to the exploitation of immigrants and the working class, but he was inflexibly puritanical in his views on sex. Not surprisingly he found *Janet March* a scandalous book. What is surprising is that he was willing to trumpet his disgust with his friend's novel so loudly in newspapers around the country. He charged that Dell was too sympathetic to the sexual curiosity and experiments of Janet and Roger in their respective early lives, and that Dell failed to point out the dangers—particularly venereal disease—of such experiments. Other reviewers around the country were equally outraged, describing the book as "disgusting," "putrid," and "violently realistic." These opinions may have actually spurred the book's sales, which numbered nearly fifteen thousand copies in the first few months alone.

Dell was wounded by the fury surrounding the novel. Sinclair's attack hurt most of all. Many years later he complained that Sinclair's review "was vicious, silly, and very damaging to me." At the time he put the best possible face on the matter, writing a long letter to Sinclair in which he actually thanked the older novelist for having expressed his opinions so frankly. He then attempted to defend himself against Sinclair's charges, arguing that there was "an unofficial censorship which resides in the minds, or rather the emotions, of people in general. This unofficial censorship has put a ban on all sorts of 'unpleasant' facts about life; and writers, ever since there have been such, have made such terms as they could with this censorship, by avoiding the mention of these 'unpleasant' facts." Dell suggested that modern writers should be willing to transgress this respectable self-censorship in order to reveal to their readers experiences and ideas with which they might otherwise remain unfamiliar. He rejected Sinclair's argument that literary works should provide explicit "guidance" for their readers. Dell said his novels were designed to promote "understanding": "As to the main purpose of fiction, I do not hesitate to define it—the purpose of it is to provide a realm of vicarious experience by which our emotional understanding of our fellow human beings may be broadened."

Dell's letter to Sinclair was successful in at least one regard: it smoothed things over between the two men and allowed them gradually to resume their friendship. But the public scandal over *Janet March* did not die. In December 1923 Knopf was informed by the New York district attorney's office that steps might soon be taken to ban the book. Similar grumblings were heard from Boston. Knopf hastily agreed to print no further copies. Dell acquiesced with Knopf's decision, and so the book was effectively, if unofficially, banned. Final copies were sold around the country, then it disappeared altogether from bookstore shelves. The novel, which had been the center of so much controversy, dropped from sight, earning Dell neither the praise nor the money he had hoped to gather from it.

HE NEVER QUITE recovered his footing as a novelist. In April 1924 Knopf brought out *Looking at Life*, the selection of his literary and political essays. Meanwhile Dell pushed forward with his "Literature and the Machine Age" essays, widely regarded at the time and afterward as the best writings ever to appear in the *Liberator.* But his reputation as a novelist had been tarnished by the controversies surrounding *Janet March.* In 1924, amid the praise he was receiving for other projects, Dell yearned to regain his standing as a novelist.

He worked on two novels in 1924 and early 1925, publishing one in the spring, the other in the fall of 1925. Both reflected, if only in indirect ways, his unhappy experience with *Janet March.* Neither is as daring as that earlier novel—not as frank about sexual matters nor as willing to celebrate youthful rebellion. In this they suggest the chastened mood that overcame Dell after the *Janet March* fiasco. Predictably, those of Dell's earlier admirers who regretted his unwillingness to contest the effort to ban *Janet March* were among those who deplored the next two novels' alleged conventionality. But if the new books were more skeptical about rebellion against the quotidian world, this was not ultimately due to Dell's fear of censorship. Rather, it reflected his increasing doubts about youthful and artistic self-absorption as well as his growing sense of the importance of communal relations and responsibilities. That neither book celebrated anarchic youth or vagabonds indicates how much they shared with the "Literature and the Machine Age" essays he was composing at the same time.

The first, *This Mad Ideal,* was to be Dell's shortest novel. More a parable than a fully developed novel, *This Mad Ideal* had little of the social detail that generally marked Dell's fiction. It focuses narrowly on its protagonist's archetypal story; even more specifically, it concentrates on the troubled inner life of that character. In this the book bears more than a passing resemblance to Hawthorne's romances—all the more so because it is set for the most part in small-town New England. Like Hawthorne, Dell examines the dilemmas faced by a willful person estranged from the society in which she lives. And as with Hawthorne, Dell's interest lies finally in the moral ambiguities at the heart of that person's solitary nature.

The story concerns Judith Valentine, born in a tiny New England town, who dreams of boarding one of the daily trains that race past her house and escaping her narrow world. That dream comes true when her solitary mother joins a singing troupe and takes her touring the country. When her mother dies, though, Judith is handed over to her stern aunt and uncle who live in a rigidly conventional town called Pompton. Although kind to her, they take no interest in her inner, imaginative life. Judith passes her time alone: reading, writing poetry, surrendering to "vague dreams, of another kind of life, among other people—dreams of flight, away from all this, into some place of her own." She is another Felix Fay, her life disrupted by outward circumstances, thrown back on her solitary, resourceful imagination. Once again Dell had returned to his own childhood for literary inspiration.

Again like Dell's earlier novels, *This Mad Ideal* centers on Judith's uncertain entrance into adulthood. She becomes entangled with several young men. First is Roy Sopwith, an aspiring artist. Like Judith, he is unsure whether to commit himself wholly to his art or to submit to the compromises of married life. Judith encourages him to go to Boston and pursue his art; she refuses early on to marry him out of fear that it will destroy both their ideals. The second man is several years older than Judith: Hugo Massinger, a dissolute journalist whose vagabond nature piques Judith's interest. But when Hugo falls in love with Judith, she again retreats before the threat of marriage.

Judith's uncompromising idealism is challenged several times in the book—and not only by the offer of marriage from two interesting men. Her boss at the town's newspaper, where Judith works on minor editorial tasks, warns her that too much idealism will leave her lonely and unfit for ordinary life. Mr. Byington praises her poetry—even publishes some of it in the *Patriot*—but he also offers his own example as a warning. Once enchanted by the English romantic poets, Byington now presents himself as a man thoroughly unsuited for happiness. He quotes her some fragments from Browning's "In a Gondola," and though he cannot quite recall the lines about "this mad ideal"—"Rescue me thou, the only real! / And scare away this mad ideal"—he paraphrases their meaning in his own rough, half-drunken way. The poet, he tells her, "wants to get rid of this ideal, he wants to chase it away, and have something familiar and human instead. . . . But ideals, you'll find, aren't so easy to chase away. The crazier they are, the more they stick to you."

Only gradually does Judith become wary of her militantly independent nature. For a long while she had refused to see Roy in Boston, for fear her presence might disrupt his artistic resolve. At last she decides to join him there. When she arrives in Boston she finds him miserable and sick, tended by his older sister who blames Judith for her brother's unhappiness. Filled with remorse, Judith approaches

Roy as he lies unconscious on his sister's bed. But at the climactic moment she is unable to bring herself to wake him. Abruptly she leaves the apartment, with plans to seek out New York's famous avant-garde.

Dell sympathized with Judith, but he was unable wholeheartedly to vindicate her decision to abandon Roy in favor of bohemia. By 1925 Judith's resolve struck Dell as at best a partial triumph, and the book ended on an inconclusive note. As Judith heads by train to New York, Dell pictures her "troubled with doubts and flushed with eagerness"—as hopeful a conclusion as he can pin on the story. Her resilient independence now seems shadowed by her failure as a lover. Her solitary nature at last seems as much a curse as a blessing.

Dell turned to much the same subject—of alienation and community—in his next book, *Runaway*, the least autobiographical of his novels to that time and dramatically different from *This Mad Ideal*. Where the preceding book centers on its heroine's unwillingness to integrate herself into society, *Runaway* is the story of a man who had deserted his family years earlier, only to return and gradually find a niche within the society he had abandoned. Clearly Dell viewed the book as an answer to *This Mad Ideal*, a hopeful response to the discontent that pervades that earlier novel. This difference in theme necessitated certain formal alterations as well. Most important, his determination to write a book about a solitary man's return to community led Dell to provide a far more detailed portrait of society in *Runaway* than he had offered in *This Mad Ideal*.

The novel is about Michael Shenstone's return to Beaumont, the medium-sized provincial town he had deserted seventeen years before in order to become a vagabond, wandering throughout Asia for the better part of two decades. Many years before, Shenstone had come to Beaumont as a young journalist and married Helena Boyce, a beautiful woman who could have married more wisely but who insisted on Shenstone, precisely for his rebellious, self-absorbed nature. Helena never demanded that he become respectable. Her generous nature is clearly patterned on that of several women in Dell's own life: Margery Currey, Marjorie Jones, and B. Marie. But Dell believed that men rarely deserve such generosity. Shenstone is destined to disappoint his selfless, forgiving wife.

Dell provides brief snapshots of his protagonist's early married life. For a while after his marriage Shenstone had felt compelled to earn money and raise himself in the town's estimation, and so he became a businessman. The couple prospered, even if Shenstone felt ruined by his life in business. Soon they were settled in a large home, the parents of a little girl. But Shenstone remained unhappy and bought himself a small cottage in town where he could read his books and dream of escape to Asia. When he finally left, sneaking out of town and boarding a late-night train, Helena refused to blame him, either publicly or at home. She seems always to have expected it of him, even to have felt he was right in saving himself from Beaumont and domesticity.

Shenstone returns seventeen years later, long after Helena has died. His plans are to stay no more than a month, get reacquainted with his daughter, then leave again for Asia. He is overtaken, however, by circumstances he had scarcely anticipated: by his resurgent love for his daughter, Amber; by a complex series of developments surrounding Amber's inheritance, which it turns out has been misappropriated by Helena's lawyer and former suitor, Ben Chivers; and by his growing friendship with George Weatherby, whom Shenstone had known years before as a boy poet but who has since become an embittered lawyer.

For all its elaborate plot machinations and conventional treatment of the romance that develops between Amber and George, *Runaway* is notable for Dell's portrait of Michael Shenstone. He is an ironic, distrustful man, unwilling to commit himself to others. In fact he is the man Dell might have become had he not found lasting love in his second marriage. But Dell sees to it that Shenstone too is rescued by love. Only gradually does Shenstone discover his subterranean sympathy for the town and daughter he had earlier fled.

Shenstone is troubled by the cynicism he detects in young, artistic people like George Weatherby. Here in the West, he tells George, "you are so rich, so proud, so confident of your mastery over the forces of nature, that you are beginning to turn back to paddle your toes in chaos for the fun of it. But the East is so poor, so humble, so afraid of Nature's anarchy, that it must treasure everything upon which man has ever set his mark—and his mark is order, which is escape from chaos. That is the meaning of its conservatism. A bad custom is better than none; for it is, at least, human."

Eventually Shenstone detects fine, human order in all sorts of unexpected places: in Amber's life with her suffragist aunt, Victoria; in George and his generous, wealthy uncle; in various of the townspeople who befriend him despite his past. To return to Beaumont, he discovers, is no simple matter. Inevitably it involves him in a web of human relationships that he finds unexpectedly powerful and gratifying. It is a conservative order that intrigues Shenstone, not the shiny radical dream of social order represented by the young revolutionary Jim Pickett, whom Shenstone describes as "sane, just, ruthlessly efficient," and who has as little patience with ordinary pleasures as he does with old-style romantic rebels like Shenstone. As unexpected as Shenstone's growing taste for conservative order is his recognition that it is finely present in Beaumont. He surprises himself by resolving, at least temporarily, to stay there.

At the end of the novel Shenstone considers the Asian figurine, a small jade dragon, that has for decades symbolized his dream of flight from ordinary life. Now it seems to him "the image of something beautiful and terrible,—outside of man's sane hopes, yet inexorably a part of man's destiny,—sometimes darkly hostile and sometimes inscrutably consoling." Here Dell made the vagabond's rejection of society more sinister—and yet more alluring—than had been the case in *This Mad Ideal*. Shenstone remains alive to the temptations offered him by flight and his solitary self. But Dell is also careful to make him a man who has discovered, much to his enchantment, that ordinary life can be as satisfying as anything he ever dreamed of finding elsewhere.

DELL FINISHED *Runaway* in the spring of 1925. Reviews of it and *This Mad Ideal* were every bit as mixed as those that had greeted *Janet March* in 1923. The *Bookman* called *This Mad Ideal* "as good as *Moon-Calf* if not better"; Edward Davison of the *Saturday Review of Literature* praised *Runaway* as "subtle, stimulating, and well-wrought." But Stuart Sherman, in a long survey of Dell's career in the *New York Herald Tribune*, detected in *This Mad Ideal* a "marked falling off in [Dell's] artistic resources"—a weak return to themes handled more robustly in *Moon-Calf*. Other reviews of Dell's two 1925 novels indicated widespread confusion as to his intentions. A reviewer in the London *Times Literary Supplement* described Dell as entirely in sympathy with Judith's quest for independence, suggesting that Dell raises that quest "to the level of inspired sanity." The *Booklist*'s reviewer, on the other hand, found little evidence of such sympathy, calling *This Mad Ideal* "more conservative than [Dell's] earlier novels."

By 1925 Dell was beginning to observe this bedlam of judgments with grim detachment. ("Why, I wonder, should anyone ever publish a book?" he was to write Ficke in 1929. "Why take so much trouble, just to be insulted by nincompoops?") Confusion over his intentions in *This Mad Ideal* and *Runaway* reflected a confusion of expectations among readers about what to expect from a Floyd Dell novel. To Dell it was plain that while he retained his affection for youthful (and not so youthful) vagabonds in these novels, he was also firmly convinced of the importance of community and tradition.

Peculiarly irksome was the fact that in 1925 he found himself surrounded by an emergent culture that seemed determined to vindicate "laissez-faire, do-nothing selfishness as a pattern of social heroism." Townsfolk in Croton still regarded him as an outlandish bohemian. But Dell knew that he wished to build, in life as in literature, on the pattern of the fine human order that Michael Shenstone had come to admire in *Runaway*. If many readers and critics now regarded him as conservative, Dell was no more inclined than Shenstone to change his ways to appease them.

However little Dell had in common with the youngest generation of American writers in 1925, he did mirror them in one respect that summer: he packed up his family and embarked for Europe, staying the whole summer and well into the fall, first in London, then in France. It was not, generally, a relaxing trip. Dell had long hated to travel (perhaps a reaction to his earlier years when his family moved often, and when a permanent sense of home had largely escaped him). In Europe he was uneasy and out of sorts, homesick for Croton and eager to return to work.

The Dells started out with ten weeks in London, staying in the small apartment they rented from Charles Hallinan, Dell's old pal from the *Chicago Evening Post*, now a journalist in London. Dell stayed busy in the English capital. He was often at the British Museum where he did research for a new, all-English edition of one of his favorite books, Robert Burton's *Anatomy of Melancholy*. He and B. Marie visited friends from the States, including Max Eastman's sister, Crystal. Mutual acquaintances introduced him to members of the Labor party at Parliament. Dell and B. Marie even had "dinner at the House of Commons with Ellen Wilkinson, a left-wing Labor M.P., and saw David Kirkwood and others, and later listened to a debate in that queer and cosy club, the House of Commons itself."

Despite such political entertainment, he hated London. It struck him as insufferably snobbish and aristocratic and made him more than a little proud of his plain, working-class American roots. "Though the Londoners were kind to us," he recalled, "I did not like London—it reeked to me of a hateful past." In a letter to Upton Sinclair, composed during the family's last days in Britain, Dell complained: "London has put me into an 18 year old mood. It is, above all, the citadel of two things both of which I hate—the surviving remnants of feudalism, and the—what shall I call it to distinguish it from our sort of highway robbery?—aristocratic finance. . . . I cannot enjoy their beauty (if they have any, which I deeply doubt), but am filled with a childish and helpless rage." He was also sick much of the time, suffering from bouts of gastritis, which he later claimed nearly killed him.

All the Dells liked Paris better—"as it seems," Dell later wrote, "that Americans always do." The family stayed on the Left Bank, enjoying the place's bohemian flavor and exploring the city. Dell visited with Simone Tery, who had translated *Moon-Calf* into French some years before. He praised the French to Ficke: "I admire their practicality, their money making instincts, their reasonableness, which is not the modern reasonableness I supposed but something earlier, older, Catholic, conventional, spacious, orderly, precise and well-adjusted to life—if that collection of adjectives means anything." After a month the family moved on to the Riviera, which Dell later remembered as "an American suburb." He saw John Dos Passos there as well as Max Eastman and Eastman's second wife, Eliena Krylenko. But Dell was not at all taken by the expatriate scene in southern France. Still sick, he was seized by nostalgia when an American acquaintance told him that the house in which he and B. Marie had lived in Greenwich Village, at 11 Christopher Street, had been torn down to make way for a modern apartment block. Quickly he composed "The Ballad of Christopher Street." Gently sentimental, leavened in spots by his familiar, ironic touch, the poem made clear how much Dell's life was anchored in America and how little he was able to share his friends' enthusiasm for life away from home.

When the family returned to Croton in mid-October, Dell was

seriously ill, having lost twenty-three pounds in Europe. Soon he began to mend, only to find himself embroiled in controversies surrounding *Runaway*. William Lyon Phelps, the Yale professor who had championed modern literature around the turn of the century, over the objections of tradition-bound classicists, wrote Dell in praise of the novel's "poetry" and "romance." But there were reproaches from old friends who saw the book as "a betrayal of the 'cause.'" Dell was wounded by these accusations; more, he was disgusted by them. "There is in America," he felt at the time, "a certain kind of 'radicalism' or 'liberalism' which consists in an ostrich-like refusal to face the realities of life, or in a Pollyannish insistence upon seeing only the brighter side of the break-up of a family. Any truthful treatment of these situations is resented, and regarded as 'reactionary.'"

Dell also found encouraging signs as he resumed his literary life in Croton. In March 1926 the "Literature and the Machine Age" essays were published by Doran in book form and titled *Intellectual Vagabondage*. The book was seriously and often enthusiastically reviewed. Dell continued its argument in an essay he published in the fall of 1926 in V. F. Calverton's *Modern Quarterly*, titled "Shell-Shock and the Poetry of Robinson Jeffers." Dell made clear at the start that he was less interested in judging Jeffers's poetry than in ascertaining what the current vogue for Jeffers revealed about "the psychology of the intelligentsia itself at [this] moment in history." He briefly summarized what he took to be Jeffers's "attitude toward life": "Mankind is a loathsome breed; an inconsiderable breed, too, mere lice on the whirling earth; and being doomed to certain extinction, its whole history in the meantime is meaningless." He laid bare Jeffers's underlying antihumanism, his suggestions that "humanity is 'the mould to break away from, the crust to break through, the coal to break into fire.'" For Dell, Jeffers's popularity lay not in his brilliance as a poet but in his espousal of certain comfortingly nihilistic sentiments: "Since life is meaningless, it is silly to try to understand it, or attempt by unraveling its secrets to get conscious and purposeful control of it. Our moralities are pitiful fictions; the true instinctive and sexual motives of life are too large and powerful to be comprehended within any merely human scheme. In so far as our sexuality is customary and civilized, it is a despicable pretense; in so far as it exceeds these bounds, it is truly interesting, picturesque, dramatic and splendid." The appeal of such a view, Dell claimed, lay in how it set young intellectuals free from any sense of their accountability to society or the future. Jeffers's world rendered all traditional responsibilities pointless: "It is a world in which politics are trash, revolution an absurdity..., science a useless but impressive revelation of our human futility, art a bitterly earnest expression of the tragic quality of human existence, love a (sometimes pleasant) madness. The role of the intellect, it will be noted, is necessarily very small in this world."

This stern commentary came ultimately out of Dell's political commitments and his deep sense of literature's essential place in a sane and just society. But he was capable of another mood in his writings as well, warm and whimsical. In 1923 Carl Van Doren, then editor of the *Century*, discussed with Dell the possibility of writing a history of Greenwich Village. Dell responded with a sheaf of stories and thinly disguised pieces of autobiographical reminiscence, all unified by memories of life in the Village and reflections on the charms and limitations of bohemia. Most of the pieces flowed out of him in a two-week burst of creativity that summer. "The Ballad of Christopher Street" followed two years later, composed on the Riviera. In late 1925 Dell wrote a few more pieces and readied the set for publication. Doran published the volume, *Love in Greenwich Village*, in May 1926, two months after *Intellectual Vagabondage* appeared and while Dell was working on his tough, uncompromising essay on Jeffers.

The atmosphere of nostalgia lies heavily on these stories, poems, and recollections. Still, they are notable for their clear-sightedness, for their air of deft, ironic detachment. The combination of fondness and insight makes the volume one of Dell's best. For all the sentiment suffusing these stories of young prewar Villagers, alienated from their families and hometowns, inspired as much by the dream of love as by their artistic ambitions, the stories are sharp and knowing, sometimes opening briefly on dark, bitter insights. Dell freely acknowledged his nostalgia for "those lost, happy years" in a Greenwich Village now given over to commercial culture and popular "uglification." He preferred the prewar Village to its new incarnation, populated with young people less idealistic than he and his companions had ever been. Of the new Village denizens Dell was fair but unsympathetic: "For them the world would never suddenly go blank of meaning. They were accustomed to its not having any meaning. I saw ourselves, in retrospect, as touched with a miracu-

lous naivete, a Late-Victorian credulousness, a faith, happy and
absurd, in the goodness and beauty of this chaotic universe. These
young people knew better." And yet Dell was never blind to the
follies of his own generation. If there is a theme uniting all the
stories and passages of reminiscence in *Love in Greenwich Village*, it
is of the failure of all the characters to reconcile their desires for
extraordinary and mundane experiences, for art and ordinary pleasures, for independence and surrender to love.

In one story, "Hallelujah, I'm a Bum!", Dell returned to the
conflict between politics and bohemia—in this case, between a
sometime political radical, Jasper Weed, and an ironic, apolitical
poet, Inez Vance. Jasper is tried, and eventually convicted and
sentenced to twenty years in prison, for his part in IWW rallies and
strikes. His radicalism places him at odds with Inez, whom he loves
and who is fond of him. He spends some time with her in the
Village, happy in their romance and detachment from the world.
But he also affirms his IWW beliefs: he wishes sincerely (if only
intermittently) to help remake the world in some better form. For
Inez, such idealism is absurd: "Don't you see that it's a kind of
madness," she tells him, "this wanting to make the world better?
The only sane ones are the dreamers and idlers. At least they don't
willfully increase the sum of human misery." When Jasper is finally
to go to prison, and so decides to escape to Soviet Russia, both agree
that they should split for good. Still, they spend one last night
together, briefly forgetting their differences, gladly escaping the great
outside world.

In this story Dell drew on his own romance with Edna St.
Vincent Millay. Like Dell in his earlier relations with Millay, Jasper
is tempted by order, permanence, and marriage in his relations with
Inez. And like Millay, Inez stoutly refuses his pleas. Jasper even uses
Dell's nickname for Millay, calling Inez "Vixen." But the autobiographical elements here are vague and fleeting. They are clearer in
"The Ex-Villager's Confession," about an affair much like the one
between Dell and Marjorie Jones during their early years in the
Village. The tale describes a principled, enlightened relation between two unmarried lovers, living together in the Village, always
respectful of each other's independence. When the two become
estranged—largely due to the man's infidelities—he is baffled by
their failure. The woman, Rosemary, understands better. She explains that they had always been afraid of what they really wanted:

"the old things—the best of them; things like homes, and permanence, and babies." She advises him to marry the next woman he falls in love with—advice he follows, and to his great happiness.

The most affecting piece of *Love in Greenwich Village* is "Phantom Adventure." Here Dell tells the story of a young banker (with "an apartment in town and a house in the country and a car and a wife and four lovely children") who has a brief flight from respectability in the form of a night spent with a stranger in the Village, a woman who is also in love with the dream of adventure. Neither is tempted to make their time together last. After the man returns to the room where he has been staying, in the house of a writer friend, he is "glad to be back in a world that had a meaning beyond the moment, a world that reached back in memory and forward in hope, the world of reality." Still, the incident stays with him, and he is shocked to discover not long afterward that the woman was a lonely schoolteacher and that she has recently died. He goes to see her corpse and is chastened to see her dead face which he had recently found so vibrantly alive.

Dell infused the story's conclusion with a telling mix of poignance and irony. One night the man tells his wife the whole story of his brief affair and its aftermath, taking care to disguise the whole as fiction. His proper wife is moved to tears by the tale—both by the depiction of the woman and by the man's willingness to break with convention and love her for one night. But the husband is shocked to discover that his wife has absolutely no suspicion that the tale is autobiographical. Quite simply, she cannot imagine that the man in the story—"the foolish adventurer of his tale"—could be her husband: "He was to her merely what he had labored for twelve years to seem to all the world." Never could he convince her that he was reckless and passionate. "He could prove nothing; his secret was fatally secure." And so he tells the story to his friend the writer, who will turn it into fiction and "sell it to other dreamers."

In "Phantom Adventure" the gap between dreams and reality, between literature and the real world, seems wider than in any other of these stories. Yet the two are also strangely intermingled here, as Dell felt was only proper. The dreamers in all the stories in *Love in Greenwich Village* are either lost to the world, like the young poets Dell describes in the Village, or unable to make their dreams a part of everyday life, like the hero of "Phantom Adventure," whose moment of adventure is doomed to remain separate from everything else in his life, no matter how hard he tries to connect the two. But these dreamers seem more real to Dell than all the faded, respectable people who flit about at the margins of these tales. As the banker's writer friend suggests, "the phantom world of fancy" is where we play out our deepest wishes, even if it is "not a part of this real life of ours at all." Dell has the banker validate his own phantom adventure as he relates his barely disguised tale to his wife: "as he talked, his confession became a passionate vindication of the rights of that phantom self for which the workaday world has so little use, and which can achieve only a pitiful and momentary freedom in what the world calls folly." Dell could chide his characters for their failure to put aside their dreams and take their place in the larger world. But he also knew that his characters were real precisely in those moments when they were unwilling to compromise their dreams.

This irony—that in their dreams and passion for escape his characters attained their greatest reality—was fully part of Dell's purpose in these stories. But there was a final irony that he could not quite control: at a time when he was living in the suburbs, a happy family man, assembling another book, *Intellectual Vagabondage*, which upbraided a whole tradition of literary dreamers and escapists, he found himself weighed down with nostalgia for the bohemian existence he had known not many years before in Greenwich Village. While Dell rejected bohemia as aery nothingness in the one book, he celebrated his bohemians in the other for the escapism that made them so vivid, so alive. It is strange that *Intellectual Vagabondage* and *Love in Greenwich Village* should come from the same author, that they were written at roughly the same time, and that they were published within eight weeks of each other in 1926. No irony was more typical of Dell, nor was there any he was less likely to master.

T W E L V E

Radical Renegade

Dell's radical credentials were endangered from the moment he decided, in January 1920, to take a leave of absence from the *Liberator* in order to write *Moon-Calf*. As the decade progressed, his ties with literary and political radicals in New York became more and more problematic. He remained friends with numerous leftists of his own generation while forming close friendships with several of the younger set. But by the early 1920s Dell was often dismissed by radicals as a renegade to the cause, an unexpectedly conventional writer and a conservative.

He never quite lived down these charges; nor was he ever entirely convinced he should try. He had long recognized "conservative" sympathies in himself, scattered among more unambiguously radical ones, and as time passed he became more certain of the rightness of those inclinations. He grew more immersed in family and community. A second son, Christopher, named for the street in Greenwich Village where Dell and B. Marie lived after their marriage, was born in 1927. Dell wrote more essays on marriage and family. He became actively involved in the effort to establish, and later to rebuild after a devastating fire, an experimental school in Croton that both his boys eventually attended. Like Michael Shenstone in *Runaway*, he found himself in the 1920s a man with the remnants of a radical reputation but without any overwhelmingly persuasive reasons why he should renounce the more traditional life to which he had returned.

At the same time Dell never fully relinquished his place in the radical community during the 1920s. He worked instead to steer literary radicals in directions other than those they were too often inclined to follow. He resisted both the fashionable cynicism of "lost generation" authors and the proletarian pretensions of militant radicals. Holding firm to the notion of a purposeful, humane radicalism, he kept his name on the *Liberator's* masthead till the magazine expired in October 1924. Nonetheless, he found himself increasingly out of step with the magazine's turn to doctrinaire, strident radicalism.

He was saddened by the *Liberator's* demise, even though he had never been willing to dedicate himself fully to the magazine. For Dell the enterprise had never inspired the camaraderie and passionate commitment that had typified the *Masses*. Novel-writing and extended leaves of absence had severed him from full absorption in the magazine. Other leaders at the magazine also grew distant from it. In early 1921 coeditor Crystal Eastman, Max Eastman's sister, married and moved to England. Later that same year business manager E. F. Mylius absconded with the *Liberator's* total cash reserves of $4,500. Max Eastman, unhappy about the prospect of raising new funds for the magazine (and eager to get a look at Soviet Russia), soon left for Europe. In his stead he appointed two younger men—the Jamaican poet Claude McKay and the militant radical Mike Gold—as coeditors. Joe Freeman, whose own importance at the *Liberator* was on the rise at this time, admitted later that few of the younger editors and writers at the *Liberator* in 1922 had the intellectual substance of "the old group."

The editorial partnership of McKay and Gold was fated for failure. Freeman called Gold "the outstanding 'proletarian' of the group. He affected dirty shirts, a big, black, uncleaned Stetson with the brim of a sombrero; smoked stinking, twisted, Italian three-cent cigars, and spat frequently and vigorously on the floor." McKay, who for several years had helped Max Eastman edit the *Liberator*, had an especially low opinion of Gold's literary tastes. "Michael Gold's idea of *The Liberator*," according to McKay, "was that it should become a popular proletarian magazine, printing doggerels from lumberjacks and stevedores and true revelations from chambermaids. I contended that while it was most excellent to get material out of the forgotten members of the working class, it should be good stuff that could compare with any other writing." McKay infuriated Gold by insisting that when it came to judging literature and art, "class labels were incidental." After tension between the two men nearly led to blows,

McKay resigned and a while afterward left for Russia. Gold followed suit, moving to California where he went to work on a novel.

Contentious and distracted editors were not the only problems facing the *Liberator*. As Freeman also realized, "the growing prosperity of the middle classes and the disillusionment of intellectuals with the social revolution deprived the *Liberator* of its old base." Literary rebels were now drawn to apolitical art journals and expatriate reviews rather than to an explicitly political magazine like the *Liberator*. In the fall of 1922, with the magazine in straitened financial circumstances and uncertain about its direction, the editorial board decided to turn the *Liberator* into an official organ of the Communist party. Dell, who had earlier refused to put up his house mortgage as collateral against the *Liberator's* mounting debts, reluctantly agreed that the Communist party, as the sole possible guarantor of the magazine's solvency, be allowed to take over. "We moved the magazine to Party headquarters on East Eleventh Street," Freeman recalled, "on the opposite side of the Village, closer to the district in which the trade-union workers lived." The move led to a more divided *Liberator*, split between "political" and "art" editors, with Dell firmly in the latter camp. Freeman later described the magazine's divided editorial setup:

> The "political editors" were for the most part members of the Central Committee of the Communist party—among them C. E. Ruthenberg, William Z. Foster, Ludwig Lore, James P. Cannon, Jay Lovestone, M. J. Olgin; the "art editors" were for the most part members of the old *Masses* and *Liberator* group including Floyd Dell, Arturo Giovannitti, Boardman Robinson, William Gropper, Lydia Gibson, Hugo Gellert, Claude McKay, Michael Gold. Not all of these were active, however; some were abroad, others lived out of town. The Party, quite naturally, wished to keep the direction of editorial policy in its own hands; the realm of art, presumably less serious, was left for the artists.

Watching all this unfold from his outpost in Croton, Dell went along with the new arrangement. But he was never happy with it. He contributed essays, most notably those in the "Literature and the Machine Age" series, but he dropped out of the battle to control the magazine's editorial policies. By 1924 he was little more than an honorary editor and an isolated contributor, no longer an insider on the magazine he had helped found a half-decade earlier.

His gradual loss of influence at the *Liberator* did not remove Dell altogether from the company of radicals. Scattered left-wing causes took up chunks of his time in the early and mid-1920s, even as he was secretly wishing he could have all his time for writing and family life. He was off and on committed to organizations with the kinds of pseudo-official names that were to inspire many other American literary radicals during the 1930s. In the mid-1920s he was secretary for a group called the "Committee for Recommending American Books to the U.S.S.R. (Russia)." Formed by the Society for Cultural Relations, a Soviet-sponsored cultural outfit, the committee was devoted to establishing cultural ties with the Soviet Union. Dell worked fitfully for the committee, soliciting suggestions from writer friends like Upton Sinclair and Theodore Dreiser for books that might be translated into Russian. He also worked briefly to establish a Labor Book Prize Committee in 1927, designed to grant a monthly prize of one hundred dollars to books on labor and radical politics. The committee counted Theodore Dreiser, Mary Heaton Vorse, and Scott Nearing (a radical economist, activist, and writer) among its other patrons. Through it all Dell remained the man he had aptly described in "A Psycho-Analytic Confession": a writer who, despite sporadic compulsions to play a sober, productive role in the political arena, was happiest in his literary and private pursuits. Radical organizations with impressive titles never inspired him for long.

The closest thing to a radical project that did engross Dell during the mid-twenties was the critical biography of Upton Sinclair that he wrote in 1926 and early 1927. It was Sinclair who first broached the idea of Dell writing such a book. In response to requests from overseas for information about his life, Sinclair wanted a biography that could be written quickly, translated into a great many languages, and sold to admirers of his work throughout the world. Dell seemed ideal for the job, with his lifelong sympathy for Sinclair's work and his radical insights into the relation between literature and politics. What's more, he had praised several of Sinclair's recent books in letters to the author. In one he called Sinclair's *Mammonart*, a sociologically based critical study, "a great work, greatly accomplished." He suggested that every child in America should read it. "It would knock that pious nonsense out of their heads that they are taught in school—the notion that true art is tame art, art made safe and harmless for the bourgeoisie! That nonsense, poisoning the minds of our finest, bravest, most clear-seeing young people even before they have learned how to write, muddying youth's purpose and degrading art's meaning for them, is robbing us of the great and vital literature they could create tomorrow. Your book is the best antidote for that spiritual poison."

Once he had begun writing the biography, however, Dell sent Sinclair the following lighthearted warning: "B. Marie says you are a very courageous man to put yourself in my hands! You've reflected, I suppose, on the fact that there are things in this universe upon which we are not in agreement. Are you willing to take your chances?" Sinclair wrote back: "When I had to differ with you concerning your books, you stood the racket like the fine soul that you are, and I will have to display equal courage. I have entire confidence in your love of truth."

Dell plowed into the task with typical energy, soliciting scores of biographical facts from Sinclair in letter after letter. Early in the summer of 1926, after the publication of *Love in Greenwich Village*, Dell, B. Marie, and four-year-old Tony took a brief trip west, visiting friends—among them, Arthur Ficke and his wife Gladys—in Santa Fe. By mid-July he was back at his desk, producing chapter after chapter of the book. In mid-fall it was heading toward completion, and Dell reported to Sinclair, in a letter dated November 8, 1926, that almost all the chapters had been prepared by a typist, that he was currently busy with corrections and rewriting, and that he would soon send Sinclair a copy of the finished typescript.

With the biography largely finished at the end of December (and with Sinclair's approval in hand), Dell confessed belatedly to another matter that had concerned him: that in drawing Sinclair's portrait he may have overstated Sinclair's progression from a rather otherworldly youth to a man fully at home in the world. "I perceive my limitations as a biographer very distinctly," Dell admitted. "I am interested in a certain psychological puzzle—how the devil a very sensitive young poet who hated the outside world became what he is today—and having shown that process, my interest refuses to linger in any detail upon the results!"

In short, Dell hinted that his biography of Sinclair was thematically allied to many of his novels. This proved to be the case. Dell traces Sinclair's progression from a bookish boy growing up in poverty in Baltimore and New York, to a young hack writer producing 56,000 words of popular magazine fiction every week, to an

unpromising—and uncompromisingly idealistic—romantic poet, to
a suddenly successful novelist with the publication of *The Jungle*, to
a radical pamphleteer, novelist, and activist during the 1920s.
Crucial to this transition from idealist to realist in Dell's view was
Sinclair's first marriage and discovery of socialism as a young man.
Especially important to Sinclair's growth as a writer, according to
Dell, "was that aspect of the Socialist philosophy which gave, to one
who had always feared and hated the world, some realistic means of
discriminating among its values, so that he could more freely and
fearlessly enter into an imaginative intimacy with it in all its crude
detail. . . . It is ultimately to the bracing influences of this new
philosophy that we owe his development into a great realistic
novelist."

Such arguments plainly carried the Dell stamp. But *Upton
Sinclair* also reflected Dell's effort to come to grips with what was
unique in Sinclair's sprawling corpus and unconventional career.
Often this led to unsympathetic judgments. He was tough on many
of Sinclair's novels, finding them often hasty, dogmatic productions.
He also disapproved of Sinclair's "puritanism": his frequent lack of
insight into his characters' sex lives, and his tendency to reduce
sexual relations to direct reflections of his characters' economic
backgrounds. This last inclination, Dell argued, revealed a blindness
to certain features of human experience. Sinclair "does not permit
himself to realize," Dell wrote, "that it is largely human nature itself
that he is condemning, rather than merely the aberrations of a
property system."

Dell argued that the pinnacle of Sinclair's achievement lay not in
his novels (not even in the world-famous *Jungle*) but in his pam-
phlets on religion, education, journalism, and literature. According
to Dell, Sinclair's exposés of how organized religion, newspapers,
and educational institutions contributed to economic and political
injustice in America added up to a vast, unsentimental, infinitely
detailed portrait of modern American life—a portrait that he never
quite equaled in his fiction: "In the realm of facts, as not always in
the realm controlled by the imagination, he is utterly assured and at
home. . . . Across these huge canvases march the multitudes of living
mankind, tricksters and deluded ones, liars and dupes, thieves and
victims, masters and henchmen, the preachers, editors, railroad
presidents, financiers, politicians, soldiers, gunmen, salesmen, teach-

ers, children: it is a panorama of contemporary American humanity, candidly, tenderly, relentlessly, magnificently displayed."

Most impressive to Dell was Sinclair's *Mammonart: An Essay in Economic Interpretation* (1925). Much like Dell's own "Literature and the Machine Age," *Mammonart* "is a handbook covering in short, vivid chapters a vast part of the world's literature, reviewing it against its own political and economic background." What Dell recognized in *Mammonart* was a "social revolutionary criticism" that "takes for granted that an artist is an interpreter of life, and judges the truth and value of his interpretation by the test of how fully he shows himself aware of what is going on in his world, with special reference to social change, and whether he helps his audience to understand and sympathize with such changes." Still, Dell was careful to define this criticism in such a way that it not be confused with the more vulgar forms of revolutionary criticism then starting to proliferate on the radical literary scene. In Dell's critical scheme, the artist "is recognized as a discriminator of spiritual values, in some sense [an indirect] creator of them." But the artist "is not asked to be consciously attempting to create such values, and least of all is he asked to believe in this or that specific program of change—he is judged as an artist and not as a politician."

This desire to preserve artistic integrity from partisan political purposes was in fact more typical of Dell than of Sinclair, a frankly political man who in 1934 was to mount a serious campaign (on the Democratic ticket) for the governorship of California. In defending a measure of imaginative autonomy for literature, however, Dell opened himself to bitter attacks from highly politicized literary radicals. Even while he was working on his biography of Upton Sinclair, Dell found himself the object of harsh criticism from young radicals. Among them was V. F. Calverton, publisher of the *Modern Quarterly*. Reviewing *Love in Greenwich Village* in the *New Masses*, the latest incarnation of the *Masses* (on whose board Dell was listed as a contributing editor), Calverton complained that Dell had abandoned radicalism for the composition of "sexy novels for adolescent Menckenians and jaded bourgeoisie."

The charge was patently unfair. Calverton was well aware that Dell himself had criticized the retreat to exclusively private and sexual themes in modern writing, characterizing it as a failure of radical purpose and nerve. In fact, Calverton not only knew that Dell had made such critical remarks in his books; Calverton had gone so far as brazenly to lift such remarks from "Literature and the Machine Age" and pass them off as his own in *Sex Expression in Literature* (1926). When Dell wrote him about these unacknowledged borrowings, Calverton admitted that he should properly have mentioned his indebtedness to Dell. He apologized for his failure to acknowledge Dell's influence and promised that he would do so in subsequent editions. Yet here was Calverton, in October 1926, lambasting Dell for precisely the kind of literary derelictions that Dell had deplored in "Literature and the Machine Age." What's more, Calverton had clearly failed to read the book under review, *Love in Greenwich Village*, with any patience. He ignored the irony (and the more explicit statements of disapproval) with which Dell dissociated himself from any unambiguous glamorization of the irresponsible bohemians pictured in the book.

In *Upton Sinclair* Dell far outdid Calverton in exposing the way in which ostensibly radical, disenchanted writers flattered the new bourgeois taste for sexual license and moral chaos in literature. "The acquisition of a considerable margin of leisure by a large part of the population which had hitherto piously believed in keeping its nose to the grindstone," Dell noted, "has resulted in a violent urban repudiation of former middle-class standards of decency and respectability. . . . A moral nihilism is the approved note at present among the shell-shocked intelligentsia, and in this comfortable doctrine the prosperous middle-class is beginning to find spiritual encouragement for the diversions which enrich its newly-found leisure."

Such passages show that Dell was better able than Calverton and other young radicals to expose the failures and hypocrisies of much contemporary literature. But Dell was not willing to adopt the ruthlessness that was becoming more common among radicals in the late 1920s. The publication of *Intellectual Vagabondage* in 1926 and *Upton Sinclair* in 1927 should have been sufficient to prove his enduring left-wing sympathies. But for radicals who required something simpler, something more dogmatic and propagandistic, Dell's commitment to literature's autonomy and his interest in experience outside the realm of explicitly political activities made him an easy target for dismissal. He continued to insist on his radical credentials in 1926 and 1927. But to many younger radicals, he looked distressingly attached to outmoded ideas about the dignity of private life, family, and the literary imagination.

*   *   *

REACTIONARY INSTITUTION OR not, family had become a constant source of interest to Dell by the mid-twenties. Cooperating with friends in Croton—a number of them old Greenwich Village radicals like themselves—the Dells supported an experimental school where Tony (and later Chris) could receive the kind of education that Dell had first described in *Were You Ever a Child?* The Hessian Hills School became the focus of much enlightened parental interest, and couples with children actually moved to Croton on the basis of the school's reputation. "The character of our part of the village," Dell noted with fond irony, "thus changed in the course of a few years from a bohemian, literary, artistic, and typically childless neighborhood, to a group of parents."

These were years during which Dell worked extraordinarily hard, producing a book, and sometimes several books—most of them novels—each year. He also churned out a good many essays and carried on a voluminous correspondence with numerous people. The attention he devoted to his sons was often of an intellectual sort—analyzing patterns in their development, taking an active interest in their education at home and in school, even applying Freudian psychology to the task of interpreting their dreams. Analyzing some of young Tony's recurring bad dreams, Dell was certain he could detect resentment against himself, much along the classic oedipal lines described by Freud. Perhaps he was right. But the fact that Dell discovered such deep-seated resentment in Tony revealed something about his own feelings as well. It suggested some underlying guilt toward his young son—guilt that he was not an entirely selfless father, but rather one who was often taken away from his family by his never-ending literary work.

B. Marie was the center of gravity in the Dells' home life, sacrificing much of her own independence in order to make possible her husband's ambitious career. She too, however, was often busy with activities outside the home. She worked at the Croton library and devoted a great deal of time to charitable causes like the Near East Relief. The boys were often left in the care of Mamie Golden, who had occasionally worked as a housekeeper for Floyd and B. Marie in Greenwich Village, and who worked for the family as a live-in housekeeper throughout much of the 1920s.

Tony and Chris also spent countless hours with the neighbors, Bob and Lydia Minor, who had no children of their own but who loved kids. Toward the end of the decade and into the next, Tony and Chris spent nearly as much time at the Minors' as at their own home. The arrangement was generally a happy one. But there was also tension between the Minors and Dell, who felt uneasy with "fighting Bob" Minor's full-blown Communist enthusiasms (Minor had largely abandoned artwork by the early 1920s in order to devote himself to the Communist party: through the twenties he was a member of the CP's central committee; he was the CP candidate for New York governor in 1932, for mayor of New York City in 1933, and for one of New York's seats in the United States Senate in 1936; in 1941 he became the party's acting general secretary). During the late 1920s Dell became increasingly unhappy with Minor's bellicose, hard-line support of the Communist party. He worried that Minor would attempt to convert his boys to the Communist faith. Years later Christopher Dell recalled an unspoken agreement between the Dells and the Minors that the latter couple would not "indoctrinate" the Dell boys while they were in the Minors' home.

No doubt Dell derived genuine satisfaction from fatherhood and marriage, which he felt humanized him after years devoted exclusively to literature, ideas, and politics. "I have gone a long way in becoming like my fellow-man," he wrote in the early 1930s, reflecting on his life as a family man, "and I think it has improved me." For the first time he developed ordinary nonintellectual pursuits. He learned to dance, which he had shied away from during even his wildest Village days. He also learned to drive a car in the late twenties, something in which he found unexpected delight ("To other people," Dell wrote, "the fact of being able to drive a car may be commonplace; to me it is still almost as strange and improbable a thing as it would be to take a trip to the Moon with Jules Verne"). Nestled in his family and among other ex-bohemians on Mount Airy Road in Croton, Dell watched himself gradually transformed into a contented father and husband. To some extent, at least, he was exactly what some radicals called him at the time: a bourgeois *paterfamilias* out in the suburbs. Dell never denied it.

The novels he wrote during the latter half of the twenties all revolved in one way or another around the theme that was occupying so much of his time and attention during those years: fatherhood. He edged around the theme in *An Old Man's Folly*, published in October 1926, only months after *Intellectual Vagabondage* and *Love in Greenwich Village*. The book is the story of Nathaniel Windle, a thoroughly unexceptional man born in Lowell, Massachusetts, in the early 1850s. As a boy Nathaniel is thoroughly influenced by his sober, hardworking father, and somewhat less by his sickly, art-loving mother, who dies when he is still a boy. Later Windle accepts his father's dying wish that he become a business-man, then resigns himself to a life as an unremarkable corset salesman. He marries a woman he never loves, who in turn bears him one child, a daughter whom he never really knows or under-stands. His brief enchantment with literature, together with an even briefer moment of intimacy with an independent-minded working girl named Ada, fades into the background of an otherwise perfectly banal life. Fatherhood only baffles and disappoints him.

Windle's dilemma echoes those of other Dell characters: he is haunted by his dissociation from the world around him. And yet his estrangement seems more hopeless—more helpless—than the es-trangement of a Felix Fay or Michael Shenstone. His dismal passivity seems to reflect Dell's enduring fears about his own charac-ter. Even when Windle seeks out the company of others—the workingmen at a local tavern and, after he inherits his uncle's wallpaper business in the California town of San Angelo, his eccentric, irascible business partner, Mr. Haik—he is unable to make significant contact. When Haik dies and an elderly Windle is eased into retirement by his ambitious son-in-law, the old man seeks solace among the radicals and misfits who gather each evening in little clusters around the town square, talking politics and redemp-tion. Windle can't understand their politics, but he is vaguely at home among these outsiders who, like himself, have no happy place in respectable society.

Windle's ironic, partial redemption is finally set in motion when he is beaten and arrested by policemen for his unexpected show of sympathy at an IWW rally on the square. Afterward he is taken into the radical community where he becomes enamored of two young people, Joe Ford and Ann Elizabeth Landor. Dell based Joe and Ann Elizabeth on himself and B. Marie; their love affair offsets the unflattering self-portrait that Dell created in Windle. Joe and Ann Elizabeth's common-law marriage, crowned by the birth of two boys and a rustic homelife in the New Jersey countryside, is to Windle an unexpected fulfillment of his own buried aspirations. Still there remains an air of detachment and regret about Windle, just as Dell recognized a surviving tendency toward estrangement in himself. If this is a tale of fatherhood, it is of a frustrated, vacant father who only late in life is redeemed by the spectacle of the love of two young people for their own children.

An Old Man's Folly was skillfully composed, ably following Windle's story from cradle to grave, with special light thrown on the old man's strangely rapt absorption in the lives of two young people whom he only partially understands. Dell provided brief snapshots of radicals—their relations within their own tiny community, and a wartime trial under the Espionage Act—that clearly reflected his own past experiences. But for all its grace and occasional innovations, the book was hardly a daring leap from Dell's preceding novels. It covered much the same territory—the conflict experienced by young people between work, ideals, and marriage—that he had explored in his earlier books. Moon-calfishness here took on a new guise in the elderly Windle—but it was moon-calfishness all the same. Composed during a year when Dell was preparing several other books for publication, the novel reflected its author's lack of attention to developing new themes, or presenting familiar ones in new ways.

THE NOVEL'S DEARTH of innovations scarcely worried Dell as he was wrapping it up in spring 1926. Three of his books were to appear that same year, testifying to abundant literary vigor, not exhaustion. Certain elements were bound to recur in his writings. Besides, he realized that among his radical dispositions he harbored certain conservative leanings that would inevitably be reflected in his novels. At times he was positively amused by the unlikely mix of views and tastes that informed his work. In a letter he wrote that spring to Arthur Ficke, Dell lampooned that mix with unmistakable delight: "I remain a pragmatic, Freudian, monogamous Bolshevik, with a conservative taste in literature; I haven't even learned to dance the Charleston; do you suppose I am becoming middle-aged? At all events, I like it." A month shy of his thirty-ninth birthday, Dell gleefully portrayed himself as a middle-aged skeptic: "I have experienced no religious or other conversions this winter, have discovered no great and wonderful and revolutionary new ideas, have become enthusiastic about no new authors, haven't fallen for a single new girl."

All the while he was girding himself for fresh literary undertakings. For several years he had often written in a modest shed in the backyard of his Croton home, where he could find the privacy he needed to compose. But without heat the studio was not suitable for work in the winter. In the spring and summer of 1926 he and B. Marie hired workmen to build an ample studio and sleeping porch on the back of their home. There Dell would be able to work year round and (as was his custom) throughout the night. He finished *An Old Man's Folly* amid the din of sawing and hammering. Rather than distract him from the work, the clamor filled Dell with happy anticipation. All that racket symbolized his renewed commitment to the literary life.

An Unmarried Father, written mainly the following spring, revealed Dell's renewed zest for novel-writing. The theme of the book—the uncontrollable compulsion of a young man to take responsibility for his illegitimate child—was not new to Dell, who had often depicted his male characters' deep-seated desire for marriage and family. What *was* new was the sharp, witty tone of the writing. Dell had often laughed at his characters, particularly male dreamers like Felix Fay. In *An Unmarried Father*, though, the satire is sharper. Dell is fond of his unmarried father, Norman Overbeck, who throws over professional success and respectability in order to adopt his son. But he also frankly reveals all that is ridiculous, incompetent, and misguided in Norman. The book, in fact, is a witty revelation of bourgeois confusion—a portrait of a respectable young man who, like his family, fiancée, and sundry lovers, has almost no insight into his own mind and nature.

Dell opens the novel with Norman ensconced in his hometown of Vickley, Illinois, now portrayed (unlike in *Moon-Calf*) as a blandly bourgeois enclave. Norman has only recently begun to work in his father's law firm. He lives with his family and is engaged to be married in a month to an eminently respectable young woman, Madge Ferris. But respectability, it becomes fast apparent, is not in the cards for Norman Overbeck. Right at the start he receives a mysterious letter from a doctor in Chicago, Martha Zerneke, who runs an adoption clinic and who asks him to contact her about a matter she declines to mention in the letter itself. Only gradually does Norman recall a sexual encounter with a young woman he had known a year earlier in Cambridge, Massachusetts, where he had been a law student at Harvard. With no evidence other than Dr. Zerneke's obscure letter and his dim recollections of a midsummer night's lovemaking in the woods near Cambridge, Norman convinces himself that he had gotten the young woman, Isabel Drury, pregnant, and that she has only recently given birth to their illegitimate child. He leaves at once for Chicago.

Dell confidently exploits the misunderstandings opened up by Norman and Isabel's brief rendezvous. When Norman reports to the doctor's office he discovers that Isabel has indeed given birth to his son. He is surprised to discover, however, that Isabel had not wanted him told about the child. What's more, Dr. Zerneke wants only to get some routine medical data in order to have a full record of the baby's parentage for purposes of putting the child up for adoption. Norman's responsibility for the child—not to mention his feelings for it—is of no consequence to these two modern women. Having come to Chicago with the expectation of being coerced into accepting responsibility for the child, Norman now finds himself baffled by the women's total indifference to him. Dell matched Norman's comic perplexity with the resolute qualities of the women around him. In a series of brief, entertaining vignettes, Norman speaks with Dr. Zerneke, who has no interest in him as a caretaker for the baby, and with Isabel, still confined to bed, who has no desire to be the baby's mother (and certainly not Norman's wife). Just as Norman is the most comically muddled of Dell's many befuddled male characters, Isabel is perhaps the boldest of Dell's many decisive women. She plans to put the baby up for adoption so that she can head for Paris where she intends to paint.

The book follows Norman's decision to move to Chicago and adopt the child himself. Once in the city, Norman proves himself a perfectly incompetent young middle-class man, unable to land a job, unable to hold one when he does land it, unable to understand his parents (who come separately to visit him), unable to understand the young women—Isabel, Madge, and his landlady's daughter Monica—with whom he is sexually allied. At last he receives a message through Dr. Zerneke that Isabel has now said she will marry him, though only to lend respectability to their child—a marriage, she lets it be known, that she will thereafter dissolve once the baby's legitimacy has been established. Dr. Zerneke complicates matters by suggesting to Norman that Isabel really wants to be a wife and mother, and that she has made this offer with the subconscious hope that Norman will make a real marriage with her. Norman sets out to telegraph her at the end of the book, intending generously to refuse her offer so that she can be free. But as he telegraphs Isabel,

Norman changes his mind and accepts her offer of marriage. "No doubt it was a crazy thing to do," he thinks afterward. "But he didn't care. He had to see this thing through with Isabel." With this unpromising resolve, he heads back to his apartment and an unpredictable future.

An Unmarried Father received mixed reviews when it appeared in October 1927. It seems apparent now that those reviewers who complained about the book's underlying conventionality missed much that was interesting and even daring about the book. For years Dell had felt that new economic conditions had disrupted the institution of marriage, undermining the patriarchal foundations of family life and leaving young people without a solid social structure within which they could work out their own private aspirations for love and family. In *An Unmarried Father,* perhaps more than in any of his previous books, Dell managed to capture that atmosphere of uncertainty and social disruption, and to do so with insight and humor. What he was already calling the breakup of paternalistic society—a society based on unquestioned male authority and economic power, and complemented by the equally unquestioned role of woman as housewife and mother—all this seemed to crumble around Norman in *An Unmarried Father,* leaving him with little more than his appalling incompetence and rampaging paternal instincts. His decision at last to try to work out a solution with Isabel, who has hitherto rejected the life of a conventional wife and mother, suggests at the very least that their future will be much different from that of the generation before theirs.

From early on Dell seems to have recognized in the humor and intricate plot of *An Unmarried Father* the makings of an entertaining play. Not long after the novel was completed he turned it into a theater piece, titled *Little Accident,* and mentioned the work to his publisher, George H. Doran. In early 1928 Doran introduced Dell to Crosby Gaige, a Broadway producer. Gaige directed Dell to Thomas Mitchell, a playwright and actor, in the hope that the book might be transformed into a witty and vaguely daring Broadway comedy. Mitchell realized immediately that Dell's preoccupation with large-scale social developments and the complex psychology of young men and women would have to be reined in in order to fashion a theatrical piece that might succeed on Broadway. He took Dell's rough draft of a script, crammed with protracted statements on society and human nature, and turned it into a punchier, more easily accessible work. The revised script was marked by rapid, racy dialogue and comic misunderstandings. All was compressed into three tightly drawn acts. The biggest changes occurred in the final act, where Norman blunders through a laundry list of paternal and romantic emotions before being joined at last by Isabel, who has frankly confronted her own maternal emotions. *Little Accident's* treatment of unmarried mother- and fatherhood may have seemed a bit scandalous in 1928, but it managed to end up in perfectly respectable fashion.

The transformation of *An Unmarried Father* into the play *Little Accident* was, on the face of it, a considerable success. Mitchell was the dominant partner in the latter stages of preparing the script: he competently transformed Dell's original into a recognizable Broadway play. Afterward Dell was able to joke about his association with Mitchell, even if the serious novelist and savvy theater man had often disagreed on how to improve the play: "All those long eloquent speeches that I wrote—some of them pages long and very Shavian— have been turned into rapid colloquial conversation." Dell laughed that Mitchell "insisted on leaving out all the statistics on illegitimacy that I gathered so carefully from the Encyclopedia Britannica and Government documents."

Dell was involved in the play's production from first to last; he helped cast the work and commented on rehearsals. But by the summer of 1928, when rehearsals picked up and promotional efforts began, Dell was as much an observer as a participant. Mitchell remained at the heart of the production, starring as Norman and continuing to take part in production decisions. The play opened in October 1928 at the Morosco Theatre, to critical acclaim. Stephen Rathbun of the *New York Sun* called it "an original and amusing comedy... fashioned from Floyd Dell's interesting sociological novel.... We heard more laughter in the Morosco last night than we have heard for a long time in the theater." Robert Coleman, writing in the *Daily Mirror,* called *Little Accident* "an ultramodern comedy" while other reviewers described it as accessible to a general audience.

Little Accident eventually ran to 289 Broadway performances and then appeared on stages around the country. It also brought Dell his first serious money in years, sometimes as much as five hundred dollars a week. He gladly participated in efforts to publicize *Little Accident:* for the *New York Times* and other papers he wrote comic pieces on what it had been like collaborating with Mitchell, and he agreed to promotional appearances, interviews, and photos. The play was later adapted twice by Hollywood, first in a 1930 production starring Douglas Fairbanks, Jr., and more than a decade later in the greatly revised *Casanova Brown*, starring Gary Cooper.

Dell accepted the play's success as an unforeseen piece of good luck—but declined to take the experience at all seriously. Certainly the play was smart and destined for success. But much of its shiny brilliance—its hilarious scenes and fast moving plot—came at the expense of the novel's underlying seriousness and insight into social disruption. *Little Accident* was more outrageous than *An Unmarried Father*, indulging often in risqué repartee and gags about sex. But it was also more conventional, ending in an entirely respectable affirmation of the patriarchal family.

In ways that were becoming commonplace by the late 1920s, the play was both titillating and conservative. Dell had long felt that conventional society, in its failure to satisfy romantic and sexual desires, tolerated certain "immoral" social practices (pornography, prostitution, and burlesque entertainment, among them) as a necessary outlet for pent-up sexual frustrations and disappointments. Such practices and institutions, he believed, served as a safety valve for the rigidly intolerant practices of paternalistic society. In *An Unmarried Father* Dell had set out to reveal the underlying perversions and wrongheadedness of such a society—a society that denied Norman his desire to be an active parent just as it frowned on Isabel's desire for intellectual and artistic fulfillment. But the play was not as far-reaching in its ambitions. Perhaps it served some subversive purpose, shaking scattered individuals in the audience into a recognition of their own frustrations. More often, though, it did what Gaige and Mitchell hoped it would do: entertain a resolutely bourgeois public without stirring people to anything so extreme as a painful examination of themselves and their family lives.

Little Accident WAS Dell's first commercial success since *Moon-Calf* and *The Briary-Bush*, and success felt good. But the popularization of his work caused him uneasiness. For the most part he handled his discomfort by resorting to irony and humor in his public statements on the work. Mitchell's changes, along with the frantic excitement of endless rehearsals and promotional appearances, left Dell nearly as baffled as Norman Overbeck himself. He described the sheer chaos surrounding the production in a fluffy newspaper piece: "I began to feel like Florenz Ziegfeld, after a week or two."

Joking aside, Dell regretted the absence of his serious reflections on modern marriage and family life from the script of *Little Accident*. He felt ever more dismay at the new celebrated fashions in American literature: the Jazz Age dissipations recounted by F. Scott Fitzgerald, the Lost Generation posturings of Hemingway, the Wasteland pessimism of Eliot. To Ficke he professed complete indifference to the whole scene (while also betraying some imperfectly controlled exasperation with it): "Present-day American literature on the whole, or that part of it which answers to the American taste of the period, bores me profoundly. I would like to skip fifty or a hundred years, for we are too slow in getting over the war or whatever ails us." Yet he knew that *Little Accident* contained none of the serious engagement with contemporary life that he imagined as an antidote to the pervasive frivolity and nihilism of 1920s literature.

The problem, to complicate matters, was not simply with popularizers like Gaige and Mitchell. Dell grudgingly admitted on occasion that, given complete freedom to write what he wanted, he too was unable to account authoritatively for the modern world. He frankly stated his wishes (and shortcomings) in a letter to the poet Elinor Wylie: "I want to *explain* things, know humbly that I can't, but am proud even of my failures." Nor, he admitted to Wylie, were the consolations of marriage and family sufficient to quell his desires for definitive accounts of both: "I have my home and take my ease more and more not in the shining perfection which is art but in the raw, crude, bewildering and contradictory chaos which is life—though that, too, is a boast, and a vain one."

Appropriately, then, his serious interests in family and fatherhood found expression in the ambiguities and hesitations—not the crystalline perfections—of literary art. This was strongly evident in the novel he completed in the fall of 1928: *Souvenir*, the third and final installment of the Felix Fay saga. The novel picks up Felix's story several decades after *The Briary-Bush*'s close. Felix and Rose-Ann have long since divorced, and Felix is now a successful dramatist living in the Connecticut suburbs, happily remarried and the father of two young girls. Autobiography clearly remained Dell's focus in the Felix Fay chronicle.

The plot revolves around Felix's relation to his son from his first marriage, Prentiss, whom he has not seen for years, but with whom he has recently resumed contact. Prentiss idolizes his father for his bohemian past. This in turn confuses Felix, who has become, in his own eyes at least, a rather conventional and successful middle-aged man. He loves his son and identifies closely with him. But there is also an unavoidable generation gap. A good many pages are devoted to Prentiss's own story as he settles in Greenwich Village and is torn between his frustrated love for Helen, an opportunistic young actress, and his left-wing political ideals. But Felix is at the center of the book, particularly his complex feelings for his son, for his own past, and for his current commitment to marriage and family.

An air of inconclusiveness and even discontent pervades *Souvenir.* Dell had melancholy and disenchantment suffuse the novel. They hover particularly around the middle-aged Felix, who is unable to resolve his uncertainties and longings. He sympathizes with his aimless son, who leaves at last for Russia, hopeful that he will be swept up in a historical movement more forceful and decisive than anything he can discover in himself. Felix also recalls his own youth—his lovers and extravagant ambitions in Greenwich Village. His young wife's jests about his middle-aged conventionality help relieve his anxiety but also add to it. Still, Felix accepts his place at home and as a successful writer without shame. He is happy to have shed his youthful alienation in favor of something that seems permanent and real. If Felix's unallayed regrets and yearnings revealed Dell's own surviving bohemian instincts, the book also clearly reflected his determination as a family man and worldly writer.

Souvenir is formless at times, lacking the crisp construction and satiric point of view that informed *An Unmarried Father.* But it also contains some of Dell's best writing: together with the complex portrait of the middle-aged Felix there are numerous scenes of Felix and his wife, Connie, among their aging, bohemian, vaguely disenchanted friends in the suburbs. The book was a necessary conclusion to the story of Felix Fay, who more than any other character had been Dell's alter ego. Reviews were mixed when the book appeared in February 1929. Dell took his lumps without regret that he had ended Felix's story—a story that so many young radicals had eagerly identified with in its earlier installments—on so sober, even resigned, a note. The book had been written out of a desire to understand his own changing life, not to please old admirers. It was a book he had needed to write.

DELL ALSO NEEDED to write the letter he sent to Mike Gold, editor at the *New Masses*, early that summer. In the 1910s Gold had been a professed follower of Dell's; Dell and Eastman, according to Gold, were "the best teachers youth could have found during those years." But Gold and Dell sparred with each other throughout the 1920s, Gold taking the more radical position, Dell relying on irony and careful analysis to debunk Gold's blustery pronunciamentos. Early in the decade they had engaged in public debates about marriage, in which Dell defended that most reprehensible of institutions and Gold proclaimed the virtues of free love. But in general their disagreements had had more to do with communism and the Soviets. As early as 1922 Dell had taken to calling Gold "Comrade Mike," a moniker clearly intended to deflate Gold's revolutionary capital. Always alert to the pretensions of literary radicals, Dell insisted in one *Liberator* article that "Comrade Mike is a literary man, an intellectual, and a member of the salaried middle class." Dell mocked Gold's exaggerated veneration of working people: as if the whole goal of revolutionary endeavor was for middle-class intellectuals to become more like underpaid, overworked textile workers, rather than the other way around! This cult of the proletarian, Dell had insisted, was typical of middle-class radicalism. Gold was only its most recent champion.

The two men tolerated each other uneasily for most of the decade. They took occasional shots at each other in print and private but agreed to some semblance of common purpose and cooperation at the *Liberator* and its successor, the *New Masses*. Gold was editor at this most radical of the subsequent incarnations of the *Masses*, and Dell appeared on each issue's masthead in a long list of prominent "contributing editors." Indeed he wrote several pieces for the *New Masses* in its early years, portraits of Upton Sinclair and Crystal Eastman prominent among them. But he had never really been on board at the magazine, and he had always felt uneasy about having his name on the masthead. Many of the magazine's regulars frankly regarded him as an outsider.

So when Dell wrote Gold in June 1929 and resigned his position at the magazine, it ought not to have surprised anyone. Dell's stated reasons for leaving were perhaps baffling and even disingenuous. He started by saying that he had kept his association with the *New Masses* "because it represented a partly Communist and at any rate rebellious literary tendency, with which I am in sympathy." Now, though, he wished to end all ties with the magazine, since "what it seems chiefly to represent is a neurotic literary and pictorial aestheticism with which I am completely out of sympathy." Signing off with a flourish, "Yours for the Revolution," Dell took what he had every reason to assume would be his final leave of Gold and company.

The next issue of the *New Masses* printed the letter in its entirety and appended a two-page *ad hominem* attack on Dell and all his writings. Gold brushed aside Dell's imputation that the magazine was not radical or political enough for him. In this Gold was undoubtedly justified: it had been clear for years that Dell was the more artistic—not to mention the less theatrically proletarian—of the two. But then Gold indulged himself in an unrestrained exercise in character assassination of the sort that was to become more common in radical publications during the coming decade. With the success of *Little Accident* clearly in mind, Gold proclaimed that "Floyd Dell is just another victim of American prosperity. He is making more money than he ever dreamed there was in the world, but deep in his mind is the knowledge of failure. He is an artistic and moral failure."

Gold went on to vent all the resentment and loathing for Dell that he had been storing up for the better part of a decade: "At no time was Floyd Dell a real revolutionist. At all times he had a distaste for reality, for the strong smells and sounds and confusions of the class struggle. . . . He was a Greenwich Village playboy. Even in those days his main interests were centred in the female anatomy." Gold complained about Dell's public attire (dress suit and tie), his recent writings (a successful Broadway play), and his audience (the despicable middle class). This last point, in fact, relied on a critique of bohemian literature and its relation to the middle class that Dell had developed long before Gold: "The war came. America became the richest country in the world. It developed a large, parvenu bourgeoisie. . . . Floyd Dell, who had always written about sex, suddenly became popular. He made, probably to his own amazement, a lot of money in sex."

Gold knew that Dell had rejected literature that catered to the middle class's newfound taste for sexual titillation and moral and social disorder. He must also have realized that Dell's works had generally aimed at a thorough dissection of social incoherence and decadence. But Gold felt no need to acknowledge Dell's radical merits. With his choppy sentences and tough-guy pose, he was determined to spill all his built-up resentment, no matter how scurrilous and dishonest his words might be. He headed toward his conclusion by dismissing Dell out of hand: "Bah! What a mess. If this is Revolution, the word has no meaning. But it is Floyd Dell, it is American literary climbing, it is bourgeois competition, it is not Revolution."

Dell never responded in print to Gold, though it is certain he was shocked and wounded by this assault. He maintained his socialist ideals and his friendships with other radicals. He also continued to write books informed by what he was certain were radical views. But Gold's attack, more than any other incident, served to detach Dell from the radical mainstream which was then turning to the Stalinism of the 1930s. In his letter to Gold, Dell's reference to his own Communist sympathies seemed, in retrospect, much out of keeping with his actual views. Perhaps he had merely wished to silence Gold by some outward expression of his own left-wing faith. In any case, his doubts about the Communists had grown throughout the 1920s, and by 1929 he was about to reject them for good. The god that failed for so many radicals in the late 1930s was one whose grave flaws Dell had discerned more than a full decade before.

THIRTEEN

Great Depression

GOLD WAS WRONG when he called Dell rich. Quite a bit of money had indeed come in from *Little Accident*, enough to provide Dell with momentary reassurance about his family's financial position. That year he even bought the vacant lot between their house and the home of Bob and Lydia Minor. But the *Little Accident* money offered only a respite from years of financial worry. Dell never saw it as more than a temporary solution.

Ever since the suppression of *Janet March* in January 1924 he had had trouble making enough money from his writings to support his family. Supplemental income came from several sources. In 1924 he, B. Marie, and Tony had passed the summer on Nantucket Island, off Cape Cod, where Dell served as a lecturer at Frederic Howe's "School of Opinion." Around the same time he began to give lectures in the New York area and elsewhere around the United States, mainly on social issues: changes in modern families; the movement for women's rights and its effect on marriage, family, and other institutions; the evolution of social institutions in the machine age; progressive education; Freudian ideas about the relations between parents and their children. Advertisements for his lectures announced Dell as a well-known novelist, though he tended to stay off literary issues in favor of social, psychological, and economic topics. Initially ill at ease in front of an audience, he gradually overcame his difficulties, becoming in time an effective and popular public speaker. He spoke easily and warmly, generally without a script. B. Marie served as his agent, booking him at gatherings around the nation. Dell hated traveling but enjoyed the lecturing itself. Certainly it brought in needed money.

At the same time he pursued arduous projects that offered little promise of monetary gain. Through much of the decade he worked with Paul Jordan-Smith (a literary journalist and independent scholar from California, whom Dell had met in 1912 when Jordan-Smith was a student at the University of Chicago) on an all-English edition of Robert Burton's seventeenth-century *Anatomy of Melancholy*. Starting in 1920 Dell and Jordan-Smith pored through editions of the *Anatomy* and, when no suitable translations of given passages were available, worked out their own transcriptions from the Latin. Their goal, as they announced in their preface to the edition they published with Farrar and Rinehart in December 1927, was "to restore to this work the unhindered appreciation which it had in its author's own day. . . . It has been our aim to produce a Burton that, in despite of any feats of future Burtonian scholarship, will still remain the edition preferred for popular and pleasurable reading."

Burton's book had fascinated both men since adolescence, largely because of Burton's intimate familiarity with every conceivable subject: "Poetry, medicine, psychology, philosophy, old wives' tales, philology, wars, antiquarian lore, theology, morals, history, climatology, food, travel, love, hate, ambition, pride, astrology, art, politics." For Dell the book was also remarkable for its insights into "morbid psychology." He regarded Burton as "a scholarly and humanistic"—though unsystematic and unscientific—"precursor to Freud." He responded powerfully to Burton's "study of people as ill at ease with life as himself," to his "revelations of the tragic and ridiculous depths of our human nature." Often melancholy himself, Dell was given to dark humors and forebodings, evident in his susceptibility to poets like Housman and Swinburne and in various of his own works, including the moody, restless *Souvenir*. In Burton's delectation of "the passionately unreasonable aspects of human nature," Dell discovered a writer after his own heart.

The work on the *Anatomy* led to another unprofitable "labor of love" for Dell: a scholarly piece published in the *Bookman*, titled "Keats' Debt to Robert Burton." Reading through the *Anatomy* page proofs in the summer of 1927, Dell had had a sudden insight: that several lines from Keats's "Ode to Melancholy"—"Ay, in the very temple of Delight / Veil'd Melancholy has her sovran shrine"—had been inspired by Burton's description of Angerona Dea ("this our goddess of Melancholy"), "to whom, in the temple of Volupia, or Goddess of Pleasure, their Augurs and Bishops did yearly sacrifice." Dell was proud and delighted to have discovered Burton's important influence on Keats. But it was the union of melancholy and delight— explored by both writers—that particularly enchanted Dell. In Keats, even more than in Burton, Dell discovered the sentiment closest to his own experience of the wonderfully pleasurable consolations of melancholy.

However rich those consolations, money worries never disappeared. What funds remained from *Little Accident* the Dells invested in the stock market in the summer of 1929—then lost it all in the crash that October. Thereafter Dell struggled to keep his projects on track even as financial anxieties closed in on him. The Great Depression taxed Dell as it did other writers, threatening his very ability to concentrate and work. Still, the books he published in the early 1930s—*Love in the Machine Age, Diana Stair,* and the autobiography *Homecoming*—were expansive and confident. Rather than betray oppressive fears and doubts, these books managed to sum up Dell's lifelong ambitions and interests.

He finished *Love in the Machine Age: A Psychological Study of the Transition from Patriarchal Society* early in 1930, working with astonishing vigor and concentration in the very months in which the nation (and his own family) descended into the throes of economic depression. Farrar and Rinehart published the book in April. In it Dell abandoned fiction for a while and indulged the desire he had confessed to Elinor Wylie two years before: the urge to explain things. The volume addressed feminism, socialism, the emergence of industrial society, psychological problems, the proper goals of intellectuals and writers, and the fate of marriage and family in a radically transformed world. A book on the order of Lewis Mumford's enormous tomes of social and cultural criticism, *Love in the Machine Age* was staggeringly ambitious. It was also eminently readable. In addition it offered a message of hope: that a rejection of patriarchal institutions and beliefs in the modern world will make possible radically renewed social institutions, including a reconstituted family. The book was seriously reviewed and won Dell considerable attention beyond the literary realm in which he was already well known. But it did not earn him much money.

Dell's concerns in *Love in the Machine Age* were ultimately personal ones, centering on the difficulties faced by individuals in their struggles to adjust happily and productively to the bewildering modern world. The roots of these problems, Dell argued, lay in enormous social changes—in the huge transformations accompanying the breakdown of the political and economic authority of earlier patriarchal forms of social organization. He described patriarchal society as an inflexibly hierarchical system founded on unequal economic and sexual relations. Dell traced this system back at least as far as the Greek city states, with their preeminent stress on landed property and on property's strictly regulated transfer from generation to generation through male family members. To varying degrees in both Athens and Sparta, Dell discovered rigidly patriarchal economic relations as well as the unfulfilling sexual relations that he regarded as an all too common consequence of patriarchalism. These involved, most importantly, marriage based on economic considerations rather than on sexual desire and romantic love. According to Dell, these city states (like all other patriarchal societies) contained sexual practices and institutions—"homosexuality, prostitution, arranged marriage, polite adultery, and sacred celibacy" —that emerged in lieu of voluntary marital arrangements. Thus patriarchal society produced a permanent emotional childishness among its members, kept as they were from free choice in the conduct of their private lives. Marriage and romantic happiness emerged in such societies as essentially unrelated matters. As a result the family, though the center of social order and meaning, became (and was to remain for many centuries) the site of unresolvable discontent, anxiety, and confusion.

Judged by contemporary standards, Dell's view of the patriarchal system was in some respects politically retrograde. Particularly troubling was his view of homosexuality as a social institution that had emerged in order to distract young men and women from their "natural" interests in one another, thereby preserving the rigidly controlled economic functions of marriage in patriarchal society. Homosexuality, Dell argued with too much confidence, was the product of a patriarchal system that frustrated natural sexual impulses, and that consequently required safety valves for the harmless release of pent-up sexual discontent. At such moments Dell fell into an error he had aptly noted in Upton Sinclair's work: the temptation to find the roots of certain sexual practices exclusively in economic and political conditions.

In other respects Dell's analysis was an up-to-date and thorough-going debunking of the patriarchal system. He portrayed the patriarchal family as "an essentially military system" that granted peremptory rights to the autocratic father. In much the same vein he described "the economics of the patriarchal family [as] military economics," with all financial power vested in the father and passed down to the eldest son. This authoritarian structure had for Dell far-reaching and deplorable implications: the patriarchal family "is thus in early European history associated with ruling castes, and with the institutions of slavery, serfdom, landed property, and the military state. These in turn have influenced the conceptions and workings of the patriarchal family, the position of wives and children being often in legal theory—however modified by natural sentiments—akin to that of slaves, serfs, or cattle." In the grand style of modern cultural criticism, Dell made connections between various levels of social organization and differing aspects of cultural belief. He described the patriarchal family as both product and source of a complex—undemocratic and unfulfilling—social system.

Dell's uncompromising repudiation of the patriarchal family suited the tastes of radical intellectuals in 1930. His fond and hopeful view of the middle class, however, did not. Much of his argument centered on the notion that it was the growth of the middle class that doomed the patriarchal family and related forms of social organization. Greater social mobility, a higher valuation of work and individual initiative, the invention of machinery that made possible high levels of productivity and widespread material comforts, the creation of a more flexible and adaptable economic system—these and other elements of the middle-class revolution profoundly undermined patriarchal authority. But Dell added that the middle class had remained largely in the dark about the implications of its own momentous rise to power:

> The middle class was destined to overthrow the aristocracy, and with it the whole patriarchal scheme. It was to destroy the absolute powers of the patriarchal State and of patriarchal religion. It was in more than one land to destroy the system of primogeniture. It was to displace the family as the economic unit, landed property as the center of economic life. It was to repudiate arranged marriage, establish love-choice, institute divorce, refuse its moral sanction to prostitution and polite adultery, and even undertake to secure paternal recognition and support for children

born out of wedlock. But it was never, at least till the present, to understand quite the significance of all these actions. While destroying the patriarchal system, it was at the same time trying to preserve and maintain all sorts of aristocratic values and ideals.

The result, he argued, was widespread social and cultural disorientation. Dell recognized decadent forms of patriarchal society everywhere around him: in the survival of autocratic parental authority within families; in a rigidly authoritarian educational system; in exaggerated ideals about sexual purity coupled with the tacit acceptance of prostitution. At the same time Dell referred to what he called "ideological overcompensations" to the breakdown of patriarchal society. These included overwrought "modern" ideas that the family should be abolished outright in favor of state-run institutions for raising children; that sex should be regarded exclusively as a source of amusement; that men have no parental instincts whatsoever; and that women should be concerned exclusively with their careers and not at all with motherhood. Dell described these ideas—these "cultural campaigns against patriarchalism, in favor of a variety of concepts of modernity"—as being "overcompensatory in their zeal. In going to extremes [the advocates of such ideas] find themselves back where they started." In rejecting the patriarchal past with such vehemence, Dell felt, these ideas were merely reactive and provocative—not genuine alternatives to patriarchal standards.

This effort to steer a course between patriarchy and its "ideological overcompensations" led Dell to a problematic set of conclusions. On the one hand he insisted that patriarchal forms of marriage be abandoned in favor of "companionate" forms in which husbands and wives are essentially equal. Companionate marriage necessarily involves "the successful use of birth-control methods, and the ability of wives to earn money in work outside the home." In a similar vein he counseled an enlightened view of adolescent development—sexual, emotional, and intellectual—arguing that young people need to escape from the distortions of the patriarchal past in order to cultivate their own affections and lives in a straightforward, wholesome manner.

Yet Dell wished to preserve at least some features of the patriarchal pattern—most prominently its insistence upon woman's crucial role as wife and mother. The overcompensatory "idea of work as a *goal*," Dell argued, "would be repudiated by working women; to them it is a *means to an end* and the end is love, marriage, children and home-making." Here Dell seemed to draw on the experience of his own marriage. B. Marie, while working part-time in libraries and for political organizations, had remained the central figure in the family's domestic life. Still, the vehemence with which Dell now argued for woman's preeminent responsibilities as wife and mother was surprising—particularly in light of his reputation as a feminist. Now that women "are out of the old patriarchal home," he insisted, "the problem is for them to get back into the home on modern and self-respecting terms."

Such statements were bound to stir controversy among leftists and feminists. Also controversial was Dell's description of art as *"a socially approved kind of symbolic behavior for the relief of anxiety."* Rejecting the notion that literature be regarded as a form of political action or pamphleteering, he argued that art's value lay in its power to please—and that it promised such pleasure equally for the artist and for the reader. What art offered, he claimed, was relief from the anxieties produced by imperfect relations with the world. "In the realms in which man is still powerless," Dell wrote, "he still needs the consolations of the helpless child and the helpless savage— though he is too intelligent to attribute to these emotional consolations any magical usefulness in altering outward realities. Their usefulness is strictly emotional: they make us feel good—and that is usefulness enough for art."

This last point, denying art's power as a political instrument and instead affirming its "permanent function of solace," was appallingly offensive to literary radicals in the early 1930s—particularly coming from a critic whose interests had once been "political." But the writers Dell was most eager to dissociate himself from were not political radicals but those champions of futility and despair—everyone from Eliot to Hemingway to Robinson Jeffers—who had gained prominence during the 1920s. In the book's opening sentences Dell announced his own purposes in unambiguous language: "This book is written in the belief that knowledge can help human beings to achieve individual emotional happiness and to enjoy responsible social and economic relations to others, and that a novelist may properly take his share in the task of public education." He wished to separate himself equally from the reactionary nihilists and the radical Stalinists whom he felt had by 1930 captured far too much cultural territory in America and Europe. On both counts he was successful. But his success served to isolate him more thoroughly than ever before on the American literary scene.

BY NO MEANS was the reception for *Love in the Machine Age* altogether negative. Birth-control advocate Margaret Sanger wrote Dell, "What fun I am having reading your 'Love in the Machine Age'! Every chapter is a college education. . . . It's splendidly written and I keep wondering when and where you get the time to do so much." Edna Millay also sent a letter to Dell in praise of the book, saying "the crisp vivid commentary is most amusing throughout" and hinting that Dell's talent for social criticism was reminiscent of Bernard Shaw's. Millay was especially taken with Dell's writing: "You've coined some new phrases . . . such as (I can't resist it) 'polite adultery' . . . That sounds very Dellesque. Dell's 'polite adultery' may become as distinctive as Veblen's 'conspicuous consumption.'"

Reviewers were equally flattering. Irwin Edman described the book in the *Forum* as "a model of lucid organization, of sober statement, of documented common sense." Harry Elmer Barnes correctly noted in the *New York Telegram* that "Dell is primarily interested in preserving the family. . . . We believe that Floyd Dell has here made one of the most important contributions to the successful solution of our contemporary sex anarchy and conjugal bankruptcy which has appeared in years."

The book's harshest critic, oddly enough, was Max Eastman, who "demolished" (his own word) *Love in the Machine Age* in a talk delivered in New York in April 1932. Eastman was willing to give Dell credit for his astute analysis of the psychological damage caused by patriarchal restrictions on adolescents and adults alike: "Just here Floyd Dell has done some magnificent thinking, studying and writing." Otherwise he found nothing in the book worthy of praise. He dismissed Dell's argument that monogamy and family are instinctive, biologically determined parts of life. In addition he highlighted—and dismissed—Dell's growing skepticism about feminism since the days of *Women as World Builders*, when (according to Eastman) Dell had glorified women's departure from the home in favor of the workplace. Most of all he rejected Dell's newfound fondness for the middle class and his championing of friction-free adaptation to the modern world: "The highest ideal he holds out for human-kind is the ideal of getting comfortably through from the uterus to the grave—getting through without any peculiarly human troubles like art or heroism or neurosis or divorce, or poetry, or sex as an amusement, or love as a peril, or anything as anything but a preparation for leaving a litter behind you when you lie down."

Eastman's presentation of himself as the champion of human complexity in the face of Dell's trouble-free utopianism was more than a little disingenuous. After all, it was Eastman, not Dell, who had been the more unconstrained utopian of the two, an outspoken proponent of the Soviet experiment and more recently of Trotsky. All the same, the charge that Dell had gone too far in indulging his desire for tidy solutions to human problems was at least partially on target. The skepticism and irony that had always figured in Dell's work were nearly absent from *Love in the Machine Age*. He had always resisted systematic explanations (whether radical or conservative) of human behavior and history. Now—for the moment at least—he seemed driven by the desire to find orderly, unqualified answers to personal and political dilemmas posed by the modern world.

Such neat answers seemed especially ill-suited to Dell's purposes as a novelist: his fiction had long been marked by the conflicts within his characters and by his own ambiguous feelings about those characters. In fact there was evidence in Dell's next novel, *Love Without Money*, that the ideas he had propounded in *Love in the Machine Age* offered him little literary inspiration. A stiff, programmatic recapitulation of the views on social change and its effect on marriage that had found direct expression in *Love in the Machine Age*, *Love Without Money* is the story of two young people, Gretchen Cedarbloom and Peter Carr, who are in love but can find no official sanction or support for their love. Much of their problem is due to the fact that they come from different social classes: Gretchen's family is wealthy, Peter's is poor. But Dell shows that their problem is more than one of class. Looking around them, Peter and Gretchen discover that society's perverse rules governing love and marriage have forced all sorts of people into unhappy compromises with their own emotions and instincts. There is Gretchen's mother, for instance, whose frustrated ambitions and desires as a woman have resulted in her barely conscious hatred of men.

All this is familiar territory from *Love in the Machine Age*, as are the predictable discussions among Peter, Gretchen, and their friends about the dilemmas facing young people. Dell offers his readers some semblance of a happy ending, granting Peter and Gretchen a monogamous relation (complete with a freshly furnished apartment) outside the socially sanctioned bounds of marriage. But this development, much like the book's dialogue, seems perfunctory and hurried. Indeed, Dell was rushing at the end, writing the last fifty thousand words in a mere ten days. Money worries hovered over him as he wrote the book, just as they hovered over his young protagonists. Perhaps that explains why *Love Without Money* is also a darker novel than Dell's earlier ones. Economic and social tyrannies seem stronger here. Something of Dell's darker cast of mind during the early 1930s is revealed in the fact that Gretchen and Peter are unable, finally, to reconcile their wholesome instincts with the society in which they have grown up.

As he was finishing the book in the summer of 1931, Dell was also concluding his second effort at theatrical collaboration with Thomas Mitchell. Another lighthearted spoof on sexual relations, *Cloudy with Showers* was plainly written in the hope of a second Broadway success. Perhaps this element of deliberate calculation made the play seem less original—and less appealing—than *Little Accident*. In any case, it was not nearly as successful as the work of two summers before. Brought to the stage in the fall of 1931, *Cloudy with Showers* was by no means a flop: it played at the Morosco Theatre for more than seventy shows. But like *Love in the Machine Age*, it provided no solution to Dell's mounting financial worries.

Some consolations could be found during these worsening times. Dell went so far as to say that he preferred depression-era America to the decade that had preceded it: "I hated the gilded days of false prosperity in America, and I feel more at home in an America which is poor—poor enough to begin to face the truth about its economic structure." On family outings into New York, Dell refused to share in B. Marie's delight in the city's fabulous skyline. He claimed to see only the ragged outline of a crumbling civilization—a Babylon whose fall gave him peculiar delight.

In the summer of 1931 he and B. Marie heard from friends about an abandoned farm for sale near Winchester, New Hampshire, in the southwest corner of the state. The house had thirteen rooms and came with thirteen acres of meadows and woodlands. Dell did not have the tiny sum—five hundred dollars—needed to buy the derelict place, but there was money saved for Tony to go to summer camp. Nine-year-old Tony, Dell recalled, "decided that we should all have the farm instead, so we bought it with his camp-money." The family painted the place and filled it with secondhand furniture. There was no electricity and no telephone—a primitive state of affairs that the family thoroughly enjoyed. Now in his mid-forties, Dell rediscovered the physical pleasures of manual labor, doing odd jobs around the house and hammering together a primitive bathhouse on the shore of a nearby lake. He even renovated the privy back of the farmhouse—with such expertise, he laughed years later, that "it made a great impression on the neighborhood, and visitors were brought to see it." The Dells passed almost the whole summer in this woody retreat, then in the fall headed back for Croton.

By October 1931 the Dells were living in gracious—and extravagantly hospitable—poverty. Their Croton household was in a constant state of flux. It now held, besides Dell, B. Marie, and their two growing boys, other regular members. B. Marie's mother, a frequent visitor throughout the 1920s, moved in permanently during the 1930s, helping out with the children—"loved and appreciated," Dell insisted, "by us all." Also a permanent member of the household was Mamie Golden, the family's beloved cook and housekeeper. Young men—writers and radicals—lived with the family for extended periods of time. Christopher Dell later recalled his mother running something like a private, ad hoc WPA for out-of-work young men. One was Hugh Hardyman, a Scotsman who served as Dell's secretary during the early 1930s. Others came and went, talking nonstop politics and literature.

The home was not unlike the chaotic, perfectly unmaterialistic one in George S. Kaufman's *You Can't Take It with You.* In the conclusion that he finally deleted from his memoirs, Dell presents a vivid snapshot of this household—a picture filled with depression details but also suffused with the romance of youthful vagabonds, good fellowship, family happiness, and hope. Dell pictures a house overrun by friends and family, all engrossed in disparate games and odd jobs. B. Marie has set several young men to work, painting the house in exchange for food, shelter, and a little money. Their work done, the lads are playing music on a xylophone and a saw. All are singing. "In the ruins of an outworn civilization," Dell concluded without bitterness, "life goes on."

IN THE MIDST of this company, Dell sat down in the early winter of 1931, not long after Farrar and Rinehart brought out *Love Without*

Money, and went to work on what was to be his longest, most ambitious, and very likely finest novel. A historical tale set in New England in the 1830s and 1840s, *Diana Stair* demonstrated Dell's prodigious grasp of American political and economic life during those years. Dell felt that in choosing those decades as the frame for his novel he was turning to a period largely forgotten by Americans. It "seems to have been known to few Americans besides the late Professor [Vernon L.] Parrington and myself, and was virgin soil in American historical fiction." He saw the radicals of that era as closely related in their democratic idealism to his own generation: "America had more of the modern spirit then than it had for a long time after the Civil War—which cut America off from full participation in the intellectual interests of Western civilization. Before the Civil War came so near as to blot out every other interest, Americans could think and talk about the same things we think and talk about today."

Diana Stair covers an extraordinary range of narrative territory, embracing both the heroine's vivid career and the turbulent political developments of the pre–Civil War era. Diana is a fascinating (if also rather outsized) character. Dell later described her as "myself in petticoats." His close identification with his heroine is apparent in how she is torn between the urge to reform the world and the desire to retreat into a private world of art, love, and self-examination. Such conflicts are familiar from the earlier novels. But *Diana Stair* is unique for the way in which this contradictory personal drama is anchored in concrete historical context. Political and economic circumstances form the indispensable reality of Diana's story. In this book Dell was more intent than ever before to show how thoroughly a person's "private life" is related to the outer social drama of the times.

In five long, densely plotted sections, Dell traces Diana's involvement with abolitionism, the awakening industrial labor movement, poetry, utopian communalism, illicit romance, and marriage. At first she is devoted to her work as a poet and teacher in a Boston girls' school. Soon she is recruited back into the abolitionist movement. When her dual careers as teacher and abolitionist are threatened by revelations about her unconventional life, she moves to a Massachusetts factory town where she is soon embroiled in labor disputes and a strike. She is taken ill in the midst of these altercations, however, and is nursed back to health in the home of a respectable Boston lawyer, Ellsworth Crocker, a middle-aged man, largely reconciled to the ways of the world but still clinging to his bohemian past and pronounced cultural interests. Safe and cherished in Crocker's home, Diana retreats for a while from political passions, devoting herself to her poetry. Her fluctuating loyalties to politics and poetry identify her most clearly as Dell's double. Eventually she marries Crocker and publishes her poems— developments that together bring her into an elite world in which she is regarded with awe.

In the novel's long final section, Diana's marriage to Ellsworth Crocker is shaken by a variety of circumstances: by her impatience with the privileged life, made to suit her career as a poet, that Crocker has constructed for her; by her brief affair with Crocker's dissolute English cousin, Tristram; and by her reawakening political enthusiasms. At last, discontented with herself and her marriage, Diana decides to separate from her husband and live in a utopian community much like Brook Farm, called Apple Farm. There she discovers the dissatisfaction and conflict seemingly endemic to utopian experiments. One adventure gains her full assent: the effort to help runaway slaves escape to Canada. This in turn leads to a trial that is based on Dell's own experience as a defendant in the *Masses* trials more than a decade earlier. The case ends, as did the *Masses* trials, with a hung jury. The book's conclusion is ambiguous, leaving the reader uncertain about Diana's future. For the moment she accepts the trial's outcome as fate's way of directing her once again to the enduring happiness and responsibilities of her marriage with Ellsworth.

Dell wrote most of this 640-page novel in six months, delivering the manuscript to Farrar and Rinehart early in the summer of 1932 and seeing it into print that same fall. The book was respectfully reviewed but received only a fraction of the attention that the Felix Fay novels had gained Dell a decade earlier. Perhaps some of that neglect was due to the book's focus on its female heroine and its frequent feminist concerns—scarcely the concerns that appealed to male radicals during the 1930s. One reviewer, Lorine Pruette, seized upon the book's feminist interests, which most male reviewers missed altogether. In a review titled "A Lady Not So Genteel" in the *New York Herald Tribune*, Pruette praised the novel's "vivid characterizations, the best ones chiefly of women." Unlike some of her male counterparts, Pruette was impressed by Dell's delineation of Diana's humanity and individuality.

In Dell's own mind *Diana Stair* vindicated his standing as a radical—and as a radical novelist. His adroit weaving of Diana's story with political narratives of the 1830s and 1840s plainly reflected his belief in the close connection between politics and private life. At the same time Dell granted Diana a large measure of freedom: her life is never overly "determined" in doctrinaire Marxist fashion by her times. As such, Dell made it clear that his brand of radicalism remained essentially "liberal," much in the American grain. Certainly it was not of the more overtly determinist sort then gaining ascendancy among American literary leftists. Perhaps this too explains why the book was not more widely hailed by American radicals.

Whatever the case, that failure to garner widespread acclaim from American radicals seems not to have shaken Dell's own convictions as a radical or as a novelist. The book struck him as a successful fulfillment of his lifelong political and literary convictions. If he were never to write another novel, Dell realized, *Diana Stair* would keep him satisfied forever.

Diana Stair WAS followed a year later by *Homecoming*, Dell's account of the first thirty-five years of his own life, culminating in the birth of his first son. "The story of a child that grew up," the book was clearly intended as the record of his own hard-earned maturity as a man and writer. Of the scores of memoirs written by Dell's contemporaries in Chicago and New York, *Homecoming* is without doubt one of the best. An artful account of his progress from boyhood in the Midwest to marriage and fatherhood in Croton, *Homecoming* has a narrative coherence and drama equaled in only the finest of Dell's novels. It echoes many of the autobiographical details he had barely fictionalized more than a decade earlier in *Moon-Calf* and *The Briary-Bush*. But the autobiography reaches a conclusion that the two novels, with their ambiguous final glances toward Felix Fay's future, carefully avoided. Closing with Dell's marriage to B. Marie, his early successes as a novelist, and the birth of the couple's first son, *Homecoming* manages to end on a note as happy as it is solid and well-earned.

Nevertheless, there were distinct hints of uneasiness tucked away in the manuscript pages of *Homecoming* that Dell decided to drop from the published book. The original version had included chapters on Dell's life during the 1920s and early 1930s. These he deleted from the final manuscript. Tony's birth, he felt, offered a more fitting note on which to end the story of his own struggle for happiness and maturity.

In some ways the omitted chapters mirrored Dell's uncertain struggle with literary fortune in the decade following Tony's birth. They were not nearly as smooth as those that came before. Choppy and scattered, they reflected the rapid succession of books that Dell wrote during these years as he raced from one project to another in an effort to earn enough money to support his family and the permanent flow of guests in his household. Also discernible were growing qualms about his place in the world—particularly in the literary world where he had once enjoyed success but had been for some time far away from the center of things. This uncertainty he tried to present as exhilarating and normal, but the worry plainly persisted. "The present is formless," he noted in one omitted chapter. His recent life he reported as "full of struggle and excitement, of disappointment and gratification, but it does not take shape in my mind as a story. I can see myself as I was; I cannot see myself as I am."

By 1933 and 1934, national and international developments were robbing Dell more and more of his peace of mind. A number of severe political worries and disappointments—the ravages wreaked on the United States by the depression; the rise of Hitler in Germany (coming after the ascendancy of Mussolini in Italy and Franco in Spain); and the final stages of "a severe case of disillusionment about Soviet Russia"—all combined to distract Dell from his writing. His growing certainty that the revolutionary experiment in Soviet Russia was turning out badly tormented him. Already in 1933 and 1934 he considered Stalin a monstrous tyrant. Years later he remarked that these concerns had given him "indigestion and almost a nervous breakdown." But he refused to ignore them.

At the same time he refused to move to the right, as did some of his acquaintances in Croton. Writing in the early 1930s to Elizabeth Lancaster, a friend from the *Masses* days, Dell complained about Croton neighbors who had "assembled at our home last night to attend Justice Holmes' birthday party over the radio. . . . I found out afterward that I had been rude in remarking that he was a much overrated man." Still talking like a determined leftist, Dell disapproved of the "States' rights basis of [Holmes'] much touted liberalism." He also deplored the fact that Holmes had run "away to Canada to avoid final appeals in behalf of Sacco and Vanzetti—Holmes being as cowardly as all the rest of that court." Dell wrote Lancaster that he felt "indignant at presumably intelligent people admiring a stuffed shirt like Holmes, and on the whole [I] feel as though I were surrounded by Rotarians."

Political disagreements among friends both saddened and exasperated Dell. In Croton, politics and debate had long been a source of stimulating, everyday pleasure. Now he found disputes among friends and acquaintances—some, like his neighbors Bob and Lydia Minor, uncompromising Communists; others moving toward "Rotarian" positions—increasingly unpleasant. Part of his reaction stemmed from his own intellectual dilemma: he was caught between his anger at left-wing naiveté and hypocrisy, and his enduring desire for substantive left-wing political principles. More and more he was left with a bad temper and frank despair. An autobiographical fragment from the early 1940s describes this worsening state of affairs in 1933 and 1934:

> I managed for a while to keep my mind on my writing, to lose myself in the imaginary world that I was creating; at times I succeeded very well. But the world's dangers and my country's dangers grew more pressing, more alarming. I would gladly have left these matters to statesmen, had there appeared to be any. It did not seem to me that I could do anything helpful. My temper became so exacerbated that I could not talk with people who had the Wall Street or the Communist point of view without yelling at them and calling them fools, idiots and lunatics. This (though perhaps true enough) did not help the world; it only left me sick with shame at my abominable manners.

Letters to friends record Dell's growing anxieties in excruciating detail. In January 1932 he sent Ficke pages of obsessive political analysis of a sort one would expect from an officer of the State Department—not from a novelist. Composed nearly a decade before Pearl Harbor, the letter includes (among other things) Dell's stunningly accurate predictions of what eventually would happen on the Asian front: "It is to Japan's interest to strike at once, if at all. The war may begin with a series of terrible disasters to the American forces, and perhaps the immediate loss of the Philippines. If America is not too badly smashed, or perhaps even if it is, the war will give [America] a chance to revive the whole structure that was built up during the last war—this time, however, with a determined effort to keep it as a permanent thing." For all its prescience, the letter reveals the extent to which politics was beginning to shove aside literary concerns in Dell's mind. Another dispatch to Ficke, from September 1933, painstakingly describes the system of royalties by which authors are paid by their publishers. The letter sketches Dell's own erratic financial rewards as an author—nearly $15,000 for more than forty thousand copies sold of *Moon-Calf*, to $1,625 for five thousand copies sold of *Love in Greenwich Village*. It concludes by portraying a literary career as, at best, a highly unpredictable proposition.

Shortly after *Homecoming* appeared, B. Marie and Dell rented out the Croton home and moved with their sons to New Hampshire. For several years the family had regarded their New Hampshire farmhouse as an enchanted refuge. Dell now hoped this retreat to the New Hampshire countryside would remove him from the political news and financial worries that were beginning to make novel-writing and other literary tasks impossible.

But the situation in New Hampshire turned out to be not much better than it had been in Croton. B. Marie and seven-year-old Chris were generally content with country life. But twelve-year-old Tony was sad to have left the Hessian Hills School in Croton. And he missed the radical political talk that had begun to fire his youthful imagination. Much like his father, Tony's political interests, fanned by the heightened urgency surrounding the depression and the situation in Europe, caught fire early on. He felt isolated in New Hampshire, surrounded by farm families indifferent to convulsions in the outside world. Dell and B. Marie agreed to let him return to Croton where he could live with friends and continue his education at Hessian Hills.

Meanwhile Dell's work did not come easily. He completed at least two light comedies for Broadway (one a collaborative effort with B. Marie), but neither made it to the stage. The novel he worked on in late 1933 and through the first half of 1934, *The Golden Spike*, was proving more difficult to write than any of his earlier ones. He wrote furiously and at incredible lengths, then tossed out huge chunks of the manuscript, only to return to the book with grim determination.

Writing at breakneck speed through the late spring and early summer of 1934, Dell managed to complete the book and see it into publication that fall. But the novel never pleased him; afterward he claimed never to have been tempted to look into its pages again.

The Golden Spike is a highly imperfect, scattered book, true enough. But it also reveals much about Dell's state of mind in 1934. It is a long work concerned with the life of Harvey Claymore, who from childhood on struggles for a respectable professional and economic position in society. As a young man, Harvey seems effectively to abandon his dreams of wealth; he becomes instead a professor of history at Franklin College. His scholarly work centers on what he calls the "golden spike"—the transcontinental railroad that in the years following the Civil War connected the Northern states with the West, thereby shattering any remaining economic solidarity between North and South. When Harvey marries Marion Ripley, a second "golden spike" enters the story: Marion's inherited wealth becomes an insurmountable source of resentment and frustration for Harvey, driving a wedge between the two and leading at last to their divorce.

More than any of Dell's earlier books, The Golden Spike is concerned with the corrosive power of money in human affairs. Significantly, Harvey is a descendant of Evelinda Sackett Lipscomb, Diana Stair's idealistic protégé in Dell's novel from 1932. What's more, Marion is descended from Diana Stair herself. But unlike the idealistic Diana and Sackett in the novel Diana Stair, Harvey and Marion are weighed down by money and the bitterness that comes with it. Set in post–Civil War America, The Golden Spike reflects Dell's view of the disintegrating idealism and accumulating power of money in that era. The optimism and energetic idealism of the 1830s and 1840s, which suffuses Diana Stair, is clearly absent from the post–Civil War world of The Golden Spike.

Harvey's failure to resist the greed and envy associated with money points to more than Dell's reading of American history. It also stemmed from Dell's deepening pessimism in 1934, as financial cares pressed in upon him. In retrospect this diffuse, unprecedentedly sour work seems an appropriate—and fateful—conclusion to Dell's career as a published novelist. The haphazardly managed plot and bitter flavor of The Golden Spike hinted that the literary career he had mapped out for himself a decade and a half before was foundering under darkening personal and national circumstances.

New Deal

DELL COMPLETED ONE last novel after *The Golden Spike*, sending the manuscript to his publishers, Farrar and Rinehart, in the spring of 1935. John Farrar reluctantly declined to publish the book. Dell—a nationally recognized author of eleven published novels and numerous other books—was stunned. He responded by going to work at once on a new book. But eighteen-hour days and constant revisions proved insufficient to bring the book into satisfactory shape. "My mind, normally so eager to do its imaginative work, had to be driven to the task," Dell recalled. "I was living on coffee and will-power."

This grim account barely captures Dell's desperation in 1935 as he made one last stab at earning his living as a novelist. Most nights he was unable to sleep. For years he had suffered from indigestion; now it plagued him without interruption. He was nearly fifty years old and found it more and more difficult to recuperate from the sleeplessness, anxiety, and persistent worries that to a lesser extent had always accompanied the composition of his novels. He began to worry that he would never recover his health. His confidence and concentration gone, Dell feared that he would no longer be able to support his family. Poverty of the sort that had afflicted Dell's parents—poverty that had smashed their family's coherence and morale—seemed to rise up before his own household. Each day Dell returned hopelessly to his writing desk.

Help came when it was least expected—and from an unexpected quarter. Jacob Baker, who in the 1920s had been an editor at the Vanguard Press, invited Dell to Washington to see about going to work for the government. In 1927 Dell had worked with Baker on a collection of stories by John Reed, *Daughter of the Revolution and Other Stories*, which Dell had edited and for which he had written an introduction. Now Baker was head of the Federal Arts Project, part of the new Works Progress Administration (WPA) established by President Franklin D. Roosevelt.

At Baker's urging, Dell went to Washington in the summer of 1935, certain it would prove a futile trip. Once in the city, though, he discovered that Baker and others had already created a position for him. At first they had considered him for the directorship of the Writers Project. But as New Deal historian Jerre Mangione notes, Dell's "reputation as a radical spokesman of the twenties was too well-established; the administration did not dare appoint him." As a result, Baker had arranged a less prominent writer's job for Dell, contingent only on his willingness to take it. This Dell was glad to do as a way out of his financial plight. Yet he remained doubtful about the job. When he moved to Washington that September, leaving his family behind in New Hampshire and staying with fellow workers at the WPA, Dell was convinced that his stint as a government employee would be a brief one.

He arrived on a Saturday, early in September, and went to work on Monday. His writing and editorial tasks, which he began without excitement, only gradually gained his sympathy. Two months later, a bit more confident that the work would last, Dell moved his family into a small apartment on Fuller Street. The family settled snugly into their Washington flat next to a park and a public school, fifteen or so minutes from Dell's office. He felt relieved to have regular work. The physical and psychological problems that had plagued him in New Hampshire began to clear up under the influence of a regular paycheck.

Dell worked on a steady stream of documents: long reports, speeches for WPA big shots, magazine articles that appeared under his own name and those of WPA administrators. In the coming years he was to be moved in and out of various departments and agencies within the WPA. All the while Dell seems to have maintained the resigned—and sometimes ostentatiously eccentric—posture of a literary man who has worked for many years alone. Yet from early on he took an interest in his work for Roosevelt's government. The political despair that had begun to overtake him in the early thirties, prompted especially by what he saw as the Soviet debacle, began to retreat in the face of his enthusiasm for the New Deal's reform programs. Almost in spite of himself, Dell began to find the work challenging, congenial, worthwhile.

This sympathy for his projects at the WPA ought not to be entirely surprising, since for many years Dell had been fascinated with politics and drawn to the cause of progressive reform. As an adolescent, politics had often seemed to him a more important and compelling cause than literature. True, during the fifteen years before his arrival in Washington he had largely pushed politics to the back burner, concentrating instead on literary and family matters. But in his last few years in Croton and New Hampshire Dell had again felt political matters come to the fore in his own mind, roughly shoving literature aside. Now the government effort to lift the United States out of the Great Depression began to appear to him as fully worthy a cause as any literary project he might imagine for himself.

Dell saw the New Deal as an endeavor which, in large and important ways, promised to fulfill his own lifelong dream of liberal socialist reform. Scattered here and there in the document he began writing that first September morning in Washington—a lengthy report titled "The Emergency Work Relief Program of the F.E.R.A. [Federal Emergency Relief Administration]: April 1, 1934–July 1, 1935"—were signs of Dell's genuine sympathy for the program. Opening with a detailed history of FERA, Dell proceeded to describe specific features of the program: the construction of schools, hospitals, courthouses, roads, bridges, and airports; the flood control and water conservation projects; the production of clothing, household goods, and food; public health services; work programs for women; the construction of public recreational facilities; government sponsorship of education for children and adults, scientific research, and the arts. Dell's name did not appear on the work, but he was pleased with it nonetheless. "This, my first government production," he noted in a diary years later, "gave me a thrill of pride. . . . I am still as proud of my governmental reports as of anything I have ever written."

In a second large report that he went to work on in January 1936—on "Government Aid During the Depression to Professional, Technical and Other Service Workers"—Dell trumpeted the government's efforts to enlist educated workers and artists of various sorts. He defended the decision to give aid to musicians, writers, and white-collar workers, noting the public need and desire for their work. The report is a welter of impressive facts about the projects and sober sympathy for them. Dell mentions the 163 symphony and concert orchestras sponsored by the Federal Music Project, as well as the 15 chamber music ensembles and 69 dance orchestras. He describes the public murals, lithographs, sculptures, etchings, posters, and photographs produced under the auspices of the Federal Art Project, and the 11,000 theatrical productions sponsored by the Federal Theatre Project. He discusses the state Guide Book series produced by many hundreds of writers and editors in the Writers Project—books that assembled "geographic, governmental, historic, cultural, sociological, recreation, industrial, and commercial information" on each state in the country.

Dell emphasized how these projects promoted the growth of native forms of American culture. The Theatre Project, he noted, produced a great number of works by young American playwrights, just as the Music Project sponsored the development of American musical forms ranging from classical to jazz. America's ethnic diversity was also encouraged by these WPA programs: "Racial or language groups—Negro, Yiddish, Anglo-Jewish, Italian and German—are doing plays out of their own life or literature." It was satisfying to write about a program that had put to work artists and other white-collar workers whose labor, Dell felt, was essential to the life of a civilized nation. He later remembered that "We were proud of the fact that our public work programs included suitable work for unemployed musicians, artists, actors, writers, teachers, doctors, dentists, engineers and clerical workers so that these were not put indiscriminately into pick-and-shovel jobs or into sewing rooms; and we were proud, too, of the fact that they did good work on these special projects."

Half a year into his sojourn in Washington, Dell felt certain that the WPA was involved in more than work relief: it was also beginning the reconstruction of American life on more enlightened and humane principles. In an article he wrote for Jacob Baker, Dell argued that "it is a stupid and un-American wish to keep our art and science and professional training in the ditch into which the depression threw it." He described the WPA's potential to transform American life: "It may be that a renaissance is beginning in America—a democratic renaissance in education and in culture. There are signs of it in the universal eagerness of our people for knowledge and beauty and all the good things of life."

His writings suggested that a humane national life required an active government, that private initiative would always neglect these finer features of national existence. In a speech for Mrs. Florence Kerr, an assistant commissioner of the WPA, Dell argued that the "privation" of the 1930s had its roots in the rapacious greed of the 1920s. That decade already saw a severe shortage of low-income housing, far too few public schools, and an appalling lack of medical care for the poorer third of the American people: "When the card-house of our foreign investments crashed, and our inflated domestic stock values tumbled after them, and our banks closed their doors, and our factories began to shut down, it took only a short time for our lowest income groups to drift into the breadlines, dragging millions more after them." The speech traced an economic cycle that led from private greed and dishonesty in the 1920s, to the government's creation of jobs and increased economic well-being in the early 1930s, to the failed effort to return to privatization in 1937 ("the result was a sudden collapse of business"), to "an enlargement of the WPA program and a resumption of government expenditures." Dell headed the speech toward its close by affirming the government's expanded role in national life: "That kind of Prosperity to which we have a right to look forward to is not a kind that pertains exclusively to private industry and business; it should be a Prosperity that includes the community as a governmental unit. The city and the State do more than govern their citizens; they also serve their citizens."

Dell plainly forwarded his own views and political passions in such documents. In writing them for others, he also surely felt the frustrations that are inevitably a part of bureaucratic, government work. He described to Elizabeth Lancaster "the anxiety-state which WPA affairs get into while Congress debates the relief appropriations," with recurring worries that WPA programs would be eliminated or severely cut back. Early on he took to referring to himself—generally with lighthearted irony—as a "minor government bureaucrat." He had a lot of work, and it was frequently revised to suit the tastes of government bosses. For a man accustomed to intellectual independence and remarkable levels of productivity, the constraints and plodding pace of the bureaucracy were often irritating, sometimes even degrading.

Still, Dell was treated with respect during his years in Washington. Many of his fellow workers regarded him with something approaching awe. Even the WPA's chief, Harry Hopkins, showed special respect for Dell when he pointedly inquired after his happiness in his new position. Verb Gabbert, a writer who worked around Dell for many of these years, later recalled that "Floyd was the star of the office. He was a nationally read author and had fed the literary appetites of many of us when we had been in our teens and twenties, I among them. Some of our crew were lavishly deferential to him, some were intimidated by him, and some were baffled or amused that so gifted a man could be so odd."

Gabbert arrived at the WPA in the late 1930s, by which time Dell had been a government employee for nearly half a decade. Dell had already worked in various capacities and buildings for the WPA when he met Gabbert. He had started at the Auditorium, where he wrote the FERA and white-collar-workers reports. Then he had been made a "supervising editor of writers' projects" and moved over to the Writers Project headquarters at the McLean Mansion—"a grandiose millionaire dwelling of another era, with a great ballroom in the middle of it, now divided up into little office cubicles." Dell claimed to be ill at ease with the writers he met there (he had become accustomed to working with engineers and bureaucrats, and he was enjoying a worklife separate from the company of writers). But in fact he was warmly received by the crowd of writers at the McLean Mansion. Like them, he was not too shy to rail against the bureaucratic procedures they were all subjected to as government employees.

It was in the spring of 1936 that Dell was moved over to the McLean Mansion. His office "was a large kitchen, with a magnificent cook-stove in it, one adequate for the preparation of a millionaire's banquet. I hoped they would leave the cook-stove there, but they took it away." Dell ended up spending little time there, since he was sent on several long trips for the WPA that same summer. He professed not to know why he had been dispatched on these field trips. Jacob Baker had merely instructed Dell to inspect WPA projects and report back to him. Dell later confessed that much of his time had been taken up listening to the gripes of frustrated administrators in various spots around the country. Apart from this largely pointless administrative chat, Dell got to see much of what the WPA was accomplishing, and he was moved by what he saw:

I went out and visited other projects—nursery schools, music projects, theatre projects, health projects, sewing projects, construction projects of all kinds. I was driven over roads built or improved by WPA workers, I saw new and renovated schoolhouses, courthouses, barracks, parks and playgrounds, swimming pools, river improvements. I talked with the local public officials who were cooperating in these activities. I got acquainted with the project supervisors, and sometimes had a chance to talk with the project workers. And I made notes on everything I saw and heard.

When he returned from the last of these trips in the fall of 1936, Dell was moved to the Lemon Building to work in the Special Reports Section of the Information Service. There he was soon made chief of the section.

It was during his time in the Information Service that Dell met Gabbert and other young writers. Some, like Gabbert, were nearly a generation younger. Treated with a respect that was generally not accorded other writers, Dell earned local renown as a hardworking, productive writer. It was a reputation he claimed to find rather baffling. He was often preoccupied and absentminded—hardly the model of an efficient bureaucrat. Still, he felt the work was important and, in its own undeniably dry way, compelling. He worked for the WPA until its dissolution in 1943, then stayed on with the Information Service four more years, completing the final report on the WPA in 1947. That same year, when he had just turned sixty, he retired on his government pension, leaving behind professional life for good.

DELL NEVER COMPLETELY sorted out his feelings about being what he once called "a Federal serf, chained to a desk from nine to five, and going meekly to bed at eleven." At times he felt it was an impossible situation, even a sad one. He referred to himself in a diary from 1939 as Mr. Flood, after Edwin Arlington Robinson's lonely, unheroic character. "Mr. Flood wishes he had somebody to talk to about writing and its problems," he notes in his diary, "as with Chicago and Greenwich Village friends once upon a time." To Elizabeth Lancaster he wrote at length about Shakespeare; then he complained that on such topics "my mind is full of opinions . . . in which not a blessed soul I know is in the slightest degree interes-

ted—so that I can't talk about it, and am sort of busting with
unexpressed views." In his diary he records "literary plots and plans
of his own, which he intends to execute of evenings and on
weekends in the year to come—a novel, no less." Still, this reference
to private ambitions is suffused with irony, suffused even with an air
of sadness and resignation.

All the same, Dell took his literary plans seriously, and he did
work intermittently on novels, stories, and poems during these years
in the government. "I have been writing poems to or on poets," he
wrote Joseph Freeman in February 1943, "including Byron, Shelley,
Keats, Milton, Browning, Leigh Hunt, Swinburne, Whittier, R. L.
Stevenson, Donne, Longfellow, Lovelace, and the author of the
Book of the Apocalypse." Praising Freeman's novel *Never Call
Retreat* (1943), which is largely political in its concerns, Dell
reminded Freeman that he, Dell, had preceded him in making
politics a respectable topic for fiction. "I can remember the time
when only Anatole France put politics in his novels," Dell wrote
Freeman; "and the time when my own Diana had more politics than
there had ever been in an American novel; now, thank heaven,
politics is recognized as being of equal importance with love as a
literary theme."

In twelve years of government service Dell amassed an astonishing
number of long, incomplete novel manuscripts and wrote scores of
finished poems on literary, political, and personal topics. These
often mocked and deplored his position as a bureaucrat. One poem
from 1943, "Poet in War Time," parodies Wordsworth's "London,
1802": "Milton! if thou wert living at this hour, / Thou wouldst be
working for the Government— / Yea, even as before, thy genius Poet
/ Up at a desk, and thy God-given power / Of thought and language,
all thy mental dower / Upon official Propaganda spent." This is
lively, self-directed satire, but it also shows a weariness that blunts its
mocking spirit.

At times Dell seemed desperate to return to the literary life, and
his poems and fiction threatened to take up all his free time and
energy. On occasion he would work all weekend on his novels,
never leaving the house, relieved, he claimed, to be back in a world
of imagination where he could forget his nine-to-five routine. All at
once the energy that had begun to desert him in the early 1930s
would come flooding back. For brief interludes, literary inspiration
seemed to transform him into a young author again. At such

moments it was easy to forget that he was a man in his fifties who, only a few years before, had worried that his inspiration and good health were gone for good.

And yet he always came back to his government job, sometimes with expressions of relief. To his close friend Elizabeth Lancaster, with whom he carried on a voluminous correspondence during the 1930s and 1940s, Dell reported one such fit of literary activity—a novel that he worked on through 1936 and intermittently for a few years afterward—that had wrenched him from family and WPA activities: "It seems to me that I have just barely escaped alive out of the clutches of the Muse." The manuscript ran to hundreds of pages, often distracting Dell from everything else. Still, when a rumor circulated in his office that he might be able to obtain a three-month vacation in order to work on his fiction, Dell quashed it. To one of his supervisors, M. E. Gilfond, he wrote: "I have in mind no private literary plans which could properly be supported by WPA funds. I did not request, do not approve, and should not consent to such an arrangement. [It] would certainly be regarded as scandalous by the public press; and which in my view would be equally dishonorable to me as a government employee and as a literary man."

What made Dell so adamant in this rejection of possible financial support for his work as a novelist and poet? Partly it was pride in his many years as a self-supporting man of letters—as a writer who had always managed (if sometimes only barely) to secure a living for himself and his family. But there were other reasons as well. Most important was Dell's urgent support for the WPA itself—for its effort to revitalize the American economy and to bring to life a dignified public culture. Dell's enthusiasm outlived the project itself, lasting right up to his retirement in 1947 and beyond.

Meanwhile he found solace and distraction in his family life. He talked politics endlessly with his two precocious, fully politicized sons. He played chess with Chris and took an active interest in Tony's photography. Verb Gabbert remembers Dell and Chris talking politics in 1939: "He and the 12-year-old carried on . . . a real conversation about the war, the kid talking like an adult and Dell replying as if he were one." Gabbert, a frequent guest in the Dell household during the 1940s and 1950s, reported "that Dell could be a wonderful father while having all the earmarks of a very bad one; that is, just not the stuff that parents are made of."

There were other distractions as well. The household was, as usual, a full one. There was B. Marie's mother, who became increasingly feeble during the early 1940s, confined often to her upstairs bedroom in the house on Ingleside Terrace that Dell and B. Marie had bought not long after moving to Washington. B. Marie's sister, Sylvia, was also a frequent member of the household. She was separated from her husband in California and confined for a while at St. Elizabeth's Hospital in Washington after she suffered a nervous breakdown. Mamie Golden was also still with the family. Reluctantly she had agreed to move to Washington, which she knew to be less racially tolerant than the community at Croton where they had lived for many years. "Ain't nothing free in Washington," she told the family, "but the streetcars and the air."

As Verb Gabbert recalled, the Dells' house had all the trappings and atmosphere of a "typical Greenwich Village apartment" from the 1910s. In a letter written shortly after Gabbert first met the Dells, he described their home in detail: comfortably cluttered and with "a colorful touch about it that you will always find about traveled people's houses—a samovar from Russia, bright, hand-woven scarfs on tables and walls from Baltic and Balkan countries; and a Greenwich Village touch because those two were so steeped in the village that I suppose it will never evaporate from their blood completely. There were batiks against the walls above and behind the sofas, and drawings by their artist friends."

For Dell there was always work at the Information Service, so he was rarely able to get away for family vacations at the farm in Winchester, New Hampshire. Many times B. Marie would take the boys up to the country house and stay a summer's month or so. Meanwhile Dell labored through the heat in Washington.

During one such interval he worked extensively with Verb Gabbert on a novel that Gabbert was writing about his earlier days as a hobo, Merchant Marine, reporter, and aspiring writer. Gabbert later recalled how differently he and Dell approached the job of writing a novel: "To me writing was no usual thing: not a job, not a passtime [sic], not a pleasure, not a craft. It was a sacrament." Dell, on the other hand, "was so much the natural writer that writing was the most natural thing he did. When doing anything else he twitched, or jerked, or shook his head or shrugged (actually *rotated* his shoulders, one after the other) or set his teeth to clicking, or combined all of these with a bit of neck-jerking into a complete St.

Vitus's dance. But when he wrote he looked as much at home and in command as the rest of us do when we talk nonsense or eat stew. This combination, Floyd and me, writer and non-writer, made collaboration difficult."

Gabbert's talent for extravagant caricature brings vividly to life Dell's literary excitement and frustrations in the course of this failed collaborative effort. Dell, he remembered, would walk back and forth across the room, pointedly—sometimes angrily—criticizing Gabbert's work. He would shove "both hands, palms outward, in his hip pockets. He clinched his fists at each step, and that raised a bulge at his seat and hitched the cuffs of his pants-legs up three inches above the tops of his shoes. He looked like a cakewalking chicken wearing a bustle." Gabbert would meekly defend his work, Dell alternately praise and deflate it. Finally Dell lost interest in their literary evenings, and the project was abandoned.

Dell lectured on occasion to various groups—mainly at colleges—on poetry and other literary topics. In 1936 he presented a series of lectures "on Poetry and Modern Life" at the Workers School for the Congress of Industrial Organizations (CIO). On Ingleside Terrace Dell became known to neighborhood children as the man who read poetry to them at the public school.

Political discussion filled much of the rest of Dell's free time, often with Gabbert and other literary friends from the WPA, sometimes in his lengthy correspondence with Elizabeth Lancaster and Joe Freeman. The revelations that came to light during the 1930s about the Soviet Union—the purge trials of 1937 and Stalin's pact with Hitler in 1939—saddened Dell. But by no means did they shock him as they did many others. Writing Elizabeth Lancaster shortly after the Nazi-Soviet pact, Dell sketched out his history of disillusion with the Soviets: "Six years ago, as if in a nightmare, I foresaw some such possibility as this, and it made novel-writing too difficult—it damn near gave me a nervous breakdown: and I've been detaching myself from that situation ever since, more and more—so that now when it is happening, though I was surprised, and am puzzled, and don't understand it, I am not as emotionally shocked and hurt as I might have been." He reserved special contempt for left-wing writers who refused to condemn the pact. In one letter he complained to Lancaster about "the Catholic-mindedness of our Communist friends, believing what they are told and changing their minds under party instruction."

At times Dell seemed to take bitter pleasure in the debacle of Soviet communism and the subsequent writhings of American radicals. In a letter to B. Marie, who was vacationing in New Hampshire during the summer of 1939, Dell commented on the recent pact. "Much fluttering in the dovecotes because of the rapproachment of Hitler and Stalin," he wrote. "I am amused to think of how hard put to it the Communists will be in explaining—and the explanations will be only the last stage of their long-drawn-out moral collapse." He worried, though, about the blow the pact would deal his idealistic seventeen-year-old son Tony.

Tony's political views—reflecting his own stubbornly youthful Communist sympathies—engaged a great deal of Dell's attention in the late 1930s, often with unhappy consequences. Inspired by the radical idealism that Dell had long since come to doubt, Tony joined the Young Communist League and the American Student Union in the late thirties. These allegiances irritated his father. In particular, Dell and his eldest son fell out on how the left should respond to the threat posed by Nazi Germany. Both had supported the antifascist forces in Spain. Beyond that father and son found less and less common ground in their political sympathies. Like other leftists during the late 1930s and on into 1940 and 1941, Tony favored neutrality in the expanding European war, arguing that it was essentially a capitalist conflict—a war between tottering capitalist empires. For a brief while his father showed reluctant, halfhearted sympathy for this view. In a letter to Elizabeth Lancaster just after Hitler's invasion of Poland in September 1939, Dell was inclined to accept arguments in favor of American neutrality: "The truth is that my imagination refuses to accept the reality of this fantastic tragedy—I don't believe it is really happening. . . . I think very little about it—far, far less than I did about the prologue in Spain. *That* was my war, but this isn't."

In the months that followed, however, Dell became convinced that neutrality was a ghastly mistake, that the United States would have to take on Nazi Germany. Christopher Dell recalls that his father's opposition to neutrality received its most public expression around 1940, when he attended a local meeting of a left-wing writers' union. The meeting had been called in order to vote on the issue of neutrality. Dell, who had stayed away from earlier meetings out of disdain for their Communist leanings, decided to see if it was possible to convince the members of the folly of neutrality.

Such gatherings were normally perfunctory affairs, with members docilely subscribing to the Communist party's official doctrines. Dell's presence at this meeting managed to disrupt, if only for an evening, the usual complacencies. Arguing passionately that a policy of neutrality would only abet Hitler's cause—that it was, in essence, a pro-Hitler stance—Dell managed to stir dissension where previously there had been passive acquiescence. When a vote was taken on the matter, a majority held out against the neutrality position, swayed by Dell's lone stance against the official party line.

Afterward Dell was congratulated by various of the writers present, not only for having led the opposition but also for having transformed the usually staid proceedings into an unprecedentedly lively debate. At the next meeting, though, when Dell failed to show up, a second vote on the matter was held, and the neutrality position easily carried the day. An article appearing shortly thereafter in the *Daily Worker*, the Communist party's official organ, claimed that Dell's arguments against neutrality had revealed him once again to be a capitalist stooge. As had been the case following Mike Gold's attack in the *New Masses* in 1929, Dell refused to respond publicly to these fulminations. Among friends Dell remarked that the Stalinists at the *Daily Worker* were intellectual lightweights whose comments warranted no serious rebuttal.

Even B. Marie, always a more determined pacifist than Dell, agreed that Nazi Germany's frightening ambitions and escalating military offensives required an armed response from the United States. In the first years of the European war Dell worried incessantly that Hitler's aggressions would go unanswered. He was an outspoken admirer of Franklin Roosevelt; but in 1940 and 1941 he grew impatient with Roosevelt's accommodation with those (many of them on the left) who argued that the United States should not declare war on Germany. That his support for armed intervention had once again alienated him from the radical fold did not bother Dell at all. He had now been certain for many years that his political sympathies lay with liberal democracy and not with any radical alternative to it. Long before the United States entered the war, Dell had concluded that the war must ultimately be fought for this essential political cause. When war was finally declared in December 1941, he accepted the country's entrance into this Second World War with feelings vastly different from those he had experienced at

the time of America's entrance into World War I in April 1917. His
mood was grim. But he was also certain that the fight was necessary.

BOTH THE DELL boys entered the armed forces during the war, Tony in
1942 and Christopher at the war's end. Dell's worries about the war—
including his chagrin over the illiberal spirit that inevitably accompanied the country's turn to wartime production and activities—were
compounded by private fears for his sons. He and B. Marie worried
through the war years that the conflagration, which they grimly
supported, would take one or both of their sons. Both were grateful
that Tony never saw service abroad and that Christopher's active
service came only after the war's conclusion.

Working in Washington for the duration of the war, Dell noted
how propaganda and war concerns darkened the optimism he and
others had felt during the heyday of the New Deal. As the war
stimulated the nation's industrial capacities to an extent that far
outstripped the earlier efforts of FERA and the WPA, these New
Deal programs seemed increasingly antiquated and superfluous. At
its peak, late in 1938, the WPA had employed nearly 3.5 million
people. One year into the war, in January 1943, that number had
fallen to fewer than 300,000. In June 1943, just before the system
was dismantled for good, only 42,000 were on WPA payrolls.

The war rendered the WPA pointless. Its demise, in turn, signaled
the end of Dell's enthusiasm for government work. On the official
memorandum announcing the end of the WPA, Dell underlined the
directive "to remove from project sites all signs indicative of WPA
project operations." He added these lines of verse: "Ay, tear the
tattered ensign down! / Long has it waved on high. / And many an
eye has danced to see / That banner in the sky." He stayed on four
more years at his desk, writing speeches, articles, and reports for the
Information Service. But his heart was no longer in the work.
Certainly he supported the war effort. But he had little interest in
most of the writing and editorial tasks that he undertook in the
aftermath of Roosevelt's New Deal.

Dell's last report was a scholarly, book-length summary of the
WPA. It is an impressive record of the agency, combining a great
deal of factual information with a thoughtful account of the WPA's
place in the history of American work-relief programs. Dell's years of
study of the transformation of the United States from a rural to a

modern, industrialized nation served him well in attempting to describe how the WPA—and FERA and the Federal Civil Works Administration before it—had represented a determined response to the need for a government-sponsored work-relief program that matched the new industrialized conditions in the United States. A graceful account of the WPA, it is a sober eulogy—a final farewell to an agency that had helped salvage American society in an era of collapsing hopes and institutions.

Dell started the report at the time of the WPA's closing down, in the summer of 1943. Working off and on for years, he finished in 1947, then made final plans to leave government work. A friend attempted to wrangle a job for him at the United Nations in New York. But Dell, convinced that the UN would turn out to be little more than an anti-Communist organization, had no appetite for the job. Instead, once he left the Information Service in 1947 he headed contentedly back to a life as an independent intellectual and literary man. Having "mustered out of government serfdom," as he put it in a July 1947 letter to Joe Freeman, Dell was glad "to be back at fictioneering."

After a twelve-year hiatus from full-time literary work he was understandably uncertain about his ability to return successfully to the literary life. He was now sixty, with four decades of hard, uninterrupted work behind him. Literary fashions had long since deserted Dell, leaving him, as he well realized, an anachronistic figure. The political catastrophes of the thirties and forties had severed him once and for all from doctrinaire radical positions. He was equally adamant in his opposition to what he regarded as the demoralizing, reactionary literary modernism exemplified by Eliot and Pound—a modernism increasingly in favor in colleges and universities across the postwar United States. Where could Dell find haven in this utterly transformed literary and political environment? What could life hold for him now, short of reminiscence and retreat?

F I F T E E N

Man of Letters

IN THE SUMMER of 1947 Dell returned full-time to the writer's trade. He pursued that life uninterruptedly, save for intervals when he was incapacitated by increasingly severe bouts of illness, until his death in 1969. Dell spent nearly all his time reading and writing, fixed at his desk in the upstairs study at the Ingleside Terrace house, or working during the summer months on the screened back porch, where he often slept at night. B. Marie continued to work as a librarian, supplementing Dell's government pension with a small but indispensable salary. Always the principled feminist, Dell claimed to see nothing objectionable in this arrangement. Privately, though, it made him uneasy to know that B. Marie, not himself, was the household's sole wage earner.

Yet this uneasiness failed to deflect him from his many literary tasks. His productivity, always great, continued unabated through the 1950s. He wrote countless pages: dozens of short stories, poems, a handful of articles, and hundreds of letters. But he submitted only a few articles and poems for publication. A bare bulb suspended over his back-porch writing desk, Dell shielded his eyesight with a green-shade cap. He wrote with uninterruptible intensity. Frequent company and talk had long been part of Dell's intellectual life. Now his primary intellectual exchanges—with Max Eastman, Upton Sinclair, Elizabeth Lancaster, Joe Freeman, the biographer Miriam Gurko, Edmund Wilson, and a handful of others—were carried on chiefly through the mails. Family members recall him writing more than he spoke.

Occasionally he ventured out for public appearances. He continued to read poetry at colleges and public schools. In 1951, after several years of correspondence with Stanley Pargellis, director of the Newberry Library in Chicago, Dell deposited his papers at the Newberry. A year later he participated in a conference there on the Chicago Literary Renaissance, of which he had been so essential a member. The next year he agreed to read some poems by William Butler Yeats over the radio in Washington, D.C. Appearances like these flattered his vanity, bolstering his sense of himself as an active literary man. But they could not overcome his growing irritation at being regarded, by scholars and literary people alike, as a man whose importance lay not in the present but in the past.

Dell himself encouraged this reputation by devoting so much time to reminiscence. In 1947, shortly after retiring from the Information Service, he wrote a fond though sharp and unpretentious memoir of his bohemian days in prewar Greenwich Village for the *American Mercury*. He stressed the modern era's rupture with the past—a rupture plastered over with false sentiment and glitz. Bourgeois tourists and young people, he wrote, found whatever little was left of the bohemian Village "picturesque; even the phoniness is picturesque, to them." He implied that the new avant-garde had lost both the idealism and independence from commercial interests that had characterized his own generation. Another essay for the *American Mercury*, titled "Memories of the Old Masses," followed in 1949, every bit as gentle (and as discerning) as the first one. Even the Yeats reading was, for Dell, charged with memory and nostalgia. In the comments he interspersed with the poems, Dell remarked on Yeats's desire to bring back the ancient tradition of oral poetry. As a young man Dell had taken that lesson to heart, passing it on to friends in Chicago, particularly to Vachel Lindsay, for whom it had been the kind of revelation that transforms a writer's life and work.

For all his willingness to indulge in reminiscence, Dell was determined to avoid nostalgic distortions of his own past. He wished to deflate what he felt were sentimental, hyperbolic accounts by a new generation of scholars in their books and articles on the Chicago Renaissance and Greenwich Village's avant-garde. At the conference at the Newberry in 1952 Dell clearly shied away from what he regarded as romanticized portraits of the Chicago Renaissance —accounts that pictured an accumulating desire for revolutionary literary change and individual self-expression. What really prompted the Chicago movement? Dell asked. The same elements that made any other insurgent literary movement: a gathering of disparate, dissatisfied literary people; comfortable places where they could meet and talk; some degree of agreement on literary matters; a particular writer or literary group—standing either as exemplar or scourge—against which they could measure themselves; and an eager, sympathetic public. No fancy or esoteric explanations would do, Dell insisted. He hinted that the new wave of critics that rushed into the universities after World War II were too eager to cook up portentous explanations for literary movements that they seemed to idolize and, partly, to envy.

Now in his sixties, Dell preferred to present himself in these scattered articles and public appearances as a realistic, down-to-earth fellow. For more than a decade he had adopted the sober demeanor of a respectable public servant. After he retired he was loath to play the part of the quaint, elderly bohemian for a new wave of writers and scholars inclined to romanticize his generation. Already there was a tendency to portray Dell's crowd as "innocent" and "lyrical." Such terms missed the earnest, problematic, often troubled features that had characterized their lives and works. Dell countered with an ostentatious show of plain, blunt sense.

As an antidote to scholarly hyperbole, this approach was fine. But the narrow boundaries of common sense scarcely allowed Dell the leeway he needed to express all his pent-up thoughts. McCarthyism and the widespread constraints of that conservative era cut him off still more from the possibility of full public expression. Free now to devote every day to his writing, he nonetheless found it difficult—for private and public reasons—to give public utterance to his most serious thoughts on politics and literature. These matters, which engaged him now as much as ever before, he addressed in astonishing long letters to old friends.

There was reminiscence here too, but of a more frank and penetrating sort. To Upton Sinclair, a friend of nearly four decades, Dell wrote that he was happy to be back at his desk, writing stories and poems every day. But he also confessed to misgivings about that kind of life. These misgivings were like the ones he had had for decades, centering on literature's power to tug one away from ordinary existence. He proudly acknowledged "some conventional and bourgeois views," such as his enduring sense of responsibility for his family, so that before retirement he had never been able to accept B. Marie's offer to support him financially while he worked on his books. At the same time he reveled in his enduring radical sympathies. He gave vent at one point to his disgust with the repressive features of American government that, he felt, had arisen since World War II's conclusion. He suspected he would not have been spared by Wisconsin Senator Joseph McCarthy and colleagues had he stayed on longer as a government employee. Upon retirement, he wrote, "I felt relieved, knowing that a man with my radical past who stayed in government work any longer would soon be dragged before a Congressional Committee, accused of subversive activities on the strength of the tittle-tattle, garbage and lies which fill the files of our wonderful, wonderful FBI, and that I might be sent to prison on the word of some ex-Communist habituated to falsehood and up to his old tricks."

Dell was able to unleash his political ire in letters to Sinclair, who in the early fifties was still something of a radical. He was more restrained in his correspondence with Max Eastman. Now in headlong flight from his Marxist past, Eastman had become an archconservative, even an outspoken defender of McCarthy. Dell mainly wished to stay off politics with Eastman for fear of wounding and alienating his old friend. It was easier, he discovered, to speak frankly about their old days together as literary radicals. Of the *Masses* and the *Liberator*, Dell wrote Eastman that they now seemed surprisingly inspired magazines, "with astonishingly good pictures and poems, and editorials and book-reviews remarkable for their independence of thought, their humor and good-nature, and their courtesy and high spirits. What terrible times they were, actually, and yet with what gusto we did enjoy them!" Eastman agreed, delighted to find that the magazines' verve was sufficient to overcome even his own newfound conservative scruples.

Surprisingly it was Dell—not Eastman—who voiced regret about the intrusion of radical political principles into the magazines' cultural pages. He saved his toughest comments for himself: "I cannot regret my own mistaken hopes, but I do blush for some of the things I did in my own field of literary criticism, not often but enough to regret, when I pushed the economic-political interpretation of literature—an interpretation so illuminating when kept within the bounds of common sense and restrained by a recognition that art has its own values—to the brink at least of absurdity, and sometimes over the edge but not so far that I couldn't climb back out again." In another letter to Eastman, Dell affirmed his loyalty to the nondoctrinaire, individualist tradition of American radicalism—a tradition that worried little about theoretical consistency. Plainly he hoped to jostle his old friend, who had once been a far more doctrinaire socialist than Dell, and who now was embracing the equally rigid (albeit reactionary) views of Joseph McCarthy and the *National Review.*

In the notebooks of poetry and reminiscence he prepared for deposit at the Newberry, Dell recalled that in 1920, amid the increasingly strident exclamations of American Marxists, he had reminded readers of the *Liberator* that American radicalism had its roots—and its sympathies—elsewhere: "We are cut off from the very tradition of protest which we are actually carrying on. We do not even know that the literature of America is above everything else a literature of protest and rebellion. . . . We only slowly come to learn that what we sometimes contemptuously call 'America' is not American at all; that it is, astonishingly enough, we who are American." Thirty years later Dell insisted that he had never lost the sense of himself as "part of a great democratic and libertarian tradition." He deplored the tendency within American radicalism to seek revolutionary principles in European models, to ignore the vitality of America's own homegrown radical heritage.

Holding fast to the long American tradition of "protest and rebellion" actually sharpened Dell's critical view of communism and its appeal to many intellectuals. His skeptical, nondoctrinal brand of radicalism made him painfully alert to communism's inevitable failures. In a letter to Upton Sinclair, dated December 14, 1953, Dell admitted that "the zeal of anti-Communism tends to corrupt the minds of writers into an anti-liberal and anti-reform and anti-democratic fanaticism." Very likely he wrote this with Max Eastman in mind. But Dell wished to distance himself just as much from the Communists, about whom he had had grave doubts by the mid-1920s, and whom he had written off for good in the early 1930s. In his letter to Sinclair he decisively rejected the notion that Stalin had betrayed the Russian Revolution, arguing instead that he had followed inevitably from it:

> I am perhaps more deeply disillusioned about Russian Communism than you, for I think that a "Socialist" regime under the "old idealists," though less brutal than Stalin's, would have been a despotism none the less. . . . I think that what we object to did not

begin with Stalin but goes back to Lenin and to Marx. This did not make me regard American capitalism as an ideal, nor does it keep me from hoping for a better society throughout the world— in that respect, if not in any doctrinaire respects, I remain a Socialist. And it appears that I am a Liberal—as, apparently, you are, too. The Communists hate Liberals, and the ex-Communists (or many of them) hate the Liberals and ally themselves with the most reactionary elements. The habit of political lying is not easily unlearned.

Dell knew that it would be best not to make remarks this blunt to Max Eastman, who had lately placed himself among those ex-Communists who allied themselves with the antiliberals on the right. Still, it was impossible to refrain from political talk altogether. Dell congratulated Eastman for having pinned down—all the way back in the 1920s, and in the pages of the *Liberator*—communism's irresistible lure for so many intellectuals: "I was deeply impressed then —and now—only by one thing you wrote on that subject [of communism]: this was the 'religious' or mystical-philosophical aspect of Marxian theory, in which the wish to change the world was imputed to the world's own nature." But Dell chided Eastman for having had then, as ever since, "a tendency to be, like the Pope and the C.P., always right no matter how much you change your views." He also reminded Eastman that he, Dell, "had already been politically disillusioned before I came to New York [in 1913], and, though disillusionments have occurred since, I was far more skeptical of the Russian Utopia than you were."

Eastman could not have missed Dell's point: that despite his criticisms of Dell for clinging to some form of left politics, it was Eastman who had always—up to the present—been compelled to follow one or another party line. Dell insisted that political doctrines and ideals must always be "held in check and resisted and contradicted by the opposite view, [or else] the results are always terrible; and I do not know of anything in Communist ideology that could be the basis for any such checks and contradictions." He concluded in a fashion clearly intended to chasten a friend too much inclined to unqualified positions: "There *is* no method of logical reconciliation of Power and Mercy (to call them that); there is no political Absolute; the best we can have in fact is a set of shifting compromises between these two principles; and that religious, economic and political dogmas are dangerous to the extent that they are consistent—there is hope for us only in contradictions that leave us free to blunder around."

Dell's faith in contradiction and compromise was not unique in the 1950s. To some extent it reflected a turn, characteristic of the age, to a position beyond ideology, prompted in part by the terrible consequences of several decades of ideological absolutism. But Dell was by no means abandoning politics, as other literary people did in the fifties. Instead he merely wished to endorse more pragmatic and humble forms of political action and thought. He remained a deeply politicized man, certain that history, economics, and politics were inextricably part of private life and culture. But he insisted that history—like culture and private experience—should not be reduced to any single cause or principle. Nor did he feel that history worked its way up from material conditions to a cultural superstructure. Ideas, idealism, free will—these remained potent, independent historical forces for Dell. His affirmation of contradiction and compromise was, in a sense, a hard-earned affirmation of American democracy and pluralism. The wisdom of such faith, however, assured Dell little influence during these years when the United States was descending into Cold War simplifications and censorship. At a time when the world was splitting itself into two hostile blocs, it was Eastman—ready to embrace still another ideological savior—who was best suited for public influence and success, not Dell.

THIS STRAINED LAST phase of Dell and Eastman's friendship reveals how changing global and American politics disrupted the lives of radicals shaped by the political and social realities of earlier times. Two world wars, the debacle of Soviet communism, the rise of the Cold War and its attendant atmosphere of fear and political polarization—these and other developments undermined the assumptions and equanimity of Eastman and Dell alike. Unlike Eastman, Dell had dissociated himself decades earlier from Marxism and the Soviet experiment. But the Cold War and the atomic bomb, the rise of mass technology and the ascendancy of Joe McCarthy, made Dell's determined brand of liberal, democratic, unsystematic leftism look increasingly anachronistic. In some ways Eastman's case was not all that different. Although he adapted more readily to the new political realities, aligning himself with Cold War zealots, he was never much at home in the new world order. Poetry, romantic literature, a residual faith in free love—Eastman clung to these old items of his radical faith through the 1950s, even as he spoke out in public and private for reactionary politics.

Yet it is not surprising that Eastman and Dell were ill at ease with each other during the postwar years. When Eastman took the liberty of passing one of Dell's poems to Florence Norton, an editor at the conservative magazine the *Freeman*, and Norton in turn printed the poem in November 1953 without Dell's knowledge, political acrimony proper broke out between the two old friends. Dell had sent Eastman the poem, "To Each His King," early in 1953, plainly intending it for nothing more than Eastman's private delectation. When Dell found that the poem had appeared in the November 1953 issue of the *Freeman*, he was livid. He wrote to Eastman, protesting this unacceptable liberty with his work. The letter, however, failed to reach Eastman. When Dell discovered that the letter had been lost in the mails, he sent a second dispatch in which he politely summarized his objections:

> I said that I didn't like to be ungracious to people who were so nice as to like my poems, but that I didn't wish to be published in the Freeman. I said that I was acquainted with the Freeman, and that, while it had improved since early days in having articles in it that were on other than political subjects, I objected to its McCarthyist line. I said that it was my hope that you would recover from this aberration, yourself. And I offered my apologies for not having made my attitude on the Freeman clear in time to save you embarrassment in regard to it and my poems.

When Eastman objected to Dell's characterization of his current political enthusiasms as an "aberration," Dell was moved to respond at greater length. After dashing off two angry letters that he wisely "wastebasketed," Dell wrote a third one that he felt was more suitably restrained. It too, however, was not without heat. Dell claimed to be thoroughly surprised that Eastman "had fallen for a nasty crook like McCarthy who was pretending to 'protect us from Communism' a la Hitler." He hinted that Eastman's willingness to entertain McCarthy's ideas as potentially respectable ones was enough to threaten their friendship. "I cannot honestly treat McCarthyism as an intellectual view," he wrote; "it seems to me a frightful lapse from reason—something intellectually disgraceful."

McCarthy, he insisted, ought properly to be understood "as an aspirant to dictatorship."

Without mentioning Eastman directly, Dell went on to comment on the phenomenon of virulent anticommunism among former Communist believers. He discussed the unmistakable hatred of "liberals" that ran through both communism and reactionary thought:

> One of the important elements in Marxian ideology is hatred and scorn of the "liberals." I reflect upon the fact that the Communists joined with the Nazis in overthrowing the German Social-Democratic regime—which was a poor thing, but better infinitely than what was to follow its overthrow. And I reflect upon the hatred and scorn of liberals that is so prominent a feature of ex-Communist ideology. The liberals, they say, are betraying us to Communism. . . . Well! Well! I think—can it be that the hatred of liberals, once learned in the Communist school, becomes an ingrained trait that persists unchanged in ex-Communists?

Then Dell complained about the inability of Communists and reactionaries alike to think in nondoctrinaire terms:

> I think of the refuge that Communism offered to people who preferred to have their thinking done for them by an intellectually authoritarian leadership. Driven from that refuge, do they seek another refuge, sometimes in an authoritarian Church, and again in an anti-Communist Crusade in which the Leader will tell them what to think, what to say, and, if they are writers, what to write?—and they will take it, for they are spiritually like the boll weevil—just a lookin' for a home, just a lookin' for a home!

Although angry, Dell had enough self-possession to show the letter to B. Marie, who convinced him not to send it to Eastman. She told Dell that Eastman would likely hand the letter over to the editor of the *Freeman*. B. Marie wagered that the *Freeman* would publish the letter together with an angry reply from Eastman. Such an outcome, the couple decided, would cause all sorts of grief for Dell. He agreed not to send the letter, and instead wrote a fourth letter—a one-page note—to Eastman. In it he merely protested the publication of his poem and told Eastman that he hoped he would soon abandon all sympathy for McCarthy.

Eastman eventually received this short letter, along with another one—very likely the one originally lost in the mails. Despite being spared Dell's full-fledged assault, Eastman was nonetheless deeply insulted by Dell's low opinion of his new political ideas. He replied with anger and arrogance. Rather than allow himself to be aligned so exclusively with McCarthy, Eastman insisted that of "my political friends, or colleagues in opinion, the closest ones, are Wilhelm Roepke and Boris Souvarine in Europe, William Henry Chamberlin, Friedrich Hayek, James Burnham, Henry Hazlitt, Ludwig Mises, Bertram Wolfe and other ex-communists in this country." For all the smug air of this recitation, Eastman was also plainly angry enough to want to wound his friend. He sneered that Dell sounded like a character from Gogol, "a welfare state *chinovnik* retired on a pension." And in a stupendously stuffy sentence (much out of keeping with his usual lively style), Eastman managed to accuse Dell of everything from hypocrisy to naiveté: "While you were working for the government, persuading yourself that its measures of social reform were all you had ever meant by socialism, my colleagues in opinion were bending all their energies to the task of studying out and thinking out the inferences that were to be drawn by those still cherishing an extreme ideal of human freedom from the total debacle of what they, and the world at large, did mean by socialism."

This exchange of letters seemed, at least for a while, to clear the air. Thereafter the friends stuck more closely to their common resolve not to take their differences in political matters quite so personally. Both pushed on with their arguments; both ventured occasional defenses of their positions. But the arguments and defenses alike were generally mild-mannered, sometimes ironic, even self-deprecating. Dell poked fun at his own political furies while gently encouraging Eastman to "not confine your reading to the books and articles of your own enchanted circle." For his part, Eastman wrote that he regretted sending Dell so foul-tempered a letter. "It seemed a boarding school girlish thing to do," he wrote by way of apology. Dell signed off his reply to Eastman's angry letter "With the regards of your old retired, pensioned-off chinovnik friend." Eastman wrote relievedly that Dell's reply had been "adroit and charming." He reminded Dell of his lifelong view of him as "a wonderful literary critic."

Sharp political differences resurfaced now and then. In one last effort to bring Eastman to a more balanced view of politics past and present, Dell noted the unqualified love of capitalism professed by ex-Communists. "There is something comical about it," he wrote. "Capitalism has always had its brighter side, and it was there to notice all along, if revolutionary preoccupations had not to some extent blinded their gaze, and if it had not been a sort of Puritanical moral duty to find nothing good in capitalism. But the defects and evils of capitalism are still there, too, and how have they been magicked out of existence." Dell warned Eastman that just as his earlier view of capitalism had been too dark, it was now too utopian; he gently chided Eastman for his "somewhat jerry-built conservatism." Once again Dell reprimanded Eastman for his loyalty to McCarthy. "It seems to me an intellectually scandalous relation," he wrote, "and a dismaying one; and you may well have premonitions of a time when you will feel surprise and shame about this misadventure. At all events," he added, "it is surely not the goal of your political history."

Eastman replied, more soberly than before, that the renunciation of communism necessarily entailed "the fight for freedom on the only terms on which it can be won, that is, a free market economy." Democratic socialism, he insisted, constituted no genuine alternative to Marxist tyranny. But Eastman also clearly wished to dissociate himself at least a bit from McCarthy. "I think McCarthy is a misbehaved and sloppy-minded person functioning in a place where the prime demand was for a well-behaved and extremely accurate and exact mind." Beyond that, however, he was not prepared to go. "The idea that [McCarthy] is a 'menace' or that he has done any more harm to the prestige or reputation of innocent people than any thorough-going congressional investigation inevitably does is a myth." Moreover, Eastman wrote, the Communist threat was real. "Communism is winning the world and simple people of common sense are aware of it." Granted that fact, he argued, it is amazing how restrained and judicious the anti-Communists have been. Dell, frightened and appalled by McCarthy, strongly disagreed. But as far as the record shows, he dropped the reawakening argument there, as if to let Eastman know that it was their friendship—not their disagreements over McCarthy—that counted most for him.

DELL AND EASTMAN remained friends largely because they devoted so much of their correspondence and conversation not to politics but to poetry—to detailed discussions of their own poems, which they sent back and forth through the mails to each other, and to rambling talks about the poets (mainly Shakespeare and the romantics) whom they each loved. In the early 1950s Eastman had asked Dell to read through the poems he was preparing for publication in a final selection of his life's work as a poet. Dell read the poems carefully, commented on them at great length, and helped Eastman develop a sense of which should be included and which not. He offered advice on how to revise many of them. Dell also read early drafts of chapters from Eastman's political memoirs, praising them highly and encouraging Eastman to go on with them at a time when Eastman seemed discouraged by the project. On more than one occasion Eastman thanked Dell profusely for his generosity in performing these tasks. Then, as often as not, he would return to politics, impatiently defending his far-right positions against real and imagined criticisms from Dell.

Away from Eastman, Dell could be more frank about his current political ideas and feelings. In a 1947 diary entry, written just after he had finished working at the Information Service, Dell foresaw a grim new world for the United States: "I expect nothing but failure of our postwar foreign and domestic policies, which are dominated by reactionary ideas, by ignorance, and by false & foolish hopes; our support of collapsing reactionary regimes abroad is wrong, our hysterical half-Nazi anti-Russia policy is silly, our atomic-bomb policy is hypocritical, our attempt to restore a dream-capitalism at home is futile." In language he would never have used with Eastman for fear of destroying their friendship forever, he imagined "a continuation of reactionary hysteria, threats against our liberties, political imbecility, and no great or decisive democratic resurgence for a while." Despite the end of the war, Dell was still racked by political worries and angers—passions so great that they continued, as had earlier ones in 1933 and 1934, to distract him from the purely literary concerns to which he would gladly have returned.

In letters to Elizabeth Lancaster, Dell wrote often about Mc-Carthy ("I hate, despise, and fear him"), the new Red Scare (more virulent and pernicious, Dell felt, than the one that had followed World War I), and the spirit of reaction sweeping the nation. He was appalled by the war in Korea, which seemed to him to represent a new imperialist and racist foreign policy for the United States. In one letter he mentioned the "fascists" in American society and politics and invoked Arnold Toynbee's notion of the "internal prole-

tariat": "all those within any civilization who no longer believe
in it because it has ceased to rule by the charm of its ideas, its
customs, its purposes, its way of life." Dell counted himself, in
the most far-reaching terms, a member of such an internal proletariat. Much of the reason for this lay in his general disgust with the
new technology-laden character of American prosperity. "I am not
charmed," he wrote Lancaster, "by our wonderful radios, television
sets and electric refrigerators." More specifically, he wished to
dissociate himself from the war effort in Korea, going so far as to
suggest that a monument be erected by the Americans in Korea,
with a macabre plaque based on Emerson's Concord Hymn: "Here,
bringing freedom and democracy to Asia, the gallant American flyers
burned to death 50 boys and girls playing in an orphanage. They
were only gooks." For Lancaster he added a gloss to the imaginary
plaque: "That is our American way of life, sister. And so far as I'm
concerned, Senator McCarthy can have it, and the Committee on
Un-American Activities can have it. But it is not good enough for
me. I am ashamed to belong to such a country, and that puts me in
the ranks of Toynbee's internal proletariat."

At other times Dell dropped the politics, if only out of disgust and
hopelessness, and wrote to Lancaster as a dear friend who had
sought like him, but with greater success, to turn away from the
nightmare of modern history in order to concentrate on family,
friendship, and cherished intellectual work. He praised Lancaster for
having "lived a rational version of the simple life, centered in family,
friends, books, painting, and the quest of truth, and not caring a
hoot about the glitter and glamour of worldly life. And I think I am
unworldly, too—," he added, in an afterthought, "too much so for
practical purposes, including practical literary purposes." He pictured himself as "a sort of anarchistic individualist, as snooty about
the rewards of our society as Thoreau, but more domestic than he;
wishing to be a hermit with a family, is to alienate oneself too much
as a writer from the chief sources of public approval."

This conflict between domestic happiness and his desire for
literary success and public influence had always been part of Dell's
life, and by the early 1950s he frankly accepted it as such. Still,
the conflict continued to rankle on occasion. And Dell felt more
isolated in the postwar years. Friends like Eastman had gone over to
the reactionary camp. Others, like Joe Freeman, were trapped in
nonliterary jobs that afforded them little satisfaction. Tastes and

values that Dell had long championed—the romantic, individualistic radicalism of the *Masses* and the pre–World War I Greenwich Village; the liberal, democratic socialism that he had first imbibed from Debs, Shaw, and Wells; the sense that history, culture, and private life are intertwined in infinitely complex and thoroughly nonsystematic ways—all these and more seemed perfectly irrelevant in the world that emerged after World War II.

In a letter to Fred Wieck, a librarian at the Newberry, Dell described how the sense of belonging to communities of like-minded men and women had inspired his early career. He also noted how that feeling had seemed to desert him altogether in the early 1930s. The rising force of fascism in Italy, Germany, and Spain; political repression (and unabashed admiration at times for the European fascists) in the United States; the disappearance of all vestiges of solidarity (in the United States as in Europe) among socialists, liberals, and Communists; the stock market crash and the onset of worldwide economic depression in 1929; Hitler's rise to power in 1933—all these combined to wipe out Dell's belief in a progressive, unified movement in the postwar world. Politics had overtaken him. Still, when he moved to Washington in 1935 and went to work for Roosevelt's government, he felt once again part "of a cheerful and hard-working band of brothers." Dell wrote Wieck that this feeling had survived, at least to some extent, until 1945, when "we dropped our devilish atomic bombs on Hiroshima and Nagasaki, . . . with Roosevelt dead, [and] liberalism in the doghouse."

Since then he had never recovered the sense of belonging to a political or cultural movement. "I feel lonely because the fascist terrorism and lying here in the U.S.A. has gone so far that people are afraid to express any decent and humane views for fear of being called Reds and hounded out of their jobs," Dell wrote Wieck. "I do not feel that I belong to a band of brothers—I feel that I am one of a scattered few intelligent and civilized and sane people in a nation of hysterical nincompoops frenzied by some of the most unscrupulous fascists that ever stabbed a man in the back." Hyperbole, perhaps. Dell finally admitted to his usual optimism. "I expect that we shall recover," he wagered, signing off, "Yours for a better world, and not so damn much politics."

Dell had written his best books, he now felt, in a mad rush before being finally overtaken by the successive stifling, terrifying waves of modern politics. Now in 1951 he was still swamped by political concerns. He sent long letters to friends and acquaintances, very likely creating more solidarity and brotherhood than he realized. But the sense of leading a fully productive literary and intellectual life had largely deserted him. His brilliant letters were vigorous protests against a world in which he was no longer at home, but they hardly set him free to resume the life he had broken off, so desperately, in 1935.

YET ALL OF Dell's correspondents led him back into the past. One such person was Edmund Wilson, with whom Dell exchanged a flurry of letters in the early 1950s. The two men, who had known each other only slightly during the 1920s and 1930s, had both been lovers of Edna Millay: Dell in 1918, Wilson a few years later. After Millay died in 1950 the two corresponded frequently for a while, writing mainly about Millay and her poetry. In the long letters they devoted to her, these two literary men provided ample evidence of her lasting power over them. Each encouraged the other to write a book-length study of Millay. When Wilson sent Dell a draft of the reflective essay on Millay that he eventually published in *The Shores of Light*, Dell praised it highly. Throughout their letters both men brought scrupulous, rigorous attention to her poems. Yet there is an obsessive quality about their brief correspondence. It was more than thirty years since either man had held Edna Millay in his arms, yet she seemed as vivid as ever to them both.

Dell heartily indulged his old obsession with Millay in these and other letters, as in occasional conversations with good friends. Even within his own family the old affair was said to obsess him still. Deep down, though, Dell knew he had been fortunate to lose her. In his long marriage to B. Marie, and in fatherhood, he had found the private life he desired. He had, as his granddaughter Jerri remarked many years later, a striking fondness for family life. Dell would always associate Edna Millay with Greenwich Village and the glamorous bohemia of the 1910s. But he had wished to escape the Village while he was there; afterward he always recalled it with a mix of irony, humor, and regret. Most of the time his poet-lover of those days seemed as distant as the prewar Village itself.

Dell's most regular correspondent through the 1950s was Joseph Freeman, his old friend and colleague from the *Liberator.* Freeman had always idolized his older friend. He had particularly admired

Dell's pathbreaking efforts to create a brand of cultural criticism that would take political and economic factors into account. To the last their friendship retained something of the mentor/pupil character it had assumed at the start. There was also genuine fondness between the men. Although Freeman had been at the center of the radical, largely Communist party–controlled literary scene of the 1930s, his friendship with Dell had never been seriously endangered. Rather, Dell had worried about Freeman's inevitable disillusionment with Marxism, much as he had worried about his son Tony's disappointment.

Their correspondence through the 1950s eventually grew to hundreds of letters, some reaching thirty and even forty pages in length. Politics and literature—part reminiscence and part current concerns—made up the bulk of the pages. Early on Freeman pressed upon Dell his view of him as "one of America's great writers," and he earnestly regretted Dell's reluctance to agree. Freeman argued that literary and political tastes had run away from Dell, but that one day they would return:

> Right now we live in a period of great reaction, an age of the breaking and making of nations, hence the fuss over the pioneer role in American literature of Pound and Eliot. They will always have a place in history. But history, like nature, is in constant flux. The pendulum will swing again; the world will return to its liberal, progressive orbit; and the literary chroniclers will rediscover the Golden Age of Millay, Lindsay, Masters, O'Neill, Dreiser, Anderson, Sandburg, Ficke, Upton Sinclair, Sinclair Lewis, Van Wyck Brooks, Waldo Frank. And when that saga is written, you will stand out in it as the best critic of that age by the common consent of your contemporary peers and because your work broke new ground which writers all over America are still working. And part of the story will be your novels and poems.

Freeman's literary list was a haphazard one. But it clearly pointed to that generation of "progressive" and "realistic" writers who had come of age early in the century, committed wholeheartedly to the American scene but destined to be ousted in a great battle of the books by more adamant modernists (from Eliot to Hemingway to Faulkner) who appeared at roughly the same moment or just afterward. Stylistic innovation and cultural pessimism—rather than realism and "liberal, progressive" faith—had carried the day. Dell, for his part, demurred at Freeman's attempt to characterize him as a neglected great author. But he must also have felt there was something to Freeman's assertion that the "progressive" literary tradition of which he was a part had been slighted in a deeply conservative age that favored writers who either endorsed conservative institutions (most notably Eliot) or who encouraged political cynicism or indifference—postures that best served the purposes of the political status quo. From childhood Dell had regarded himself as part of a progressive, idealistic literary tradition, going back at least as far as his beloved Shelley, and spanning, in its American incarnation, Emerson, Whittier, and Whitman on through to magazines like the *Masses* and the *Liberator.* More than once Dell made it clear that he regarded *Diana Stair* as one of the recent monuments of this progressive literary tradition.

On questions of contemporary literary taste Dell was notably straightforward, sometimes disarmingly blunt. Whenever Freeman expressed admiration for the celebrated modernists of the preceding three decades, Dell responded with disdain. In one letter he ticked off a few determinedly traditionalist opinions, stating his preference for Homer over Proust, Wells over Dos Passos, even H. G. Bailey's detective novels over James Joyce. "I especially dislike the products of that School of Old Maidish Fantasy presided over by Auntie James Joyce," he wrote. "I don't like Magic Mountainish fiction or Wastelandish verse." Above all, Dell hated the writings of T. S. Eliot. He despised Eliot's abstruseness, elitist air, reactionary politics, British cultural sympathies, Anglican Church posturings, and desolate tone. Dell correctly recognized in such verse a renunciation of romantic literature and progressive politics. In both of these latter movements Dell had plainly established a lifelong stake. He realized that the seemingly universal prestige enjoyed by Eliot in the postwar world had as its inevitable counterpart the greatly diminished reputation of the literary and political movements to which Dell had belonged.

When Freeman wrote in praise of Proust, Joyce, Gide, Kafka, and other preeminent European modernists, Dell felt called upon to outline his objections to these writers. He argued against what he perceived to be the modernist tendency toward excessive inclusion of facts, thoughts, experiences—the apparent effort to capture life in all its chaotic details and the stream of uninterrupted, spontaneous consciousness. For Dell, literature was inevitably an artful arrangement of facts and consciousness, a carefully edited, deliberately shaped account of human experience. "Certain things have to submit to transmogrification before they go into novels," he wrote Freeman, "and this process may add or, more often, subtract from the original. . . . This is the reason why biography and autobiography is more real in some respects than fiction. It is (I believe) idle to pretend that fiction can have these other values; it can't, and this is the nature of things; art and life are different, and if we try to get too much of the undoctored incident into art we are in danger of losing the special and important magic of art."

Although Dell firmly believed that political concerns and incidents could be built into successful novels, he also warned Freeman against literary works with explicit, uncompromising political agendas. He worried about novels that combined an interest in contemporary life with explicit political interests. Such books, he suggested, were almost always barely disguised propaganda, not literature. Rather, he admired writers who managed to integrate political concerns into their literary works without employing those political elements for propagandistic purposes. "In your review of politics in literature," he wrote Freeman, "you left out Shaw and Ibsen, who showed how long political speeches can be an essential part of the action. . . . You left out 'Diana Stair,' in which there are many 'political' speeches, all a part of the action and expressive of the characters."

Dell felt that a writer like Dos Passos allowed his politics to run roughshod over his novels. He had even less sympathy for what he felt was the rather maudlin nihilism of "lost generation" writers. In Hemingway's *The Sun Also Rises*, Dell wrote Freeman, "the sentimentality [is] unendurable." Dell granted some exceptions to his general disdain for contemporary fiction. He agreed with Freeman, for instance, that Raymond Chandler deserved to be read "as an important social critic." But for the most part his literary sympathies—both in stylistic and thematic matters—lay farther back in the past.

Dell's letters to Freeman were by no means confined to intellectual topics. Occasionally they offered entertaining accounts of his family, including the two granddaughters, Jerri and Katie, born to Christopher and his wife Barbara. When Freeman's mother died unexpectedly, Dell's brief letter was a model of heartfelt condolence. His affection for Freeman was unmistakable. Always Dell had regarded Freeman as a younger writer who was carrying on the literary and political concerns he had represented in his own writings for decades. Now that they were both older men—Dell retired and heading toward seventy, Freeman well into his fifties—they seemed more alike than ever. In their correspondence they aimed to preserve a species of progressive culture and political idealism to which they had each, in differing ways, devoted their lives. Now that they recognized those causes as beleaguered, they sometimes gave in to anger and bitterness. More often they devoted themselves with renewed hope to the spirit of uninhibited talk and intellectual companionship that had brought them together at the start.

True Riches

D ELL SPENT THE 1950s rooted at his writing desks at Ingleside
Terrace, surrounded by family and a small circle of friends. The
friends he saw most often were Verb Gabbert, his coworker from
Information Service days, and Ted Hines, a much younger man but
"intellectually grown up," as he wrote Freeman in 1951, and
"immensely a reader of books." Hines had met B. Marie at the
public library where she worked; she in turn had brought him home
to meet Dell. He seemed to fill a gap for Dell that had opened up
when Tony and Christopher moved out of the house. Still in his
twenties, Hines served as a conduit for Dell to the intellectual
excitement and optimism of youth.

In 1951, just weeks after his first granddaughter, Jerri, was born,
Dell spoke about poetry and his own literary past at Christopher's
graduation from Goddard College. The speech was a success, the
weekend an occasion for Dell to feel once again the effect of his
oratorical powers upon an audience. Stefano Sarragato, a poet who
attended the ceremony, wrote a brief, impressionistic poem afterward, recording Dell's appearance and behavior at a gathering of
literary people at Goddard that same week: "his trembling fingertips," smoking constantly, speaking of Dreiser and Pound and William Carlos Williams, reciting occasional poems, "his cataclysmic
smile, / his crackling voice, his jittering / poise his blissful face." In a
letter to Freeman in which he quoted Sarragato's poem in full, Dell
cracked that he had not made any of the poem up himself. He was
flattered by the attention.

His sense of his place in the world grew increasingly narrow during the 1950s and on into the 1960s. His eccentricities, his frequent air of preoccupation, his black moods and fits of ill temper—B. Marie bore all with good grace. The two were, as Verb Gabbert once wrote, genuinely fond of each other. She worked at Mount Pleasant public library in Washington through much of the 1950s and early 1960s, encouraging her husband in all his literary and intellectual projects. Dell, in turn, encouraged B. Marie to write down the vivid stories about her family and her early years that she loved to tell. A favorite story was that of B. Marie's paternal grandfather who had gone out to California in 1849 in search of gold, found precious little of it, but then made fortunes several times over herding livestock out west. There were tales about B. Marie's parents and their early years as farmers in Minnesota. Most affecting of all was an anecdote about B. Marie's mother, Stella, who had come to live with B. Marie and Dell some years after her husband died. Stella, who had doubted her love for her husband early on in their marriage, had come finally to love him wholeheartedly. After he died, B. Marie remembered, her mother would go to the cemetery alone and plant sweet peas on his grave.

Dell recorded many of B. Marie's stories in letters to Joe Freeman. He was delighted to have a wife with so colorful a family. Many years after their marriage in 1919, she continued to inspire him with love and gratitude. She was larger than him, bigger boned and more robust, with pale, translucent skin. Meanwhile Dell, never large to begin with, seemed to shrink as he grew older. He weighed 120 pounds or less and stood no more than five feet six inches. He dressed like a respectably retired Washington bureaucrat, often in a jacket and tie. But there was still much of the bohemian about B. Marie, dressed in her peasant smocks and light moccasins. Thanks mainly to her, their house at Ingleside Terrace still had about it the air of Greenwich Village. Perhaps Gabbert was right: the Dells had imbibed too much of the early Village ever to get it out of their blood. For Dell the pleasures of bohemia had come to be mixed inseparably with love for his wife. In 1950, in one of the birthday poems he wrote for her every year, he described how his world had contracted to the domestic happiness she had created for him: "The great world is a queer world, / Its light withdrawn. / But our small world is a dear world— / Blue eyes shine on."

*   *   *

IN HIS LAST years the world became still smaller for Dell. There was always, it seemed, news of the death of some dear friend. Arthur Ficke had died a painful death of throat cancer back in 1945. Dell had written shortly before his death: "Dear Arthur: I have been thinking a great deal about you lately. . . . I thought of our old times together in Chicago and New York, and how gay and—though we did not know it then—how wise we were." Verb Gabbert had brought Dell news of Edna St. Vincent Millay's death in 1950; Dell had been devastated. Then in 1954, precisely when they were contending over politics past and present, Dell wrote Eastman with news that Marjorie Jones had died suddenly of a heart attack in Pasadena—"Dear, beautiful, generous-hearted MJ," he wrote. Dell had loved M.J. in Chicago and Greenwich Village, where they had lived together for several happy years, both their names emblazoned on the mailbox at the foot of the stairs. M.J. had remained friends with Dell and B. Marie all these years. Lately she had become— inexplicably, it seemed to Dell—an old woman, crippled with arthritis. "She was such a lovely and lovely-looking girl," Eastman wrote in response to Dell's news of her death. "There's so much bad news these days. My friends are dropping around me like trees in a hurricane."

When Eastman's wife of many years, Eliena Krylenko, died in 1956, Dell wrote his friend at once, recalling Eliena and the times when they had all been together. It took a while before Eastman wrote back: "I have delayed a long time answering that lovely letter you wrote to me when Eliena died. I know you will understand why. Your eloquent and beautiful memories of her meant a great deal to me." He added that he was happy they had all been able to get together the previous fall, before Eliena's death, for a "reunion." Politics, which had once threatened to divide the two men, was no longer an issue between them.

Dell worked on into the sixties on a handful of projects. He corresponded at great length with the writer Miriam Gurko when she was at work on a biography of Edna St. Vincent Millay. Dell himself wrote several essays on Millay in which he recalled the bohemian world in which they had both flourished, and to which their names were destined to remain inextricably tied. The radical movements of the sixties, combining politics and culture in ways not entirely different from that of Dell's own generation, interested him occasionally. Once a young socialist came to visit Dell in Washington, asking for support in the effort to reestablish the Socialist party in America. Dell was curious and sympathetic. But by the mid-sixties he was too old, too frail, to take an active part in new radical movements. His world continued to narrow, the domestic sphere occupying nearly all his loyalty.

A series of strokes in the mid- and late sixties left Dell increasingly feeble. Emphysema, following a lifetime of heavy smoking, robbed him of the little that was left of his surviving strength. Glaucoma took an eye—hard loss for a man who wrote and read nearly all day, every day. (He also managed some humor about it. When his granddaughter Jerri discovered him sitting before a full-length mirror, she teased him, "Floyd, Floyd, vanity is all." "Vanity!" he fired back. "I need it to stick in my glass eye!") Halfway through the decade Dell and B. Marie sold their home on Ingleside Terrace to Tony and moved out of the city, settling in a smaller house in Bethesda, Maryland. In 1967, surfacing after a long period of illness, Dell wrote his last words on Millay, revising a long, lucid piece in which he recalled their romance in vivid, unsentimental details. He mailed it off to the Newberry, thereby bringing to a close his productive life as a public writer. He was eighty years old, and his days as a bohemian and literary man in Davenport, Chicago, Greenwich Village, and Croton now seemed very distant indeed.

Dell lived to see his fiftieth wedding anniversary in February 1969. By then he was confined to his bed with emphysema, in need of an oxygen mask and frequent medical attention. On the day of their anniversary B. Marie was also laid up in their bed, recovering from a recent fall. The family was on hand, and granddaughter Jerri told them how wonderful she thought it was that, in the United States and in times of family fracture and divorce, they had managed to stay married for so long and so happily. Dell, never inclined to let anyone else have the last word, replied in typical fashion: "Wonderful, hell! It took a lot of goddamn hard work." B. Marie, who knew best of all, agreed. "Right, a lot of damn hard work."

Dell died July 23, 1969, in Bethesda. By then emphysema and illness had wasted him down to eighty-five pounds. He had announced some years earlier in a poem to B. Marie that he wanted his ashes scattered, with hers, in the countryside near their summer home in Winchester, New Hampshire. With B. Marie still alive, the family decided the best plan would be to bury his ashes in Winchester, in safe keeping, so to speak, until their ashes could be scattered together. Most of Dell's closest friends from the days in Chicago and New York were already dead—Eastman had died only a few months earlier, in March—deaths that only added to the impression that Dell's time had passed for good. Nevertheless, he affirmed up to the end the literary and political principles that had inspired him all his life, and that he felt were as vital and essential in 1969 as they had been in 1919.

Among those principles had been several that, however much they clashed with one another, had steered him away from serious pursuit of worldly fame and success. These principles he had followed until they brought him a full life's share of happiness. He called them "true riches," and in a letter to Elizabeth Lancaster in the 1950s he had spelled them out directly:

> These [riches] include several things, and first of all two things that are in fact more or less opposed. . . . One is freedom. And the kind of freedom is illustrated by a bit of verse that springs to my mind, remembered from my seventeenth year: "Here are true riches, Here is Golconda, Here are the Indies, Here we are free—" and the freedom was that of Vagabondia, or, actually, Bohemia, freedom from the necessity of holding a job, free from the constraints and hypocrisies of a commercial civilization— "Free to be oddities, Not mere commodities, Stupid and salable, Wholly available, Ranged upon shelves." This still seems to me one of the most golden kinds of true riches. The second kind, however, is one of a simple domestic life with a wife and children—which, after considerable experience, I still hold to be one of the most golden kinds of true riches. In the kind of world we live in, we must ordinarily give up the first to gain the second, and vice versa, and those are lucky who can by hook or by crook and compromise have both for a while.

Dell mentioned other riches to Lancaster as well: "possession of aesthetic sensibilities and some creative powers," a handful of close friends, "a place to live which is a refuge from the world but not too remote from civilization." And he added that true riches "do *not* include any kind of activities intended to improve the world—these being a duty, perhaps, or a necessity, even, but not a kind of true riches."

In 1951, disheartened by McCarthyist reaction and the collapse of all radical dreams, it is understandable that Dell should have added this last caveat, this renunciation of political idealism and engagement. But in fact political conscience and activism had always been a part of his life and work, and just as surely they had enriched both. The desire for personal freedom and private happiness had always been strong in Dell: above all he identified it with bohemia. But such desire had always been tempered by his commitment to public life and by his faith in progress and human decency. From the start these items of faith had given him a saving perspective on himself and his comrades—a perspective that many of those same comrades lacked. Commitment to public life and progress had added irony and detachment to his bohemian tastes; alert democratic sympathies to his potentially elitist brand of radical politics; a disdain for escapism, nihilism, and the absurd in literature and culture generally, even while he recognized in literature something quite different—more perfect, better formed—than life itself. These items of faith had also been indispensable to his belief that friendship, marriage, family, and society itself are enduring, enriching parts of human experience—matters on which he had been willing to stake his imagination and his heart.

Bohemia, socialism, literature, criticism, marriage, family, activism, retreat—Dell's life had been made up of many contradictory things. After his own fashion, though, he was certain he had found some reconciliation among them. Essential to this adjustment had been his view of life as something like a literary project, to be fashioned into a whole that makes sense, in which one can take wholehearted satisfaction and pride. Reality, he had written Elizabeth Lancaster, should be understood at least in part as a fiction, as a text constructed by writers and nonwriters alike. "Life, insofar as it is worth living, is an artistic creation, a pattern-finding and design-creating activity, a story, a dream, not any the less a story or a dream when it is most completely lived—and *this* process involves turning away from the whole rush of reality—'bodiless, soulless, formless, senseless, meaningless, worthless'—to an inner refuge, a garden, a green isle in the sea." What is essential is "the selection, out of the meaningless welter of reality, of parts which can be put together in a significant pattern and *lived.*" Dell had hammered his own lived reality out of literature and politics, bohemia and family, public action and private pleasures. "The man—poet or businessman or whatever—who fails to make a life worth living out of his domestic relations, his marriage and family, his friendships, his human relations generally, often does so because he does not know how to select from the huge clutter of reality the elements that *can* be composed into a story that has a form, a design, a meaning."

How much design and meaning had he managed to find and create in his own life? Never enough, perhaps, to suit this literary man with tastes that ran to precise, well-crafted designs. Politics seemed to crash in on him, particularly in the years after 1933, disrupting the well-composed life he craved. But in the end he accepted his unquenchable political ideals, passions, and disappointments as well—if not quite as riches, then at least as his human duty. From the start he knew that the disruptions of politics, like all disruptions, must be accepted as part of life's pattern, even if they made that pattern irregular, distressing, uncontrollable in places. However much life may be like fiction—something to be planned and shaped like a literary work—it was also something that remained resiliently different from fiction, something in which chaos, spontaneity, and other freewilled people also played necessary, life-giving parts. Delight in life's unexpected nature—bringing sadness, to be sure, but also great pleasure—such delight had been part of Floyd Dell's abundant, lifelong faith.

NOTES

In these notes I have used abbreviations for several periodicals, individuals, and libraries, as noted below.

PERIODICALS
Chicago Evening Post: CEP
Friday Literary Review: FLR
Tri-City Workers Magazine: TCWM

INDIVIDUALS
George Cram Cook: GCC
Floyd Dell: FD
Theodore Dreiser: TD
Max Eastman: ME
Arthur Davison Ficke: ADF
Joseph Freeman: JF
Upton Sinclair: US

LIBRARIES
Beinecke Library, Yale University: BLYU
Lilly Library, Indiana University: LLIU
Newberry Library: NL
The Floyd Dell Papers at the Newberry Library are designated by the abbreviation: FDPN.

PREFACE

p. xi, "conspiring to cause mutiny": quoted in FD, *Homecoming* (New York: Farrar & Rinehart, 1933), 313.
p. xi, "a scene from": FD, *Looking at Life* (New York: Knopf, 1924), 153.
p. xii, "I sometimes wondered": FD, "Colors of Life," *Liberator* I (December 1918), 44–45.
p. xiii, "love encounters": Day, *The Eleventh Virgin* (New York: Boni, 1924), 169.
p. xiv, "a textbook case": Emily Hahn,

Romantic Rebels (Boston: Houghton Mifflin, 1967), 177.
p. xiv, "Grand Economic": quoted in Daniel Aaron, *Writers on the Left* (New York: Oxford University Press, 1977), 218.
p. xv, "stood for fun": FD, *Homecoming*, 251.
p. xv, "its characteristic": Irving Howe, "To the *Masses*—With Love and Envy," in William L. O'Neill, ed., *Echoes of Revolt: The Masses 1911–1917* (Chicago: Ivan R. Dee, 1989), 7.

One: MIDWEST BOYHOOD

p. 4, "grim and generous": FD, epigraph to *Moon-Calf* (New York: Knopf, 1920).

p. 4, "young idealism": quoted in Heywood Broun, "Books," *New York Tribune*, October 27, 1920, 10.

p. 4, "I have just": TD to FD, November 20, 1920. FDPN.

p. 5, "In a manner": Robert H. Wiebe, *The Search for Order* (New York: Hill and Wang, 1967), 44.

p. 6, He railed regularly: Christopher Dell to author, March 1991.

p. 7, "Adam was only": FD, *Moon-Calf*, 16.

p. 9, "The first jobs": FD, *Homecoming*, 5.

p. 9, "the Lawgiver": FD, *Homecoming*, 6.

p. 11, "clever but unreal": FD, *Homecoming*, 27, 28.

p. 11, "I spent": FD, *Homecoming*, 17.

p. 11, "cruelly disillusioned": FD, *Homecoming*, 23, 22.

p. 12, "created in the public": FD, *Homecoming*, 37.

p. 13, "brisk, handsome, well-ordered": Mark Twain, *Life on the Mississippi* (New York: Airmont Publishing, 1965), 272.

p. 13, "interested in art": Twain, *Life on the Mississippi*, 272.

p. 14, "old wooden bedsteads": FD, *Homecoming*, 42.

p. 14, "a series": FD, *Homecoming*, 42.

p. 15, "Socialism was not": FD, *Homecoming*, 55.

p. 15, "It told about Greek": FD, *Homecoming*, 64.

p. 15, "less a rebel": FD, *Moon-Calf*, 101.

p. 15, "I was engaged": FD, *Homecoming*, 55.

p. 16, "What if my father": FD, *Homecoming*, 55–56.

p. 16, "the obligation": FD, *Homecoming*, 57.

p. 16, "That was a glorious evening": FD, *Looking at Life*, 147.

p. 17, "love exists": FD, *Homecoming*, 45.

p. 17, "a kind of Slavic Forest": FD, *Homecoming*, 63–64.

p. 17, "My life seemed": FD, *Homecoming*, 73.

p. 18, "I enjoyed each moment": FD, *Homecoming*, 77.

Two: TRI-CITY REBEL

p. 19, "Floyd Dell was": Harry Hansen, *Midwst Portraits* (New York: Harcourt, Brace, 1923), 209.

p. 19, "commonplace and uninteresting": FD, *Homecoming*, 83.

p. 20, "Port Royal": FD, *Moon-Calf*, 219.

p. 20, "some native American": FD, *Homecoming*, 170.

p. 20, "Davenport was": FD, Poetry Notebook I. FDPN.

p. 20, "prove a troublesome": FD, *Homecoming*, 104.

p. 21, "Floyd Dell was": Hansen, *Midwest Portraits*, 212.

p. 21, "some expression": FD, omitted chapters, *Homecoming*, 486. FDPN.

p. 21, "read and knew": FD, *Homecoming*, 81.

p. 22, "Darwin, Emerson": FD, Poetry Notebook I. FDPN.

p. 22, "a foolish consistency": FD, Poetry Notebook I. FDPN.

p. 22, "an extraordinarily beautiful": FD, *Homecoming*, 90–91.

p. 23, "Nat Tyler": FD, Poetry Notebook I. FDPN.

p. 25, "of a semi-possessive": FD, Poetry Notebook II, 130. FDPN.

p. 25, "that an older": FD, "The Kinsey Report." FDPN.

p. 26, "No knowledge": Susan Glaspell, *The Road to the Temple* (New York: Frederick A. Stokes, 1927), 188.

p. 27, "the most important thing": FD, *Homecoming*, 119.

p. 27, "In reaching out": FD, *Homecoming*, 146.

p. 27, "What I learned": FD, *Homecoming*, 119.

p. 28, "You have been mooning": FD, *Moon-Calf*, 189.

p. 28, "romantic nonsense": FD, *Moon-Calf*, 191–195.

p. 28, "would have less": FD, *Homecoming*, 119.

p. 28, "Your family will": FD, *Homecoming*, 120.

p. 29, "capturing 'personal' items": Hansen, *Midwest Portraits*, 210.

p. 29, "full of rabbinical": FD, "Dr. William Fineshriber." FDPN.

p. 29, "one of the pagan": FD, "Dr. William Fineshriber." FDPN. FD, *Homecoming*, 121.

p. 30, "of a broad": FD, "Dr. William Fineshriber." FDPN.

p. 30, "I was on guard": FD, Poetry Notebook I. FDPN.

p. 30, "slow subtle destiny": quoted in FD, *Homecoming*, 106–107.

p. 30, "In all the world": "Salutatory," *TCWM* I, 1 (November 1905), 1.

p. 30, "As a reporter": FD, *Homecoming*, 133.

p. 31, "Workingmen of the tri-cities": J. C. Gibson, "A Call to Action," *TCWM* I, 4 (February 1906), 19.

p. 31, "In any sanely": "Thersites" (FD), "Diphtheria in Davenport," *TCWM* I, 1 (November 1905), 6.

p. 31, "Under Capitalism": "Thersites" (FD), "Why People Go to Brick Munro's," *TCWM* I, 11 (September 1906), 3.

p. 31, "Incredible, amazing romanticists": FD, *Homecoming*, 96.

p. 31, "the Profit": FD, "Why People Go to Brick Munro's," 4.

p. 32, "I watched last night": FD, *Homecoming*, 97.

p. 33, "imperious, wild": FD, Poetry Notebook II, 137. FDPN.

p. 34, "clarify the political atmosphere": Milo Mitchell Clapp, "Socialists and the I.W.W.," *TCWM* I, 11 (September 1906), 12.

p. 34, "conclusively dedicated to": FD, Poetry Notebook I. FDPN.

p. 35, "It was a magical": FD, *Homecoming*, 162.

p. 35, "In being true": FD, *Homecoming*, 162, 163.

p. 35, "I was puritanically": FD, "Daughters of Dreams and of Stories" (hereafter "Daughters of Dreams"). FDPN.

p. 35, "All this, though": FD, *Homecoming*, 163.

p. 36, "Certainly I could not": FD, *Homecoming*, 166.

p. 36, "without scenes": FD, "A Summer Romance in the Middle West." Unpublished essay. Papers of Christopher Dell.

p. 36, "for insolence": FD, *Homecoming*, 169.

p. 37, "the critic": GCC, clipping, *Davenport Democrat*, 1912. FDPN.

p. 38, "the queer fish": Glaspell, *The Road to the Temple*, 193.

p. 38, "The cock-sure": Glaspell, *The Road to the Temple*, 182, 181.

p. 38, "In the whole history": Glaspell, *The Road to the Temple*, 181.

p. 39, "disorderly, pig-sty": FD, *Homecoming*, 148.

p. 39, "the Transcendental movement": FD to George Bernard Shaw (not sent), 1908. FDPN.

p. 40, "What I mean": FD to "My Dear Doctor," May 16, 1908. FDPN.

p. 40, "fiercer iconoclast": FD to George Bernard Shaw, 1908. FDPN.

p. 40, "American Union": FD to George Bernard Shaw, 1908; FD to "My Dear Doctor," May 16, 1908. FDPN.

p. 41, "sweethearts": FD, "Daughters of Dreams." FDPN.

p. 41, "She had been": FD, "Daughters of Dreams." FDPN.

p. 42, "his romanticism": FD, "Daughters of Dreams." FDPN.

Three: LITERARY JOURNALIST

p. 45, "shock city": A connection between turn-of-the-century Chicago and Asa Briggs's concept of a "shock city" is made in James Gilbert, "The Capital of Nature," *Atlantic Monthly*, June 1991, 113–117.

p. 46, "a gracious": FD, *Homecoming*, 181.

p. 46, "is in many respects": F. H. Stead, "The Civic Life of Chicago," *Review of Reviews*, August 1893, 179. This and other turn-of-the-century impressions of Chicago are found in Ross Miller, *American Apocalypse* (Chicago: University of Chicago Press, 1990).

p. 47, "some kind of": FD, *Homecoming*, 187.

p. 48, "to find order": FD, *Homecoming*, 185.

p. 48, "She was at home": FD, *Homecoming*, 185.

p. 49, "She was a girl": FD, *Homecoming*, 185.

p. 49, "a very beautiful": FD, *Homecoming*, 193.

p. 50, "I asked if": FD, *Homecoming*, 193.

p. 50, "If my wife": FD, *Homecoming*, 198.

p. 51, "That means that": FD, *Homecoming*, 190.

p. 51, "in financial news": FD, *Homecoming*, 188.

p. 51, "intellectual brilliance": FD, *Homecoming*, 188.

p. 53, "We agree with": Francis Hackett, "Why Read Literature," *FLR*, July 9, 1909, 4.

p. 53, "futility and fatuity": FD (Unsigned), review of Hutchins Hapgood's *An Anarchist Woman*, *FLR*, June 4, 1909, 2.

p. 53, "a definition": Francis Hackett, review of *Socialism in Theory and Practice*, by Morris Hillquit, *FLR*, March 19, 1909, 1.

p. 54, "to understand socialism": Hackett, review of *Socialism in Theory and Practice*, 1.

p. 54, "cover all the affairs": "Announcement," *FLR*, March 12, 1909, 4.

p. 54, "the sole literary": "Announcement," *FLR*, March 12, 1909, 4.

p. 55, "teems with ideas": Hackett, review of H. G. Wells's *Tono-Bungay, FLR,* March 26, 1909, 1.

p. 55, "The novel": Hackett, "Reticence in Fiction," *FLR,* March 19, 1909, 4.

p. 56, "It is a matter": FD, review of *Nirvana Days,* by Cale Young Rice, *FLR,* September 10, 1909, 2.

p. 57, "a towering figure": FD (Unsigned), "Minor Mention," *FLR,* June 11, 1909, 2.

p. 57, "Ten years ago": GCC to FD, September 10, 1909. FDPN.

p. 58, "discriminate between": FD (Unsigned), "A Point in Criticism," *FLR,* May 28, 1909, 4.

p. 58, "It is necessary": FD to ADF, March 23, 1914. FDPN.

p. 59, "would really have": FD, "Daughters of Dreams," 15. FDPN.

p. 59, "I find myself": Mollie Cook to FD (undated). FDPN.

p. 60, "a genius for friendship": Eunice Tietjens, *The World at My Shoulder* (New York: Macmillan, 1938), 18.

p. 62, "relieved [Floyd] of": Anderson, *My Thirty Years' War* (New York: Horizon, 1969), 37.

p. 62, "If most European": quoted in FD, *Homecoming,* 198.

p. 62, "some restlessness": FD, "Daughters of Dreams," 16. FDPN.

p. 63, "There was a girl": FD, *Homecoming,* 212.

Four: "A NEW ERA"

p. 65, "There was always": FD, *Homecoming,* 189–190.

p. 65, "he was called": Fanny Butcher, *Many Lives—One Love* (New York: Harper and Row, 1972), 71.

p. 66, "working for some": FD, Poetry Notebook III, 16. FDPN.

p. 66, "a kind of prescience": Butcher, *Many Lives—One Love,* 69.

p. 66, "the standards for": FD, Editorial, *FLR,* July 28, 1911, 2.

p. 67, "she wrote well": FD, *Homecoming,* 228.

p. 67, "Friday book section": Anderson, *My Thirty Years' War,* 36.

p. 67, "Floyd's injunctions": Anderson, *My Thirty Years' War,* 36–37.

p. 67, "Poets have always preached": FD (unsigned), "Literature and Life," *CEP,* June 6, 1913, 9.

p. 68, "In heaven's name": FD, *Homecoming,* 228.

p. 69, "On the way": FD, "Daughters of Dreams," 11. FDPN. Dell's account here does not include names, but here and elsewhere it is clear that the other participants are Augusta and Lucian Cary.

p. 69, "to put me": FD, "Daughters of Dreams," 16. FDPN.

p. 69, "it is all right": FD, "Daughters of Dreams," 11. FDPN.

p. 70, "it was now accepted": FD, "Daughters of Dreams," 17. FDPN.

p. 70, "I think that Margery": FD, "Daughters of Dreams," 17. FDPN.

p. 70, "was not the behavior": FD, "Daughters of Dreams," 17. FDPN.

p. 70, "a beautiful year": FD, *Homecoming,* 229.

p. 70, "the fiddles are tuning": quoted in Alfred Kazin, *On Native Grounds* (New York: Harcourt Brace Jovanovich, 1982), 165.

p. 71, "the year when": Butcher, *Many Lives— One Love,* 69.

p. 71, "It was the year": FD, *Homecoming,* 218–219.

p. 71, "as a muddy pathway": FD, "Robert Herrick's Chicago," *FLR,* January 26, 1912, 1.

p. 72, "is not a cruel place": FD, "Mr. Dooley's Chicago," *FLR,* February 2, 1912, 1.

p. 72, "The poetry of Chicago": FD, "Theodore Dreiser's Chicago," *FLR,* February 23, 1912, 1.

p. 73, "a place of": FD, "Theodore Dreiser's Chicago," 1.

p. 73, "would have been": Butcher, *Many Lives—One Love,* 71.

p. 74, "newer ideal": FD, "A New Idealism," *FLR,* December 29, 1911, 1.

p. 74, "She treats of love": FD, "A New Idealism," 1.

p. 74, "in conflict with": FD, "A New Idealism," 1.

p. 75, "dream of the perfect": FD, "A New Idealism," 1.

p. 75, "as a sociological abstraction": FD, *Women as World Builders* (Chicago: Forbes, 1913), 1.

p. 75, "is, first of all": FD, *Women as World Builders,* 24.

p. 75, "In this 'home'": FD, *Women as World Builders,* 25.

p. 76, "exaggerates the": FD, *Women as World Builders,* 24.

p. 76, "one which cannot": FD, *Women as World Builders,* 24, 22.

p. 76, "to raid parliament": FD, *Women as World Builders,* 37.

p. 76, "send women into": FD, *Women as World Builders*, 42.

p. 76, "has the gift": FD, *Women as World Builders*, 34.

p. 76, "She has made": FD, *Women as World Builders*, 43.

p. 76, "the body is": FD, *Women as World Builders*, 50

p. 77, "wonders if": FD, *Women as World Builders*, 63.

p. 77, "a future more": FD, *Women as World Builders*, 64.

p. 78, "woman's movement": FD, *Women as World Builders*, 19, 20.

p. 78, "It is, then": FD, *Women as World Builders*, 20–21.

p. 78, "provocative [. . .] well worth": review of *Women as World Builders*, *New York Times Book Review*, May 4, 1913, 266.

p. 78, "an exhilarating book": Elia Peattie, review of *Women as World Builders*, *Chicago Tribune*, April 19, 1913, 9.

p. 78, "Your articles": Frances Bjorkman to FD, August 5, 1912. FDPN.

Five: SOUTHSIDE BOHEMIAN

p. 80, "Why does all": Arthur Davison Ficke, *Selected Poems* (New York: Doran, 1926), 185.

p. 81, "Well, it is": FD, "Syndicalism," *FLR*, December 27, 1912, 1.

p. 81, "A Word With": *FLR*, December 6, 1912.

p. 82, "For a moment": FD, "Mothers and Daughters," *International* V (January 1912), 28.

p. 83, "unconventional form": FD, review of Ezra Pound's *Provenca*, *FLR*, January 6, 1911, 5.

p. 83, "Ezra Pound": FD, "To a Poet," *FLR*, April 4, 1913, 4.

p. 83, "unpublishable poem": FD, "Jessica Screams," *Smart Set* XXXIX (April 1913), pp. 113–120. All subsequent quotations from the story are to this appearance in the *Smart Set*.

p. 85, "It must be": FD quoted in Hahn, *Romantic Rebels*, 183.

p. 87, "It is 11:30 p.m.": FD to ADF, May 26, 1913. FDPN.

p. 88, "a prose still-life": ADF to FD, June 3, 1913. FDPN.

p. 89, "a more psychological": FD, "The Littlest Theater," *Harper's Weekly*, November 29, 1913, 22.

p. 89, "Floyd Dell went": Maurice Browne, *Too Late to Lament* (Bloomington: Indiana University Press, 1956), 129.

p. 89, "I have always felt": Anderson, *My Thirty Years' War*, 37.

p. 90, "Nicholas Vachel Lindsay": FD, review of Vachel Lindsay's *The Tramp's Excuse*, *FLR*, October 29, 1909, 8.

p. 90, "From time to time": Lindsay to FD, September 13, 1911. FDPN.

p. 90, "You . . . are living": Lindsay to FD, January 21, 1910. FDPN.

p. 91, "an artist with": FD, *Homecoming*, 224.

p. 92, "I learned": FD to ADF, June 19, 1913. FDPN.

p. 93, "A man I": Sherwood Anderson, *Sherwood Anderson's Memoirs* (New York: Harcourt, Brace, 1942), 236.

p. 93, "She was one": *Sherwood Anderson's Memoirs*, 240.

p. 94, "a slender, delicate": FD, *Homecoming*, 237.

p. 94, "Floyd walked up": *Sherwood Anderson's Memoirs*, 243.

p. 94, "Sherwood and Floyd": Anderson, *My Thirty Years' War*, 39.

p. 95, "a gay happy time": *Sherwood Anderson's Memoirs*, 248, 249.

p. 95, "Candor was more": FD, *Homecoming*, 239–242.

p. 96, "wear a high collar": FD, *Homecoming*, 234.

p. 96, "You'll be sorry": FD, "The Portrait of Murray Swift," FDPN. All subsequent quotes from this story are from this manuscript.

p. 98, "I guess I mean": Margery Dell to FD, 1913. FDPN.

p. 99, "The life at Provincetown": FD to ADF, September 5, 1913. FDPN.

p. 100, "reason and logic": FD to Fineshriber, Fall 1913. FDPN.

Six: "REVOLUTIONARIES WITHOUT A REVOLUTION"

p. 102, " 'They' had been rebels": Malcolm Cowley, *Exile's Return* (New York: Viking, 1951), 72.

p. 103, "authentic bohemian": FD, "Rents Were Low in Greenwich Village," *American Mercury* LXV (December 1947), 663.

p. 103, "This [new] Village": FD, "Rents Were Low in Greenwich Village," 663.

p. 103, "for a time": Allen Churchill, *The Improper Bohemians* (New York: E. P. Dutton, 1959), 27.

p. 103, "The wartime": FD, "Rents Were Low in Greenwich Village," 665.

p. 105, "'a beautiful girl": FD, *Homecoming*, 247.

p. 105, "a play to produce": FD, *Homecoming*, 247.

p. 106, "of all the tin": H. L. Mencken to TD, October 16, 1916. Quoted in W. A. Swanberg, *Dreiser* (New York: Charles Scribner's Sons, 1965), 209.

p. 106, "a satire on": FD, *Love in Greenwich Village* (New York: George H. Doran, 1925), 29.

p. 106, "What! you've": FD, *Love in Greenwich Village*, 29.

p. 107, "to immense applause": FD to ADF, December 8, 1913. FDPN.

p. 107, " 'in the Chinese manner' ": FD, *Homecoming*, 250, 262.

p. 107, "For a while": FD, *Homecoming*, 261.

p. 107, "divine adventurousness": FD, "Ibsen Revisited," *King Arthur's Socks and Other Village Plays* (New York: Knopf, 1922), 145, 146.

p. 107, "a mocking footnote": FD, *Homecoming*, 262.

p. 108, "the two great riddles": FD, "Mona Lisa and the Wheelbarrow," *Harper's Weekly* LIX (July 4, 1914), 7.

p. 108, "There goes your": ME, *Enjoyment of Living* (New York: Harper and Brothers, 1948), 444.

p. 109, "The magazine didn't pay": FD, *Homecoming*, 249.

p. 109, "You are elected": ME, *Enjoyment of Living*, 394.

p. 109, "Floyd, you are going": FD, "Memories of the Old Masses," *American Mercury* LXVIII (April 1949), 481–482.

p. 109, "Bohemian ways": FD, "Memories of the Old Masses," 482.

p. 110, "We plan a": ME, "Editorial Notice," *Masses*, December 1912.

p. 111, "This magazine is owned": *Masses*, February 1913.

p. 111, "the most perfect": ME, *Enjoyment of Living*, 443.

p. 111, "I never knew": ME, *Enjoyment of Living*, 443–444.

p. 112, "I am the managing": FD to ADF, December 8, 1913. FDPN.

p. 112, "Floyd brought": ME, *Enjoyment of Living*, 444.

p. 113, "Oh my God, Max": Mary Heaton Vorse, *A Footnote to Folly* (New York: Farrar & Rinehart, 1935), 42.

p. 113, "Louis Untermeyer": FD, "Memories of the Old Masses," 483.

p. 113, " 'Bourgeois!' he": Churchill, *The Improper Bohemians*, 108.

p. 113, "Sure—sure": Louis Untermeyer, *From Another World* (New York: Harcourt, Brace, 1939), 48–49.

p. 114, "a war of": ME, *Enjoyment of Living*, 548.

p. 114, "some kind of": FD, "Memories of the Old Masses," 483.

p. 115, "the Rebel Rich": FD, "Memories of the Old Masses," 485.

p. 116, "My room": Orrick Johns, *Time of Our Lives* (New York: Stackpole & Sons, 1937), 215.

p. 116, "like a dock laborer": Johns, *Time of Our Lives*, 215.

p. 116, "like a true": FD, "Daughters of Dreams," 17. FDPN.

p. 116, "In the Village": FD, *Homecoming*, 249.

p. 117, "We held the same": FD, *Love in Greenwich Village*, 240.

p. 117, "The laws of": FD, *Love in Greenwich Village*, 242–243.

p. 118, "I want to be": FD to ADF, March 23, 1914. FDPN.

p. 118, "it ought to": FD to ADF, March 23, 1914. FDPN.

p. 119, "We have inherited": FD to ADF, March 23, 1914. FDPN.

p. 119, "in the same": ME, *Enjoyment of Living*, 453.

p. 120, "had mainly regarded": FD, "Change in American Life and Fiction," *New Review* III (May 1915), 13.

p. 121, "social approach to books": JF, *An American Testament: A Narrative of Rebels and Romantics* (New York: Farrar & Rinehart, 1936), 114.

p. 121, "I was impressed": JF, *An American Testament*, 114.

p. 122, "white pants": Churchill, *The Improper Bohemians*, 107.

p. 122, "shy and unsocial": FD, "Rents Were Low in Greenwich Village," 665.

p. 123, "actually quiet, sober": FD, Poetry Notebook III, 22, FDPN.

p. 124, In it he: FD, "Apologia," *Poetry* VI (May 1915), 67.

p. 124, "I remember the revelation": FD, "Who Said That Beauty Passes Like a Dream?" *Masses* VII (October 1916), 270.

p. 124, "This is the morning": FD, Poetry Notebook III, 31. FDPN. A slightly different version of this poem appeared in the *New York Tribune* on February 4, 1915.

p. 125, "Poor pretty little": FD, Poetry Notebook III, 27. FDPN.

p. 126, "was writing a semi-mystical": FD, *Homecoming*, 274.

p. 127, "supernormal [or] queer": FD to

Sherwood Anderson, 1920 (?). Anderson Papers, NL.

p. 128, "the long-sustained": FD, "A Great Novel," *FLR*, November 3, 1911, 1.

p. 128, "I have put off": FD to TD, 1913 (undated). TD Papers, Van Pelt Library, University of Pennsylvania.

p. 128, "mountainous manuscript": FD, *Homecoming*, 269.

p. 128, "the result shows": FD, "The 'Genius' and Mr. Dreiser," *New Review*, December 15, 1915, 362.

p. 129, "an intellectual species": FD, "Mr. Dreiser and the Dodo," *Masses* V (February 1914), 17.

p. 129, "Look, this world is changing,": quoted in Swanberg, *Dreiser*, 192.

p. 130, "I believe the Masses": FD to ADF, December 17, 1915. FDPN.

Seven: LOVE IN GREENWICH VILLAGE

p. 131, "On two important": FD, Poetry Notebook III, 9. FDPN.

p. 131, "stability of opinion": ME, *Love and Revolution: My Journey Through an Epoch* (New York: Random House, 1964), 223.

p. 132, "made it clear": JF, *An American Testament*, 115.

p. 133, "sees his own foibles": Randolph Bourne, *Youth and Life* (Boston: Houghton Mifflin, 1971), 125.

p. 133, "his beautiful mind": FD , *Homecoming*, 311.

p. 133, "what the Village meant": FD , *Homecoming*, 271.

p. 134, "mountain health-resort": FD, *Homecoming*, 272.

p. 134, "The news of the village": FD to ADF, December 17, 1915. FDPN.

p. 135, "back of the Palisades": FD, Poetry Notebook III, 34. FDPN.

p. 135, "Only two": FD, "Daughters of Dreams," 24, FDPN.

p. 136, "M.J. and I": FD to ADF, November 2, 1916. FDPN.

p. 136, "among its first families": FD, *Homecoming*, 280, 279.

p. 136, "associated one with Europe": Henry May, *The End of American Innocence: A Study of the First Years of Our Own Time, 1912–1917* (New York: Oxford University Press, 1979), 281.

p. 137, "I found that I": FD, *Homecoming*, 280–281.

p. 138, "an extraordinarily snobbish": FD, *Homecoming*, 280.

p. 138, "intellectually compatible": FD, "Daughters of Dreams," 25, 54.

p. 138, "to get into love": FD, "Daughters of Dreams," 39.

p. 138, "All the young": *Sherwood Anderson's Memoirs*, 243.

p. 138, "Everybody in the Village": FD, *Homecoming*, 291.

p. 139, "at grips": FD, "Speaking of Psychoanalysis" *Vanity Fair* V (December 1915), 53.

p. 139, "the necessity": FD, "The Science of the Soul," *Masses* VIII (July 1916), pp. 30–31.

p. 139, "I wasn't living": FD, "How It Feels to be Psychoanalyzed." FDPN.

p. 139, "I wanted to be set free": FD, *Homecoming*, 291.

p. 140, "My psychoanalyst": FD, *Homecoming*, 293–294.

p. 141, "There was a look": Dorothy Day, *The Eleventh Virgin* (New York: Albert and Charles Boni, 1924), 296.

p. 141, "an awkward": FD, *Homecoming*, 296.

p. 142, "a supremely right thing": quoted in William D. Miller, *Dorothy Day* (New York: Harper and Row, 1982), 80.

p. 142, "should really": Day, *The Eleventh Virgin*, 169.

p. 144, "then we knew": Glaspell, *The Road to the Temple*, 253.

p. 144, "during the winter": Churchill, *The Improper Bohemians*, 203.

p. 145, "Nothing was too mad": FD, *Homecoming*, 266.

p. 145, "Give it all": see Glaspell, *The Road to the Temple*, 266.

p. 145, "I did not like": FD, *Homecoming*, 267.

p. 145, "playwright, stage designer": FD, *Homecoming*, 265.

p. 146, "She had a beautiful voice": FD, *Homecoming*, 299.

p. 147, "to have Millay": FD, "Not Roses, Roses All the Way." FDPN. Unless otherwise noted, subsequent quotations on Dell's romantic involvement with Millay come from this unpublished essay.

p. 149, "This door": Edna St. Vincent Millay, "Bluebeard," *Renascence and Other Poems* (New York: Mitchell Kennerley, 1917), 44.

p. 150, "an iniquitous arrangement": FD, *King Arthur's Socks and Other Village Plays*, 96, 97–98.

p. 152, "These first two lines": FD, *Homecoming*, 301.

p. 153, "In my previous love affairs," FD, Poetry Notebook III, 52. FDPN.

p. 154, "at moments": FD, *Homecoming*, 302.

Eight: WARTIME

p. 155, "sinister psychology": FD, "Not Without Dust and Heat," *Looking at Life*, 153. This article first appeared in slightly different form as "The Story of the Trial," *Masses* I (June 1918), 7–18.

p. 155, "George Cook and I": FD, *Homecoming*, 260.

p. 155, "All existing": Hutchins Hapgood, *A Victorian in the Modern World* (New York: Harcourt, Brace and World, 1939), 393.

p. 156, "The world was"; FD, "Rents Were Low in Greenwich Village," 665.

p. 156, "no longer the resultant": ME, *Enjoyment of Living* 550.

p. 157, "that Sloan, Davis": ME, *Enjoyment of Living* 554.

p. 158, *"The Masses* has no": see ME, *Enjoyment of Living* 557–558.

p. 158, "This paper belongs": see ME, *Enjoyment of Living* 558.

p. 159, "The 'Renaissance' ": FD, *Homecoming*, 292–293.

p. 159, "It is strange": FD, *Homecoming*, 293.

p. 160, "either support": Bourne, in Carl Resek, ed., *War and the Intellectuals* (New York: Harper and Row, 1964), 13.

p. 160, "there was something": FD, "Memories of the Old *Masses*," 486.

p. 161, "There are some laws": FD, "Conscientious Objectors," *Masses* IX (August 1917), 29.

p. 161, "within the scope": see ME, *Love and Revolution*, 60.

p. 162, "conspiring to cause": quoted in FD, *Homecoming*, 313.

p. 163, "fallen in love": ME, *Love and Revolution*, 83–84.

p. 164, "Are you prejudiced?": FD, *Looking at Life*, 157.

p. 165, "It was with": FD, *Looking at Life*, 152–153.

p. 166, "I had always": see ME, *Love and Revolution*, 94.

p. 166, "so slight": ME, *Love and Revolution*, 94.

p. 166, "I found in": FD, *Looking at Life*, 163.

p. 166, "These men": see ME, *Love and Revolution*, 97–98.

p. 167, "the defendants": FD, *Looking at Life*, 160–161.

p. 168, "that opinion": see ME, *Love and Revolution*, 96.

p. 168, "as a pro-German": ME, *Love and Revolution*, 98.

p. 168, "I am not ashamed": FD, "Colors of Life," *Liberator* I (December 1918), 44–45.

p. 168, "The whole thing": FD, *Looking at Life*, 168.

p. 169, "When it grew dark": FD, Poetry Notebook III, 40. FDPN.

p. 170, "The sunny": FD, *Pearson's Magazine*, December 1918, 78.

p. 171, "Child of the lightning": FD, "On Reading the Poems of Edna St. Vincent Millay," *Liberator*, October 1918, 41.

p. 173, "declared that anyone": ME, *Love and Revolution*, 122.

p. 174, "very much the Richard": Day, *The Long Loneliness* (New York: Harper and Brothers, 1952), 68.

p. 175, "cried, Desdamonaishly": Dell, "Edna St. Vincent Millay," *New York Herald Tribune*, May 3, 1931.

p. 175, "It looks as": FD, "Not Roses, Roses All the Way." FDPN.

p. 175, But within a few: FD, "Not Roses, Roses All the Way." FDPN.

Nine: POSTWAR NOVELIST

p. 176, "Greenwich Village had become": FD, *Homecoming*, 324–325.

p. 177, "a show-place": FD, *Homecoming*, 325.

p. 178, *"bohemianism* and *radicalism":* Cowley, *Exile's Return*, 66.

p. 178, "It now occurs": FD, "Not Roses, Roses All the Way." FDPN.

p. 179, "truth is reality": FD, *Were You Ever a Child?* (New York: Knopf, 1919), 153.

p. 179, "the values which": FD, *Were You Ever a Child?*, 11.

p. 180, "is content to live": FD, *Were You Ever a Child?*, 121.

p. 180, " 'The artist must not": FD, *Were You Ever a Child?*, 122.

p. 182, "She must have": FD, Poetry Notebook III, 52–53. FDPN.

p. 183, "her youth and courage": FD , *Homecoming*, 330.

p. 183, "I fell in love": FD, *Homecoming*, 330.

p. 185, "outside toilet": FD, "Rents Were Low in Greenwich Village," 667.

p. 186, "soldiers, seamen and citizens": "Militant Suffragists Start Riot Near Broadway While Trying to Burn Wilson Speech," *New York Tribune*, March 5, 1919.

p. 186, "Not only that I love you": FD, *Homecoming*, 334.

p. 187, "This is the Mount": FD, *Homecoming*, 334.

p. 187, "studied audacity": review of *Were You Ever a Child?*, *Dial* 67 (November 15, 1919), 464.

p. 188, "exhilarating . . . absurd": Elia W. Peattie, "The New Education," *Chicago Tribune*, January 31, 1920, 13.

p. 188, "carrying packs": FD, *Homecoming*, 336.

p. 189, "I 'associated' ": FD, *Homecoming*, 338.

p. 189, "too polished": FD, *Homecoming*, 339.

p. 189, "a simpler and": FD, *Homecoming*, 341.

p. 190, "I left out": FD, *Homecoming*, 340.

p. 191, "I should define": *New York Tribune*, February 27, 1921. Clipping in the BLYU.

p. 191, "he and Joyce": FD, *Moon-Calf*, 284–285.

p. 192, " 'was an outdoor;' ": FD, *Moon-Calf*, 340, 341.

p. 192, "Drop whatever": Heywood Broun, "Books," *New York Tribune*, November 19, 1920, 10.

p. 193, "the clearest": Harry Hansen, "His First Novel—and Fame," *Chicago Daily News*, October 27, 1920, 12.

p. 193, "very competent writing": H. L. Mencken, review of *Moon-Calf*, *Smart Set* 64 (February 1921), 141.

p. 193, "a fine, free": Fanny Butcher, review of *Moon-Calf*, *Chicago Sunday Tribune*, November 7, 1920, sec. 1, p. 9.

p. 193, "The book makes": Sherwood Anderson to FD, 1920. FDPN.

p. 193, "I have called": US to FD, 1920. FDPN.

p. 193, "an intimate": TD to FD, November 20, 1920. FDPN.

p. 193, "the best sellers": FD, *Homecoming*, 343.

p. 194, "I knew better": FD, *Homecoming*, 344

Ten: "LITERATURE AND THE MACHINE AGE"

p. 196, "I'd like to": FD, *The Briary-Bush*, 418.

p. 196, " 'We were afraid": FD, *The Briary-Bush*, 425.

p. 197, "I was happy": FD, *Homecoming*, 352.

p. 198, "had always seemed": FD, *Homecoming*, 354.

p. 198, "like a pilgrim": FD, *Homecoming*, 355–356.

p. 199, "it is the father": FD, *Homecoming*, 358.

p. 199, "the most important novel": Harry Hansen, review of *The Briary-Bush*, *Chicago Daily News*, November 9, 1921, 12.

p. 199, "hovers over": Carl Van Doren, review of *The Briary-Bush*, *Nation* 114 (January 4, 1922), p. 19.

p. 200, "the silliness": John Peale Bishop, "Three Brilliant Young Novelists, No One of Whom Is Over Twenty-Five," *Vanity Fair*, October 1921, 8; and John Peale Bishop, review of *The Briary-Bush*, *Vanity Fair*, November 1921, 10.

p. 200, "decidedly genteel": Francis Hackett, review of *The Briary-Bush*, *New Republic*, December 14, 1921, 78.

p. 200, "the break-up of": FD, *Homecoming*, 362.

p. 200, "there was a non-aristocratic": FD, *Homecoming*, 349.

p. 201, "part and parcel": FD, *Homecoming*, 350.

p. 201, "We had debates": FD , *Homecoming*, 350.

p. 201, "almost as if": quoted in O'Neill, *Echoes of Revolt: The Masses 1911– 1917*, 21.

p. 201, "to co-ordinate": FD, *Homecoming*, 350.

p. 201, "taste for chaos": FD, *Homecoming*, 360.

p. 202, "It was characteristic": F. Scott Fitzgerald, *The Crack-Up and Other Stories* (New York: Penguin, 1986), 10.

p. 202, "A more skeptical": Bourne, *War and the Intellectuals*, 64.

p. 202, "against the encroachment": Harold Laski, "The Liberalism of Randolph Bourne," *Freeman* I (May 19, 1920), 237.

p. 203, "Where does Mr. Laski": FD, "The Creative Sceptic," *Freeman* I (May 26, 1920), 254.

p. 203, "A liberty that": Harold Laski, "The Liberalism of Randolph Bourne," 237.

p. 204, "Yes, intellectual": FD, "The Creative Sceptic," 254.

p. 205, " 'we are going' ": FD, "A Psycho-Analytic Confession," *Liberator*, April 1920, 18.

p. 205, " 'It's impossible": FD, "A Psycho-Analytic Confession," 19.

p. 206, "why, toward the end": FD, "Psychanalysis and Recent Fiction," in *Psyche and Eros*, July 1920, 39.

p. 206, "the advent": FD, "Psychanalysis and Recent Fiction," 41.

p. 202, "compromise effected": FD, "Psychanalysis and Recent Fiction," 42.

p. 207, "As capitalism": FD, "Psychanalysis and Recent Fiction," 42–43.

p. 207, "perceptions of social": FD, "Psychanalysis and Recent Fiction," 48.

p. 208, "a kind of Marxian": FD, *Homecoming*, 337.

p. 208, "raised socialist criticism": Bernard Smith, *Forces in American Criticism* (New York: Harcourt, Brace, 1939), 296.

p. 210, "a plea in defense": FD, *Intellectual Vagabondage* (New York: Doran, 1926), xv.

p. 210, "It will be": FD, *Intellectual Vagabondage*, 173–174.

p. 211, "Querulous and": FD, *Intellectual Vagabondage*, 229.

p. 211, "Can you create": FD, *Intellectual Vagabondage*, 233.

p. 211, "The future": FD, *Intellectual Vagabondage*, 240.

p. 211, "Facing an ironic": FD, *Intellectual Vagabondage*, 241, 242.

p. 212, "It is evident": FD, *Intellectual Vagabondage*, 249.

p. 212, "view of life": FD, *Intellectual Vagabondage*, 251.

p. 212, "the intelligentsia": FD, *Intellectual Vagabondage*, 260.

Eleven: UNDER FIRE

p. 215, "Something in "Dell's": JF, *An American Testament*, 242.

p. 215, "that as a citizen": JF, *An American Testament*, 242.

p. 215, "Ideas flowed": JF, *An American Testament*, 246.

p. 215, "a magic little": JF, *An American Testament*, 247.

p. 216, "genius for friendship": JF, *An American Testament*, 247.

p. 217, "This is not": review of *King Arthur's Socks and Other Village Plays*, New York *Evening Post Literary Review*, December 9, 1922, 300.

p. 217, "progressively weaker": JF, *An American Testament*, 247–248.

p. 217, "an attempt to": Dell, *Homecoming*, 361.

p. 218, "Not strange": FD, *Janet March* (New York: Knopf, 1923), 213.

p. 218, "Strange, that it": FD, *Janet March*, 215–216.

p. 219, "'disgusting . . . putrid'": see George Thomas Tanselle, "Faun at the Barricades," Ph.D. dissertation, Northwestern University, 1959, 316–317.

p. 220, "was vicious, silly": FD to US, 1923. FDPN. Dell penciled these words onto the letter many years later.

p. 220, "an unofficial censorship": FD to US, 1923. FDPN.

p. 222, "vague dreams": FD, *This Mad Ideal* (New York: Knopf, 1925), 72.

p. 222, "this mad ideal": FD, *This Mad Ideal*, 203.

p. 224, "you are so": FD, *Runaway*, (New York: Doran, 1925), 123.

p. 225, "sane, just": FD, *Runaway*, 177.

p. 225, "the image of": FD, *Runaway*, 303–304.

p. 225, "as good as": review of *This Mad Ideal*, *Bookman*, April 1925, 216; Edward Davison, "Middle-Class Life," *Saturday Review of Literature*, October 17, 1925, 210.

p. 225, "marked falling off": Stuart Sherman, "The Coast of Bohemia," *New York Herald Tribune Books*, March 15, 1925, 1.

p. 225, "to the level": review of *This Mad Ideal*, London *Times Literary Supplement*, July 23, 1925, 497.

p. 226, "more conservative than": review of *This Mad Ideal*, *Booklist*, May 1925, 302.

p. 226, "Why, I wonder": FD to ADF, February 11, 1929. BLYU.

p. 226, "laissez-faire": FD, *Intellectual Vagabondage*, 175.

p. 226, "dinner at the House": FD to US, July 22, 1925. US Papers, LLIU.

p. 227, "Though the Londoners": omitted chapters, *Homecoming*, 494a1. FDPN.

p. 227, "London has put": FD to US, July 22, 1925. US Papers. LLIU.

p. 227, "as it seems": FD, omitted chapters, *Homecoming*. FDPN.

p. 227, "I admire their practicality": FD to ADF, September 1925. BLYU.

p. 227, "an American": FD, omitted chapters, *Homecoming*. FDPN.

p. 228, "poetry [and] romance": in FD to William Lyon Phelps, November 2, 1925. BLYU.

p. 228, "a betrayal of": FD to ADF, November 4, 1925. BLYU.

p. 228, "There is in": omitted chapters, *Homecoming*, 504. FDPN.

p. 228, "the psychology of": FD, "Shell-Shock and the Poetry of Robinson Jeffers," *Modern Quarterly* III (September–December 1926), 268.

p. 228, "attitude toward life": FD, "Shell-Shock and the Poetry of Robinson Jeffers," 268–273.

p. 229, "those lost, happy": FD, *Love in Greenwich Village*, 320.

p. 229, "For them the world": FD, *Love in Greenwich Village*, 320–321.

p. 230, "Don't you see": FD, *Love in Greenwich Village*, 175–176.

p. 231, "the old things": FD, *Love in Greenwich Village*, 250.

p. 231, "an apartment in town": FD, *Love in Greenwich Village*, 79.

p. 231, "glad to be back": FD, *Love in Greenwich Village*, 90.

p. 231, "the foolish adventurer": FD, *Love in Greenwich Village*, 98.

p. 232, "the phantom world": FD, *Love in Greenwich Village*, 83.

p. 232, "as he talked": FD, *Love in Greenwich Village*, 97.

Twelve: RADICAL RENEGADE

p. 234, "the old group": JF, *An American Testament*, 256.

p. 234, "the outstanding 'proletarian' ": JF, *An American Testament*, 257.

p. 234, "Michael Gold's idea": Claude McKay, *A Long Way from Home* (New York: Harcourt Brace and World, 1937), 139.

p. 235, "the growing prosperity": JF, *An American Testament*, 308.

p. 235, "We moved the magazine": JF, *An American Testament*, 309.

p. 235, "The 'political editors' ": JF, *An American Testament*, 310.

p. 236, "a great work": FD to US, 1925. US Papers, LLIU.

p. 237, "B. Marie says": FD to US, March 5, 1926. US Papers, LLIU.

p. 237, "When I had": US to FD, March 16, 1926. US Papers, LLIU.

p. 237, "I perceive": FD to US, December 30, 1926. US Papers, LLIU.

p. 238, "was that aspect": FD, *Upton Sinclair* (New York: Doran, 1927), 97–99.

p. 238, "does not permit": FD, *Upton Sinclair*, 155.

p. 238, "In the realm": FD, *Upton Sinclair*, 169.

p. 239, "is a handbook": FD, *Upton Sinclair*, 173.

p. 239, "social revolutionary": FD, *Upton Sinclair*, 173, 174.

p. 239, "sexy novels": see Aaron, *Writers on the Left*, 215 (originally in the *New Masses*, October 1926, 28).

p. 240, He apologized: V. F. Calverton to FD, undated. FDPN.

p. 240, "The acquisition": FD, *Upton Sinclair*, 157–158.

p. 241, "The character": FD, omitted chapters, *Homecoming*. FDPN.

p. 242, Years later: Christopher Dell to author, March 21, 1992.

p. 242, "I have gone": omitted chapters, *Homecoming*, 512-A. FDPN.

p. 242, "To other people": FD, omitted chapters, *Homecoming*, 521. FDPN.

p. 244, "I remain a pragmatic": FD to ADF, May 18, 1926. BLYU.

p. 247, "No doubt it": FD, *An Unmarried Father* (New York: Doran, 1927), p. 301.

p. 248, "All those long": unidentified newspaper clipping. FDPN.

p. 248, "an original": Stephen Rathbun, *New York Sun*, October 10, 1928.

p. 248, "an ultramodern comedy": Robert Coleman, " 'Little Accident' Big Hit," *Daily Mirror*, October 10, 1928.

p. 250, "I began to feel": unidentified newspaper clipping. FDPN.

p. 250, "Present-day American": FD to ADF, April 18, 1928. BLYU.

p. 250, "I want to *explain*": FD to Elinor Wylie, April 5, 1928. BLYU.

p. 252, "the best teachers": Michael Gold, "May Days and Revolutionary Art," *Modern Quarterly* 3 (February–April 1926), 160–164.

p. 252, "Comrade Mike": FD, "Explanations and Apologies," *Liberator*, June 1922, 25–26.

p. 253, "because it represented": FD, Letter, *New Masses*, July 1929.

p. 253, "Floyd Dell is": Mike Gold, "Floyd Dell Resigns," *New Masses*, July 1929, 10.

p. 253, "At no time": Gold, "Floyd Dell Resigns," 10, 11.

Thirteen: GREAT DEPRESSION

p. 256, "to restore to": FD and Paul Jordan-Smith, Preface to Robert Burton, *The Anatomy of Melancholy* (New York: Farrar & Rinehart, 1927), v, viii.

p. 256, "Poetry, medicine": Jordan-Smith, *The Anatomy of Melancholy*, ix–x.

p. 256, "morbid psychology": FD, *The Anatomy of Melancholy*, xiii.

p. 256, "study of people": FD, *The Anatomy of Melancholy*, xiv.

p. 256, "labor of love": see FD, "Keats's Debt to Robert Burton," *Bookman* LXVII (March 1928), 13–17. Dell's description of his work on *Anatomy* as "a labor of love" occurs in FD, omitted chapters, *Homecoming*, FDPN.

p. 258, "homosexuality, prostitution": Dell, *Love in the Machine Age* (Farrar & Rinehart, 1930), 6.

p. 259, "an essentially military": FD, *Love in the Machine Age*, 17.

p. 259, "The middle class": FD, *Love in the Machine Age*, 22.

Notes

p. 260, "cultural campaigns": FD, *Love in the Machine Age*, 117, 118.
p. 260, "the successful use": FD, *Love in the Machine Age*, 357.
p. 260, "idea of work": FD, *Love in the Machine Age*, 139.
p. 261, "are out of": FD, *Love in the Machine Age*, 144.
p. 261, "a socially approved": FD, *Love in the Machine Age*, 371.
p. 261, "In the realms": FD, *Love in the Machine Age*, 373.
p. 261, "This book is written": FD, *Love in the Machine Age*, 3.
p. 262, "What fun I am": Margaret Sanger to FD, May 1, 1930. FDPN.
p. 262, "the crisp vivid": Millay to FD, May 13, 1930. FDPN.
p. 262, "a model of lucid": Irwin Edman, "Moon-Calf Grown Up," *Forum* 83 (June 1930), xiv.
p. 262, "Dell is primarily": Harry Elmer Barnes, review of *Love in the Machine Age*, *New York Telegraph*, April 4, 1930, 8.
p. 262, "Just here Floyd": ME, "Floyd Dell's Double Life," *Art and the Life of Action* (New York: Knopf, 1934), 138.
p. 262, "The highest ideal": ME, *Art and the Life of Action*, 156.
p. 264, "I hated": FD, omitted chapters, *Homecoming*, 525–526. FDPN.
p. 264, "decided that we": FD, omitted chapters, *Homecoming*, 521. FDPN.
p. 265, "it made a great": FD, "Diary Notes." FDPN.
p. 265, "In the ruins": FD, omitted chapters, *Homecoming*, 527.
p. 266, "seems to have": FD, omitted chapters, *Homecoming*, 524. FDPN.
p. 266, "America had more": FD, *Diana Stair* (New York: Farrar & Rinehart, 1932).
p. 266, "myself in petticoats": FD, "Notes, Private." FDPN.
p. 267, "vivid characterizations": Lorine Pruette, "A Lady Not So Genteel," *New York Herald Tribune Books*, October 23, 1932, 6.
p. 269, "The present": FD, omitted chapters, *Homecoming*, 512-A. FDPN.
p. 269, "a severe case": FD, autobiographical fragment. FDPN.
p. 269, "indigestion and almost": FD to B. Marie Gage, undated. FDPN.
p. 269, "assembled at our": FD to Elizabeth Lancaster, March 9, 1931. FDPN.
p. 270, "I managed for": FD, autobiographical fragment. FDPN.

p. 270, "It is to Japan's": FD to ADF, January 1932. BLYU.

Fourteen: NEW DEAL

p. 273, "My mind": FD, autobiographical fragment. FDPN.
p. 274, "reputation as a": Jerre Mangione, *The Dream and the Deal: The Federal Writers' Project, 1935–1943* (New York: Avon, 1972), 57.
p. 275, "This, my first": FD, autobiographical fragment. FDPN.
p. 276, "geographic, governmental": "Government Aid During the Depression to Professional, Technical and Other Service Workers" (1936), government report by FD, uncredited.
p. 276, "Racial or language": "Government Aid During the Depression to Professional, Technical and Other Service Workers."
p. 276, "We were proud": FD, autobiographical fragment. FDPN.
p. 276, "it is a stupid": article, by FD, for Jacob Baker (undated). FDPN.
p. 277, "When the card-house": "Bridging the Economic Gap," speech, by FD, for Florence Kerr. FDPN.
p. 277, "the anxiety-state": FD to Lancaster, Summer 1936. FDPN.
p. 278, "Floyd was the star," Verb Gabbert to Jerri Dell, January 28, 1974. From the papers of Christopher Dell.
p. 278, "a grandiose millionaire": FD, autobiographical fragment. FDPN.
p. 278, "was a large kitchen": FD, autobiographical fragment. FDPN.
p. 279, "I went out": autobiographical fragment. FDPN.
p. 279, "a Federal serf": FD, autobiographical fragment. FDPN.
p. 279, "Mr. Flood wishes": FD, "Diary Concerning Mr. Flood." FDPN.
p. 279, "my mind is full": FD to Lancaster, Summer 1936. FDPN.
p. 280, "literary plots": FD, "Diary Concerning Mr. Flood." FDPN.
p. 280, "I have been writing": FD to JF, February 1943. FDPN.
p. 280, "Milton! if thou wert": FD, Poetry Notebook II, 180. FDPN.
p. 281, "It seems to me": FD to Lancaster, Summer 1936. FDPN.
p. 281, "I have in mind": FD to Gilfond, January 9, 1940. FDPN.
p. 281, "He and the 12-year-old": fragment of a letter by Verb Gabbert. Papers of Christopher Dell.
p. 282, "Ain't nothing free": Christopher Dell to author, August 1992.

p. 282, "typical Greenwich Village": Verb Gabbert to Jerri Dell, January 28, 1974. Papers of Christopher Dell.

p. 282, "a colorful touch": fragment of a letter from Verb Gabbert. Papers of Christopher Dell.

p. 282, "To me writing": Verb Gabbert to Jerri Dell, January 28, 1974. Papers of Christopher Dell.

p. 283, "Six years ago": FD to Lancaster, 1939. FDPN.

p. 284, "Much fluttering": FD to B. M. Gage, ca. September 1939. FDPN.

p. 284, "The truth is": FD to Lancaster, 1939. FDPN.

p. 284, a left-wing writers' union: This episode was related by Christopher Dell to author, August 1992.

p. 286, "Ay, tear the tattered": Papers of Christopher Dell.

p. 287, "mustered out": FD to JF, July 1947. FDPN.

Fifteen: MAN OF LETTERS

p. 289, "picturesque; even the": FD, "Rents Were Low in Greenwich Village," 668.

p. 291, "some conventional": FD to US, January 21, 1954. US Papers, LLIU.

p. 291, "with astonishingly": FD to ME, October 26, 1951. ME Papers, LLIU.

p. 291, "I cannot regret": FD to ME, October 26, 1951. ME Papers, LLIU.

p. 292, "We are cut off": FD, Poetry Notebook IV, 79. FDPN.

p. 292, "the zeal of": FD to US, December 14, 1953. US Papers, LLIU.

p. 292, "I am perhaps": FD to US, December 14, 1953. US Papers, LLIU.

p. 293, "I was deeply": FD to ME, November 12, 1953. ME Papers, LLIU.

p. 293, "held in check": FD to ME, November 12, 1953. ME Papers, LLIU.

p. 295, "I said that I": FD to ME, February 17, 1954. ME Papers, LLIU.

p. 295, "had fallen for": FD to ME, March 10, 1954 (letter not sent). FDPN.

p. 296, "One of the important": FD to ME, March 10, 1954 (letter not sent). FDPN.

p. 297, "my political friends": ME to FD, May 14, 1954. ME Papers, LLIU.

p. 297, "not confine your": FD to ME, May 15, 1954. ME Papers, LLIU.

p. 297, "It seemed a": ME to FD, June 27, 1954. ME Papers, LLIU.

p. 297, "With the regards": FD to ME, May 15, 1954. ME Papers, LLIU.

p. 297, "adroit and charming": ME to FD, June 27, 1954. ME Papers, LLIU.

p. 298, "There is something": FD to ME, July 10, 1954. ME Papers, LLIU.

p. 298, "the fight for": FD to ME, September 16, 1954. ME Papers, LLIU.

p. 299, "I expect nothing": FD, Diary entry, November 20, 1947. FDPN.

p. 299, "I hate, despise": FD to Lancaster, May 31, 1951. FDPN.

p. 300, "all those within": FD to Lancaster, March 23, 1951. FDPN.

p. 300, "I am not charmed": FD to Lancaster, March 23, 1951. FDPN

p. 300, "lived a rational": FD to Lancaster, February 5, 1951. FDPN.

p. 301, "of a cheerful": FD, to Fred Wieck, April 12, 1951. FDPN.

p. 301, "I feel lonely": FD to Fred Wieck, April 12, 1951, FDPN.

p. 303, "one of America's": JF to FD, January 25, 1951. FDPN.

p. 304, "I especially dislike": FD to JF, August 1947. FDPN.

p. 305, "Certain things have": FD to JF, April 3, 1951. FDPN.

p. 305, "In your review": FD to JF, April 3, 1951. FDPN.

p. 305, "as an important social": FD to JF, April 3, 1951. FDPN.

Sixteen: TRUE RICHES

p. 307, "intellectually grown up": FD to JF, May 14, 1951. FDPN.

p. 307, "his trembling fingertips": FD to JF, October 5, 1951. FDPN.

p. 308, "The great world": FD, Poetry Notebook III, 128. FDPN.

p. 309, "Dear Arthur": FD to ADF, October 24, 1945. BLYU.

p. 309, "Dear, beautiful": FD to ME, January 8, 1954. ME Papers, LLIU.

p. 309, "She was such a lovely": ME to FD, January 29, 1954. FDPN.

p. 309, "I have delayed": ME to FD, December 3, 1956. FDPN.

p. 310, "Vanity is all": Jerri Dell to author, March 1992.

p. 310, "Wonderful, hell!": Jerri Dell to author, March 1992.

p. 311, "true riches": FD to Lancaster, February 7, 1951. FDPN.

p. 311, "possession of aesthetic": FD to Lancaster, February 7, 1951. FDPN.

p. 312, "Life, insofar": FD to Lancaster, August 30, 1951. FDPN.

INDEX

Adams, Frances, 182, 184
Addams, Jane, 75
American Mercury, 289
American Student Union, 284
America's Coming-of-Age (Brooks), 207
Anarchism, 17–18, 106
Anarchist Woman (Hapgood), 53
Anatol (Schnitzler), 89
Anatomy of Melancholy (Burton), 226, 256–257
Anderson, Cornelia, 94
Anderson, Karl, 93
Anderson, Margaret, 67, 89, 94
Anderson, Sherwood, xiii, 5, 106, 112, 121, 138, 174, 193, 208, 303; disagrees with FD, 125–127; influenced by FD, 93–95
Appeal to Reason, 15, 39
Arabian Nights, 11
Aristophanes, 57
Armory Show (Post-Impressionist Show), 71, 104
Arnold, Benedict, 18
Arnold, Matthew, 130, 209
Arrow of Gold (Conrad), 189
Art Institute (Chicago), 87, 96
Ashcan School, 11, 157
Atlantic Monthly, 132–133
Avant-garde, xiii, xiv–xv, 88–89, 104, 115, 122, 130, 201–202, 289–290. *See also* Bohemia.

Bailey, H. G., 304
Baker, Jacob, 273–274, 276, 278
Baker, Martha, 60, 61
Ballantine, Edward J., 144
Banks, Charles, 23
Barker, Granville, 57

Barnes, Djuna, 112
Barnes, Earl, 166–168, 172–173
Barnes, Harry Elmer, 262
Barns, Cornelia, 113, 166
Barry, Ill.: character of, 5–8; FD in, 5–12
Becker, Maurice, 107, 113, 156–157
Bell, Josephine, xi, 112, 162, 163
Bellamy, Edward, 16, 209
Belloc, Hilaire, 57
Bellows, George, 107, 113, 158
Belmont, Alva, 115
Benet, William Rose, 112
Bennett, Arnold, 57, 67, 81
Beresford, J. D., 208
Bergson, Henri, 81
Berkman, Alexander, 163
Bishop, John Peale, 200
Bjorkman, Frances Maule, 78–79
Blake, William, 57, 214
Blunt, Wilfrid Scawen, 22, 214
Bohemianism, 5, 25, 39; in Chicago, 85–88, 99; in Greenwich Village, 102–106, 114, 130; commercialization of, 176–178, 289–290
Boni, Albert, 106
Boni, Charles, 106
Boni and Liveright, 106
Booklist, 225
Bookman, 108, 225, 256
Bound East for Cardiff (O'Neill), 143–144
Bourne, Randolph, xii, 112, 174; on ironic radicalism, 132–133; on World War I, 160, 202–204
Boyce, Neith, 143
Branchard, Katarina, 116
Brest-Litovsk, Treaty of, 165
Briggs, Asa, 45
Brooke, Rupert, 124–125

327

Brooks, Van Wyck, 56, 174, 207–208, 303

Broun, Heywood, 192

Brown, John, 18

Brown, Robert Carlton, 113

Browne, Maurice, 61, 71, 87, 88–89, 145

Browning, Robert, 21, 209, 280

Brubaker, Howard, 113, 115

Bryant, Louise, 143, 144

Burnham, James, 297

Burr, Jane, 184–185

Burton, Sir Robert, 226, 256–257

Butcher, Fannie, 65, 66, 71, 73, 193

Butler, Samuel, 67

Bynner, Witter, 112

Byron, George Gordon, Lord, 209, 210, 280

Cabell, James Branch, 201, 202, 217

Calverton, V. F., 201, 228, 239–240

Cannan, Gilbert, 132

Cannon, James P., 235

Carlyle, Thomas, 17

Carmen, Bliss, 22

Carr, Michael Carmichael, 89, 96

Cary, Augusta, 60, 68–70, 89, 100, 107

Cary, Lucian, 60, 68–69, 81, 89, 100

Casanova Brown, 249

Cather, Willa, 116

Century, 23, 229

Chamberlain, Kenneth Russell, 111, 113, 156

Chamberlin, William Henry, 297

Chandler, Raymond, 305

Change Your Style (Cook), 143

Chasm (Cook), 42

Chesterton, G. K., 57, 81, 169

Chicago, Ill.: character of, 43–46; FD in, 43–101

Chicago Commons Settlement House, 34, 45

Chicago Daily News, 100, 193, 199

Chicago Daily Socialist, 43

Chicago Evening Post, 47, 51–53, 65, 81, 92, 99–100, 226. *See also Friday Literary Review* (Chicago).

Chicago Literary Renaissance, xiii, 289

Chicago Symphony Orchestra, 44, 49

Chicago Tribune, 47, 65, 78, 188, 193

Churchill, Allen, 103, 122

Civil War (American), 5, 20, 266

Clapp, Milo Mitchell, 34

Coleman, Glenn, 111, 113, 156–157

Coleman, Robert, 248

Coleridge, Samuel Taylor, 209

Columbian Exposition (1893), 86

Communism, 283–285, 292–294, 296–299. *See also* Communist party; Marxism.

Communist party, 235, 242, 270, 283–285, 303

Connecticut Yankee in King Arthur's Court (Twain), 11

Conrad, Joseph, 189

Constancy (Boyce), 143

Contemporaries (Steele), 143

Cook, George Cram (Jig), 99, 116, 155; in Chicago, 61, 63, 81; in Davenport, 25, 30, 37–42, 57–59; and Provincetown Players, 142–146

Cook, Mollie. *See* Price, Mollie.

Cooper, Gary, 249

Covington, Annette, 87

Cowley, Malcolm, 102, 103, 178–179

Cram, Ralph, 34

Crane, Stephen, 67, 116

Cummings, e. e., 112

Currey, J. Seymour, 49, 100, 135

Currey, Margery, 42, 100, 138, 196, 198, 223; divorce from FD, 134–135, 136; hosts literary salon, 60–62, 85–90, 92–94; influence on FD, 48–49, 55–56; marriage with FD, 49–51, 62–64, 69–70, 79, 80, 91–92, 95, 98–99

Daily Mirror (New York), 248

Daily Worker, 285

Darwin, Charles, 22, 129

Daughter of the Revolution and Other Stories (Reed), 274

Davenport, Iowa: character of, 19–20, 44; FD in, 19–42, 58–59

Davenport Democrat, 34, 36–37

Davenport Times, 28–30, 33, 34

Davies, Arthur B., 112, 158

Davis, Richard Harding, 174

Davis, Stuart, 111, 113, 156–157

Davison, Edward, 225

Day, Dorothy, xiii, 112, 141–142, 151, 162, 174–175, 183–184

Debs, Eugene, 27, 45, 172, 301

Defoe, Daniel, 11, 209

Dell, Anthony (father), 3, 6–12, 14–16, 21, 197–198, 269

Dell, Anthony (son), 198–199, 215, 241–242, 264–265, 271, 281, 285, 303, 310

Dell, Berta Marie Gage (wife). *See* Gage, Berta Marie.

Dell, Charles (brother), 7, 12, 15

Dell, Christopher (son), 230, 241–242, 265, 271, 281, 285, 305

Dell, Cora (sister), 8, 9, 12

Dell, Floyd (*see also* WRITINGS OF *at end of biographical entries*): birth of, 5; childhood in Barry, 5–12; adolescence in Quincy, 3–5, 12–18; relations with parents, 7, 9–10, 15–16, 197–198; youthful literary tastes, 11, 14, 16–18, 21–22; becomes a socialist, 15–18, 26–34; in Davenport, 19–42; as young poet, 21–25; writer and editor at *Tri-City Workers Magazine*, 30–34; first love affair, 35–37; lives on Jig Cook's farm, 37–42; moves to Chicago, 43–45; in Chicago, 45–101; meets and marries Margery Currey, 42, 49–50; marriage to Margery Currey, 49–51, 62–64, 69–70, 79, 80, 91–92, 95, 98–99; assistant editor at *Friday Literary Review*, 51–64; editor-in-chief at *Friday Literary Review*, 65–101; hosts Chicago literary salon, 60–62, 88–96; love affairs in Chicago, 63–64, 68–70, 73, 79, 91–92; essays on Chicago literature, 71–73; views on feminism, 73–79, 261; writes early stories, 82–85, 96–98, 123; leader among Chicago bohemians, 85–101; befriends and influences Sherwood Anderson, 93–95; resigns at *Chicago Evening Post*, 100; moves to Greenwich Village, 104; leads Liberal Club theatricals, 105–108; editor at the *Masses*, 108–115, 117–120, 122–123, 126, 129–130, 132, 137, 139, 141–142, 147; contributor to the *New Review*, 119–121, 128–130; relations with Marjorie Jones, 92, 100, 116–117, 134–136, 138, 230; literary disagreements with Sherwood Anderson, 125–127; views on Dreiser, 72–73, 120, 127–130; and literary modernism, 126, 130, 137, 206–208, 210–215, 304–305; and Freudianism, 134, 138–140, 151, 178, 201, 241, 255, 256; and Provincetown Players, 142–151; relations with Edna St. Vincent Millay, 146–154, 169–172, 174–175, 181–182, 230; defendant in the *Masses* trials, xi–xii, 160–169, 172–173; on progressive education, 179–182; meets and marries B. Marie Gage, 182–186; marriage to B. Marie Gage, 196, 198–199, 204, 241–242, 261, 264–265, 268, 271, 282, 284, 285–286, 288, 290, 296, 302, 308, 310–311; takes trips to western U.S., 197–198, 237; birth of son

Anthony, 198–199; place in postwar literary world, 199–215, 216–217; life in Croton-on-Hudson, N.Y., 215–216, 233–234, 241–242, 265, 269–271; takes trip to Europe, 226–227; birth of son Christopher, 233; works on biography of Upton Sinclair, 236–240; theatrical success on Broadway, 247–250; disputes with Mike Gold, 201, 252–254, 285; scholarly projects on Burton and Keats, 255–257; and Great Depression, 257, 264–265; on lecture tours, 255–256; views on patriarchal family, 200, 258–260; political anxieties during early 1930s, 269–272; works for WPA and U.S. Information Service, 273–287; falls out with Communists, 204–205, 254–256, 283–286; retirement, 288–313; political disputes with Eastman, 288, 291–299; deplores cold war America, 299–301; correspondence with Freeman on literature, history, 302–306; speaks at son Christopher's graduation, 307; deaths of friends, 309; fiftieth wedding anniversary, 310; death of, 310–311

Dell, Floyd, WRITINGS OF: *Angel Intrudes*, 146–148; "Apologia," 124; "Ballad of Christopher Street," 227, 229; "Beating," 123; *Briary-Bush*, 195–201, 214, 216, 217, 219, 249, 250, 268; "Builders," 30; "Change in American Life and Fiction," 120–121; *Cloudy with Showers*, 264; *Diana Stair*, 257, 266–268, 272, 304, 305; *Enigma*, 107; "Ex-Villager's Confession," 230–231; *Golden Spike*, 271–273; "Hallelujah, I'm a Bum!," 230; *Homecoming*, 257, 268–269, 271; *Ibsen Revisited*, 107; *Idealist*, 107; *Intellectual Vagabondage*, 208–214, 220–221, 228, 229, 232, 235, 240, 242; *Janet March*, 214, 217–221, 225, 255; "Jessica Screams," 83–85; *King Arthur's Socks*, 144, 214; "Literature in the Machine Age," *see Intellectual Vagabondage*; *Little Accident*, 247–250, 253, 255, 257; *Long Time Ago*, 144–145; *Looking at Life*, 214, 220; *Love in Greenwich Village*, 229–232, 237, 239, 240, 242, 271; *Love in the Machine Age*, 257–264; *Love Without Money*, 263–264, 265–266; "Memories of the Old Masses," 289; "Mona Lisa and the Wheelbarrow," 108; *Moon-Calf*, xiii, 4, 20, 27, 35, 125, 189–197, 199, 204, 209, 216, 225, 227, 233, 245, 249,

Dell, Floyd, WRITINGS OF (cont.):
268, 271; "Mothers and Daughters,"
82–83; "Mr. Dreiser and the Dodo,"
129; *Old Man's Folly*, 242–245; "On
First Seeing Isadora Duncan's School,"
124; "On Reading the Poems of Edna
St. Vincent Millay," 171–172; *Perfect
Husband*, 107; "Perfectly Good Cat,"
109; "Phantom Adventure," 231–232;
"Portrait of Murray Swift," 96–98;
"Psychanalysis and Recent Fiction,"
206–208; "Psycho-Analytic Confession,"
204–206, 236; "Railroad Riots of 1877,"
49; *Runaway*, 214, 223–226, 227, 230;
Saint George in Greenwich Village,
106–107; "Saturday Night," 33; "Shell-
Shock and the Poetry of Robinson
Jeffers," 228–229; "Socialism and
Anarchism in Chicago," 49; *Souvenir*,
250–252, 256; *Sweet and Twenty*,
148–150; "Tamburlaine," 23; *This Mad
Ideal*, 214, 221–223, 225–226;
Unmarried Father, 245–250, 251; *Upton
Sinclair: A Study in Social Protest*,
237–240; *Were You Ever a Child?*,
179–181, 187–188, 241; *Women as
World Builders*, 75–79, 262
Dell, Harry (brother), 8, 12
Dell, Jerri (granddaughter), 302, 305, 307,
310
Dell, Kate (mother), 3, 7–12, 14, 16,
197–198
Dell, Katie (granddaughter), 305
Dell, Margery Currey (wife). *See* Currey,
Margery.
Demuth, Charles, 143
Depression of 1873, 5, 7
Depression of 1893, 10
Depression of 1907, 37
Depression of 1929. *See* Great Depression.
Deutsch, Babette, 112, 188
Dewey, John, 160, 179
Dial, 115, 187
Dickens, Charles, 11, 209
Dodge, Mabel, 103, 105, 115, 143
Donne, John, 22, 24, 280
Doran, George H., 214, 247
Dos Passos, John, 112, 227, 304, 305
Dostoevsky, Fyodor, xi, 120
Drayton, Michael, 22
Dreiser, Theodore, xiii, 103, 106, 116,
126, 190, 236, 303, 307; FD's writings
on, 72–73, 120, 128–130; praises *Moon-
Calf*, 4, 193; relations with FD, 90–92,
99, 127–128

DuBois, W. E. B., 119
Duncan, Isadora, 75, 76, 124
Dunne, Finley Peter, 71–72

Eastman, Crystal, 226, 234
Eastman, Max, 106, 119, 131, 143, 144,
215, 227, 300, 309, 311; criticizes *Love
in the Machine Age*, 262–263; defendant
in *Masses* trials, xi, 147, 156–158,
161–162, 164–166, 168; editor of the
Masses, xiii, 108–115, 141, 160–161,
173; editor of the *Liberator*, 169, 189,
234; political disputes with FD, 288,
291–299
Edman, Irwin, 262
Egoists (Huneker), 56
Eleventh Virgin (Day), 141
Eliot, Charles William, 52–53
Eliot, George, 209
Eliot, T. S., 207–208, 217, 250, 261,
287, 303, 304
Ellis, Charles, 153
Emerson, Ralph Waldo, 17, 22, 40, 57,
67, 304
Engels, Friedrich, 22, 42
Enjoyment of Poetry (Eastman), 110
Espionage Act, xi, xiii, 147, 160, 161,
162, 182, 244
Euripides, 89
Evans, Ernestine, 87
Evanston, Ill., 42, 49–50

Fairbanks, Douglas, 249
Farrar, John, 273
Farrar and Rinehart, 256, 257, 265, 267,
273
Faulkner, William, 303
Federal Arts Project, 274, 276
Federal Emergency Relief Administration
(FERA). *See* Works Progress
Administration (WPA).
Federal Guide Book series, 276
Federal Music Project, 276
Federal Theatre Project, 276
Federal Writers Project, 276
Feminism, xiii, 5, 50, 66, 73–79, 108,
118, 183, 200, 255, 257, 261, 262,
267–268
Feuchter, Fred (Fritz), 26–29, 37
Ficke, Arthur Davison, 30, 61, 80, 87–88,
92, 95, 106, 107, 112, 116–119, 130,
134–135, 136, 185, 197, 237, 250,
270–271, 303, 309; affair with Millay,
153–154
Ficke, Gladys, 237

Fielding, Henry, 67
Fineshriber, Rabbi William, 20, 29, 37, 49–50, 100
Fitzgerald, F. Scott, xiii, 194, 202, 217, 250
Flaubert, Gustave, 56
Forum, 262
Foster, William Z., 201, 235
France, Anatole, 132, 280
Franco, Francisco, 269
Frank, Waldo, 189, 303
Fredericks, Henry C., 168
Freeman (1920s), 115, 202–204
Freeman (1950s), 295, 296
Freeman, Joseph: relations with FD, 121, 132, 201, 215–216, 217, 280, 283, 287, 288, 300, 302–306, 307; and the *Liberator*, 234–235
Freeman, Marilla, 22–24, 26, 30, 41, 45–47, 60
Freewoman, 77
Freud, Sigmund, 138, 139, 153, 241, 256
Friday Literary Review (Chicago), 51–58, 60–62, 65–68, 70–81, 83, 88, 89, 90, 92, 96, 108, 118, 120, 200. See also *Chicago Evening Post*.
Fuller, Henry Blake, 43–44

Gabbert, Verb, 278–279, 281–283, 307, 308, 309
Gage, Berta Marie, 196, 197–199, 204, 216, 223, 226, 241–242, 243, 261, 264–265, 268, 271, 282, 284, 285–286, 288, 290, 296, 302, 308, 310–311; meets and marries FD, 182–188
Gaige, Crosby, 247, 250
Gale, Zona, 193
Galsworthy, John, 55, 67
Game (Bryant), 144
Gellert, Hugo, 235
"*Genius*" (Dreiser), 128–130
Gibson, Lydia, 198, 235, 241–242, 255, 270
Gide, André, 304
Gilfond, M. E., 281
Gillmore, Inez Haynes, 103
Gilman, Charlotte Perkins, xiii, 75–76, 96
Giovannitti, Arturo, 119, 158–159, 235
Glaspell, Susan, 26, 30, 37–38, 42, 59, 61, 99, 103, 112, 142–144
Glintenkamp, Henry, 111, 113, 156–158, 161, 162
Godwin, Grace, 176
Godwin, William, 202

Gogol, Nikolai, 297
Gold, Michael, 201, 234–235, 252–255, 285
Golden, Mamie, 183, 241, 265
Goldman, Emma, 41, 57, 75, 77, 163
Gotsch, Jo, 107
Great Depression, 257
Greenwich Village: character of, 102–106, 176–178; FD in, 102–199
Gropper, William, 235
Gumberg, Alexander, 182, 184
Gurko, Miriam, 288, 309

Hackett, Francis, 47, 51–57, 58, 60, 65, 66, 67, 68, 200
Haeckel, Ernst Heinrich, 22, 38
Hallinan, Charles Thomas, 47, 60, 89, 100, 226
Hand, Judge Augustus, 162–163, 168, 172
Hand, Judge Learned, 161–162, 164
Hansen, Harry, 19, 21, 29, 47, 193, 199
Hapgood, Hutchins, 53, 106, 143, 155
Harding, Warren G., 202
Hardyman, Hugh, 265
Harper's, 23, 89, 108
Harris, Frank, 72, 174
Havel, Hippolyte, 113, 143
Hayek, Friedrich, 297
Haymarket riot, 43, 48, 49
Hazard of New Fortunes (Howells), 200
Hazlitt, Henry, 297
Hecht, Ben, 95
Heine, Heinrich, 22, 130
Hemingway, Ernest, 202, 217, 250, 261, 303, 305
Henley, William, 130
Herrick, Robert (novelist), 43–44, 56, 71–72, 120
Herrick, Robert (poet), 22, 214
Hillquit, Morris, 53, 162–164, 167–168, 172
Hines, Ted, 307
Hitler, Adolf, 269, 283, 285, 301
Holladay, Polly, 105, 113
Holmes, Judge Oliver Wendell, 269–270
Homer, 304
Hopkins, Harry, 278
Housman, A. E., 21, 256
Howe, Frederic, 255
Howe, Irving, xv
Howells, William Dean, 200
Hoyt, Helen, 112
Hufaker, Lucy, 134–135
Hugo, Victor, 11
Hull House, 47

Huneker, James, 21, 56
Hunt, Leigh, 280
Hyman, Elaine (Kirah Markham), 91–92, 99, 107, 143, 144

Ibsen, Henrik, 55, 56, 67, 77, 209, 304
Industrial Workers of the World (IWW), 33–34, 43, 104, 230, 243
Ingersoll, Robert, 3, 18, 209
Innocents Abroad (Twain), 11
Intellectuals, 28, 71, 136–138, 202–213. *See also* Avant-garde.
International, 82
Introduction to Metaphysics (Bergson), 81

James, Edna, 144
Jeffers, Robinson, 228–229, 261
Jennie Gerhardt (Dreiser), 127–128
Johns, Orrick, 116
Johnson, Raymond, 87
Jones, Marjorie, 61, 87, 107, 140, 143, 197, 223; relations with FD, 92, 100, 116–117, 134–136, 138, 230; death of, 309
Jones, Robert Edmond, 143
Jonson, Raymond. *See* Johnson, Raymond.
Jordan-Smith, Paul, 256
Joyce, James, 137, 201, 208, 304
Jung, Carl, 139
Jungle (Sinclair), 39, 193

Kafka, Franz, 304
Karb, David, 142
Kaufman, George S., 265
Keats, John, 166, 256–257, 280
Kemp, Harry, 143, 144
Kenton, Edna, 61, 134–135
Kerr, Florence, 276
Key, Ellen, 73–75, 77, 117, 138
Kipling, Rudyard, 21, 81
Kirkwood, David, 227
Knopf, Alfred A., 187, 190, 198, 214, 219, 220
Korean War, 299–300
Kreymborg, Alfred, 106, 143
Kropotkin, Peter, 17, 22, 203
Krylenko, Eliena, 227, 309

Lancaster, Elizabeth, 269, 277, 279, 281, 283, 284, 288, 299–300, 311–312
Laski, Harold, 202–204
Lawrence, D. H., 208
Lenin, V. I., 173, 189, 293
Lenin: The Man and His Work (Williams), 189

Lewis, Sinclair, xiii, 4, 192–194, 201, 217, 303
Lewisohn, Adolph, 115
Liberal Club (New York City), 105, 107–108, 115, 122, 143, 145, 154
Liberator, 137, 166, 169, 170, 171, 179, 188, 189, 198, 201, 204–205, 208, 214, 221, 233, 234, 252, 291, 292, 293, 302, 304; taken over by Communist party, 235
Life on the Mississippi (Twain), 13
Lindsay, Vachel, 89–90, 112, 169, 303
Lippmann, Walter, 119
Little Theater (Chicago), 71, 87, 88–89, 91, 96, 108
Liveright, Horace, 106
London, Jack, 57, 120
Longfellow, Henry Wadsworth, 280
Looking Backward (Bellamy), 16
Lore, Ludwig, 235
Lovelace, Richard, 280
Lovestone, Jay, 235
Lowell, Amy, 112
Lyric Opera (Chicago), 49
Lyric Year, 71, 81

McCarthy, Joseph, 291, 292, 294, 295–296, 297, 298, 299, 300
McCarthyism, 290, 291, 295–296, 311
McClure's, 19, 23
Macdougall, Allan, 145
McKay, Claude, 234–235
Mad Hatter (New York City), 176
Main Street (Lewis), xiii, 4, 192–194, 201
Malone, Dudley Field, 162–164, 168, 172
Mammonart (Sinclair), 236–237, 239
Manage, Blanche, 87
Mangione, Jerre, 274
Manton, Judge Martin, 172–173
Markham, Kirah. *See* Hyman, Elaine.
Marsden, Dora, 75, 77
Marvel, Ik, 17
Marvell, Andrew, 22
Marx, Karl, xiv, 3, 22, 26, 38, 200, 293
Marxism, xiv–xv, 26, 201, 205, 208, 268. *See also* Communism; Marx; Soviet Union.
Masses, xiii, xv, 33, 108–115, 117–120, 122–123, 126, 129–130, 132, 137, 139, 141–142, 147, 169, 188, 189, 214, 215, 235, 269, 299, 301, 304; and artists' strike, 156–158; and World War I, 156, 158–162; and Espionage trials, xi–xii, 154, 162–169, 172–173, 175

Masters, Edgar Lee, 92, 303
May, Henry F., 136–137
Mencken, H. L., 56, 106, 127, 189, 193
Mestre, Pat, 198
Mid-American Chants (Anderson), 126
Millay, Edna St. Vincent, xi, 71, 81, 112,
    262, 302, 303, 310; relations with FD,
    147–154, 165, 169–172, 174–175,
    181–182, 230; death of, 309
Millay, Norma, 153
Milton, John, 22, 280
Minor, Lydia. *See* Gibson, Lydia.
Minor, Robert, 158, 241–242, 255, 270
Mises, Ludwig, 297
Miss Lulu Bett (Gale), 193
Mitchell, Tenn., 93, 94
Mitchell, Thomas, 247–248, 250, 264
Modern Quarterly, 228, 239
Modernism, 130, 137
Moline, Ill., 19, 31
Monroe, Harriet, 71, 89, 124
Moody, William Vaughn, 22, 81
Moore, George, 121
Moore, Lou Wall, 87
Morality of Women, and Other Essays
    (Key), 73–74
Morris, William, 16, 209
Mother Earth, 41, 77
Mumford, Lewis, 257
Murger, Henri, 132
Mussolini, Benito, 269
Mylius, E. F., 234

Nation, 199
National American Woman Suffrage
    Association, 78
National Review, 292
Nearing, Scott, 236
Never Call Retreat (Freeman), 280
New Left, 132
New Masses, 239, 252–253
New Republic, 115, 133, 160, 200
New Review, 119–122, 128–129, 137
New York Herald Tribune, 225, 267
New York Sun, 248
New York Telegram, 262
New York Times, 54, 78, 248
New York Tribune, 186, 191, 192
Newberry Library, 86, 289, 292, 301, 310
News from Nowhere (Morris), 16
Nietzsche, Friedrich, 38, 56, 57, 209
Nirvana Days (Rice), 56
Nordfeldt, Bror, 87, 96, 143, 144, 185,
    216
Nordfeldt, Margaret, 87

Norris, Frank, 17, 39, 46, 56–57, 67,
    116, 120
Norton, Florence, 295

Octopus (Norris), 17
"Ode to Melancholy" (Keats), 256–257
Olgin, M. J., 235
On Baile's Strand (Yeats), 89, 91
O'Neill, Eugene, 143–144, 201, 303
Oppenheim, James, 112
Osbourne, Lloyd, 198
Our America (Frank), 189

Pankhurst, Emmeline, 75, 76
Pargellis, Stanley, 289
Parrington, V. L., 266
Past and Present (Carlyle), 17
Pater, Walter, 56
Paterson Pageant, 104, 132
Pearson, Ralph, 87
Pearson's Magazine, 170, 174
Peattie, Elia W., 47, 48, 78, 188
Phelps, William Lyon, 227
Poe, Edgar Allan, 18, 40
Poetry, 71, 83, 89, 124
Poole, Ernest, 120
Pound, Ezra, xiii, 57, 83, 287, 303, 307
Powys, John Cowper, 93
Prejudices (Mencken), 189
Price, Mollie, 38, 41–42, 46, 58–60, 61,
    63–64, 70
Price, James Russell, 46, 47
Progressive education, 5, 178, 179–181
Proust, Marcel, 304
Provincetown Players, 142–151, 154
Pruette, Lorine, 267–268
Psychology of the Unconscious (Jung), 139
Puck, 108
Pullman strike, 43

Quincy, Ill.: character of, 3, 12–14; FD
    in, 3, 12–18

Randolph, Mary, 87
Rathbun, Stephen, 248
Rauh, Ida, 107, 143, 145
Reed, John, xiii, 106, 108–110, 112, 113,
    143, 156, 160, 162, 172, 174–175, 274
Reilly, Leigh, 54, 99
Renascence (Millay), 71, 81, 147,
    151–152, 170, 171
Reveries of a Bachelor (Marvel), 17
Rice, Cale Young, 56
Robins, Margaret Dreier, 75
Robinson, Boardman, 111, 158, 161, 215,
    235

Robinson, Edwin Arlington, 279
Rock Island, Ill., 19, 30
Rodman, Henrietta, 105, 106, 107
Roepke, Wilhelm, 297
Rogers, Merrill, xi, 142, 162, 163, 166, 167
Rolland, Romain, 132
Roosevelt, Franklin D., 274, 285, 301
Rousseau, Jean Jacques, 209
Ruskin, John, 209
Russell, Bertrand, 112
Russia. *See* Soviet Union.
Ruthenberg, C. E., 235

Sandburg, Carl, 89, 112, 174, 303
Sanger, Margaret, 262
Sappho, 39
Saturday Review of Literature, 225
Schnitzler, Arthur, 57, 89
Schreiner, Olive, 75, 76
Scripps, E. W., 115
Seven Arts, 115, 133, 160, 164, 174
Sex Expression in Literature (Calverton), 240
Shaffer, John, 54, 99–100
Shakespeare, William, 22, 279, 299
Shaw, George Bernard, 22, 39, 55, 57, 67, 209, 211, 262, 301, 304
Shelley, Percy Bysshe, 21, 40, 166, 280, 304
Sherman, Stuart, 225
Shores of Light (Wilson), 302
Shropshire Lad (Housman), 21
Sinclair, Upton, xiii, 39, 46, 57, 67, 106, 112, 120, 193, 227, 290–291, 292–293, 303; criticizes *Janet March*, 219–220; subject of FD's biography, 236–240
Sister Carrie (Dreiser), 72, 92, 127, 190
Slavery, 6, 40–41
Sloan, John, 103, 109, 111, 112, 113, 123, 156–158
Smart Set, 83–85
Smith, Bernard, 208
Socialism, xiii, 5, 15–17, 20, 22, 26–28, 37, 39, 52, 53–54, 66, 80–81, 118, 200, 257
Socialism, Utopian and Scientific (Engels), 42
Socialism as It Is (Walling), 80–81
Socialism in Theory and Practice (Hillquit), 53
Socialist party, 3, 15–17, 24, 27–28, 43
Song of Myself (Whitman), 22
Southey, Robert, 130
Souvarine, Boris, 297

Soviet Union, xiv–xv, 165, 170, 172–174, 182, 188, 204–205, 212, 234, 235, 263, 269–270, 283, 294
Spanish-American War, 12, 37
Spanish Civil War, 284
Spingarn, Joel Elias, 112
Stalin, Josef, 269, 292, 293
Stedman, Seymour, 172–173
Steele, Wilbur Daniel, 143
Steffens, Lincoln, 116
Stein, Gertrude, 126
Stendhal (Marie Henri Beyle), 137
Stevens, Doris, 163–164
Stevenson, Robert Louis, 198, 280
Stirner, Max, 22
Sun Also Rises (Hemingway), 305
Suppressed Desires (Cook and Glaspell), 143
Swinburne, Algernon Charles, 22, 209, 256, 280
Syndicalism, 81. *See also* Industrial Workers of the World (IWW).
Synge, John Millington, 47, 67

Tannenbaum, Samuel, 140, 147
Taylor, Graham, 34, 45
Ten Days That Shook the World (Reed), 174
Tennyson, Alfred, 21, 206, 209
Tery, Simone, 227
Thackeray, William Makepeace, 11
This Side of Paradise (Fitzgerald), xiii, 194
Thoreau, Henry David, 67
Tietjens, Eunice, 60, 89, 112
Times Literary Supplement (London), 225
Titan (Dreiser), 91
Tobey, Berkeley, 108, 113
Tolstoy, Leo, 57, 203
Tono-Bungay (Wells), 55
Toomer, Jean, 112
Toynbee, Arnold, 299–300
Tri-City Workers Magazine, 30–34
Trilling, Lionel, xii
Trojan Women (Euripides), 89, 91
Trotsky, Leon, 263
Turgenev, Ivan, 57
Twain, Mark, 11, 13, 57, 67

University of Chicago, 22, 86, 87
Untermeyer, Jean Starr, 112
Untermeyer, Louis, 112, 113, 188

Van Doren, Carl, 199, 229
Van Doren, Mark, 112
Vanity Fair, 139, 146

Veblen, Thorstein, 87, 262
Verne, Jules, 11, 209
Volkenburg, Ellen Van, 61, 88
Voltaire (François Marie Arouet), 209
Vorse, Mary Heaton, 103, 113, 143, 156, 236

Walling, William English, 80–81, 113, 119
Washington Square Players, 154
Webb, Beatrice, 75, 77
Wells, H. G., 11, 22, 55, 67, 132, 155, 191, 209, 211, 301, 304
Westley, Helen, 106, 107
Wharton, Edith, 120
Wheeler, Kathleen, 87
Whitman, Walt, 21, 22, 40, 55, 120, 209, 304
Whittier, John Greenleaf, 40–41, 280, 304
Wiebe, Robert, 5
Wieck, Fred, 301
Wilde, Oscar, 21
Wilkinson, Ellen, 226–227
Williams, Albert Rhys, 188–189
Williams, William Carlos, 112, 307
Wilson, Edmund, 112, 288, 302
Wilson, Woodrow, 71, 163, 178, 186
Windy McPherson's Son (Anderson), 5, 93, 125–126

Winesburg, Ohio (Anderson), 112, 126
Winslow, Horatio, 108
Winter, Alice Beach, 113
Winter, Charles A., 113
Wirt, William, 179
Wolfe, Bertram, 297
Woman's suffrage movement, 106. *See also* Feminism.
Women and Labor (Schreiner), 76
Wood, Clement, 107, 141
Wordsworth, William, 21, 280
Works Progress Administration (WPA), xiv, 274–279, 283, 286–287
World Columbian Exposition (1893). *See* Columbian Exposition (1893).
World War I, xi, 155–156, 299
World War II, 284–287
Wright, Willard Huntington, 84
Wylie, Elinor, 112, 250, 257

Yeats, John Butler, 70
Yeats, William Butler, 89, 90, 91, 289
You Can't Take It with You (Kaufman), 265
Young, Art, xi, 103, 111, 113, 156–157, 161–162, 167
Young Communist League, 284

Zorach, William, 143

A NOTE ON THE AUTHOR

Douglas Clayton was born in New York City and studied at the University of Chicago, the University of the South, and Northwestern University. He has taught literature at the University of Illinois, Chicago, and at Northwestern, where he was also a *Tri-Quarterly* Fellow. His articles on American culture have appeared in the *American Scholar*, *Chicago History*, and other journals and magazines. He is now humanities editor at the University of Nebraska Press.